The Letter of the Roman Church to the Corinthian Church from the Era of Domitian: 1 Clement

Classic Studies on the Apostolic Fathers

Edited by Jeremiah Bailey and George Kalantzis

Volume 1

"Many of Harnack's analyses and insights into *1 Clement* retain their value in today's marketplace of historical inquiry. Cerone's adept translation has done a great service to Anglophone scholarship, by converting this wealth into usable currency. Critical readers will discover a worthy return on investment."

—**Paul Hartog**, Professor of Theology, Faith Baptist Theological Seminary

"Jacob Cerone's edition of Adolf von Harnack's seminal study of *1 Clement* is an outstanding premiere to what promises to be an impressive series, Classic Studies on the Apostolic Fathers. From the characteristically erudite introduction to Harnack's essay by Prof. Larry Welborn, to the smooth translation of Harnack's influential 'farewell gift' to his church history students, to the four still-valuable articles on 1 Clement by Harnack appended to the essay, this volume shines with insight. For anyone interested in 1 Clement—which should be any student of early Christianity—this is a must-have volume."

—**David J. Downs**, author of *Alms: Charity, Reward, and Atonement in Early Christianity*

"This fine little volume provides a clear and lucid rendering of a classic German study not widely known and only rarely used by English readers of 1 Clement. The vibrant contemporary style and careful sensitivity to von Harnack's original emphasis is admirable. Cerone's careful work is much appreciated, and serious students of the Apostolic Fathers do well to have this publication available for their own research."

—**Clayton N. Jefford**, Professor of Scripture, Saint Meinrad Seminary and School of Theology

"Scholarly study of *1 Clement* must begin with Adolf von Harnack's treatments of it. Jacob Cerone has done a great service in furnishing an English translation of his essays. Complemented by Larry Welborn's introduction both to the letter and Harnack's interpretations, this collection will be an invaluable resource for the study of *1 Clement* for years to come. I heartily recommend it."

—**Harry O. Maier**, Professor of New Testament and Early Christian Studies, Vancouver School of Theology

"Adolf von Harnack's introduction and interpretation of the 'First Letter of Clement,' though published ninety years ago, is still one of the most important contributions for the study of the history of the early church. We can be grateful now to have an excellent translation which opens this book to the worldwide community of scholars working on early Christianity. Four appendices represent the development of Harnack's studies on this topic; the bibliography gives an overview on modern publications. L. Welborn in his essay 'Harnack's "Testament"' gives a critical survey on the historical context of Harnack and his work."

—**Andreas Lindemann**, co-author of *Interpreting the New Testament*

"Jacob Cerone provides scholars with a long-needed translation of Adolf von Harnack's so-called scholarly Testament: a famous small booklet on 1 Clement. Cerone manages to cast Harnack's often old-fashioned and at times a bit pretentious German in a pleasant and readable English and supplies the reader with all sorts of invaluable information in his accompanying notes. A must for all interested in 1 Clement or in von Harnack as an academic scholar."

—**David du Toit**, Professor of New Testament Studies, University of Erlangen-Nuremburg, Germany

"It is fortunate and salutary that this collection of influential studies on 1 Clement—including Harnack's last monograph—is now competently translated for a broader readership. Bearing a peculiar scholarly flavor today, these studies will certainly be of direct interest to scholars of 1 Clement and early Christianity, and at the same time they will provide students with select material for incursions into the history of the field."

—**Dan Batovici**, author of *The Shepherd of Hermas in Late Antiquity*

The Letter of the Roman Church to the Corinthian Church from the Era of Domitian: 1 Clement

With a Collection of Articles on 1 Clement by Adolf von Harnack

Adolf von Harnack

EDITED AND TRANSLATED BY
Jacob N. Cerone

FOREWORD BY
Larry L. Welborn

PICKWICK *Publications* · Eugene, Oregon

THE LETTER OF THE ROMAN CHURCH TO THE CORINTHIAN CHURCH FROM THE ERA OF DOMITIAN: 1 CLEMENT
With a Collection of Articles on 1 Clement by Adolf von Harnack

Classic Studies on the Apostolic Fathers 1

Copyright © 2021 Jacob N. Cerone. All rights reserved. Except for brief quotations in critical publications or reviews, no part of this book may be reproduced in any manner without prior written permission from the publisher. Write: Permissions, Wipf and Stock Publishers, 199 W. 8th Ave., Suite 3, Eugene, OR 97401.

Pickwick Publications
An Imprint of Wipf and Stock Publishers
199 W. 8th Ave., Suite 3
Eugene, OR 97401

www.wipfandstock.com

PAPERBACK ISBN: 978-1-7252-7378-8
HARDCOVER ISBN: 978-1-7252-7379-5
EBOOK ISBN: 978-1-7252-7380-1

Cataloguing-in-Publication data:

Names: Harnack, Adolf von, 1851–1930, author. | Cerone, Jacob N., editor and translator. | Welborn, Larry L., 1953–, foreword.

Title: The Letter of the Roman Church to the Corinthian Church from the Era of Domitian: 1 Clement : With a Collection of Articles on 1 Clement by Adolf von Harnack / Adolf von Harnack ; edited and translated by Jacob N. Cerone ; foreword by Larry L. Welborn.

Description: Eugene, OR: Pickwick Publications, 2021 | Classic Studies on the Apostolic Fathers 1 | Includes bibliographical references and index

Identifiers: ISBN 978-1-7252-7378-8 (paperback). | ISBN 978-1-7252-7379-5 (hardcover). | ISBN 978-1-7252-7380-1 (ebook).

Subjects: LCSH: Clement I, Pope. First epistle of Clement to the Corinthians. | Clement. | Early church, 30–600. | Church history—Primitive and early church, ca. 30–600. | Christianity and culture.

Classification: BR65 C64 H27 2021 (print). | BR65 (ebook).

For students of Early Christianity and 1 Clement

Contents

Series Foreword: Classic Studies on the Apostolic Fathers | ix
Preface: Adolf von Harnack and 1 Clement | Jacob N. Cerone | xi
Acknowledgments | Jacob N. Cerone | xvii
Foreword: Harnack's Testament | Larry Welborn | xix

Preface | 1

Introduction | 3

1. The Transmission of the Letter | 7

   The Letter | 10

2. The Author | 40
3. Characteristics of the Letter and Its Religious Content | 43
4. The Sources of Clementine-Roman Christianity | 54

   1. The Old Testament | 54
   2. Christ and the Christian | 58
   3. The Rational-Moralistic Idealism of the Age and Its Literary and Aesthetic Forms | 65

   Excursus: The Political Stance | 70

5. The Struggle in Corinth over the Ecclesiastical Officials and the Order of the Office | 72

   Section I | 72

   Section II | 74

   Section III | 76

   Excursus: Is the Attitude of the Letter Specifically Roman? | 80

6. Problems That Have not yet Been Conclusively Investigated Posed by 1 Clement, Which Can Also Be Addressed in Seminars | 82
7. A Look at the Development of Church History, Which the Letter Grants and That Should Be Studied | 84
8. Concluding Word | 86

    Notes | 88

Appendix I: The Recently Discovered Latin Translation of 1 Clement | 109

Appendix II: New Studies on the Recently Discovered Latin Translation of 1 Clement | 123

Appendix III: The First Letter of Clement: A Study to Determine the Character of the Oldest Form of Gentile Christianity | 144

Appendix IV: The Epithet "Servant of God" Used of Jesus and Its History in the Ancient Church | 169

Bibliography | 203

Index to 1 Clement by Harnack | 209

Index of Authors | 217

Index of Subjects | 219

Index of Ancient Sources | 227

Series Foreword

Classic Studies on the Apostolic Fathers

The late scholar of early Christianity Larry Hurtado described the second century as "the Cinderella century," because it occupies the liminal space between the apostolic period of the New Testament and the world of the apologists at the end of the second century and beginning of the third. The post-apostolic era was a vibrant period of development as early Christians struggled to narrate their beliefs about the person of Jesus, decide the structure of their assemblies, find their place in the vastness that was the Roman Empire, and tackle the social issues that arose when a Jewish sect took on a massive influx of gentiles.

Some of the earliest voices of this period are found in the grouping of texts that is commonly called "The Apostolic Fathers." These texts are a record of early Christian self-expression composed without the limits of later creeds and bear witness to the hard work of identifying one's own theological boundaries or rejecting the boundaries that others have created. The presentation of these texts as a collection, however, is an artificial construct of scholarship, which is reflected in the variety of genres found within: the corpus includes epistolary material (both corporate and individual; both pseudepigraphic and genuine), a sermon, an apology, and an apocalypse. In many respects, it is precisely this variety that makes the Apostolic Fathers an excellent entry point to the broader second century.

Even though in the last few decades there has been an increase in interest in the *Apostolic Fathers*, the volume of scholarship remains small. There are likely many causes for this neglect, but two seem particularly prominent. First is the inherent difficulty of any transitional period to fit comfortably within the delineations of historical scholarship. To those who were trained in New Testament studies, the boundaries of that corpus have more recently tended to exclude the post-apostolic writings, while those trained in Patristics or Late Antiquity sometimes gloss over the second century in favor of the action-packed third and fourth centuries. Hurtado argued (and we agree), however, that the study of the second century makes the scholars working on either side of that century better. When we skip over these texts, we erase important strata of early Christian theological development.

Another significant cause of this neglect is access to scholarship. The student who wishes to study these texts closely is already faced with the challenge of greatly expanding their Koine vocabulary and, if they desire to engage in textual criticism, acquiring Latin, Coptic, and Syriac. Having accomplished these things, the would-be student of the Apostolic Fathers is then confronted by the reality that most of the secondary literature is in German, French, or Italian. In addition, much of the important English language scholarship is out-of-print and/or prohibitively expensive to acquire. Studying these texts beyond a surface level might, therefore, seem quite daunting.

The goal of *Classic Studies on the Apostolic Fathers* is to bridge this gap by bringing back to print some of the most important but hard-to-find resources in English and by providing translations of important works of scholarship on the Apostolic Fathers into English for the very first time. It is our hope that *Classic Studies on the Apostolic Fathers* will allow students and scholars to see for themselves the promise of these texts and engage this vital period anew.

—Jeremiah Bailey
and
George Kalantzis

Preface

Adolf von Harnack and 1 Clement

ALTHOUGH THE BROADER CORPUS of Adolf von Harnack's research and scholarly output has received a wide reception throughout the world and has even been translated into several languages, his final work entitled *Einführung in die alte Kirchengeschichte: Das Schreiben der römischen Kirche an die korinthische aus der Zeit Domitians (I. Clemensbrief)*, published by Hinrichs in 1929, has remained untranslated for the English-speaking world. To be sure, Harnack's occupation with 1 Clement had an impact on Clement studies during his own era and continues to impact contemporary studies on 1 Clement,[1] nevertheless it has remained out of reach for those who cannot read German. With the ever-increasing interest in the so-called Apostolic Fathers and the sources of the earliest expressions of Christianity, it seems there is no better time to present a translation not only of Harnack's *Introduction to Ancient Church History* but also four significant journal articles he penned on 1 Clement for the Preußischen Akademie der Wissenschaften prior to his *Introduction*.

The first half of this volume consists of Harnack's *Introduction to Ancient Church History*. Shortly before his death in 1930, Harnack composed the volume as a farewell gift for the students of his church history seminar. The composition of the work is specifically aimed at his students: For example, Harnack includes a translation of the letter (partly for those whose Greek was sub-par and partly as a means of expounding the meaning of the letter), and he uses significantly fewer extensive Greek and Latin passages scattered throughout the volume than, for example, the essays he published on 1 Clement in the second half of this volume. Furthermore, he includes two lists towards the end of the *Introduction* providing his students possible avenues for future investigations, many of which were taken

---

1. See Larry Welborn's foreword in this volume.

up and addressed later by his students or students of 1 Clement in general. In addition to these features, Harnack's *Introduction* includes discussions on the transmission history of 1 Clement, authorship, the characteristics and religious content of the letter, the sources of Clement's Roman Christianity (e.g., the Old Testament, Christ, and the rational-moralistic idealism of the age and its literary forms), an excursus on Clement's attitude towards the political rulers and power structures of his day, an extensive section on ecclesiology and ecclesiastical offices, and finally notes on the text of 1 Clement. The arrangement and translation of this text follows that of the original publication by Hinrichs in 1929 and not the reprint by Brill in *Encounters with Hellenism*.

In the second half of the volume, there are four appendixes. Each appendix contains one of Harnack's articles on 1 Clement written between the years 1894 and 1926. The first two journal articles, both published within months of one another in 1894, beam with the excitement of a newly discovered Latin translation of 1 Clement. The first, "The Recently Discovered Latin Translation of 1 Clement" (appendix 1), begins with an examination of the extant manuscripts of 1 Clement and their respective value, including an assessment of how matters have now changed in light of Morin's discovery of a Latin translation of the text. Having provided an overview of the current state of affairs, Harnack turns to a number of peculiarities in the Latin translation overlooked by Morin. The text has undergone a number of scribal alterations. The translator has omitted the word "our" in the phrase "our soldiers" (37.1) and in the phrase "our leaders" (60.2). Furthermore, the prayer for "our leaders" and the submission of all Christians to their earthly rulers has been inverted. Instead of Clement praying that Christians might be submissive to their rulers, the prayer exhorts the rulers to submit themselves to the church, more specifically, to the pope. Harnack is certain these readings were not present in the original translation of the letter (which he dates to the second century) nor did they originate with the copyist of the eleventh-century manuscript now in our possession. Instead, he holds out hope that a catalog from the Lobbes Monastery might shed further light on the origin of the forgery. Notwithstanding the criticisms Harnack himself addresses in the subsequent article (see appendix 2), his judgment on the forgery present in this Latin manuscript continues to be positively received in contemporary Clement scholarship. Harnack himself notes Knopf's positive reception of his assessment in his *Introduction*,[2] and Grant, Lindemann,

---

2. See Harnack, *Introduction*, 107.

and Lona all cite this article as evidence of the tendentious readings present at times in this Latin translation.[3]

In the second appendix, "New Studies on the Recently Discovered Latin Translation of 1 Clement," Harnack provides further investigations into the Latin text. The first portion of the essay begins where Harnack broke off in the previous essay, with a report on the contents on the Lobbes Monastery catalog. This catalog witnesses the presence of a Latin translation of 1 Clement within its library, which stood alongside the works of Cyprian and Cassiodori. The fact that it is not connected to 2 Clement and is placed alongside Cyprian attests to the antiquity of the original translation and its significance. In the second section, Harnack discusses ancient citations of the Latin text of 1 Clement, specifically by Ambrose and Lactantius, which reliably dates the translation to no later than the end of the third century. Section three turns to the internal evidence: the vocabulary employed by the translator, specifically terms for ecclesiastical offices, dates the translation to Rome in the second century. The essay concludes with a fourth section, wherein Harnack engages with critics of his forgery theory offered in the previous essay along with a proposal for how the forgery arose: a marginal reading from a previous manuscript had been mindlessly and uncritically copied into a new manuscript. Once again, Harnack's philological judgments have found a welcome home in Clement scholarship: By and large, the modern assessment of the extant eleventh-century manuscript is that it originated from an earlier, second or early third-century translation.[4]

Appendix 3 contains the essay "The First Letter of Clement: A Study to Determine the Character of the Oldest Form of Gentile Christianity." This essay was published in 1909 and represents an earlier investigation into the characteristics of 1 Clement as a whole. It is, in essence, the *Introduction* in its infancy. As Harnack himself notes, much of this essay has been brought into the *Introduction* word-for-word. There are of course interesting differences between the former and later works. Of particular note is the absence of a translation, the absence of textual notes, the presence of a rough outline of 1 Clement in a footnote, the use of lengthy Greek and Latin citations from primary source texts, a substantially different introduction for the work, and the inclusion of an excursus that addresses ecclesiastical *termini technici* attested to for the first time in 1 Clement. I have included this essay here within this volume, despite the large overlap in material with his

---

3. See Grant, *First and Second Clement*, 3–4; Lindemann, *Die Clemensbriefe*, 173–74; Lona, *Der erste Clemensbrief*, 607n3.

4. For the impact of Harnack's essay on the current views about the original Latin translation, see Lona, *Der erste Clemensbrief*, 15, 15n2–3.

Introduction for those interested in investigating the development of Harnack's thoughts on 1 Clement.

The final essay, which Harnack published in 1926, is a detailed investigation into all the uses of the epithet "servant of God" (παῖς θεοῦ) for Jesus up until the Apostolic Constitutions and Canons (see appendix 4). Harnack's goal in this essay is to answer the question: Why has ὁ παῖς θεοῦ as an epithet for Jesus penetrated the churches and their history despite the fact that it was never a common name for him in the New Testament? To answer this question, he charts the origins of the phrase (a translation of the Hebrew *ebed YHWH*) and analyzes every documented instance of its usage within the literary remains of the early church. He concludes that παῖς θεοῦ ("servant/son/child of God") was not widely used because of the baser meaning (i.e., "servant") that could have been associated with it. Nevertheless, this epithet conveyed intimacy and a sacredness that had penetrated into the liturgy and prayers of the church, ensuring that its usage endured longer than it otherwise would have, until it was gradually and inevitably replaced by υἱὸς θεοῦ ("son of God") because this designation for Jesus did not have the uncomfortable baggage associated with παῖς θεοῦ. Although the reception of this article in later Clement research is sporadic,[5] Hermut Löhr engages with Harnack throughout his own extensive investigation of this epithet and its meaning in 1 Clement.[6]

Before bringing this preface to its overdue conclusion, it is important to make the reader aware of the translator's approach to Harnack's articles along with a number of features of the translation itself. Throughout this translation, I have attempted to render his words as faithfully as possible into a smooth English idiom. Sentences of unbearable length or complexity have been broken up into smaller and more manageable pieces. Incomplete sentences, which were prolific throughout Harnack's comments on the text of 1 Clement, have been expanded and completed in numerous places where the phrasing was awkward or where the meaning might have otherwise been obscured. Translator's Notes (marked by the abbreviation TN within the footnotes) have been added to explain idiomatic expressions, provide alternate translations for difficult constructions, or in rare instances provide an explanation of Harnack's choice of terminology. There was at least one instance—in Harnack's essay on "servant" as an epithet for Jesus—where a paragraph spanning three pages was divided into smaller sections. It is my hope that this attention to English aesthetics makes for a more pleasant reading experience.

---

5. For instance, there is no reference to this work in Lona, Lindemann, Grant.
6. See Löhr, *Studien*, 318–34.

Additional features of this translation should be identified. Those familiar with Harnack's work on 1 Clement in German may notice that I have made a number of changes to his text. None of these changes have a bearing on content, but instead attempt to conform Harnack's works to the stylistic norms of contemporary academic literature. Abbreviated citations, which at times only included an author's name and the date of the publication, have been filled out wherever possible and a full bibliography of works cited has been provided. Additionally, Harnack's tendency to quote phrases, clauses, or whole verses from 1 Clement and only reference the chapter and not the specific verse(s) cited has not been maintained. While Martin Rumscheidt in his reader *Adolf von Harnack: Liberal Theology at its Height* begrudgingly tolerated this practice because of the work it would have required to repair it,[7] I have provided this additional information: Where citations of quoted text were missing, they have been supplied; where only the chapter has been provided by Harnack and it is clear that he was referencing a specific verse within that chapter, the verse has been supplied; in all matters that were unclear, no action was taken and Harnack's texts remain as they once did. Students of Harnack and 1 Clement will, I believe, benefit from more precise citations of the source texts as well as the accompanying index of ancient sources for the *Introduction* and all the appendixes. Finally, Harnack's original works—as I am certain will also be true of this edited compilation—contained numerous typographical errors (e.g., missing or incorrect versification in his translation of 1 Clement, incorrect accentuation or misspellings of Greek words, and incorrect references to the text of 1 Clement, to mention only a few). These errors—where I have become aware of them—have been corrected within this translation. Should one object to this liberality with Harnack's works, the original German texts are freely available online and can be consulted at the reader's discretion.

—Jacob N. Cerone

---

7. Rumscheidt writes: "The reader will become aware of Harnack's irritating habit of quoting a variety of poets, writers, and journalists without citing the source. The editor decided that the absence of such references, which to search out would have been a huge task, does not reduce the clarity of the image of Harnack's life and work" (Rumscheidt, "Introduction," 41). Clearly Rumscheit's decision was prudent when one considers the scope of literature Harnack interacted with in his more extensive works as well as the fact that Rumscheidt did not have the aid of modern electronic search tools.

Acknowledgments

When I began gathering sources for my doctoral work on 1 Clement, Harnack's *Introduction* was one of the first texts I encountered. At the time, my family and I had not yet moved to Munich to begin my studies, but I could already see Harnack would be a big part of the academic landscape. At first, the process of working through the text was painfully slow. I remember asking Jeremiah Bailey if he knew of an English translation. There was none. I began translating portions of Harnack's *Introduction* for my personal studies. Now, many translation projects later, I am proud to share the full translation of these texts, which would not have been possible without the support and encouragement of numerous individuals.

I am especially thankful to my Doktorvater David S. du Toit, who drew my attention to 1 Clement, encouraged me as I progressed in my German acquisition, and gave me opportunities to translate theological articles into English for publication. I am also thankful for Jeremiah Bailey for his conversations about Harnack and 1 Clement, his inclusion of this translation as the inaugural volume in this series on the Apostolic Fathers, as well as his careful review of the translation before its submission. I offer my sincerest thanks to Wayne Coppins, Christoph Heilig, Andrew Bowden, Nara Kim, Kathrin Hager, and David Lincicum for their comments and suggestions whenever I encountered particularly tricky German constructions. I am also thankful for Nathaniel Cooley and Zane Derven, who proofread the translation and offered necessary corrections, as well as my wife Mary Beth, who offered helpful suggestions throughout the process that have helped shape it into the volume it is.

Finally, it has been nothing but a pleasure working with both Jeremiah Bailey and George Kalantzis, the editors of this new series on the Apostolic Fathers, as well as the staff at Wipf and Stock, especially Jim Tedrick, Michael Thompson, George Callihan, and Calvin Jaffarian. Without them, their attention to detail, and their professionalism, this project would never have come to fruition.

—Jacob N. Cerone

Foreword

Harnack's Testament

THE SMALL, VALEDICTORY MONOGRAPH on 1 Clement[1] that Adolf von Harnack bequeathed to participants in his seminar on church history,[2] and to future generations of students,[3] was the culmination of a lifetime of research on the first of the so-called Apostolic Fathers,[4] but was also, in a deeper sense, Harnack's "intellectual testament,"[5] in which he sought to convey what was essential for an understanding of Christian history. As an historian, Harnack regarded 1 Clement as "the most important document we have received from earliest church history," after the writings of the New Testament, because in this epistle "the great church of the Greeks and Romans . . . the mother of all churches . . . represents itself in spirit and essence," so that without difficulty "one is able to foresee its further development into the catholic church."[6] As a Protestant theologian, Harnack found in 1 Clement a "pure" and "simple morality," expressed in humility, love and service, rooted in a consciousness of the reality and sovereignty of God,[7] an ethical idealism that Harnack saw

---

1. Harnack, "Das Schreiben der römischen Kirche."

2. On the conclusion of Harnack's seminar, see Zahn-Harnack, *Adolf von Harnack*, 436.

3. Emphasized by the term "Studierende" in the title and the explicit statement of purpose in the foreword, Harnack, *Das Schreiben der römischen Kirche*, 3 (1).

4. On the centrality of 1 Clement to Harnack's work, see Harnack, *Das Schreiben der römischen Kirche*, 3 (1); "Ansprachen," 7–15. In 1876, Harnack published a critical edition of 1 Clement in *Patrum Apostolicorum Opera*, followed a year later by a second edition, which added numerous manuscript variants. For a more detailed account of Harnack's engagement with 1 Clement throughout his academic career, see Markschies, "Harnack's Image of 1 Clement and Contemporary Research," 54–69.

5. So characterized by Unnik, "Studies on the So-Called First Epistle of Clement," 116.

6. Harnack, *Das Schreiben der römischen Kirche*, 5 (3).

7. Harnack, "Der erste Klemensbrief," 42–43 (148–49); *Das Schreiben der römischen*

threatened by the impending crises of the early twentieth century.[8] Harnack committed his understanding of the history and theology of the church to a monograph of only 128 pages, in the hope that students would learn from 1 Clement "the strength and purity of a will to goodness and to the building up of a new humanity energetically devoted to the welfare of others."[9] Were Harnack's hopes fulfilled?

I

Without doubt, Harnack's most important insight was that the Scriptures of Israel (in Greek translation) are the wellspring of Clement's religiosity: "The Christianity of Clement's epistle finds its God-given, plenary and sufficient foundation in the Old Testament, and consequently is nothing other than a religion of this book."[10] Harnack recognized that Clement's appropriation of Scripture differed from that of the Epistle to the Hebrews and the Epistle of Barnabas, indeed, differed most from that found in Paul: in Clement, there is no caesura in the meaning of the text, occasioned by the coming of Christ, requiring allegorical interpretation; rather, the words of Scripture apply directly to the lives of the "elect" to whom Clement writes, providing instructions for conduct and examples of nurture.[11] Harnack did not hesitate to draw the consequences: "In its foundation and its religious attitude, the Roman epistle belongs to the history of Old Testament religion and of ancient Judaism."[12]

Harnack was so convinced of the importance of Scripture in 1 Clement that he gave the insight to his most brilliant student, William Wrede, as a topic for research, to which Wrede then devoted the second half of his doctoral dissertation.[13] Scholars have continued to build upon Harnack's insight. Annie Jaubert emphasized Clement's knowledge of Levitical

---

Kirche, 58 (48).

8. Harnack, "Funfzehn Fragen," 6–8; "Review of Heinrich Hoffmann," 409–10.

9. Harnack, *Das Schreiben der römischen Kirche*, 103 (87).

10. Harnack, "Das Schreiben der römischen Kirche," 53 (54). Harnack counted one hundred twenty quotations and allusions, along with seven citations from the Apocrypha ("eine ungeheure Zahl!"); this and all future page references are to the reprint of Harnack's monograph in *Encounters with Hellenism*.

11. Harnack, "Das Schreiben der römischen Kirche," 56–57 (57–58).

12. Harnack, "Das Schreiben der römischen Kirche," 57 (58). "Ancient Judaism" translates Harnack's "Spätjudentum," in accordance with current usage.

13. Wrede, *Untersuchungen zum ersten Klemensbriefe*, 58–107.

traditions.[14] Donald Hagner devoted a third of his meticulous study of 1 Clement to the author's use of the Old Testament.[15] More recently, Peter Tomson has examined Clement's references to Jerusalem, its temple, priesthood and cult.[16] Scholars have been slower to engage Harnack's inference about Clement's place in the history of Judaism. Only recently has a productive debate been joined between Joseph Verheyden and James Carleton Paget: the former asserts that Clement's references to Israel, few though they are, imply a polemical attitude toward Jews and Judaism,[17] while the latter argues that Clement's extensive use of Scripture reveals a positive attitude toward Judaism, characteristic of "an erstwhile God-fearer, who retained a respect for his Jewish heritage."[18]

As a second element in Clement's formation, Harnack identified the "specifically Christian content."[19] Harnack endeavored to assess Clement's Christology on its own terms, that is, without reference to Paul. In this way, Harnack discovered a plentitude and diversity of christological formulations that he found "astonishing" in such an early writing.[20] Harnack summarized his results in an overview of the passages in which Clement uses the phrase "in Christ," or describes the church as the "flock of Christ," or focuses attention upon the "blood of Christ," etc.[21] Harnack inferred that behind Clement's statements about Christ and his salvific work was a broad stream of primitive tradition that was independent of Paul and Paulinism.[22] Nevertheless, Harnack judged that Clement's Christology, for all its breadth, was superficial and unreflected, merely repeating the formulas of tradition.[23]

Harnack's insight into the Christology of 1 Clement has produced little impact upon subsequent scholarship, apart from echoes in the commentaries.[24] William Wrede formulated the paradox identified by his teacher in an extreme manner: Christology is ultimately dispensable for Clement, since what matters is obedience to the commandments of God found in

---

14. Jaubert, "Thèmes lévitiques dans la Prima Clementis," 193–203.
15. Hagner, *Use of the Old and New Testaments in Clement of Rome*, 21–132.
16. Tomson, "Centrality of Jerusalem and Its Temple," 97–112.
17. Verheyden, "Israel's Fate in the Apostolic Fathers," 237–62.
18. Paget, "1 Clement, Judaism, and the Jews," 218–50.
19. Harnack, "Das Schreiben der römischen Kirche," 58–65 (58–65).
20. Harnack, "Das Schreiben der römischen Kirche," 58 (58).
21. Harnack, "Das Schreiben der römischen Kirche," 58–61 (58–61).
22. Harnack, "Das Schreiben der römischen Kirche," 61–62 (61–62).
23. Harnack, "Das Schreiben der römischen Kirche," 63 (62–63).
24. Fischer, *Die Apostolischen Väter*, 13; Lindemann, *Die Clemensbriefe*, 112–13.

Scripture.[25] The only monograph devoted to the Christology of 1 Clement, that of H. B. Bumpus, circumvents the problem diagnosed by Harnack, by positing the influence of intertestamental literature upon Clement.[26] Only Horacio Lona resumes Harnack's approach, in an excursus to his erudite commentary, listing all of Clement's christological statements, organized systematically: from preexistence to resurrection, and the sending of the apostles;[27] within this framework, Lona ascribes special importance to the function of Christ as "mediator" of the saving work of God.[28]

Harnack's third insight into the sources of Clement's thought was that the letter is permeated by a Hellenistic-Roman idealism, epitomized by the works of contemporary Stoics and Platonists, such as Epictetus and Plutarch.[29] Harnack called attention, in particular, to the ideology of "peace and concord" found throughout the epistle, the counsel of voluntary exile in chapter 54, and the view of the natural world as a harmonious whole in chapter 20, adducing parallels from philosophers and orators.

Developing Harnack's insight into the Hellenistic milieu, Louis Sanders adduced numerous parallels between passages in 1 Clement and the writings of Epictetus, Dio Chrysostom, and Seneca, which locate the Roman epistle in proximity to the popular Stoicism of the early Empire.[30] Martin Dibelius and Adolf Ziegler demonstrated that the *agon* motif in 1 Clem 5–7 reflects the tradition of the Cynic-Stoic diatribe.[31] In a seminal monograph that takes its point of departure from Harnack, W. C. van Unnik demonstrated that 1 Clement belongs to the "deliberative genre," a kind of discourse regularly discussed by writers on rhetoric after Aristotle, and instanced in the speeches "On Concord" by Dio Chrysostom and Aelius Aristides.[32] Recently, Cilliers Breytenbach has investigated the sources of Clement's encomium of cosmic concord in chapter 20, as a model of the harmony he seeks to nurture in the Christian community.[33] Breytenbach finds the closest parallels to 1 Clem 20 in the deliberative discourses of Dio Chrysostom and Aelius Aristides, and in

---

25. Wrede, *Untersuchungen zum ersten Klemensbriefe*, 103.

26. Bumpus, *Christological Awareness of Clement of Rome and Its Sources*.

27. Lona, *Der erste Clemensbrief*, 401–3.

28. Lona, *Clemensbrief*, 403–4.

29. Harnack, "Das Schreiben der römischen Kirche," 65–70 (65–69).

30. Sanders, *L'Hellénisme de Saint Clément de Rome et Le Paulinisme*; preceded by Bardy, "Expressions stoïciennes dans la 1ᵉ Clementis," 73–85.

31. Dibelius, *Rom und die Christen im ersten Jahrhundert*, 192–99; Ziegler, *Neue Studien zum ersten Klemensbrief*, 24–37.

32. Unnik, *Studies over de zogenaamde Eerste Brief van Clemens*; followed by Bakke, *Concord and Peace*.

33. Breytenbach, "Civic Concord and Cosmic Harmony," 259–73.

pseudo-Aristotle's *De mundo*, where Stoic cosmology is placed at the service of arguments for civic concord.[34]

A final, crucial contribution of Harnack's monograph was his analysis of Clement's attitude toward the Roman state.[35] Harnack rightly recognized that Clement's orientation is entirely positive. In evidence, Harnack pointed to the liturgical prayer at the close of the epistle, where Clement petitions: "grant that we may become obedient to our rulers and governors upon the earth … to whom God has given the exercise of sovereignty" (60.4–61.1). From this, Harnack drew two consequences: first, that the earthly regime of Rome is parallel to the heavenly kingdom of God; and second, that Clement permits no right of resistance to those who must be subservient; rather, resistance to the temporal authorities is resistance to the will of God (61.1).[36]

Harnack puzzled over the apparent incongruity between Clement's attitude toward the Roman state and his knowledge that Christians had suffered persecution under Nero (chapters 5–6). Harnack concluded that Clement's attitude toward the Roman state was a defensive posture calculated to protect the Christian community: "that our Roman community-writing represents this attitude, despite the Neronian and Domitianic persecution, must have been of the greatest importance. Recognition of the right of the authorities and a passive posture were alone able to protect the political existence of the church."[37] As a concrete instance of the danger facing the Christian community, Harnack pointed to 47.6–7, where Clement alleges that the "report" that "the church of the Corinthians is in revolt … has not only reached us, but also those who are of a different allegiance from us, so that you are creating danger for yourselves." Harnack suggested that Clement raises here the specter of action by the Roman authorities, in response to the discord in the church at Corinth: "indeed, it seems that in Corinth an intervention by the police was at least threatened (a house-search in consequence of the conflicts?)."[38]

Paul Mikat built effectively upon Harnack's hypothesis in his investigation of the importance of the concepts *stasis* and *aponoia* for an understanding of 1 Clement.[39] On the basis of a close reading of 47.7 and 54.2, Mikat concluded that Clement saw the Corinthian church threatened by a dangerous situation: the intervention of the Roman authorities, in order to put an end to the conflict in the house churches. Mikat explained: "The prayer

34. Breytenbach, "Civic Concord and Cosmic Harmony," 263–70.

35. In the excursus "Die politische Haltung" in Harnack, *Das Schreiben der römischen Kirche*, 71–72 (70–71).

36. Harnack, "Das Schreiben der römischen Kirche," 71 (70).

37. Harnack, "Das Schreiben der römischen Kirche," 71 (70).

38. Harnack, "Das Schreiben der römischen Kirche," 99 (104).

39. Mikat, *Bedeutung*.

for the rulers of this world in 1 Clement arises from the concern that a persecution may occur; so long as the *stasis* continues, there is a risk that the temporal authorities will be provoked to intervene. If there are Christians whose conduct can be plausibly described as *aponoia*, the authorities may suspect that the movement is a *superstitio*, rather than a *religio* which affirms its support for the welfare of the empire through its cult."[40]

II

Toward the end of the monograph, before the notes to his felicitous German translation, Harnack listed eighteen problems posed by the Roman epistle which had not been fully resolved, and which might be profitably pursued in future seminars.[41] Several of these issues have since become the subject of research, as we have seen: the Old Testament citations in 1 Clement, the engagement of the author with the ideals of Greco-Roman culture, the rhetorical style and genre of the letter, etc. Recently, Clare Rothschild has taken up one of the issues raised by Harnack, namely, the Pauline character of Clement's epistle. In a thorough investigation of the reception of First Corinthians in 1 Clement, Rothschild demonstrates that Clement borrows the authority of Paul's voice, while simultaneously altering Paul's message.[42] When Clement makes use of Paul's language, it is mostly for rhetorical effect; his thought is generally at odds with Paul's theology, or else Clement adds to Paul's text what he really wishes to say.[43]

It is instructive to consider which issues were omitted from Harnack's list of "not yet fully investigated problems." First among these is the matter of the date of the epistle, which Harnack confidently assigned to the final years of the reign of Domitian.[44] In this, Harnack followed the suggestion of the first editor of the epistle, Patrick Young (1633 CE), who interpreted the mention of "sudden and repeated misfortunes and hindrances which have befallen us" in the preface to the epistle (1.1) as an allusion to the persecution of the Christians of Rome by Domitian,[45] a view that was popularized by J. B. Lightfoot,[46] and that by the time of Harnack had become the scholarly consensus.[47]

40. Mikat, *Bedeutung*, 39.
41. Harnack, "Das Schreiben der römischen Kirche," 82–83 (82–83).
42. Rothschild, "Reception of 1 Corinthians in 1 Clement," 35–60.
43. Welborn, "Take up the Epistle of the Blessed Paul the Apostle," 345–57.
44. Harnack, "Das Schreiben der römischen Kirche," 87 (88–89).
45. Young, *Clementis ad Corinthios epistola prior* (1st and 2nd ed.).
46. Lightfoot, *Clement of Rome*, 1:27, 81, 346–58, 383.
47. See the list of early proponents—Cotelier, Ritschl, Reuss, Hilgenfeld, Gundert, Tischendorf, Lightfoot, Zahn, et al.—in Gebhardt and Harnack, *Patrum Apostolicorum*

In an article published in 1984, I challenged this consensus by demonstrating that no linguistic basis exists for interpreting the language of 1 Clem 1.1 as a reference to persecution.[48] The most serious event denoted by the hendiadys συμφοραί ("misfortunes") and περιπτώσεις ("hindrances") relates to the incidence or consequence of civil strife (στάσις).[49] When one takes account of the genre of 1 Clement as a deliberative appeal for concord, the function of the first sentence of the epistle becomes clear: it serves as a *captatio benevolentiae*, guarding against the impression that the Roman church is lording it over their Corinthian brothers and sisters by intervening in their conflict.[50] What Clement means to suggest by mentioning the "misfortunes and hindrances" that had delayed the Roman church from responding to the crisis at Corinth is made explicit in 7.1: "We are writing these things, beloved, not admonishing you alone, but also reminding ourselves; for we are in the same arena, and the same struggle lies before us." The impact of my article upon scholarship has been to sever the long-postulated connection between the language of 1 Clem 1.1 and the Eusebian tradition of a persecution by Domitian, throwing open the question of the date of the Roman epistle. In retrospect, Harnack's failure to list the date of 1 Clement among the "not yet fully investigated issues" did much to consign the matter to scholarly oblivion for more than two generations.

A second matter that Harnack evidently regarded as settled was the occasion of the Roman epistle: the church of the Corinthians had unjustly removed some of its presbyters from their ministry (44.3–6; 47.6).[51] Harnack did not inquire further into the motive for the revolt, concluding that it was merely a quarrel between cliques, without any foundation in principle.[52] But reflecting upon the influence that a few prominent persons (1.1; 47.6), the instigators of the uprising (51.1; 57.1), had been able to win over the entire Corinthian community, Harnack made the following suggestion (in a footnote): "That the majority [of the rebels] counted among its members especially many young people, and that some women also made their influence felt here, has, in light of 1.3; 3.3; 21.6–7 (note the bitter irony), a high probability."[53]

In the first volume of his magisterial history of the early church, a work dedicated to the memory of Adolf von Harnack, Hans Lietzmann took up Harnack's tentative suggestion about the motive for the revolt and

---

Opera, lix–lx.

48. Welborn, "On the Date of First Clement," 35–54.

49. Welborn, "On the Date of First Clement," 46–48.

50. Welborn, "On the Date of First Clement," 47.

51. On the precision with which the occasion of 1 Clement can be determined, see Harnack, "Das Schreiben der römischen Kirche," 75 (74–75).

52. Harnack, "Das Schreiben der römischen Kirche," 76 (75–76).

53. Harnack, "Das Schreiben der römischen Kirche," 76n60 (76n11).

the identity of the perpetrators, and put forward the hypothesis that the conflict at Corinth in the time of Clement was inter-generational in character: "The younger generation revolted against the regime of the older and deposed the bishops and deacons from their office."[54] In a monograph published in 2018, I sought to confirm this hypothesis by analysis of the rhetoric and argumentation of 1 Clement, with attention to the themes and motifs that recur frequently in ancient accounts of generational conflict.[55] I also argued that certain women provided financial support for the young men who deposed the established presbyters.[56] Among the motives for the revolt, I posited frustration at the routine exclusion of the young from church office,[57] and a revival of the memory of a Pauline polity in which age was not a qualification for leadership.[58]

The most serious—and poignant—omission from Harnack's monograph is the absence of any critique of Clement's attitude toward the Roman state. To be sure, Harnack rightly judged that Clement provides no basis for resistance to the temporal authorities. As we have seen, Harnack explained Clement's subservience as a defensive posture calculated to protect the Christian community. But, unfortunately, Harnack did not stop there: he added that, through compliance, the church became a "positive factor" for the Roman state.[59] And worse, Harnack foresaw that by endorsing the government as a divinely-willed institution on earth, Clement prepared the way for a later day when the church itself would assume temporal authority.[60] Harnack's uncritical stance toward the church-state relationship led him to greet the Concordat between the Roman Catholic Church and the Fascist government of Italy as a "rekindling" of the spirit manifest in 1 Clement.[61] The tragic denouement of Harnack's blindness was revealed fifteen years after the publication of his monograph, when the senior student in Harnack's seminar, Dietrich Bonhoeffer, was put to death in Flossenburg prison for his resistance to the Nazi regime.[62]

---

54. Lietzmann, *Geschichte der Alten Kirche*, 201.
55. Welborn, *Young Against the Old*, esp. 21–48, 129–72.
56. Welborn, *Young against the Old*, 189–94.
57. Welborn, *Young against the Old*, 200–202.
58. Welborn, *Young against the Old*, 202–6, building upon a suggestion of Barclay, who devoted a paragraph of his essay, "There Is Neither Old Nor Young?" (235–36), to 1 Clement.
59. Harnack, "Das Schreiben der römischen Kirche," 71 (70).
60. Harnack, "Das Schreiben der römischen Kirche," 71–72 (70–71).
61. Harnack, "Das Schreiben der römischen Kirche," 4 (6).
62. Marsh, *Strange Glory*.

III

Harnack's life-long interest in 1 Clement was not merely antiquarian. Rather, the monograph discloses that Harnack resonated deeply with the religious character of the Roman epistle. Harnack saw the religion of 1 Clement as "a moral movement based upon a monotheism of the greatest seriousness and highest vitality: or better, based upon the reality of God."[63] As the truest heirs of Clement's religiosity, Harnack pointed to Calvin in Geneva, and the Puritans in New England.[64] The epilogue to the monograph reveals the hope—a hope also expressed in Harnack's lectures and letters—that an encounter with the "classic" Christianity of 1 Clement would somehow serve to maintain the relationship between the Reformation and the Enlightenment that Harnack viewed as essential for the future of humanity.[65]

Almost a century after the publication of Harnack's farewell monograph, it seems that Harnack's highest hope has been disappointed. The spirit of Reformation and Enlightenment has departed, and not only from Berlin.[66] The attack upon history-writing from a Protestant perspective by J. Z. Smith in his widely acclaimed *Drudgery Divine* has discredited Harnack's project in the academy.[67] Even Christoph Markschies, Professor of Ancient Christianity at the Humboldt-Universität zu Berlin, concludes that Harnack's research method was "denominationally dictated," and moves along one of the "dead-end streets from today's perspective."[68] Whether this will be the ultimate legacy of Harnack's "testament" is in the hands of readers of this long-delayed translation of Harnack's monograph.

—Larry Welborn

---

63. Harnack, "Das Schreiben der römischen Kirche," 47 (48).

64. Harnack, *Das Schreiben der römischen Kirche*, 47 (48).

65. Harnack, "Das Schreiben der römischen Kirche," 85–86 (86–87).

66. Following a conference on "The Rise of Early Christianity in Greece" at the Humboldt-Universität in May 2017, I asked a post-doctoral research assistant if he might guide me to the Zionskirche, where Dietrich Bonhoeffer once served as a pastor, for Sunday worship services. The research assistant replied, "Haven't you heard that Christianity has left Berlin?"

67. Smith, *Drudgery Divine*.

68. Markschies, "Harnack's Image of 1 Clement and Contemporary Research," 68–69.

Preface

WITH THE PUBLICATION OF the following pages, I conclude my seminar on Church History, which I led in Leipzig, Gießen, Marburg, and Berlin for fifty-four years (1874–1928) and which was the focus of my academic work. A large number of studies on church history and monographs by fellow students have come out of the seminar, but I have certainly learned more from these exercises than did my students. For this, I thank them most sincerely, but above all I thank them for the cordial trust I have always found to be characteristic of them. These pages are my farewell. They are to remind my colleagues of the spirit shared in the hours on Thursday evenings. It was a serious and a joyful spirit. May it remain true with them even in difficult times. — *Non potest non laetari qui sperat in domino*!

Berlin, June 1929
von Harnack

Introduction

THE DEEPEST GRATITUDE THAT Christianity owes to tradition relates to the collection and preservation of the writings of the New Testament. However, next to the transmission of the New Testament is the most important foundational document (*Urkunde*) we have received from the earliest history of the church: the so-called 1 Clement, that is, the extensive letter from the Roman Church, the congregation of the capital of the world, to the Corinthian Church, the congregation of the Greek metropolis, which originated during the reign of Domitian. Rome and Greece appear here together in the transition from the apostolic age to the post-apostolic age, and Rome is the spokeswoman. This is of utmost importance; but the requisite consequence does not follow from this fact. Neither the Roman Church, which is primarily in view in this letter, nor the Protestant churches, nor historical-theological scholarship appreciate this writing as it deserves in their research and teaching. What it is ultimately about can be summarized in one sentence: From the New Testament writings, one cannot grasp the essence and spiritual structure of the great church of the Greeks and Romans, how it was formed in the first century and how it became the mother of all churches—one can only approach it tentatively and with uncertainty from here—however, in 1 Clement, the oldest church of the Gentiles presents itself in spirit and essence, and one can by means of simple analysis both ascertain its elements and foresee its continued development into the Catholic Church. Therefore, this letter forms directly the foundation for the study of the ancient history of the church, while the majority of the writings compiled in the New Testament are testimonies to the short, paleontological epoch[1] (so to speak) of the history of Christianity. This classical epoch has been denied a direct continuation.[2]

From here arises the necessary conclusion that the study of ancient church history must begin with 1 Clement, since there is no other foundational document (*Urkunde*) that is able to compete with it with respect to its historical significance. From this insight, the following work emerged: a presentation in an elementary form that does not deal with many individual and sublime foundational questions.[3] It is a necessary addition to the textbooks that exist on church history and hopes to introduce every student of theology to the most ancient history of the church through 1 Clement. If this happens, the student will be placed upon a firm foundation, will understand the development that begins here, and will be protected from the greatest danger that lurks here, namely overestimating particular phenomena (e.g., primitive, gnostic) within the development of the earliest history of the church, and letting it cloud one's view of the main elements. The one who has worked through and understood 1 Clement is immune to the mistakes of taking a measure of the particular phenomena of the most ancient church history and substituting a distorted, generalized picture in place of the genuine one.[4]

---

1. TN: Harnack uses the expression "paläontologische Epoche" numerous times throughout his works. Christoph Markschies explains that Harnack's use of the expression refers to "the entire writings of Early Christianity from the first three centuries" ("Harnack's Image of 1 Clement and Contemporary Research," 58). For a more in depth explanation of Harnack's usage of this expression and its meaning, see Markschies, "Harnack's Image of 1 Clement and Contemporary Research," 59–60.

2. The distinction made here is not to be understood as an absolute distinction. From the New Testament writings, lines can be drawn to the nascent Catholic Church, and, on the other hand, 1 Clement evidences original Christian features of the first order. Nevertheless, in the main, the distinction rightly exists.

3. The predecessor of this work is an investigation which I published in 1909 in the proceedings of the Prussian Academy, "Der erste Klemensbrief. Eine Studie zur Bestimmung des Charakters des ältesten Heidenchristenums" (translated in this volume under the title "The First Letter of Clement: A Study to Determine the Character of the Oldest Form of Gentile Christianity," 144–168). I have taken over a number of lengthy constructions, word-for-word, from that publication, and so this new work can be understood as a greatly expanded and augmented reworking of the earlier one. Among the foundational questions, I consider to be of significance those that pertain to the emergence of church law and, similarly, those which one can and has linked with the letter. Whether and to what extent one wishes to deal with them must remain open.

4. One could argue that the doctrinal development of the church in the following period could not be understood from 1 Clement, because it remains silent about the heresies. Yet this argument is inaccurate. Granted, one cannot foresee from this letter what theses and in what forms the heresies would appear; nevertheless, how the churches will answer them with firm doctrines of faith and knowledge is clearly evident in it, and this is the main point because it will determine the fight decisively. But what

We have excellent detailed commentaries on the letter, especially those by Lightfoot (1890)[5] and by Knopf (1920)[6]—see also my commentary (1876)[7]—and I can only hope that they are being worked through. They do not, however, make superfluous the attempt to target directly the historical understanding of this foundational document (*Urkunde*) directly through analysis, and at the same time to introduce it into the basic repertoire of theological education. Therefore, I have also provided a German translation[8] here, partly to explain the letter through the translation itself, and partly to make it possible for those who still have difficulties reading it in the original language, because unfortunately we must reckon with this state of affairs in a large number of students. However, they too should interact with the explanations and remarks given here, which in many cases refer to the Greek text.[9]

When I published the letter together with my friend von Gebhardt (†) in 1875, there was only one manuscript, and that manuscript itself was incomplete. Today, we have six, not more or less indifferent copies,[10] but rather six principal manuscripts (two Greek, one Old Latin, one Old Syriac, and two Coptic). The transmission of the letter is therefore firmly established, and also in this respect (the richness and goodness of ancient tradition) it comes alongside the writings of the New Testament. The manuscript discoveries of the last fifty years have not come anywhere near as close to any ancient Christian writing like that of 1 Clement. They also show the high esteem in which the writing was held in ecclesiastical antiquity. It is the purpose of this work to give back to it—a letter that had been entirely forgotten from the thirteenth to the seventeenth century, which then gradually reappeared—its status as the oldest and most distinguished foundational document (*Urkunde*) of the ancient church of the Greeks

---

it contains about the moral and ecclesiastical principles of life, about the community in order and worship, and about ministry is to be taken as the immediate starting point for subsequent developments.

5. Lightfoot, *Clement of Rome*, vol. 1.
6. Knopf, *Die Lehre der Zwölf Apostel*.
7. Gebhardt and Harnack, *Patrum Apostolicorum Opera*.
8. TN: Here rendered into English.
9. With these remarks, I do not intend to explain the letter with an evenly prepared commentary, but instead I have deliberately proceeded eclectically and have essentially limited myself to what I deemed necessary for the purpose of this work. With regard to translation, I am grateful to older translations for some apt expressions. I have not, however, compared them methodically.
10. TN: Harnack's use of "gleichgültige" ("indifferent") establishes, by way of contrast, the value of all extant manuscripts. Among the extant manuscripts of 1 Clement, none are insignificant.

and the Romans. By following my monograph on Marcion published nine years ago with such a monograph on 1 Clement, I am guided by the intention to make the two most important phenomena of the post-apostolic age as clear and bright as possible and to influence the teaching of church history accordingly, this time in a form expressly intended for students since I often treated 1 Clement in seminars and gave a one hour lecture on it in the winter semester of 1928/1929.

The noble, in the best sense of the word, letter of 1 Clement belongs to the Church of Rome; even today it may strengthen its Catholic self-confidence. The peace treaty between the Vatican and Fascist Italy that we have just witnessed has rekindled this self-confidence. An eloquent proof of this is the treatise by the important Italian church historian Chiappelli "Gesù e Roma" ("Nuova Antologia," Nov. 1, 1928) with the motto from Dante "Di quella Roma onde Cristo è Romano." Here, Jesus and Rome—strangely without respect to 1 Clement—are presented according to a hyper-historical method as the great syzygy, chosen by Jesus, who has determined and dominated the history of the church. Forty-three years ago, in a chapter entitled "Katholisch und Römisch" in the first edition of my *Lehrbuches der Dogmengeschichte*[11]—which is as far as I know the first in Protestant historiography—I established the historical connection between these two great phenomena of church history and strengthened this proof in subsequent editions. But to form the syzygy "Jesus and Rome" lies outside critical-historical possibility and can only be achieved by political speculation which leaves the domain of real history. Nevertheless, Chiappelli tried it and placed the eternal Rome according to the wish of Jesus (!) on the throne next to Jesus. Fascist Italy and the Roman Church will gratefully welcome this new theology of history, but historical research must reject it and at the same time fear that eccentric speculation will discredit the true realization that "Catholic" and "Roman" really belong very closely together. Jesus and Rome cannot be connected with each other on any historical line without the mediating role of Hellenism and the Greek Church.

---

11. Harnack, *Lehrbuch der Dogmengeschichte*.

1. The Transmission of the Letter

Codex A = Codex Alexandrinus, fifth century, in the British Museum,[1] which contains the entire Bible. The letter is at the end of the New Testament, after Revelation. The Patriarch Cyrillus Lukaris gifted this codex to the king of England in the year 1628. Junius published it in the year 1633. It lacks a leaf (1 Clem 57.6–63, to the end). Otherwise, the codex has defects due to damage to the edges and illegibility. A phototype was produced in 1879.

Codex H[2] = Codex Hierosolymitanus (Patriarchal Library), written in the year 1056, discovered and published (1875) by Bryennios. The letter is placed after Barnabas and before 2 Clement and the Didache (thus placed together with the *antilegomena*, but not among the works of the New Testament). A photographical facsimile is in Lightfoot's edition, published in 1890.

Codex S = A Syriac codex (Cambridge, Add. Mss. 1700), written in the year 1170, described and first used by Lightfoot (*loc. cit.*), published by Bensly and Kennet (1899). The letter is within the New Testament, after the Catholic Epistles and before 2 Clement and the Pauline Epistles, and is divided into lections.

Codex L = A Latin codex (Seminary at Namur, previously the Monastery of Florennes) from the eleventh century. The translation

---

1. TN: In Harnack's day, Codex Alexandrinus was housed in the British Museum, of which the Library was a part. However, the Library detached itself from the British Museum in 1972. Codex Alexandrinus is, therefore, no longer housed in the Museum but instead within the British Library.

2. TN: In previous works, Harnack has used the abbreviation C for this manuscript because it was often called Codex Constantinopolitanus. This practice has inadvertently bled into this work, despite the fact that he claims to use the abbreviation H here. This inconsistency has been repaired within this translation.

however probably belongs to the second century. The codex was discovered and published by Morin (Maredsous, 1894). The letter stands in a miscellaneous collection, after the letter of Pseudo Clement to James and before Bede's *De locis sanctis*.

Codex C¹ = A Coptic codex[3] (papyrus, Akhmimic dialect, housed in the Staatsbibliothek of Berlin, formerly in the White Monastery of Shenute), fourth century, or (early) fifth. Five leaves (1 Clem 34.5—42.2) have been lost. The codex was discovered and published by Karl Schmidt, *Texte und Untersuchungen zur Geschichte der altchristlichen Literatur*, vol. 32.1, 1908.

Codex C² = A Coptic codex[4] (papyrus, Akhmimic dialect, but a different translation than C¹, Straßburg, probably fifth century, preserved only in fragments, extending to around 1 Clem 26. Edited by F. Rösch, *Bruchstücke des 1 Clemensbriefs* (Straßburg: M. Du Mont Schauberg, 1910).

In the indirect tradition, only Clement of Alexandria (containing numerous quotations and allusions) is of both great and substantial significance.

All the manuscripts are valuable, and not a one of them is clearly better than the others (A is not much better than H); C¹ and C² are closer to AH than S and L.

If SL agree with one of the four manuscripts (AHC¹C²), there is a very high probability that it is the original reading; agreement between AHC¹C² does not however guarantee the correctness of the reading. Very sparse are the cases in which a singular manuscript has preserved the correct reading; nevertheless, even S and L sometimes have a singular reading that is correct. The history of the letter, which begins with Ignatius, Polycarp, Hermas, Dionysius of Corinth, Hegesippus, and Irenaeus, thus presenting itself in an incomparably good series of witnesses,[5] cannot be dealt with in short; it

---

3. TN: This codex is also known as Codex Berolinensis.

4. TN: This codex is also known as Codex Argentinensis.

5. Ignatius writes to the Romans (3:1), "You have never mistreated anyone, you have taught others . . . " It is highly probable that this refers to 1 Clement.

In his letter to Philippi, Polycarp used numerous passages from 1 Peter and 1 Clement without naming his sources. (He proceeds differently, however, with respect to Paul.)

Hermas (Vis. II.4) claims to have received the following order from the "church" in the form of an old woman, "Write two books and send one to Clement, the other to Grapte. Clement should then send it to the cities abroad. For this is his duty (ἐπιτέτραπται: the word is unfortunately ambiguous—*ad hoc* or entirely?), but Grapte should instruct the

is however discussed in detail by me in my edition *Patrum Apostolicicorum Opera* (1876)[6] and in my *Altchristlichen Literaturgeschichte I* (1893).[7]

widows and orphans." It is generally accepted that the Clement mentioned is our Clement, and that the reference here is to 1 Clement.

Eusebius writes, "A letter to the Romans is circulated also by Dionysius (bishop of Corinth, ca. 170) with the address to the then bishop Soter . . . . In this letter, Dionysius also mentions the letter of Clement to the Corinthians, stating that this letter has been read in the Corinthian Church for a long time due to old habits. His words are as follows, 'Today we have observed the holy day of the Lord, on which we have read your letter aloud, which we will continue to read [in the church assembly] for our admonition, as well as the previous one which you wrote to us through Clement'" (*Hist. eccl.* IV.23.9f).

Eusebius writes, "That at that time [of Domitian] in Corinth [i.e., in the Christian congregation there] a revolt took place. Hegesippus (ca. 180) is a credible witness to this" (*Hist. eccl.* III.16). Eusebius also notes in IV.22.1f. that Hegesippus had said some things about the letter of Clement to the Corinthians in his work (*Hypomnemata*) before he came to speak about his stay in Corinth.

In his list, Irenaeus (*Haer.* III.3.3) calls Clement the third bishop of Rome, but interrupts the list at this point and, because of the great importance of the matter, inserts the following, "Clement also saw the blessed apostles and came into contact with them and had the *kerygma* of the apostles and their tradition still present and before his eyes . . . . When at his time there was a not insignificant uproar among the brethren in Corinth, the Church in Rome prepared a very proper letter to the Corinthians. It aligns them with peace, renews their faith, and proclaims the tradition that was recently received from the apostles: the one Almighty God, the creator of heaven and earth, the Maker of man who brought about the flood, who called Abraham, who led the people out of Egypt, who spoke to Moses, who gave the law, who sent the prophets, and who prepared the fire for the devils and his angels. That this Father of our Lord Jesus Christ (also) is proclaimed by the churches can be learned from this writing, by those who wish to learn it, and can bring to light the apostolic tradition of the Church, for this letter is older than today's false teachers."

Clement of Alexandria, who plundered the letter of his namesake, quotes it as "The Letter of Clement," but also as the "Letter of the Romans" (*Strom.* V.12.80) and calls Clement "Apostle" (*Strom.* IV.17.105).

6. Gebhardt and Harnack, *Patrum Apostolicorum Opera*.

7. Harnack, *Geschichte der altchristlichen Literatur bis Eusebius*, 1:40ff.

The Letter

THE CHURCH OF GOD, which lives as a stranger in Rome, to the church of God, which lives as a stranger in Corinth, by the will of God through our Lord Jesus Christ. May grace and peace be granted to you in abundance by Almighty God, through Jesus Christ![1]

1.1 The sudden and abrupt misfortunes and adversities that took place among us, brothers, have, as we see it, somewhat delayed our attention to the disputes that have arisen among you, (beloved), that abominable and unholy dissension that is foreign and indecent to God's chosen ones, which has ignited a few reckless and insolent people to such an extent of folly that your venerable, infamous, and beloved reputation has suffered severe damage. (2) For what visitor has not approved of your firm faith, endowed with all virtues? Who does not admire your prudent and gentle piety for Christ? Who does not proclaim your great practice of hospitality? Who does not praise your perfect and secure knowledge? (3) For it was your habit to do everything without regard for the person and to walk in God's statutes, subordinating yourselves to your leaders and showing the honor due to the old. You commanded the young to be of a moderate and honorable mind, and you instructed your women to do everything with an impeccable, noble, and pure conscience, with a proper love for their husbands. You also taught them to abide by the rules of subservience and to furnish their household with dignity, full of respectability.[2]

2.1 Furthermore, you were all of humble mind, without any arrogance, submitting rather than giving orders, giving rather than taking, content with the provisions of Christ and holding them close to you. You carried his words carefully in your heart, and his sufferings stood before your eyes.[3] (2) And so a deep and fruitful peace was given to all and an

---

1. 1 Cor 1:1f. (1 Peter 1:1f., 17).
2. (Titus 2:5).
3. (Acts 20:35); (Gal 3:1).

insatiable desire to do good was instilled, and the Holy Spirit was poured out over all of them in full measure. (3) Being filled with a holy purpose, you stretched out your hands to the Almighty God in good spirits and with pious confidence, imploring him to grant his grace if you sinned against your will.[4] (4) A battle lay before you day and night for the whole brotherhood, that by mercy and . . . the number of his elect might be saved. (5) You were pure and innocent, and you did not hold malice against each other. (6) Every turmoil and every schism was an abomination to you; you mourned the missteps of your neighbors; you regarded their shortcomings as your own. (7) You never repented of a good deed; you were ready for every good work. (8) Adorned with a venerable walk full of all virtues, you performed everything in the fear of him; the commandments and statutes of the Lord were written on the tablets of your heart.[5]

3.1 Every sort of glory and enlargement were given to you, and that which was written has been consummated, "My beloved ate and drank, and was enlarged, and became fat, and kicked out."[6] (2) From this came evil zeal and envy, strife and sedition, persecution and decay, war and captivity. (3) Now the ignoble rose against the noble, those with no name against those with a high reputation, the ignorant against the intelligent, the young against the old.[7] (4) Therefore, justice and peace were far away, because each one abandoned the fear of God and became blind with regard to faith in him, not walking in the statutes of his commandments, nor conducting his life after Christ, but walking according to the desires of his evil heart, cherishing unjust and godless zeal, through which death also penetrated into the world.[8]

4.1 For it is written, "And it happened after several days that Cain brought God an offering from the fruits of the earth, and Abel also brought such an offering from among the first born of the sheep and from their fat. (2) And God looked at Abel and his gift. However, he paid no attention to Cain and to his offering. (3) And Cain was very sad and his countenance fell. (4) And God said to Cain, 'Why have you become so sad and why has your countenance fallen? Did you not sin, if you offered rightly but did not divide rightly? (5) Calm down. He (Abel) will turn to you and you will rule over him.' (6) And Cain said to his brother Abel, 'Let's go to the field!' And it happened, when they were in the field that Cain rose up against his brother

---

4. TN: Or, "sinned inadvertently."
5. (Prov 7:3).
6. Deut 32:14f.
7. (Isa 3:5).
8. (Isa 59:14); (Phil 1:27).

Abel and killed him."[9] (7) See, brothers, evil zeal and envy have resulted in fratricide! (8) Our father Jacob, persecuted by evil zeal, fled from the face of his brother Esau.[10] (9) Evil zeal caused Joseph to be persecuted up to death's edge and to the point of slavery.[11] (10) Evil zeal forced Moses to flee from the face of king Pharaoh of Egypt when he heard from his fellow countryman this word, "Who appointed you judge and ruler over us? Will you kill me as you killed the Egyptian yesterday?"[12] (11) Evil zeal brought about the expulsion of Aaron and Miriam from the camp.[13] (12) Evil zeal brought Dathan and Abiram down into Hades alive because they revolted against Moses, the servant of God.[14] (13) Evil zeal not only provoked the disfavor of foreign tribes against David, but he was even persecuted by king Saul.[15]

5.1 But let us put aside the old examples and turn to the warriors closest to us. Let us take the noble examples of our own age![16] (2) Because of evil zeal and envy, the greatest and most pious pillars were persecuted and fought to the death.[17] (3) Let us place the heroic apostles before our eyes. (4) Peter, who was affected by unjust zeal, did not take upon himself one or two, but a whole number of afflictions from battle, and thus stepped out as a confessor to the place of glory due him. (5) Paul, who was persecuted by evil zeal and strife, showed the victory prize of endurance. (6) Seven times in shackles, forced to flee, stoned, a herald in the East and in the West, he received the magnificent glory of his faith.[18] (7) After he taught piety to the entire world and had come to the boundaries of the West, and had given his testimony before the rulers, he was liberated from the world and taken up to the holy place. Thus, he became the greatest example of perseverance!

6.1 To these men of pious conversion were added a great multitude of elect, who suffered many abuses and torture because of evil zeal and thereby set the most excellent example among us. (2) Because of evil zeal, women—Danaids and Dircae—were persecuted and suffered monstrous and sacrilegious torments. Upon the certain path of faith, they ran the course and attained the precious gem, despite being weak in body. (3) Evil zeal alienated

---

9. 1 Clem 4.1ff; Gen 4:3–8.
10. Gen 27:41ff.
11. Gen 37.
12. Exod 2:14.
13. Num 12.
14. Num 16.
15. 1 Sam 21, 29, 18f.
16. (Phil 1:15).
17. (Gal 2:9).
18. (Acts 14:19) — 2 Tim 1:11.

wives from their husbands and altered the word of our father, Adam: "This is bone of my bone, and flesh of my flesh."[19] (4) Evil zeal and strife have destroyed great cities and wiped out great nations!

7.1 We are writing this to you, beloved, not only for your admonition, but we also hold it before ourselves. For we stand in the same arena, and the same battle lies before us.[20] (2) Therefore, let us dispense with empty and vain thoughts, and let us go on to the glorious and venerable rule of our tradition, (3) and let us see what is good, what is pleasant, and what is pleasing to the one who created us.[21] (4) Let us look upon the blood of Christ and know how precious it is [to God and] to his Father because, for the sake of our salvation, it has brought the gracious gift of conversion[22] to the whole world.[23] (5) Let us go through all generations and learn that generation after generation the Master has given the opportunity of conversion to those who wish to be converted to him.[24] (6) Noah proclaimed conversion, and the people who listened to him were delivered.[25] (7) Jonah proclaimed to the Ninevites their demise. But they converted from their sins, were reconciled to God by supplication, and received salvation, even though they were strangers to God.[26]

8.1 The (appointed) servants of the grace of God spoke about conversion through the Holy Spirit. (2) Even he himself, the Master of all things, spoke about conversion with an oath, "For as I live, says the Lord, I do not wish for the death of the sinner, but repentance,"[27] adding also an excellent word, (3) "Convert, house of Israel, from your lawlessness. Say to the sons of my people, 'Even if your sins reach from earth to heaven, and even if they are redder than scarlet and blacker than sackcloth, and you convert to me with all your heart and say, "Father," I will hear you like a holy people.'"[28] (4) And in another place he says thus, "Wash yourselves and be cleansed. Remove the wickedness of your souls from before my eyes. Put away your wickedness, learn to do good, seek (righteous) judgment, deliver the one

---

19. Gen 2:23.

20. (Phil 1:30).

21. Ps 132; (1 Tim 2:3).

22. TN: Harnack uses "Bekehrung" here, which means "conversion." Most English translations for this and subsequent passages, however, use "repentance."

23. (1 Pet 1:19).

24. (Wis 12:10).

25. (Sib. Or. 1.128f).

26. Jonah 3 — (Eph 2:12).

27. Ezek 33:11.

28. What is the source? Perhaps Ezekiel Apocryphon?

who suffers injustice, do justice to orphans, and treat the widow justly. Now come, let us reason together, says the Lord. Even if your sins are crimson, I will make them white like snow. Even if they are like scarlet, I will make them white like wool. And if you are of good will and you listen to me, you will enjoy the goods of the land. But if you will not and do not listen to me, the sword will devour you. For the mouth of the Lord has said these things."[29] (5) Since he wanted to make all his beloved partakers of conversion, he confirmed it through his almighty decision.

9.1 Therefore let us obey his exalted and glorious will, and pleading for his mercy and goodness, let us fall down before him and turn our feet in the other direction towards his compassionate ways and dismiss the pointless toil, the strife, and the evil zeal that leads to death! (2) Let us look at those who have perfectly served his sublime glory. (3) Let us take Enoch, who, being found just (pious) in obedience, was transferred (to heaven) without dying.[30] (4) Noah, being found reliable (believing) in his service, proclaimed a new beginning of the world, and through him the Lord saved the living beings who entered the ark in harmony.[31]

10.1 Abraham, who was called "friend" (of God), was found trustworthy because he subordinated himself obediently to the words of God.[32] (2) In obedience he departed from his country and from his relatives and from his father's house, so that he might inherit the promises of God by giving up a small country and few relatives and a small house. (3) "Go out from your land and from your relatives and from your father's house into the land that I will show you and I will make you a great people and bless you and make your name great, and you will be blessed and I will bless those who bless you and all the tribes of the earth will be blessed in you."[33] (4) And again, when he separated from Lot, God said to him, "Raise your eyes and look from the place where you stand now to the north and to the south and to the east and to the sea. For all the land you see, I will give you now and your seed forever. (5) And I will make your seed like the sand of the earth. If anyone can count the sand of the earth, so will your name also be counted."[34] (6) And again he says, "God led Abraham out and said to him, 'Look up to heaven and count the stars if you can count them. Your name will be like the stars.'

---

29. Isa 1:16–20.
30. 1 Clem 9.3ff.: Gen 5:24; Heb 11:5 (or 11:5–10).
31. Gen 6:8ff.
32. Isa 41:8 (2 Chr 20:7).
33. Gen 12:1ff.
34. Gen 13:14ff.

And Abraham believed God, and it was counted to him as righteousness."[35] (7) Because of faith and hospitality a son was given to him in old age, and because of obedience he offered him to God as a sacrifice on one of the mountains he had shown him.[36]

11.1 Because of hospitality and piety, Lot was saved from Sodom, while the whole land around was judged by fire and brimstone. The Master made it clear that he does not abandon those who hope in him, but judges with punishment and torment those who are of a different mind.[37] (2) For since his wife went out with him but was of a different mind and was not in harmony with him, he set up a sign by making her into a pillar of salt unto this day, so that all may know that double-minded people and those who doubt the power of God will become a sign of judgment and a symbol for all generations.[38]

12.1 Because of faith and hospitality, the whore Rahab was saved.[39] (2) When spies were sent to Jericho by Joshua, son of Nun, the king of the land realized that they had come to spy out their land, and he sent men to capture them, in order to kill them. (3) But the hospitable Rahab took them in and hid them in the upper chamber, under stalks of flax. (4) And when the king's agents came and said, "The spies in our land have come to you. Bring them out, for the king commands it," she replied, "The men you are looking for have certainly come to me, but they immediately went out." Then she pointed them in the opposite direction the spies went. (5) And then she said to the men, "I am certain that the Lord God has given this land over to you. For fear and trembling of you has afflicted its inhabitants. Now, when it happens and you take the land, save me and my father's house." (6) And they said to her, "It will be for you as you have said to us. When you see that we are approaching, gather all of your people together under your roof, and they will be saved. For all that is outside of the house will perish." (7) Additionally, they gave her a sign that she should hang a piece of scarlet outside of her house. Thereby, they made it known that through the blood of the Lord, salvation is given to all those who believe in God and hope in him. (8) Behold, beloved, not only faith, but also prophecy was in the woman!

13.1 Let us therefore be humble, brothers, discarding all arrogance and conceit and ignorance and wrath, and let us obey what is written. For the Holy Spirit says, "Let not the wise man boast of his wisdom, nor the

35. Gen 15:5f.
36. Gen 21f.
37. 1 Clem 11.1f.: Gen 19.
38. Wis 10:7
39. 1 Clem 12:1f.: Josh 2 — (Heb 11:31).

strong man of his strength, nor the rich man of his wealth, but let the one who boasts boast of the Lord, seek him out zealously, and execute judgment and righteousness."[40] Above all, bearing in mind the words of the Lord Jesus, which he spoke, teaching gentleness and patience. (2) For he said, "Show mercy so that mercy may be shown to you. Forgive so that you may be forgiven. As you do so also it will be done to you. As you give so also it will be given to you. As you judge so will you be judged. As you show kindness so also will kindness be shown to you. With whatever measure you measure, so also will it be measured out for you."[41] (3) With this commandment and these exhortations, let us strengthen ourselves in order to walk obediently in humility in his holy words. For the Holy Word says, "Upon whom will I look, except upon the gentle and the quiet, and upon the one that trembles at my sayings?"[42]

14.1 It is right and pious, beloved brothers, to obediently submit ourselves to God rather than follow the leaders who are boastful and destroy his orders in shameful zeal. (2) For we will incur upon ourselves no small injury, but rather a great danger, if we, taking these dangers lightly, surrender ourselves to the will of people who incite strife and riots with the result that we alienate ourselves from our peaceful condition. (3) Greet one another in kindness according to the compassion and kindness of the one who created us. (4) For it is written, "The kind will be the inhabitants of the land, and those who are not wicked will be left in it. But the unlawful will be cut off from it."[43] (5) And again it says, "I saw the wicked high and lifted up like the cedars of Lebanon. And I passed by, and behold, he was no more, and I looked for his place, and I did not find it. Keep innocence and look to that which is right, for there is a remnant (progeny) bestowed upon the peaceful man."[44]

15.1 Therefore, let us join together with those who piously practice peace, and not those who wish for it hypocritically. (2) For this is what he says in one place, "This people honors me with their lips, but their hearts are far from me."[45] (3) And again, "They blessed with their mouths, but they cursed in their hearts"[46] (4) And again he says, "They loved him with their mouths, and with their tongues they lied to him. Their hearts were not

---

40. Jer 9:23f; 1 Sam 2:10; 1 Cor 1:31
41. (Matt 5:7; 6:14; 7:1f; 12; Luke 6:31, 37f).
42. Isa 66:2.
43. Prov 2:21f; Ps 37:39.
44. Ps 37:36–38.
45. Isa 29:13 — (Matt 15:8; Mark 7:6).
46. Ps 62:4.

honest with him, nor were they found faithful to his covenant."[47] (5) Therefore, "let the deceitful lips that speak against the righteous law be silenced."[48] And again, "The Lord will cut off all the deceitful lips, the boastful tongue, the people who say, 'Let us praise our tongue, our lips are ours. Who is our Lord?'[49] (6) Because of the need of the beggars and because of the sighing of the poor, I will now arise, says the Lord. I will bring them to the place of salvation. I will pronounce judgement freely there."

16.1 Christ is with the humble portion, not those who rise above his flock. (2) The scepter (of the majesty) of God, the Lord Jesus Christ, did not come with the splendor of greatness or superiority, though he could have done so, but instead came humbly, as the Holy Spirit said of him.[50] For he says, (3) "Lord, who believed our words, and the Lord's arm, to whom was it revealed? We proclaimed concerning him, 'Like a little child, like a root in thirsty earth.' He had no form or glory. We saw him, and he had no attractiveness or beauty. Instead, his appearance was contemptible, beneath that of human attractiveness. He was a mistreated and afflicted man, knowing how to endure weakness, for he has to turn his face away. He was despised and considered to be nothing. (4) This is the one who bears our sins and suffers pain for us, and we considered he was subject to plagues, blows, and mistreatment (by himself). (5) But he has been wounded for our sins and afflicted for our lawlessness. The punishment for our peace lay upon him, and by his wounds we were healed. (6) We all went astray like sheep—each one of us erred upon his own path—(7) and the Lord gave him over for our sins. And he did not open his mouth during his affliction. Like a sheep he was led to the slaughter, and like a lamb he went silently before his shearer, such that he does not open his mouth. In his humiliation, justice was abolished. (8) Who will tell his descendants, for his life is taken away from the earth? (9) For the lawlessness of my people, he meets his death. (10) And I will give the wicked for his burial and the rich for his death, because he committed no transgression, nor was there deceit found in his mouth. And the Lord desires to clean him from his punishment. (11) If you make (him) an offering for sin, your soul will see offspring who live long. (12) And the Lord desires to remove the torment of his soul to show him light to form (??) him by understanding, to justify the righteous one who has served many well, and it is he who will bear their sins. (13) Therefore, he will have many as heirs and will share the spoils of the strong, because his soul has been given over

---

47. Ps 78:36f.
48. Ps 31:19
49. Ps 12:3f.
50. (Heb 1:8; Ps 45:6; Phil 2:5f).

to death, and he was counted among the transgressors. (14) And he bore the sins of many, and was given up for their sins."[51] (15) And again, he himself says, "I am a worm and not a man, a reproach of men and a contempt for the people. (16) Everyone who saw me mocked me. Their lips spoke, and they shook their head, 'He has hoped in the Lord, let him pull him out, let him deliver him, for he takes pleasure in him.'"[52] (17) See, beloved men, what sort of example has been given to us! For if the Lord was so humble, what should we do, we who have come under the yoke of his grace?

17.1 Let us be imitators of those men who went about in goatskins and sheepskins and proclaimed the coming of Christ. We mean Elijah and Elisha, and also Ezekiel, the prophets, and those who received the testimony (from God).[53] (2) Abraham received a glorious testimony, and he was called "friend of God," and with regard to the glory of God, he humbly says, "I am but dirt and ashes."[54] (3) Furthermore, the following has been written about Job: "Job was righteous and blameless, true, one who feared God, far from all evil."[55] (4) But he accused himself with these words: "Nobody is clean of dirt, even if his life lasts only one day."[56] Moses received the name "faithful in the entire area of his house" (i.e., God's house) and God used him to judge Egypt through the scourges and plagues. But even he, who was gloriously honored, did not give a boastful speech, but instead when the oracle was given to him from the thorn bush, he said, "Who am I that you should send me? I stammer and have a slow tongue."[57] (6) And again he says, "I am but steam from a boiling pot."[58]

18.1 But what should we say about David, who was certified (by God), to whom God said, "I have found a man after my heart, David, the son of Jesse. I have anointed him with eternal mercy."[59] (2) But he also says to God, "Have mercy on me, God, according to your great mercy and according to the fullness of your compassion, erase my iniquity. (3) Wash me thoroughly of my iniquity, and purify me from my sin, for I know my iniquity, and my sin is always before me. (4) Against you alone have I sinned and done evil before you, that you may be justified in your words and have

---

51. Isa 53:1–12.
52. Ps 22:6ff.
53. (Heb 11:37).
54. (Isa 41:8) — Gen 18:27.
55. Job 1:1.
56. Job 14:4f.
57. Num 12:7 (Heb 3:2); Exod 3:11; 4:10.
58. Where does this citation come from?
59. Ps 89:21 (1 Sam 13:14).

victory when you are called into judgment. (5) For behold, I was brought forth in iniquities, and in sin my mother conceived me. (6) For behold, you have loved truth; the dark and hidden things of your wisdom you have revealed to me. (7) You will sprinkle me with hyssop and I will be clean. You will wash me and I will be whiter than snow. (8) You will fill my ear with rejoicing and joy; the bones lying on the ground will rejoice. (9) Turn your face away from my sins and erase all my iniquities. (10) Create a pure heart in me, God, and give me a renewed spirit in my inner being. (11) Do not cast me away from your face, and do not take your Holy Spirit away from me. (12) Return to me rejoicing in your salvation, and strengthen me by the guiding spirit. (13) I will teach the lawless your ways, and the wrong doers will convert to you. (14) Snatch me out of blood guiltiness, God, the God of my salvation. (15) My tongue will proclaim your righteousness, O Lord. You will open my mouth, and my lips will proclaim your praise. (16) For if you wished for sacrifice, I would have offered it; but you will not accept burnt offerings. (17) A sacrifice for God is a contrite spirit; a contrite and humble heart God will not despise."[60]

19.1 The humility and submissiveness of so many and of men with such excellent repute has not only improved us by their obedience, but also the generations before us, namely those who received his oracles in fear and sincerity.[61] (2) Now that we have become partakers of many great and glorious deeds (through the examples given), let us hasten to the goal of peace that was handed down to us from the beginning, and let us look to the Father and creator of the whole world and flock to his glorious and exalted gifts of peace and his benefactions! (3) Let us look at him with the spirit and let us look with the eyes of the soul at his long-suffering will. Let us note how free of anger he is towards all his creation!

20.1 The heavens, set in motion by his rule, obey him peacefully. Day and night punctually run the course prescribed by him, without hindering one another. (3) Sun, moon, and the chorus of stars orbit their prescribed regions in unison, according to his order without any riot. (4) According to his will, the fertilized earth brings forth all kinds of food in abundance, at the appropriate times, for humans, animals, and all living beings on it, without rebelling or changing anything in his commandments. (5) The inscrutable depths of the abysses and the indescribable courts (areas?) of the underworld are held together by one and the same set of laws. (6) The torrent of the immense sea, held together "in accumulations" according to his plan for creation, does not exceed the limits set for it, but just as he

---

60. 1 Clem 18.2ff.: Ps 51:3–19.
61. (Heb 12:1).

commanded the sea, so it does.[62] (7) For he said, "Come this far, and your waves will shatter within you."[63] (8) The ocean, which is boundless to humans, and the worlds that lie beneath it are governed according to the same orders of the Master. (9) The spring, summer, autumn, and winter seasons alternate peacefully. (10) The posts of the winds perform their duty at certain times without fault. The inexhaustible springs, created for enjoyment and wellbeing, grant humankind without end their life-giving powers, and the smallest living beings form their unions in harmony and peace. (11) To all these the great Master craftsman of all has prescribed that it[64] might exist in peace and concord, giving benefactions to all, but abundantly to us who have taken refuge in his mercies through our Lord Jesus Christ. (12) To him be glory and majesty forever! Amen.

21.1 See to it, beloved, that his many favors do not become a judgment for us if we do not walk worthy of him, doing what is good and pleasing before him in harmony. (2) For he says somewhere, "The Spirit of the Lord is a light that searches out the inner parts of the body."[65] (3) Let us note how close he is and that none of our thoughts nor of our dialogues, which we conduct, are hidden from him. (4) It is therefore right that we do not depart from his will as deserters. (5) We would rather offend those who are foolish and ignorant and boastful and those who brag about their speech than offend God.[66] (6) Let us revere the Lord Jesus, whose blood has been shed for us, let us fear our rulers with reverence, let us teach the young in the fear of the Lord, and let us guide our wives towards that which is good. (7) Let them demonstrate an amiable disposition of noble purity, show their sincere will to be meek, reveal their gentleness with the silence of their tongue. Let them not show their love in a cliquish fashion, but in piety equally towards all who fear God.[67] (8) Let our (your?) children take part in the teaching of Christ. Let them learn how strong a humble mind is before God, what chaste love can do before God, and how the fear of God is something beautiful and great and saves all those who walk in it in holiness with a pure mind. (9) For he is the searcher of thoughts and deliberations. His breath is in us, and if he desires, he will take it back.[68]

---

62. Gen 1:9.

63. Job 38:11.

64. TN: "Es" ("it") is most certainly a reference to "all these things" or rather "all," everything God has created.

65. Prov 20:27.

66. (James 4:16).

67. (1 Tim 5:21).

68. (Heb 4:12; Ps 104:29).

22.1 But all these things are certified by faith in Christ, for he himself calls us to himself through the Holy Spirit, "Come, children, hear me. I will teach you the fear of the Lord. (2) Is there anyone who desires life, who wants to see good days? (3) Hold your tongue from evil, and your lips, that they might speak nothing deceitful. (4) Avoid evil and do good, (5) seek peace and pursue it. (6) The eyes of the Lord are upon the righteous, and his ears upon their supplication, but the face of the Lord is against those who do evil, to cut off their memory from the face of the earth. (7) The righteous one has called, and the Lord has heard him and saved him from all his afflictions."[69] (8) "The afflictions of the righteous are numerous, and the Lord will tear him away from all of them." Then, "The scourges of the sinner are numerous, but those who hope in the Lord will be surrounded by mercy."[70]

23.1 The all merciful and beneficent Father has a heart for those who fear him. He distributes his gracious gifts gently and benevolently to those who come to him with a simple disposition. (2) Therefore, let us not be double-minded, nor let our souls run wild with desires in connection with his effusive and glorious gifts. (3) Let this Scripture not be true of us, which says, "Those who are wretched are those who are divided in their souls, those who doubt saying, 'We have already heard these things in our fathers' time, and behold, we have grown old and none of this has happened to us.' (4) Oh, you who do not understand! Compare yourselves to the tree, or the vine. First, it loses its leaves, then the bud comes, then the leaves, then the blossom, and then the sour grape, then the ripe grape."[71] You see, in such a short period of time, the fruit of the tree grows to maturity. (5) Truly his purpose will be accomplished quickly, and suddenly the Lord will come into his temple and the Holy One whom you expect.[72]

24.1 Let us observe, beloved, how the Master continues to show us that the coming resurrection will take place, of which he made the Lord Jesus Christ the first-fruit by raising him up.[73] (2) Let us consider, beloved, the resurrection that takes place within the normal course of time. (3) Day and night make it known to us: the night comes to rest and the day rises up; the day disappears and the night comes. (4) Let us consider the fruit: How and in what manner do things proceed with the seed? (5) The sower goes out and throws out seed after seed upon the earth. They fall into the earth, dry

---

69. Ps 34:11–17.
70. Ps 32:10.
71. From where does this text come? (See 2 Peter 3:4).
72. Isa 13:22; Mal 3:1.
73. (1 Cor 15:20, 36f)

up, and disintegrate. Then, the Master's powerful providence resurrects them from decay, and from one he makes many arise and bear fruit.[74]

25.1 Let us consider the meaningful, paradoxical phenomenon that appears in the East, in the regions of Arabia. (2) There is a bird called the phoenix. It is a unique specimen, and it lives five hundred years. When it is close to the time of its dissolution, it builds for itself a nest of incense, myrrh, and other fragrances, and when its time is up, it goes into the nest and dies. (3) While its flesh rots, however, a worm develops that feeds on the carcass of the dead animal and it grows feathers. Then, when it is fully grown, it takes its nest, in which the bones of its predecessor lie, and traverses the distance between Arabia and Egypt, bearing its load to the city called Heliopolis. (4) And during the day, in plain sight, it flies to and places the bones upon the altar of the sun, and then it returns again. (5) Then, the priests search the annals and discover that it came after the conclusion of five hundred years.

26.1 Therefore, can we still consider it something great and wonderful that the craftsman of everything will raise up those who have piously served him in the assurance of a good faith when he shows us the greatness of his promise through a bird? (2) For he says somewhere, "And you will raise me up, and I will praise you,"[75] and also "I fell asleep and slept; I was raised up because you are with me."[76] (3) And again, Job says, "And you will raise up this flesh of mine, which has endured all these things."[77]

27.1 With this hope, therefore, our souls should bind themselves to him who is faithful to his promises and just in his judgments.[78] (2) He who commanded not to lie will all the more not lie himself, for nothing is impossible with God except lying.[79] (3) Therefore, let faith in him be kindled in us, and let us remember that all things are near to him. (4) By one word of his power he has brought all things about and by one word he can destroy them. (5) "Who can say to him, 'What have you done,' or who can resist the power of his strength?"[80] He will do everything when he wills it and how he wills it, and nothing of what he has commanded will be nullified. (6) All things are before his face and nothing is hidden from his will. (7) "The heavens tell the glory of God, and the firmament

74. (Mark 4:3, including its parallels.)
75. From where does this citation come? Ps 28:7?
76. Ps 3:5 and Ps 23:4.
77. Job 19:26.
78. (Heb 10:23).
79. (Heb 6:18).
80. Wis 12:12 and 11:22.

proclaims the work of his hands: one day proclaiming the word to another, and one night proclaiming the knowledge to another. There are no words or sounds whose voices cannot be heard."[81]

28.1 Since all things are seen and heard (by God), let us fear him and abandon the abominable desires for evil deeds so that we may be protected from the coming judgments by his mercy. (2) For where can we flee from his powerful hand, and what world will receive one who wishes to depart from him on his own path? For it says somewhere in the Writings,[82] (3) "Where shall I go and where shall I hide from your face? If I ascend to heaven, you are there, and if I depart to the most extreme part of the earth, your right hand is there. If I pitch my camp in the abyss, your Spirit is there."[83] (4) Where then can one go to escape or run away from the one who encompasses all things?

29.1 Let us now approach him with a pious heart, raising holy and undefiled hands to him, in love to our benevolent and merciful Father, who has made us a part of his elect.[84] (2) For thus it is written, "When the Most High divided the nations, when he scattered the sons of Adam, he set the limits of the nations according to the number of the angels of God. His people, Jacob, became the Lord's portion. Israel became his possession."[85] (3) And in another place, he says, "Behold, the Lord takes a people from among the nations, just as a man takes a first fruit from his threshing floor, and the holy of holies will come out from this people."[86]

30.1 Since we are a holy portion (of God), let us do all that is holy and let us flee from slander, abominable and filthy embraces, intoxication and rebellious sentiments and shameful desires, abominable adultery and shameful pride. (2) For "God," it says, "resists the arrogant but gives grace to the humble."[87] (3) Let us, therefore, join with those to whom grace is given by God. Let us equip ourselves with concord, a humble mind, abstinence, distance from every whisper and slander, presenting our righteousness with works and not with words. (4) For it says, "He who speaks much must also listen to objections, or does the chatterbox think himself to be

---

81. Ps 19:1–3.

82. TN: The German here is "Schriftwort" and can mean "Writing" or "Scripture." In his comments on 28.2 at the end of this volume, Harnack remarks that the term likely refers to the third division of the Old Testament. For this reason, I have opted for the translation "Writings" instead of "Scripture."

83. Ps 139:7ff.

84. (1 Tim 2:8).

85. Deut 32:8f.

86. Deut 4:34; 14:2; Num 18:27; 2 Chr 31:14; Ezek 48:12.

87. Prov 3:34.

right? (5) Blessed is the one born of the woman whose life is brief. Do not speak many words."[88] (6) Let our praise be with God and not of ourselves, for those who praise themselves hate God.[89] (7) The testimony of our good deeds should be given to us by others, as it was given to our fathers, the righteous ones. (8) Impudence and presumptuousness and audaciousness are for those who are cursed by God, but mildness and humility and gentleness for those who are blessed by God.

31.1 Let us therefore come under his blessing and let us see what the paths of blessing are. Let us reconsider what has happened from the beginning. (2) Why was our father Abraham blessed? Was it not because he worked righteousness and truth through faith?[90] (3) Isaac, confidently aware of what was to come, was glad to be offered as a sacrifice.[91] (4) Jacob humbly left his land because of his brother and went to Laban and served him, and the twelve scepters of Israel were given to him.[92]

32.1 If someone pays attention to each one of these matters, he will know the glories of the gifts given by him (God? Jacob?). (2) For from him (Jacob) come the priests and Levites, all of whom serve at the altar of God. From him comes the Lord Jesus according to the flesh. From him come the kings and rulers and leaders through Judah. But (also) the other tribes have no small glory since God promised, "Your seed will be like the stars of heaven."[93] (3) Now, all of these were glorified and made great not by themselves, nor by their own work, or by the righteous deeds which they did, but by his will.[94] (4) Therefore, even we who are called by God's will in Christ Jesus are not justified by ourselves, nor by our wisdom or insight or piety or works which we have done in holiness of heart, but by the faith by which the Almighty God justified all from the beginning. To him be glory forever and ever. Amen.

33.1 What then should we do, brothers? Should we be sluggish in doing good and abandon love? May the Master never let this happen to us, but instead let us hasten with endurance and zeal to do every good work.[95] (2) He himself, the craftsman and Master of the universe, rejoices in his works, (3) for through his majestic power he has established the

---

88. Job 11:2f.
89. (Rom 2:29).
90. (Rom 4:1f; Gal 3:6f; James 2:21f).
91. Gen 22:7f.
92. Gen 28f.
93. (Rom 9:4f); Gen 15:5 (22:17; 26:4).
94. 1 Clem 32:3f. (Paul: Gal and Rom; Titus 3:5).
95. (Rom 6:1f).

heavens, and with his incomprehensible understanding he adorned them. He separated the earth from the water flowing around it, and founded it on the secure foundation of his will. The animals that walk upon it were brought into existence by his command. The sea and the living beings in it he prepared beforehand, and kept them in check by his power. (4) Above all this, he made the most excellent and noble work, man, through his holy and undefiled hands as the impression of his own image. (5) For God says thus, "'Let us make man in our own image and our own likeness.' And God formed man, male and female, he made them."[96] (6) And when he had finished all these things, he praised them and blessed them, saying, "Increase and multiply."[97] (7) Let us recognize that all who are righteous have received their adornment with good works, and that the Lord himself rejoiced in the good works with which he adorns himself. (8) Now, since we have this example, let us join in his will without hesitation. Let us accomplish the work of righteousness with all our strength!

34.1 The efficient worker receives bread for his work in confidence; the lazy and nonchalant worker does not dare to look at his employer.[98] (2) Therefore it is our duty to be willing to do good, for everything comes from him. (3) For he has told us in advance, "Behold the Lord and his reward before him, to repay everyone according to his work."[99] (4) Therefore, he admonishes those of us who trust in him with all our heart not to be sluggish and nonchalant towards any good work.[100] (5) Let our renown and our confidence be in him. Let us obey his will. Let us contemplate the whole multitude of his angels, how they serve his will as satellites.[101] (6) Scripture says, "Ten thousand ten thousands always surround him, and thousands of thousands serve him, and they call out loudly, 'Holy, holy, holy is the Lord of hosts. All creation is filled with his glory.'"[102] (7) And we also, spiritually gathered together in harmony in the same place, wish to call out to him continuously as if with one mouth so that we may have a share in his great and glorious promises. (8) For he says, "No eye has seen and no ear

---

96. Gen 1:26f.
97. Gen 1:28.
98. (Sir 4:29).
99. Isa 40:10; 62:11.
100. (2 Tim 2:21).
101. TN: Satellites, which is a translation of the German "Trabanten," has the idea of "those beside him" or at his guard.
102. Dan 7:19; Isa 6:3.

has heard and it has not come into the heart of a man what the Lord has prepared for those who wait for him."[103]

35.1 How exhilarating and wonderful are the gifts of God, beloved, (2) life in immortality, joy in righteousness, truth with candor, faith with confidence, self-control with holiness, and all these things lie within the realm of our understanding. (3) But what then are the good things that will only be prepared for those who have endured? The craftsman and Father of the eons, the Most Holy one, he alone knows their greatness and their beauty. (4) Now let us struggle to be found among the number of those who persevere, that we might receive the promised gifts. (5) How, beloved, will this happen? If our mind is firmly bound with God through faith if we eagerly seek to be pleasing and acceptable to him, if we do what corresponds to his blameless will, and walk by the way of truth and cast off from us all injustice and lawlessness, greed, strife, wickedness and deceit, whispering and slander, hostility to God, arrogance and boastfulness, vanity and inhospitableness,[104] (6) for those who do these things are enemies of God, and not only them, but also those who approve of such behavior. (7) For the Scripture says, "God says to the sinner, 'Why do you discuss my statues and put my covenant in your mouth? (8) You yourself hate discipline and cast my words behind you. When you see a thief, you run with him, and you make common cause with adulterers. Your mouth piles up wickedness, and your tongue lays cords of deceit. You sit against your brother and slander him, and against your mother's son you do outrageous things. (9) You do this, and I am silent. And you think, lawless one, that I am like you, (10) that I will convict you and place you before your own eyes. (11) Know this, you who have forgotten God, so that he does not take you like a lion and there be no one to save you. (12) A sacrifice of praise will glorify me, and this is the path upon which I will show him the salvation of God.'"[105]

36.1 This, beloved, is the path on which we have found our salvation, Jesus Christ, the high priest of our offerings (prayers), the patron and helper of our weakness.[106]

> (2a) Through him, we look into the heights of the heavens,
>
> Through him we see as in a mirror God's blameless and most venerable face,
>
> Through him the eyes of our hearts have been opened,

---

103. What is the source of this quotation? Is it the Apocalypse of Elijah? (1 Cor 2:9; Isa 64:4).
104. (Rom 1:29–32).
105. Ps 50:16–23.
106. (Heb 2:17; 3:1; 4:14f; etc.)

Through him our darkened mind blossoms again into the light,

Through him the Master has made us taste immortal knowledge.

(2b) "He who is the reflection of his majesty, is so much greater than the angels because he has received a more excellent name."[107] (3) For so it is written, "He who makes his angels spirits and his servants flames of fire."[108] (4) But in relation to his Son, the Master has said thus, "You are my Son. Today I have begotten you. Ask of me, and I will give you the nations for your inheritance and the ends of the earth for your possession."[109] (5) And again he says to him, "Sit at my right hand until I make your enemies into a footstool for your feet."[110] (6) Who are the enemies? The wicked and those who oppose his will.

37.1 Let us now, brothers, with tenacious perseverance serve as soldiers according to his blameless commands. (2) Let us look at those who serve as soldiers under our military leaders, how ordered, compliant, and obedient they are as they carry out their orders. (3) Not all are prefects, chiliarchs,[111] hekatontarchs,[112] or a pentekontarchs,[113] but each one carries out the command of the kings and the military leaders according to his rank.[114] (4) The great cannot exist without the small, nor can the small exist without the great. Everywhere a kind of mixture is necessary, and through it usefulness arises. (5) Let us consider our bodies: the head is nothing without the feet, and the feet are nothing without the head. And the lowliest members of our body are necessary and useful to the whole body. Even more, all are united and under one leadership so that the whole body may remain safe.[115]

38.1 Let our whole body (corporate identity) remain safe and sound in Christ Jesus, and let everyone order himself with respect to his neighbor in accordance with the *charisma* of his neighbor.[116] (2) Let the strong take care of the weak, but let the weak have respect for the strong. Let the rich give to the poor, and let the poor thank God that he has given him one through whom

---

107. (Rom 1:21; Eph 4:18); (1 Pet 2:9); Heb 1:3ff.

108. Ps 104:4; Heb 1:7.

109. Ps 2:7; Heb 1:5.

110. Ps 110:1; Heb 1:13.

111. TN: A chiliarch is a commander of one thousand men.

112. TN: A hekatonarch, also known as a centurion, is a commander of one hundred men.

113. TN: A pentekontarch is a commander of fifty men.

114. (1 Cor 12:29f; 15:23; 1 Peter 2:13f).

115. (1 Cor 12:12f).

116. (Eph 5:21; 1 Peter 5:5; 4:10; 1 Cor 7:7).

his need is fulfilled. Let the wise man show his wisdom not in words but in good deeds. Let the humble not testify to his own humility, but let someone else do it. Let the one who is chaste not boast, but instead let him know that it is another who grants him his abstinence. (3) Let us consider, brothers, from what material we are made, how we were created, and who we were when we entered the world, and from what grave and darkness our Sculptor and craftsman led us into the world, having already prepared his benefactions before we were born![117] (4) Having all this from him, let us give thanks to him in all things, to whom be the glory forever and ever. Amen.

39.1 Foolish, ignorant, stupid, and uneducated men jeer and mock us and wish to exalt themselves through that which they contrive.[118] (2) But what can a mortal do, and what can the power of the earth-born do? (3) For it is written, "No form stood before my eyes; I heard only a breath of air and a voice.[119] (4) Well then? Will the mortal man be clean before the Lord, or a man blameless in his deeds if he does (not even) trust his children and perceives wrongdoing in his angels? (5) Not even heaven is clean before him, how much less the inhabitants of houses of clay, to which we also belong, having been made of the same clay. He struck them like a moth, and from early morning until evening they are no more; because they could not help themselves, they perished. (6) He breathed on them, and they died because they had no wisdom. (7) Call out, see if there is someone to answer you or if you will see one of the holy angels. For wrath drives away the foolish, and zeal kills those who go astray. (8) But I saw the foolish take root, and yet the place they were standing was immediately swallowed up. (9) May their children remain far away from salvation, be mocked at the doors of the lowly, and no savior be found for them. For the righteous will eat what was prepared for them, and they themselves will not be saved from evil."[120]

40.1 Since this is quite clear to us now, and since we have gained insight into the depths of the divine *gnosis*, we must do everything in an orderly manner that the Master ordered to be done at the prescribed times. (2) The sacrifices and (cultic) services are to be performed according to his will, not carelessly or disorderly, but at certain times and hours. (3) Where and through whom he desires them to be fulfilled he himself has determined by his supreme will, so that everything done in a holy manner and according to his will might be pleasing to him. (4) Therefore, those who offer their sacrifices at the appointed times are acceptable to him and certain of their

---

117. (Ps 139:15).
118. (Ps 44:14; 69:4).
119. Job 4:16ff.
120. Job 15:15; 4:19–5:5.

salvation. (5) For the high priest is given his own services, and the priests are given their own places, and the Levites have been given their own *diakonien*. The layman is bound to the regulations for the layman.

41.1 Let each of you, brothers, be pleasing to God, with a good conscience in his own place of order, without transgressing the law of his ministry, but acting with dignity. (2) It is not everywhere, brothers, that daily offerings, freewill offerings, sin offerings, and trespass offerings are made, but only in Jerusalem, and not in every place there, but in front of the temple building, on the altar, after the offering has been examined for blemishes by the high priest and by the aforementioned servants. (3) Therefore, whoever does something against his will shall be punished by death. (4) See, brothers, the greater the *gnosis* we have been consider worthy of receiving, the greater the danger that threatens us.

42.1 The apostles were entrusted with the gospel for us by the Lord Jesus Christ, and Jesus Christ was sent by God. (2) Therefore, Christ is from God and the apostles are from Christ. Accordingly, both are from God in an orderly manner according to the will of God. (3) After they had received their commissions, had attained full conviction through the resurrection of the Lord Jesus Christ, and were strengthened in the Word of God, they went out in the persuasive power of the Holy Spirit and proclaimed the good news that the kingdom of God is coming soon. (4) Preaching in countries and cities and baptizing those who obeyed the will of God, they appointed their firstfruits, after being tested in the Spirit, as bishops and deacons for the future believers. (5) And this was not an innovation, for written long ago was a word of Scripture that says, "I will appoint their bishops in righteousness and their deacons in faithfulness."[121]

43.1 And how can one be surprised that those to whom God has entrusted such a work in Christ appointed the aforesaid, since the blessed "true servant in the entire house," Moses, recorded in the Holy Books all that was commanded to him, and the other prophets follow him, joining their witness to what he recorded as laws?[122] (2) For when a fight arose about the priesthood and the tribes quarreled about which of them was to be adorned with this glorious name, he commanded that the leaders of the twelve tribes should bring him staffs inscribed with the name of each tribe. He took them, bound them together, sealed them with the signet rings of the leaders of the tribes, and deposited them in the tent of the testimony on the table of the Lord. (3) And he shut up the tent, sealed the locks as well as the staffs, (4) and said to them, "Brothers, the tribe whose staff sprouts is the tribe God

---

121. Isa 60:17.
122. Heb 3:5 (Num 12:7).

has chosen to be his priests and servants." (5) The next morning, he called all of Israel together, 600,000 men, showed the seals to the leaders of the tribes, opened the tent of the testimony, and took out the staffs. And it was discovered that Aaron's staff had not only sprouted, but also that it bore fruit. (6) What do you think, beloved? Did Moses not know in advance that this would happen? He certainly knew it, but so that no rebellion might arise in Israel, he acted in such a way that the name of the True and Only One might be glorified. To him be glory forever and ever. Amen.

44.1 Through our Lord Jesus Christ, our apostles also came to the realization that there would be a dispute about the name (office) of the bishop. (2) Therefore, having possession of complete foreknowledge, they established the aforementioned and then issued the additional decree that if some of the aforementioned die, other tried and tested men would assume their office. (3) The men now appointed by them (the apostles) or later by other respected men, with the consent of the whole church, will, in our judgment, be unjustly and unfairly deposed from their ministry, when they have served the flock of Christ blamelessly in a humble manner, peaceably, and not with pettiness, and have received from all for a long time a praiseworthy testimony. (4) For it will be no small sin for us if we depose from the office of bishop those who have brought the offerings[123] blamelessly and in holiness. (5) Blessed are the presbyters who have already traversed their journey through life and experienced an end, crowned with the fruits of perfection. For they need not fear that someone will push them out of the position prescribed for them. (6) And yet we see that you have removed some, in spite of their excellent conduct, from the ministry which they administered blamelessly and honorably.

45.1 Exert yourselves, brothers, in a zealous struggle for all that belongs to salvation. (2) Search deep in the Holy Scriptures, which are true, which were written by the Holy Spirit. (3) Know that there is nothing unrighteous or wrong in them. You will not find in them that the righteous have ever been deposed by holy men. (4) The righteous were persecuted, but by lawless men. They were imprisoned, but by the unrighteous. They were stoned, but by the wicked. They were killed, but by a people of a vile and unrighteous zeal. (5) They endured such suffering in a praiseworthy manner. (6) What shall we say, brothers? Was Daniel thrown into the lion's den by the godly?[124] (7) Or were Ananias, Azarias, and Mishael locked up in the fiery furnace by the worshipers of the supreme and glorious cult of the Most High? By no means! Who are the people that do this? Those who hate God

---

123. TN: "Opfer" can be translated as "offerings" or "sacrifices."
124. Dan 6:16f.

and who, being burdened with all wickedness, have increased their rage to such heights that they have brought down to ruin those who serve God with holy and blameless intent, not knowing that the Most High fights for them and protects those who serve his excellent name with a pure conscience. To him be the glory forever and ever. Amen.[125] (8) But those who have persevered in confidence will receive glory and honor, and will be exalted and recorded by God in his memory forever and ever. Amen.

46.1 We, brothers, must follow such examples. (2) For it is written, "Join the holy ones, for those who join them will be sanctified."[126] (3) And again in another place it says, "United with an innocent man, you will be innocent, and with the elect you will be elect, and with the perverse, you will do perverse things."[127] (4) Therefore, let us now join ourselves with the innocent and with the righteous. They are God's elect. (5) Why are there disputes and heated outbursts, and divisions, and schisms, and war among you? (6) Or do we not have one God, and one Christ, and one Spirit of grace poured out upon us, and one calling in Christ?[128] (7) Why do we pull and tear apart the members of Christ and revolt against our own bodies, and go so far into madness that we forget we are members in a shared identity? Remember the words of Jesus our Lord.[129] (8) He said, "Woe to that man. It would be better for him if he had not been born than give offense to one of the chosen ones. It would be better for him to have a millstone attached to him and to be sunk into the sea than to pervert one of my elect."[130] (9) Your schism has perverted many, plunged many into faint-heartedness, many into doubt, all of us into mourning, and yet your rebellion persists.

47.1 Take the letter of the blessed Paul, the apostle, in your hands. (2) How did he write to you at the beginning of the proclamation of the Gospel? (3) Truly pneumatically, he informed you by letter about himself and about Cephas and about Apollos, because you had already formed parties at that time.[131] (4) However, this formation of parties brought you into a lesser sin, for you split yourselves into parties of apostles certified (by God) and of a man who stood in great esteem by them. (5) Now, on the other hand, think about those who have perverted you and diminished the dignity of your universally recognized brotherly love! (6) It is shameful, indeed a great

---

125. Dan 3:19f.
126. What is the source of this citation?
127. Ps 18:25f.
128. (Eph 4:4f).
129. (Rom 12:5).
130. (Matt 26:24; 18:6; Mark 9:42; Luke 17:2).
131. 1 Cor 1:10f.

shame, beloved, and it is disgraceful for your conduct in Christ when one hears that the secure and ancient church of the Corinthians is in rebellion against its presbyters because of one or two people. (7) And this news has not only reached us, but also those who are of a different mind than us, so that your foolishness provokes blasphemies against the name of the Lord, but also puts you yourself in danger.[132]

48.1 Now, let us dismiss this quickly and fall down before the Master and implore him with tears that he may reconcile us in grace and restore us to our venerable and pure conduct in brotherly love. (2) For this is the gate of righteousness opening to life, as it is written, "Open up for me the gates of righteousness. As I enter them, I will praise the Lord. (3) This is the gate of the Lord. The righteous will enter there."[133] (4) Many gates are indeed open, but the gate of righteousness is the gate of Christ. All who enter here are blessed, and they conduct their travels in piety and righteousness, steadfastly accomplishing all things. (5) A man may have faith, he may be able to expound his *gnosis*, he may be wise in judging thoughts (speeches?), he may be holy in his deeds.[134] (6) The greater he thinks he is, the more humble of mind he must be, and must strive for that which is useful to the whole, and not just to himself.[135]

> 49.1 Whoever has love in Christ obeys the commandments of Christ.
>
> (2) The bond of God's love, who can describe it?[136]
>
> (3) The sublimity of his beauty, who can speak of it?
>
> (4) The heights to which love drives us is inexpressible.
>
> (5) Love binds us to God,
> Love covers a host of sins,
> Love can endure anything; it is patient in all things.
> There is nothing mean in love, nothing arrogant.
> Love has no division,
> Love causes no rebellion,
> Love does everything in unity.
> In love, all the elect of God are made perfect.
> Without love, nothing is pleasing to God.[137]

132. (Rom 2:24).
133. Ps 118:19f.
134. (1 Cor 12:8f).
135. (Matt 23:11; 1 Cor 10:24, 33).
136. (Col 3:14).
137. (1 Peter 4:8; 1 Cor 13:4, 7).

(6) In love, the Master received us. For the sake of the love which he has for us, Jesus Christ our Lord gave his blood for us according to the will of God, and his flesh for our flesh, and his spirit[138] for our spirit.

50.1 Behold, beloved, what a great and wonderful thing love is; its perfection is indescribable! (2) Who is able to be found in it except those God finds to be worthy? Let us now plead and beg for his mercy that we might be found blameless in love without being a party to the factions of men. (3) All generations from Adam to this day have passed away. But those perfected in love have, according to God's grace, the place of the pious. They will be revealed when the day of the kingdom of Christ comes.[139] (4) For it is written, "Go into the chambers for a short period of time, until my wrath and indignation pass by, and I will remember the opportune day and raise you up from your graves."[140] (5) Blessed are we, beloved, if we continue to obey the commandments of God in harmony and love, so that our sins may be forgiven through love. (6) For it is written, "Blessed are those whose transgressions against the law are forgiven, and whose sins are covered. Blessed is the man to whom the Lord does not reckon sin, in whose mouth there is no deceit."[141] (7) This beatitude is brought into relation with those chosen by God through Jesus Christ our Lord. To him be glory forever and ever. Amen.

51.1 For all the sins we have done and all the sins we committed as a result of the insidious calculations of the adversary, let us ask for forgiveness. But those who created the rebellion and the division must look to the hope common to all. (2) For those who conduct their walk in fear and love would prefer that they, instead of their neighbors, fall into tribulation, and would prefer to belittle themselves than the concord so gloriously and appropriately handed down to us. (3) For it is nobler for a man to confess his transgressions than to harden his heart, as those who have hardened their hearts in rebellion against the servant of God, Moses. Their judgment is manifest.[142] (4) They went into hell while living, "and death leads them to pasture."[143] (5) Pharaoh and his army, and all the noblemen of Egypt, and their chariots and horsemen, were sunk into the Red Sea and perished for no other reason than

---

138. TN: The German "Seele" here can mean as many things as the Greek ψυχὴν: spirit, soul, life.

139. (1 Peter 2:12).

140. Isa 26:20; Ezek 37:12; and where else?

141. Ps 32:1f.

142. (Rom 3:8).

143. Num 16:32f; Ps 48 (49):14.

that they hardened their hearts after the signs and miracles were done in Egypt by the servant of God, Moses.[144]

52.1 The Master of all things needs nothing, brothers, and he requires nothing at all, only that one confesses to him. (2) David, the chosen one, says, "I will confess to the Lord. This will be more pleasing to him than a young calf with horns and hooves. The poor will take note of this and rejoice."[145] (3) And again he says, "Sacrifice to God the sacrifice of praise and offer your prayers to the Most High and call out to me in the day of your tribulation, and I will pull you out and you will glorify me.[146] (4) For a sacrifice to God is a broken spirit."[147]

53.1 You indeed know the Holy Scriptures, beloved, you know them well and have gained deep insights into the sayings of God. Therefore, we only write the following as a reminder. (2) When Moses ascended the mountain and spent forty days and forty nights in fasting and humiliation, God said to him, "Moses, Moses, descend quickly. For your people, whom you brought out of Egypt, have acted against the law. For they quickly deviated from the way you showed them. They made images for themselves."[148] (3) And the Lord said to him, "I have spoken to you more than once, 'I see this people and behold, they have a stiff neck. Let me exterminate them, and I will extinguish their name from under heaven, and I will make you a great and wonderful people, a much greater people than this.' (4) And Moses said, 'Not so, Lord! Forgive this people their sin, or remove me from the Book of the Living.'"[149] (5) What great love! What perfection that cannot be increased! The servant speaks to the Lord with such boldness. He asks for forgiveness for the congregation or wishes to be struck down along with it himself.

54.1 Who then is noble among you, who is sincere, who is filled with love? (2) Let him say, "If rebellion and strife and schism have arisen because of me, I will go away to wherever you want me to go, and I will do whatever the congregation commands, only let the flock of Christ live in peace, together with the appointed presbyters!" (3) If he does so, he will obtain great glory in Christ, and every place will receive him, "for the earth is the Lord's and all that is in it."[150] (4) This is how those who have walked

---

144. Exod 14:33f; Num 12:7; (Rom 1:21).
145. Ps 69:31f.
146. Ps 49 (50):14f.
147. Ps 51:19
148. Exod 34:28; Deut 9:9; Exod 32:7f; Deut 9:12f.
149. Exod 32:32.
150. Ps 24:1.

according to God's order for life, without any change of mind, have acted and this is how they will act.

55.1 But we wish to produce examples from the nations of the world. Many kings and leaders have handed themselves over to death after receiving an oracle at the time of a plague in order to save their fellow citizens through their blood. Many emigrated from their native cities so that they would no longer remain in rebellion. (2) Also among us (Christians) we have news that many allowed themselves to be shackled in chains for the freedom of others. Many have gone into slavery and fed others with the money received for it. (3) Many women, strengthened by the grace of God, have done many manly deeds. (4) The blessed Judith asked the elders, when the city was besieged, to allow her to go to the camp of the foreigners.[151] (5) Surrendering herself to danger, she went out of love for her homeland and her people who were besieged, and the Lord gave Holofernes "into the hand of a woman." (6) Esther, who was perfect in faith, also exposed herself to no less danger in order to save the twelve tribes of Israel, who were on the brink of extinction. For through her fasting and her humiliation she presented the matter to the all-seeing Master, the God of the eons. And when he saw the humility of her soul, he saved the people for whose sake she put herself in danger.[152]

56.1 And now let us intercede for those who are guilty of any offence, that humble willingness will be given to them, not to submit to us, but to the will of God. For in this way, the compassionate remembrance addressed to God and the saints will bring full fruit.[153] (2) Let us accept discipline, beloved, about which no one should be unwilling. The practice of exhorting one another is good and of utmost use, for it joins us to the will of God. (3) For this is what the Holy Word says, "The Lord has disciplined me with a harsh discipline. He has not handed me over to death.[154] (4) For the Lord chastens the one he loves, and he swings the scourge upon every son he accepts."[155] (5) "He who is righteous will chastise me," it is said, "with mercy and will convict me. But may the oil of sinners not wet my head."[156] (6) And again, he says, "Blessed is the man whom the Lord convicts. Do not reject the exhortation of the Almighty. For he inflicts suffering and restores. (7) He strikes, and his hands heal. (8) Six times he pulls you out of emergency, and the seventh time nothing bad comes upon you. (9) In famine he will save you from death, and

---

151. Judith 8ff; 13:15.
152. Esther 7ff; 4:16.
153. (Gal 6:1).
154. Ps 118:18.
155. Prov 3:12.
156. Ps 141:5.

in war he will release you from the hand that wields the sword. (10) And he will hide you from the scourge of the tongue, and you will fear no evil to come. (11) You will laugh at the wicked and the lawless, and you will not fear the wild beasts. (12) For the wild beasts will greet you peacefully. (13) Then you will know that your house is at peace, and that the supply of your tent will not be reduced. (14) You will know that your seed will be numerous and your children like the plants of the field. (15) But you will enter the grave like ripe grain, brought in at the right time, and brought together like sheaves on the threshing floor."[157] Behold, beloved, what protection those chastised by the Lord enjoy. For the Father, who is a good Father, chastises us with his holy discipline, in order to have mercy upon us.

57.1 Now, you who have laid the foundation of the rebellion, obey the presbyters and, bowing the knees of your heart, let yourselves be chastised to repentance.[158] (2) Put aside the boastful and arrogant exaltation of your tongue and learn obedience. For it is better for you to be little and honored in the flock of Christ than appear as a great lord and be expelled from the common hope. (3) For thus says all-virtuous Wisdom, "Behold, I will recite to you a word from my spirit; I will teach you my word. (4) Because I called again and again and you did not hear, and because I extended my words and you did not respect them, but instead rendered irrelevant my intentions, therefore I will laugh at your downfall and rejoice when disaster comes upon you, when sudden turmoil strikes you and catastrophe comes like a sudden gust of wind, or when tribulation and distress come upon you. (5) It will happen that when you call upon me, I will not hear you. The wicked will seek me, and they will not find me. For they hated wisdom, but rejected the fear of the Lord. Nor did they wish to take notice of my intentions. They mocked my reproaches. Therefore, they will eat the fruits of their own chosen way, and they will fill themselves with their iniquities. (7) For they will be murdered for their injustice against minors, and a judgment will destroy the wicked. But whoever hears me will dwell confidently in hope and will rest with all confidence from every evil."[159]

58.1 Let us, therefore, flee from the threats which Wisdom has foretold to the rebellious, and let us obey his holy and glorious name, that we may dwell in peace, in confidence in his pious and majestic name. (2) Receive our counsel; you will not regret it. For as the true God lives, and the Lord Jesus Christ, and the Holy Spirit, and the hope of the elect, whoever, with a humble mind, steadfast meekness, and without regret, fulfills the laws and

---

157. Job 5:17ff.
158. 1 Peter 5:5.
159. Prov 1:23ff.

the commandments issued by God will be added and counted among the number of those (people?) saved by Jesus Christ. Through whom be glory to him forever and ever. Amen.

59.1 But if some refuse to obey what he has spoken through us, they should know that they entangle themselves in transgression and in no insignificant amount of danger. (2) But we will be blameless for this sin, and we will pray unceasingly and petition that the craftsman of everything may preserve unharmed the number of his elect throughout the whole world, through his beloved servant Jesus Christ, through whom he called us from darkness to light, from ignorance to knowledge of the glory of his name,[160] (3) to hope in your name, which contains the archetypal principle of all creation. . . . You have opened the eyes of our hearts "that we might know you, who alone is the Highest among the Highest, the Holy One who rests among the holy, the one who humbles the pride of the exalted, who brings to nothing the attacks of the nations, who exalts the humble, who humbles the exalted, who makes rich and poor, who kills <and heals> and makes alive, the only benefactor of the spirits and the God of all flesh, who looks down into the abysses, who watches over the works of men, who helps those who are in danger, the savior of the desperate, the creator and the guardian of all spiritual things, who causes the nations to increase and chooses out from them all those who love you through Jesus Christ, your beloved servant, through whom you instructed, sanctified, and honored us.[161] (4) We ask you, O Master, to be our helper and protector. Free those among us stricken by grief, have mercy on the oppressed, raise up the fallen, make yourself present to the needy, heal the weak, bring back the lost ones of your people, feed the hungry, free our prisoners, raise up the dejected, comfort the despondent. Let all nations know that you are God alone and Jesus Christ is your servant and we are your people and the sheep of your pasture."[162]

60.1 "For you have revealed the eternal order of the world through your prevailing power. You, Lord, have created the world, you are reliable in all generations, just in your judgments, wonderful in strength and majesty, wise in creation and knowledgeable in preserving what exists, good in what is seen and friendly to those who hope in you. Merciful and benevolent one,

---

160. (1 Peter 2:9).

161. (Eph 1:17f) — (Isa 57:15) — (Isa 13:11) — (Ps 33:10) — (Job 5:11) — (1 Sam 2:7) — (Deut 32:39) — (Ps 115:7) — (Num 16:22; 27:16) — (Sirach 16:18f) — (Ps 32 [33]:13) — (Judith 9:11; Isa 29:19) — (Zech 12:1; Amos 4:13; Isa 57:16) — (Job 10:12; 1 Peter 2:25).

162. (Ps 118 [119]:114) — (Ezek 34:16) — (1 Thess 5:14) — (1 Kings 8:60; 2 Kings 19:19) — Ps 99 (100):2.

forgive us our unlawfulness and injustice and missteps and transgressions.[163] (2) Do not reckon sin to your slave men and slave women, but purify us with the purification of your truth, and direct our steps to walk in piety of heart and to do that which is good and pleasing before you and before our rulers.[164] (3) Indeed, Master, let your face shine upon us for good in peace so that we may be shielded by your powerful hand and delivered from all sin by your strong arm, and deliver us from those who hate us unjustly.[165] (4) Give us and all inhabitants of the earth harmony and peace, as you have given them to our fathers when they called upon you piously in faith and truth, obedient to your almighty and glorious name."[166]

61.1 You, O Master, have given our leaders and rulers the power of their kingdom by your great and ineffable power, that we, recognizing the glory and honor that you have bestowed upon them, may obey them, resisting nothing of your will. Bestow upon them, O Lord, health, peace, harmony, well-being, so that they may lead without difficulty the dominion you have given them.[167] (2) For you, O heavenly Master, king of the ages of the world, bestow glory and honor and power on the children of men over that which is on earth. You, O Lord, direct their will to that which is good and pleasing before you so that they may exercise the power you have given them with a pious mind, in peace and meekness, and become partakers of your grace.[168] (3) You, who alone are able to do this and even more good for us, we praise you, the high priest and the patron of our souls Jesus Christ, through whom be glory to you and majesty now and from generation to generation and forever and ever. Amen."

62.1 About what belongs to our worship of God—which is quite necessary for those who wish to live a virtuous life, piously and justly—we have sufficiently written to you; (2) for we have dealt with every subject regarding faith, repentance, genuine love, abstinence, moderation, and perseverance, exhorting you that you must be pleasing in righteousness, truthfulness, and perseverance to the Almighty God, with a pious mind, with love and peace, with inexhaustible gentleness without holding a grudge, in harmony, just as our aforementioned fathers were pleasing, because they were of a humble mind with respect to the Father and God and creator, and that you must be pleasing to all men. (3) And we were

---

163. (Deut 7:9).
164. (Num 14:18) — (Ps 39 [40]:3; Ps 118 [119]:133) — (1 Kings 9:4; Deut 13:18).
165. (Ps 66 [67]:1) — (Jer 21:10) — (Isa 51:16; Exod 6:1, etc.).
166. (Ps 144 [145]:8).
167. (1 Peter 2:13, 15; Rom 13:2).
168. (1 Tim 1:17).

especially happy to give this exhortation, because we know very well that we write to faithful and especially distinguished men, who have gained deep insight into the sayings of the teaching of God.

63.1 Therefore, it is right and proper to follow such beautiful and countless examples, to bow the neck, and to join us in obedience to the leaders of our souls so that we, ending this senseless insurrection, may reach the goal set before us in truth without any blame. (2) And you will bring us joy and happiness when you become obedient to what we have written by the Holy Spirit and eradicate your wicked anger in accordance with the admonishment we have addressed (to you) in this letter regarding peace and harmony. (3) We are also sending reliable and prudent men who have walked among us from youth until old age. They will be witnesses between you and us. (4) But we do this so that you may know that our concerns have been and continue to be centered on this: that you may come to peace as quickly as possible.

64.1 Moreover, may the omniscient God, the ruler of the spirits, and the Lord of all flesh, who has chosen the Lord Jesus Christ, and through him makes us a special people, may he grant to every soul that calls upon his majestic and holy name, faith, fear, peace, perseverance, long-suffering, abstinence, purity, and moderation, that they might be pleasing to his holy name, through our high priest and patron Jesus Christ. Through whom to him be glory and majesty, power and honor now and forever and ever. Amen.[169]

65.1 The ones sent by us, Claudius Ephebus and Valerius Bito, together with Fortunatus, send them back to us in peace and with joy as soon possible, so they may announce to us as soon as possible the much wished for and desired state of peace and harmony, so that we too may rejoice over it as soon as possible.[170] (2) May the grace of our Lord Jesus Christ be with you and with all those everywhere who are called by God through him, through whom be glory, honor, power, and majesty, and eternal dominion forever and ever. Amen.[171]

---

169. 1 Clem 64: (Num 27:16; Heb 12:9) — (Eph 1:4; Deut 14:4).
170. (1 Cor 16:11).
171. (1 Cor 1:2).

2. The Author

As is said in the opening of the letter, the Roman congregation names itself as the author. The text of the letter maintains this claim throughout, from beginning to end, and Codex C[1] even maintains it within the letter's *subscriptio*. Officials who represent the congregation are not identified for either the Roman or Corinthian community. Even the "witnesses" sent to Corinth (see 1 Clem 63.3; 65.1) are indeed characterized as "old," but the mention of any official designation—even that of "presbyter"—is avoided. Therefore, as we can see here, both congregations still appear to function as pure, Christian democracies wherein no one rules.[1]

Thus, attribution of the letter to Clement is based only on the tradition that a man named Clement is its author. Nevertheless, it is valuable because it is an ancient and unanimous tradition that was already written down in Hermas Vis. II.4 (making it virtually a contemporaneous witness).

Irenaeus clearly says that this Clement was "bishop"; but according to the words of Hermas, this is only a strong suggestion. Irenaeus says even more. He describes Clement as the only bishop in Rome during his time or rather places him in a monarchial list of bishops, which from the beginning demonstrates the existence of monarchical bishops in a closed succession. This cannot be correct, but is rather constructed from a later vantage point. For the letter itself does not give the slightest indication of it, and the Shepherd of Hermas knows of only "bishops" in his native Roman community and shows no knowledge of a monarchical bishop. However, it cannot be ruled out that *de facto* Clement was the most outstanding and therefore leading bishop among his Roman bishop colleagues. Indeed it is quite probable that this is the case because the letter shows such insight,

---

1. The letter of Polycarp to the Philippian congregation written about twenty years later is different. The address reads, "Polycarp and the presbyters with him to the church of God that dwells in Philippi as foreigners." But even here, the addressees are not regimentally differentiated.

prudence, and strength that it is difficult to imagine that the Roman community possessed several such wise and energetic minds and Christian characters at that time and that Clement had to share his representation of the community with others.

The fabulous legend beginning in the third century knows much of this Clement, who is never called by his surname. However, the certified history (Irenaeus) reports of only the important fact that he still saw the blessed apostles (Peter and Paul) and that he was in contact with them (see above; there is no reason to object to this information as invented). Therefore, we have before us a man whose life still partly belongs to the apostolic age and who is connected to the historical Jesus through an intermediary link. The name Clement connects him simultaneously with the consul Titus Flavius Clemens, who was executed under the very probable suspicion of Christianity, as well was with both Domitillas, the Domitilla catacombs, and numerous inscriptions found therein. Alone, this provides no solution. An identification with the consul is not possible, for this would not have been forgotten by the ancient tradition, not to mention its unlikelihood for other reasons. It is obvious that the author was a freed man or a slave of the consul. Because of his excellent knowledge of the (Greek) Bible, one would like to conclude that he was born a Jew; however, this conclusion is very uncertain. Would it have been possible for a born Jew to have set aside Judaism like our author, who additionally has left behind no knowledge of Hebrew? On a certain Roman patriotism present within the letter, see below. If we know nothing about the author of the letter from the literature, he himself provides ample material for his characterization; for what we will say about the Christian and moral character of the Roman epistle applies first and foremost to the author of the epistle itself. To a greater degree, one is struck by the literary characteristics of the letter, and it may be said here that he possesses the usual rhetorical-philosophical education, but not more. He is a man who knows how to write to an extent, but lacks a higher philosophical education; who likes to be dramatic, though lacking aesthetic taste; whose strength does not lie in recognition and knowledge but in good will, in humility towards God, and in the sense of order, obedience, and moderation. Here, however, he is quite excellent and he connects this sense with a solidarity that is based on Christian fraternity, unity and peace, and the rejection of anything eccentric. In every century of the Roman Church, he would be welcomed as a characteristic and worthy representative, and one might make judgments about his secular education as always and the analysis of his letter may make him appear more independent or dependent—the ability and strength to confidently move in religious traditions and experiences and to be a leader for others cannot be denied him.

The letter falls into the very last period of Domitian's reign, and is, therefore, just as old as John's Revelation, which *toto coelo* is different from him, indeed represents the antithesis to him in Christian literature. Whoever wishes to deal with this letter must first acquire a basic knowledge of the external and internal context of the empire at that time. The works particularly recommended here can be found in every textbook of church history.

3. Characteristics of the Letter and Its Religious Content

THERE CAN BE NO doubt about the intention and purpose, method and means of the letter. It is clear, transparent, and definite from the first to the last leaf. The charge that the letter is poorly planned and contains superfluous remarks is unjustified.[1] The disputes that have broken out in the Corinthian community, which have resulted in the dismissal of some presbyters (bishops and deacons), are to be abolished as soon as possible, so that the masterminds of the deposition are prosecuted as the culprits. But since the whole congregation either approved of the deposition by a majority decision or—more probably—did not oppose it, the Romans recognize in this behavior the symptom of a general weakness of the Christian community that has seized the so respected and famous Corinthian congregation. According to this, it is first necessary to strengthen the Christianity of the sister congregation. It is the conviction of the Romans that only after they have been strengthened (i.e., after they possess the knowledge and strength) will they be in a position to resolve the disputes. Therefore, the letter is divided into two parts. In the first, larger portion, Christianity as it is and should be is presented to the Corinthian community as a gift and a task in continued exhortations (always taking into account the particular occasion of the letter). In the second portion of the letter, the Roman judgment in relation to the disputes is prepared, reasoned, formulated, and executed with its consequences in the most careful manner

---

1. It is not necessary to give a detailed explanation of the letter's structure. Everyone can discover it for himself, as soon as he has realized that after the introduction (chapters 1 and 2), the main caesura falls between chapter 36 and 37 and that 59 to 65 functions as a conclusion. The structure may even be described as tight. Excursuses may be noted in a few places, but they are not disturbing. For this very reason, the assumption that the author used older pieces from sermons is unjustified, even though not all the compositions in the letter are original.

(1 Clem 37ff). The Romans look back primarily to the first portion of the letter when writing, "About what belongs to our worship of God—which is quite necessary for those who wish to live a virtuous life, piously and justly—we have sufficiently written to you; for we have dealt with every subject regarding faith, repentance, genuine love, abstinence, moderation, and perseverance" (1 Clem 62.1–2).

Whatever one may think of the remarks about Christianity in the letter, the Roman congregation will receive lasting recognition, as it has grasped the present task of eliminating an evil dispute, not as a particular one, even less by going into concrete details and gossip, but out of the knowledge that one must strengthen the roots, the faith, and the moral vitality, if a weakness shows itself in the leaf and the blossom.[2] This knowledge is truly apostolic, for this is how Paul proceeded. At the same time, it corresponds to the decision of the Roman community to intervene in the turmoil of the sister community at all, for it has thereby demonstrated a Christian common sense that also corresponds to the apostolic view that one should come to the aid of a suffering member.[3] The whole letter in both its parts can be brought under the heading that the Roman congregation itself casually formulated "an exhortatory petition concerning peace and harmony" (1 Clem 63.2).

The extensive prayer, into which the writing concludes (1 Clem 59–61), is not merely the climax of the edifying admonition, but also expresses a special formal peculiarity: The Roman congregation closely unites itself with the sister congregation; therefore the reproaches and admonitions are always given in the first person plural and not in the second person. Yes, the Romans feel themselves to be standing together with the Corinthians in an assembly before God's eyes and celebrating a worship service when writing (see, above all, 1 Clem 34.7). Therefore, the great prayer at the end—which some wished to separate as a later addition because the overall attitude of the letter was not understood and appreciated—does not come as a surprise, but organically follows the previous one. By joining

---

2. It is also very remarkable that the Roman congregation consistently avoids speaking of itself or even presenting itself as an example in the letter. That makes the worthiest impression! It is completely occupied with the task of making peace in Corinth. Even the difficult experiences that have recently come upon it (the Domitian persecution) only appear at the beginning of the letter to excuse its belated care, and then leaves it aside entirely without any complaint. It wants to help, but does not demand any help itself. The words of prayer, "Deliver our prisoners" (59.4) and "Deliver us from those who hate us unjustly" (60.3) could also have been written in a so-called time of peace.

3. The Roman community has intervened unsolicited (1.1 does not say περὶ τῶν ἐπιζητουμένων παρ' ὑμῶν πραγμάτων, but rather παρ' ὑμῖν). On the fact that it indeed intervenes at all and also demonstrates a domineering attitude, see below.

3. CHARACTERISTICS OF THE LETTER AND ITS RELIGIOUS CONTENT 45

forces with the Corinthian congregation, the Romans removed from the outset all sharpness from its admonitions and made it impossible for the Corinthians to complain about pedantry and arrogance. The Roman congregation, therefore, is all the more capable of giving its admonitions and instructions all the more urgently and emphatically.

As far as the religious and theological character of the letter is concerned, first of all a fundamental methodological error has to be eliminated which has burdened the understanding of the letter in all theological camps since the time of Baur and his school. Although Wrede[4] vigorously opposed him, and Knopf[5] liberated himself from him in a commendable way, there is still much to be done for his complete extermination. The error consists in the fact that one attempts to understand the religious character of the epistle from the Pauline epistles, or even from other Christian writings and ways of thinking, either by the assumption that the writing is a compromise between Pauline thought and Jewish Christianity, which abrades and weakens both in the interest of peace, or by the other related assumption that the author of the epistle had wanted to theologically balance different NT doctrinal terms in their intentions and formulas and, so to speak, reduce them to a common denominator. This is the view of Lightfoot[6] and others, that of Baur and the Tübingen school. Against Baur, it has to be said that in the whole letter neither Judaism nor Jewish Christianity finds the slightest consideration—this important observation will be considered later—and that there is no reason why this should be explained by "compromising diplomatic intentions." In any case, Baur's explanation of the paradoxical deficiency remains understandable and debatable because there really was a great contrast and struggle between Paul and Jewish Christianity in the past. What is entirely incomprehensible to us today, however, is Lightfoot's view, which is at the same time a particularly clear proof of how fundamentally the historical judgment has changed in recent decades. Lightfoot states in his "Introduction" that the letter is marked by three characteristics: (1) comprehensiveness, (2) sense of order, (3) moderation. Then, he writes the following about the first point (I have to cite the entire passage despite its length because it unfortunately still has followers among us today):

> The comprehensiveness is tested by the range of the Apostolic writings, with which the author is conversant and of which he makes use. Mention has already been made of his co-ordinating the two Apostles S. Peter and S. Paul in distinction

---

4. Wrede, *Untersuchungen zum ersten Klemensbriefe*, 58ff.
5. Knopf, *Clemensbriefe*, vol. 1.
6. Lightfoot, *Clement of Rome*, 1:95ff.

to the Ebionism of a later age, which placed them in direct antagonism, and to the factiousness of certain persons even in the apostolic times, which perverted their names into party watchwords notwithstanding their own protests. This mention is the fit prelude to the use made of their writings in the body of the letter. The influence of S. Peter's First Epistle may be traced in more than one passage; while expressions scattered up and down Clement's letter recall the language of several of S. Paul's Epistles belonging to different epochs and representing different types in his literary career.

Nor is the comprehensiveness of Clement's letter restricted to a recognition of these two leading Apostles. It is so largely interspersed with thoughts and expressions from the Epistle to the Hebrews, that many ancient writers attributed this Canonical epistle to Clement.

Again, the writer shows himself conversant with the type of doctrine and modes of expression characteristic of the Epistle of S. James. Just as he coordinates the authority of S. Peter and S. Paul, as leaders of the Church, so in like manner he combines the teaching of S. Paul and S. James on the great doctrines of salvation (this is justified from 1 Clem 31–35). We have thus a full recognition of four out of the five types of Apostolic teaching, which confront us in the Canonical writings. If the fifth, of which S. John is the exponent, is not clearly affirmed in Clement's letter, the reason is that the Gospel and Epistles of this Apostle had not yet been written, or if written had not been circulated beyond his own immediate band of personal disciples.

This consideration starts from the premise that Lightfoot and those theologians related to him apparently take for granted that the apostolic writings (or the oldest Christian literature) had been available to the congregations in the empire as peculiar "doctrinal concepts" that they, as such, had to study eagerly and convey, since the inspiration of these writings guaranteed their full uniformity and consistency. But with this presupposition, everything that follows is incorrect. There is, therefore, something tragic about the fact that the most learned and merited exegete of 1 Clement has fallen to it; for (1) what bore the name of Christ and what one read as a Christian was read in the churches of the post-apostolic era in the kingdom first of all for edification, that is, to recognize the will of God and to strengthen obedience according to this will. (2) A church theology did not yet exist at all (neither an internal nor an external compulsion to acquire such a one), but only certain firm basic features of the proclamation, beside them hundreds of *disjecta membra* of a theological kind and of a most diverse origin, on which one

3. CHARACTERISTICS OF THE LETTER AND ITS RELIGIOUS CONTENT 47

indiscriminately built oneself up. (3) The Old Testament was exclusively the inspired *litera scripta* (see below), and in every respect it was considered a sufficient divine, foundational document (*Urkunde*). The word of Christ and the "pneumatics" of the apostles, the prophets, and teachers or even the congregations competed with this foundational document (*Urkunde*), but did not yet present itself as a divine dictate and was therefore of a different kind than this, that is, not a regulation of faith but support. (4) Compared to the novelty and power of the fundamental proclamation and the overwhelming impression of the Old Testament interpreted in Christian terms, "doctrinal concepts" could at first only have a subordinate meaning. However, they could offer other difficulties and impulses in detail in addition to edification. (5) The contrasts of the apostolic age (Jewish Christianity in various forms, Paul) were extinguished for Rome, Corinth, and the west of Asia Minor around the year of 100 CE, (6)—especially with regard to 1 Clement—the compilation of Peter and Paul in the letter has nothing to do with the contrast that once prevailed here, nor with Peter's doctrine; but additionally, the material that is related to 1 Peter, James, and Hebrews in the letter must not be used in the way that Lightfoot uses it, even if it were certain that Clement read the letter of James and knew 1 Peter as Peter's letter.[7] These letters are cited without the authors' names or rather, they were not at all cited but the author takes individual sentences (in no way especially characteristic) from them tacitly into his own constructions. The fact that here, in addition to the all-dominant edifice, another intention prevailed, or that the author wanted to introduce authorities and convey doctrinal concepts, is therefore entirely excluded. Only in relation to Paul, whose letter is explicitly cited (1 Clem 47), is the situation different. Here, the author has made an effort to conform himself to the apostle at a very important point (see below).[8]

---

7. The doubt as to whether 1 Peter was handed down as Petrine is based on the observation that it is also abundantly written out in Polycarp's letter, as it is in our letter, but also tacitly and without the author's name, while there, as here, Paul was cited by name and cited as an authority. It should also be remembered that 1 Peter is missing within the Muratorian Fragment.

8. The most remarkable thing about post-apostolic literature—which is regularly overlooked—is its autonomy and its total or essential independence from the literature of the most ancient time, or rather the apostolic age. Clement, Ignatius, Hermas, 2 Clement, Barnabas—everyone has his own Christianity, in which Paul or other ancient figures only plays a role. Dutch critics have recognized this and concluded that the oldest literature is not authentic. This is, of course, fundamentally wrong; but to make artificial connections with this literature among the post-apostolic fathers in order to derive their doctrine from the apostolic doctrines is no less wrong. The different forms of Christianity in the century from ca. 50 to 150 are almost exclusively connected to the Old Testament and the *kerygma* of God and Christ. For the Christians of the second

The strongest impression one gets from the letter is that the new religion was primarily not a cultic, nor an enthusiastic, nor a gnostic or speculative-mysterious movement, but rather a moral movement founded on the basis of the monotheism felt with the highest seriousness and liveliness, or better, on the basis of the reality of God. It is about a holy life, about the knowledge and observance of the will of God and about the performance of the good, or rather good works (see 1 Clem 2.2; 32.1ff; etc.). From the first to the last leaf, this fundamental character is strongly expressed in the letter, and one must descend to Calvin in Geneva, the Puritans of England and the New England states, in order to find in the common religion the sovereignty of God's holy laws so naturally as the Alpha and Omega of all living things. But the conviction that those who have received this salvation owe it to the election of God, which cannot be fathomed any further, who has provided a fixed number as the people of his property, also can be found here. Ultimately the content of the moral law of God (δικαιώματα) is similar in Clement and the Puritans: for there and here it is by no means antithetically directed towards the world, as if the world itself was the evil principle, but directs itself towards the positive ideals of obedience, moral purity, and sublimity (ἁγνότης, σεμνότης) as well as to the peace that can be won by gentleness and humility, love and service, and that presents itself in corporate unity. The moral ideal is not escapism and asceticism—it is esteemed as a special gift of God (1 Clem 35.4), but rarely mentioned, and where it is remembered, ascetics receive a warning against arrogance (1 Clem 38.2)—but the complex of all the positive virtues that produce a holy and pure, a peaceful and charitable (1 Clem 48.1) life with others. It is, in a word, simple morality, illuminated by the presence and power of God, which is what matters to the Roman Christians. The natural forms of existence and the differences between one another on the basis of possessions and education are taken for granted and should be regarded as gifts from God and used for the good of the whole. In the sense and in the style of the "Haustafeln" (household codes) of the Pauline epistles, warnings are repeatedly given to the old and young, the spouses, women, and educators. Clement writes, "Let our whole body remain safe and sound in Christ Jesus, and let everyone order himself with respect to his neighbor in accordance with the *charisma* of his neighbor. Let the strong take care of the weak, but let the weak have respect for the strong. Let the rich give to the poor, and let the poor thank God that he has given him one through whom his need is fulfilled. Let the wise man show his wisdom not in words but in good deeds. Let the humble not testify to his own humility, but let someone else

---

and third generation, this is only praiseworthy.

3. CHARACTERISTICS OF THE LETTER AND ITS RELIGIOUS CONTENT   49

do it" (1 Clem 38.1–2). These admonitions culminate in the repeated praise of love, which intensifies into a hymn (1 Clem 49; 50). No morbid addiction to martyrdom, no ostentation, and no complacent reflection disturbs the serene and simple seriousness of the whole posture and determined will to love. To such an extent all *échauffement* is missing, and it seems so self-evident that the congregation is given the leeway to really do what is good everywhere, that in many places one believes to have before one's eyes a letter from a time in which Christianity has carried out its assimilation to the world without relinquishing or curtailing its ideals. The pneumatic element is present as much as is the memory of the imminent return of Christ (1 Clem 23). Both topics must be discussed later; here it suffices to say that "the full outpouring of the Holy Spirit" (1 Clem 2.2) is seen in its most important consequences not in the ecstatic, but in the production of the Christian state itself and its essential traits, and that at the same time the delay of the return of Christ in judgment is explained with an intensification of the imminent judgment. Neither element provokes a stormy or even an intensified inner agitation within the author.

All the more versatile and animated is the testimony of the one living God, the creator and ruler. Indeed, we have no work from the ancient Gentile church before Origen, in which it is pronounced with such inwardness and in such a richness of relationships. A great number of the constructions in the letter serve it. Here, we can clearly see what the former Gentiles experienced and felt first and foremost in the new religion, which brought them into an indissoluble relationship with the living source of all things. Everything else receded behind this continuing experience; God in nature, his creative will, his lawful administration, and his orders are praised; God in his work in history, establishing an end and determining boundaries; God as the power that has foretold and prepared everything; God who peers into what is hidden; God as judge; God as the redeemer and as the giver of all good gifts; God as the force that alone leads to himself, *a deo per deum ad deum*. All convictions and sentiments awakened by living theism are offered here in astonishing reverence and joy.[9] One could claim from every individual construction that it is not original; but he who is unable to feel the joy and the full seriousness of the simple knowledge of

---

9. In the foreground is God as Master (δεσπότης) or as the πατὴρ καὶ κτίστης τοῦ σύμπαντος κόσμου (1 Clem 19.2) or ὁ μέγας δημιουργὸς καὶ δεσπότης τῶν ἁπάντων (20.11), indeed, in truth, everything has already been said with it. The name "Father" in the ethical sense is completely relegated to the background. Here, there is a clear difference from the New Testament letters. Note, however, the importance Clement attaches to emphasizing God's nearness (see, for example, 21.3: Ἴδωμεν πῶς ἐγγύς ἐστιν, καὶ ὅτι οὐδὲν λέληθεν αὐτὸν τῶν ἐννοιῶν ἡμῶν οὐδὲ τῶν διαλογισμῶν ὧν ἐποιούμεθα) and his mercy (see 20.11: ἡμεῖς οἱ προσπεφευγότες τοῖς οἰκτιρμοῖς θεοῦ).

God in these testimonies which are constantly springing up in the letter, and to distinguish them from religious stylistic exercises, must be denied the ability to distinguish the articulation of sincere religious life from the semblance of such a life. But if it is argued that the poetic prose and the rhetorical clothing of numerous passages cast doubt on that sincerity, it must not be forgotten that it was caused by the example of the Psalms, which was an indispensable garment that could not be missing from a document that, in times of diminishing taste, went from one cosmopolitan city to another and was to be read out loud publicly. The author has the greatest difficulty in escaping the aesthetic taste of the day, even if he is convinced of the objective purity of his ideas. However, one must say this of the letter: No polytheistic sub-tone, base intention, and no selfishness disturbs the articulation of a living knowledge of God.

The author has the highest admiration for the order of the divine world government, and the fact that he hardly speaks of miracles at all is probably connected with it. This great chapter in the history of ancient Christianity is almost completely omitted by him. Neither do miraculous phenomena have a place where he draws the ideal picture of a Christian community (1 Clem 1; 2), nor where he describes God's work. He certainly was not "afraid of miracles." He reminds his readers of Old Testament miracles, and he bases the hope of the resurrection, in addition to a cosmic-rational line of reasoning, on the story of the phoenix (1 Clem 24; 25).[10] The choice of this common Greek narrative, which does not present the process as a miracle, but rather as a natural phenomenon, is significant. The work of God is everywhere natural law and miraculous simultaneously. But he is either unaware of contemporary Christian miracles, which would be applicable here, or he is afraid to use such singularities. The vast field of miraculous healings and the exorcisms of demons, be it by Christ or by others in the present, is not even touched upon, as the author hardly has anything to do with demons, Satan, or the devil anywhere.[11]

The organ that establishes the connection with God is faith. But this—apart from the passage where Pauline propositions are thought of—is only

---

10. Jesus' resurrection is considered only as the first case of the resurrections.

11. The devil appears as "the adversary" only once (1 Clem 51). The later traits of ascetic self-disparagement are still completely absent, as Tertullian, for example, shows. How humility is to be understood in the letter is shown immediately by 1 Clem 2. It is contrasted with pompousness and arrogance. Especially characteristic is 1 Clem 48.5-6: "A man may have faith, he may be able to expound his knowledge, he may be wise in judging thoughts (speeches?), he may be holy in his deeds. The greater he thinks he is, the humbler of mind he must be, and must strive for that which is useful to the whole." See my treatise, von Harnack, "'Sanftmut, Huld und Demut' in der alten Kirche," 113–29.

3. CHARACTERISTICS OF THE LETTER AND ITS RELIGIOUS CONTENT

clear to the author as an active obedience of faith. Faith means to accept God as creator and Lord and to obey his will through good works. But there is also an important additional feature: the humility associated with meekness is inseparable from obedience of faith. It is one of the central concepts of the letter[12] and imbues faith with the manner in which the author conceives of it. The fear of the judge is not absent, but it does recede. This can be explained by the fact that the author is aware of God's unrestrained mercy, which looks at sins and forgives them. Sin is spoken of rather frequently in the letter, but it is spoken of within the context of the comforting maxim that God at all times and always granted the possibility for a change of mind (repentance), and that the remission of sins follows after the change of mind, and that all men were and are able to change their mind, that is, to perform obedient faith. For Christians, another special aspect is that they have escaped the dominion of sin, are therefore capable of sinlessness, and sin only involuntarily. The author also considers the grave sins of the Christian to be among involuntary sins, and here too he does not doubt their inheritance. However, it requires a hard and constant struggle of the brotherhood on behalf of the sinning brother, and above all, the conversion and repentance of the sinner himself. Nevertheless, the most joyful optimism dominates the author's disposition, for repentance is always available. Through renewed faith and love, God's mercy for forgiveness is always won anew. The proof that "the grace of repentance" is always accessible is almost the main purpose of the letter (see 1 Clem 2; 50; 51). Therefore, there is a lack here of the agonizing and restless fear of God and the oscillation between fear and hope that is characteristic of so many Gentile Christian monuments[13] (see, e.g., Hermas and 2 Clement). Admittedly, this optimistic conviction of faith is miles away from Paulinism, since Clement is unable to bear clear witness either to the tenacity of sin or to its characteristic of guilt, despite the quotations of the Psalms which it expresses.[14] In the Pauline and Augustinian churches, this whole view will be perceived as religiously poor and flat, but it is close to numerous sayings of Jesus, and one cannot deny

---

12. See 1 Clem 2; 13; 16–19; 21; 30; 31; 38; 44; 48; 53; 55; 56; 58; 59; 62.

13. TN: Here, Harnack uses the word "Denkmäler," which could be translated as monuments, memorials, statues, etc. In his address at the *Studentenkonferenz* in Aarau, Switzerland, Harnack uses the same term and clarifies his meaning. He writes, "There are the monuments from all epochs of the last two thousand five hundred years and beyond. By monuments, I mean all that which is still extant from bygone ages, be it buildings, statues, inscriptions, coins, documents, handwriting, etc." (Harnack, "What Has History to Offer," 48).

14. For more about this and about a conflict between the author and Paul, see below.

a congregation that follows it its place in Christianity. Such a congregation will have deeper experiences later.

Knowledge (*gnosis*) is highly esteemed, indeed it belongs beside the main elements of the new religion along with faith, piety, and hospitality (see 1 Clem 1).[15] However, it does not pass over to external areas, but instead remains entirely within the understanding of the revelations of the creator God within the visible world[16] and the regulations of the Old Testament, and receives its deepest content through Christ. For it is through him that knowledge is supposedly raised to a new, higher level and makes accessible "the immortal *gnosis*," that is, the *gnosis* that has the invisible and eternal within itself as its content and transmits it as a possession (see 1 Clem 36). If the letter thereby opens a vista towards the development of the next subsequent period, wherein "the immortal *gnosis*" plays an important role, it is nevertheless quite far from the author himself to paint this *gnosis* and to shape it with philosophy or the resources of some wisdom cult. No post-apostolic writing bears so few "gnostic" characteristics as this letter.[17] When Clement speaks of "the depths of divine knowledge" (βάθη τῆς θείας γνώσεως; 1 Clem 40.1), into which Christians gain insight, he also means here exclusively or mainly the proper understanding of the Old Testament in its theistic and moral respects.[18] Nevertheless, he also attests to the fact that *gnosis* is different and grows among Christians, and that increased knowledge means increased responsibility (1 Clem 41; 48).

Baptism is mentioned once in passing (1 Clem 42.5) and the Lord's Supper is alluded to several times and is highly esteemed (1 Clem 7.4; 12.7; 21.6; 44; etc.). But the author did not deal with these sacred acts in detail. In an intimate and detailed letter to Christians, this is conspicuous, and one can assume from this silence in the context of the whole letter that he rationalized the mysteries, even if Christianity was a mystery religion to him, which can be proved by his thoughts about the blood of Christ.

---

15. The compilation is not random. The mention of hospitality in this context is particularly noteworthy (cf. 1 Clem 10–12: "faith and hospitality" or "hospitality and piety"). It proves that under the circumstances of the time, this virtue was particularly necessary, that many virtues converged in it, as in a focal point, and that it must have formed a *nota confessionis* against the ruling greed.

16. TN: That is, within nature.

17. A narrow path leads over to the apologetic *gnosis*, and none at all to the *gnosis* of the excited apocalyptic and the mysteriosophy.

18. "The depths of divine knowledge" must have been a well-known term at that time, though not a common one. Paul uses it (1 Cor 2:10) and John speaks of "the depths of Satan" (Rev 2:24). But then, in Christianity, the term is attested among the Gnostics (see Iren. *Haer.* II.22.3; II.28.9; Tert. *Val.* 1; Hipp. *Haer.* V.6).

3. CHARACTERISTICS OF THE LETTER AND ITS RELIGIOUS CONTENT

"The blood of Christ": what the author has to say about Christ, he offers not as his own *gnosis*, but as an expression of a fact of which he only has to remember. But this fact dominates all statements, because everything for the author is determined "in Christ" and "through Christ" so that, according to the author, "Christ" must be consulted as coefficient to every religious contemplation, statement, and function, be it with regard to God or to human beings. Therefore, in order to avoid great repetitions, I am content with this statement and will return to his "Christianity," in the specific sense of the word, in the following analysis. But it may already be said here that ability to recognize the meaning of Christ and to make a statement does not correspond to the pan-Christism[19] of the words.

In 1 Clem 35.1–3, the author summarizes the gain of the Christian religion: "How exhilarating and wonderful are the gifts of God, life in immortality, joy in righteousness, truth with candor, faith with confidence, self-control with holiness, and all these things lie within the realm of our understanding. But what then are the good things that will only be prepared for those who have endured? The craftsman and Father of the eons, the Most Holy one, he alone knows their greatness and their beauty." Each individual piece and its compilation are not entirely transparent. But it is certain that, compared with the Gospels and Pauline Epistles, there is something different here. Whence comes this *fructus religionis* and the knowledge on which it is founded?

---

19. TN: The word "Panchristismus" in German is an invention of Harnack's, and I have decided to maintain it in the translation. The term reflects Harnack's previous statement that Christ is everywhere (*pan*) the coefficient to every religious act within the letter.

4. The Sources of Clementine-Roman Christianity

1. The Old Testament

IN THE SECOND HALF of his work *Untersuchungen zum 1 Clemensbrief*, in the section titled "Der 1 Clemensbrief und das AT,"[1] Wrede examined the relationship of the letter to the Old Testament quite excellently and corrected it against an earlier misunderstanding. But even he has not yet spoken the last word. It must read: The Christianity of 1 Clement recognizes its complete and sufficient God-given foundation in the OT and therefore is nothing other than the religion of this book.[2] Any analysis of the religious content of the letter is wrong that does not put this proposition at the forefront. This Christianity simply identifies itself with the religion of the Old Testament.[3]

---

1. Wrede, *Untersuchungen zum ersten Klemensbriefe*, 58–107 (ET: "1 Clement and the OT").

2. See here Wrede, *Untersuchungen zum ersten Klemensbriefe*, 59 (also 75f). "The value that the letter of the Roman congregation possesses as a historical, foundational document (*Urkunde*) for the Christianity of the first century lies not least in the manner of its use and valuation of the Old Testament, and this use and valuation is essential for the author's overall Christian disposition." Apart from Scripture and the *kerygma* (see also 1 Clem 44), there is no "tradition" for the author, for the singular use of the expression ὁ κανὼν τῆς παραδόσεως (7.2; cf. 19.2; 51.2) is not yet a technical term. Instead, it describes the content of Scripture and the gospel message as tradition.

3. Already outwardly and materially, the Christianity of the letter presents itself as the religion of the Old Testament. I count approximately 120 Old Testament citations and allusions in the letter (apart from the linguistic reminiscences; the letter itself speaks the language of the OT; it is the religious language for him), a tremendous number! To them are added 7 "apocryphal" citations, which the author, however, has treated as Old Testament texts; the writings from which they originated were handed down to him together with the Old Testament. A close examination of the quotations shows that careful compilations of similar passages can be found and that the author has both quoted from memory and copied (see Wrede, *Untersuchungen zum ersten Klemensbriefe*, 64f). To what extent he already stands under a tradition within

4. THE SOURCES OF CLEMENTINE-ROMAN CHRISTIANITY

The appraisal of the Old Testament and this consciousness are therefore presented more precisely:

(1) The Old Testament is the divine word (i.e., the dictation of God) and as *litera scripta* it is the highest and final authority. Therefore, it is objectively irrelevant from which Old Testament book a verse is drawn, who the human author is, when and to whom the word is spoken, etc.[4]

(2) The Old Testament was given by God to the prophets/holy men, but is intended for a circle of elect, whose number is gradually being fulfilled and is now coming to perfection by those who belong to the church (the "brothers" and "sisters," the "sanctified"; the name "Christian" does not appear).[5]

(3) The Old Testament contains the self-revelation of God in relation to the world and his will to mankind, which is presented in the form of "statutes" and "regulations." But these legal statutes—that they at the same time represent an ethical book of examples is just as important—also include his gracious and merciful will in love and forbearance, which has always existed, that is, even before Christ, and has always been active in the same way.[6] The fact that the Old Testament also contains prophecy recedes, but is not absent; however, nothing would be more contrary to Clement's meaning than the view that the Old Testament is a book of prophecy of future grace and salvation, and that its content of grace will come into force only through future acts of salvation (that is, through Christ). The "Scripture," that is, the Old Testament, is itself the book of

---

his citations is difficult to determine. Only a few citation compilations point to such a tradition, and not with any certainty.

The Septuagint is the basis throughout. The addition of apocryphal traits to Old Testament stories must belong to an accompanying, i.e., Jewish exegetical tradition. The practice of wandering through the Old Testament and its history for the purpose of paraenesis is a part of Jewish tradition. It is found in the Christian lectures from the very beginning and has never ceased.

4. This does not require proof. In a few places, the Holy Spirit or Christ is made the subject of the words of Scripture (see 13.1; 16.2; 45.2; 16.2, 15; 22.1 [Christ through the Holy Spirit]). There are exceptions and rare cases where one learns in which book of the Old Testament the saying in question is written (26.3, Job; 52.2, David; 57.3, the πανάρετος σοφία, i.e., the Proverbs).

5. See 1 Clem 50.6f; 2.4; 29.1 (ἐκλογῆς μέρος ἡμᾶς ἐποίσεν) and the large congregational prayer. The Old Testament prophets etc. are "the fathers," "our fathers"; they have nothing to do with Judaism. It is certain that Scripture is exclusively for the elect because a different subject is never mentioned. Therefore, the idea of the covenant is entirely reduced, for the elect are a mere heap. There is no covenant made with one partner, let alone two covenants. Therefore, the term "people" in the church (59;64) should not be pressed. It is only a reminiscence and means nothing more than a heap.

6. It is especially important to recognize and note this. On the unrestrained mercy of God, see 1 Clem 7; 8, and above at chapter 3.

grace and mercy and therefore the foundation and the source of God's church. See below about what comes through Christ.[7]

(4) The fact that the Old Testament prophets and pious men all belonged to the people of Israel can be seen immediately from the letter; however, this people is no longer significant, and there is no talk of an effective covenant of salvation with this people, followed by a new covenant.[8] There has always been only one and the same goal of divine revelation: to call the elect and to make full their number. Nothing can be said about what Clement thought about Judaism in general due to his complete silence.

(5) The binding content of the revelation of Scripture is religious-moralistic. All ceremonial, ritual, priestly, organizational, etc. provisions can only be considered to be typological, analogous, and exemplary for the present, and in this way they have an important significance. Yet, at the time when they were given up until the appearance of Christ—as the author will have to be understood—it was pious and good to fulfill them. Further details cannot be ascertained because of Clement's absolute silence, nor can the distinction between the religious and the ceremonial be satisfactorily made, which in any case is not easy to make.[9]

---

7. The Old Testament also contains prophecies (about Christ) according to Clement. But they are not very frequently brought into discussion (1 Clem 12; 16; 17; 23; 21; 26; 50). For the author, standing in the foreground are the Old Testament passages that are used as types or used analogously. The examples of pious men in the Old Testament "have not only improved us but also the generations before us (19.1), namely those who received the scriptural oracles (τὰ λόγια) in fear and sincerity." This is their primary meaning.

8. Since there is no reason to think of this silence as finicky, the composition of the Roman congregation must have changed substantially since the days of Paul, or Paul had misjudged this composition in his letter? At the time of Clement, not only must the church have been completely separated from the synagogue, but also the national Jewish element in the church must have completely receded. The attitude of the letter cannot be understood otherwise. It is not possible to determine the extent to which the Roman congregation's attitude towards Judaism had diminished, how much it denied it possession of the Old Testament and its covenant with God.

9. The facts presented here are highly paradoxical. On the one hand, it is obvious that Clement or the Roman (and Corinthian) congregation does not recognize the ceremonial law—it has completely disappeared from them—but, on the other hand, they do not in any way reinterpret it allegorically-spiritually (this kind of interpretation differs from Philo among others), but rather let it (a) exist for an earlier time in relation to pious men, use it (b) analogously, exemplarily, and typologically for the ecclesiastical present, and recognize in it (c) prophecies of various kinds, especially as they relate to the ecclesiastical institutions of the present (in the persons and in the processes). For these reasons, even the ceremonial law, according to Clement, is written "for us." On (a) and (b), see 1 Clem 32; 40f; 43, etc. Even the non-religious, moral material in the Old Testament is founded upon God's will and order, and requires understanding and respect, even though it is not binding. In this respect, we can compare Luke's point of

4. THE SOURCES OF CLEMENTINE-ROMAN CHRISTIANITY

This assessment and appropriation of the Old Testament in Rome is neither like that of the Epistle to the Hebrews, nor that of Barnabas or Justin, and least of all that of Paul. It is instead much simpler and at the same time more violent than that of Paul. It represents the attempt in which it could remain impossible to ignore Judaism entirely, as if it did not exist in the past or in the present, to claim the holy "Scriptures" were exclusively given to the church (and its precursors, the ancient men of God), and yet not recognize the ceremonial law as law. The contradictory, astonishing simplicity of this view suggests that it is incomplete and would not seem so paradoxical if the author had spoken about Judaism. Such an inquiry is not possible because what Clement has said about Scripture leaves no room for Judaism, that is, no room for its possession of the Old Testament or of its covenant with God.

What consequences did this treatment of "Scripture" have from an objective point of view? They have already become sufficiently clear. The new Christian religion is not new, but is the revealed religion of the Old Testament. It is a religion of the book; it is a religion of the law; its valuable contents are God's commandments (δικαιώματα καὶ προστάγματα τοῦ θεοῦ), in which his essence and his will are made evident. This view is quite consistent with the basic religious character of ancient Judaism, namely within its Hellenistic formation. However, we may add that this Christianity conflates with ancient Judaism because it originates from it; the church received this view of ancient Judaism along with the Old Testament. It accepted Scripture, but radically rejected everything national therein. It is not Paulinism, even if in a weakened form, that lies behind this Christianity—a Paulinism that abolishes the significance of the people of Israel is no Paulinism—but

---

view on the matter, for whom the ceremonial law is also meaningless, but who admires and esteems the ancient pious ones because of their law-abiding attitude. For Clement as well, in addition to the priests and the Levites (see 1 Clem 32), the Jewish kings and judges etc. were glorious gifts of God. On (3), the passage in 1 Clem 42.5 is of particular importance. Clement writes: Ἐκ πολλῶν χρόνων ἐγέγραπτο περὶ ἐπισκόπων καὶ διακόνων· οὕτως γάρ που λέγει ἡ γραφή (Isa 60:17)· Καταστήσω τοὺς ἐπισκόπους αὐτῶν ἐν δικαιοσύνῃ καὶ τοὺς διακόνους αὐτῶν ἐν πίστει. So the appointment of bishops and deacons was already prophesied by Scripture in ancient times! In doing so, Clement adjusted the text according to that permission, also constructed by Philo, that one is permitted and must illuminate and safeguard by correction a text left dark by the Holy Spirit for pedagogical reasons. Also, the references to the Old Testament cult and priestly orders in 1 Clem 40f are, according to Clement's meaning, not to be understood as justification for the existing orders in the church (since the bishops and deacons are hardly conceived of as continuations of the priests and the Levites; the church does not yet have any priests), but are to be regarded as important examples according to which one must follow in analogy. Such an incomplete and inadequate attitude, which caused hundreds of doubts to awaken, could not be sustained in the long run.

is instead the religion of ancient Judaism in its simplest, strongest form, not with the specific subtleties and speculative insights of Philo or the "Wisdom of Solomon,"[10] but of the Proverbs and the moral sayings of Job, etc.[11] These Gentile Christians were either Jewish proselytes themselves before they were baptized, or were won by baptized Jewish proselytes. According to its foundation and religious attitude, this Roman letter belongs to the history of the Old Testament religion and ancient Judaism.[12]

But this cannot possibly be the last word, for not only is Judaism here so strongly rejected that it has completely disappeared, but there is also a new religious community in the place of the synagogue. How did this come about? What is the Christianity of this "brotherhood," this *ecclesia* of God"?

2. Christ and the Christian Tradition

Anyone who undertakes the task of examining the Roman letter for its specific form of Christianity will be astonished to discover what a rich Christian content the proclamation of the Roman congregation at the time of Domitian already included. To put it briefly, everything is already contained in its proclamation in surprising completeness through tradition, and the expectations which the address—formulated according to apostolic example—raises in this regard are not disappointed. An orderly survey should prove this:

(1) The religious statements in the letter are immersed in the repeated testimony "in Christ" or "through Jesus Christ": piety in Christ (1.2); conduct life according to Christ (3.4); teaching of Christ (21.8); faith in Christ

---

10. The echoes of these are extremely sparse. The matter is different in Hebrews, Barnabas, and the Apologists.

11. A special preference for certain Old Testament writings cannot be proven in my opinion. Isaiah 53 and Ps 22 and 51 are quoted, but did not disturb the author's moralism. By the way, the long quotations by the author suggest that he does not count on his reader's familiarity with them.

12. On what power it had succeeded in eliminating the national Jewish and ceremonial law, see the following chapter. The basic features of the religious attitude of ancient Judaism as strictly monotheistic legalism and redemption through obedience, which leads to a morally pious life accompanied by good works—their achievement is the ultimate goal (see 1 Clem 2.2; 33.1; 34.1ff; etc.)—and which will receive its reward, must be assumed to be known here. For these ideas determine the author; what he observes about faith and justification is so un-Pauline (see below for details). Affiliation with the history of ancient Judaism can also be seen in the Jewish exegetical and historical tradition, which was adopted along with the Old Testament. In the notes at the end, I have provided numerous proofs. This affiliation is just as evident in the great congregational prayer at the end of the letter and in many places in the liturgical and homiletic tradition.

4. THE SOURCES OF CLEMENTINE-ROMAN CHRISTIANITY

(22.1); the calling in Christ (32.4; 46.6); salvation in Christ Jesus (38.1; see also 36.1: our savior Jesus Christ); missional work is entrusted to the apostles in Christ (43.1); the walk in Christ (47.6); the gate of justice is the gate in Christ (48.4); love in Christ (49.1); glory in Christ (54.3). In addition to these passages where besides the authoritative work of God the mediation through Christ is emphasized again and again as an inseparable unity, see especially 20.11, "we are those who have taken refuge in his mercies through Jesus Christ."

(2) The congregation speaks of itself not only as the "*ekklesia* of God," but also as "the flock of Christ" (16.1; 44.3; 57.2; 59.4), and the kingdom of God (42.3) is also called the "kingdom of Christ" (50.3). The technical self-designation of the congregation as "those chosen by God through Christ" corresponds to the fact that Christ is also designated as chosen by God (1 Clem 64).

(3) Christ is "the Lord": this is the sole title he has (12.7; 16.17; 44.1; without the addition of Jesus Christ). Only in the prayer at the end of the letter is he called "the servant" several times, but with the messianic addition "the beloved," for he is "the Son" (36.4f; 7.4).

(4) Christ, along with the Holy Spirit, belongs to God in an exclusive manner. On the Holy Trinity, see 1 Clem 46.6, "Do we not have one God, and one Christ, and one Spirit of grace?" and 58.2, "For as God, the Lord Jesus Christ, and the Holy Spirit live, also faith and the hope of the elect"; see also 42.3.

(5) Christ spoke already in the Holy Scriptures before his temporal appearance (see above). He is the scepter of God and could have come to earth in divine glory (16.2). Thus, his pre-existence is certain.[13]

(6) In the most important relationships, the word of God and the work of Christ are interchangeable. For example, 16.17 says, "We have come under the yoke of the grace of Christ through him," and 2.1 says that all spiritual nourishment from which the spirits live is called the "provisions of Christ" (Codex Alex. has "God"). Instead of the commandments of God, Clement also says "the commandments of Christ" (49.1).

(7) The letter says of the "sufferings of Christ" that they are always before the eyes (of the righteous Christians), and the blood of Christ is of supreme importance to the author. First Clement 7.4 says, "Let us look upon the blood of Christ and know how precious it is (to God and) to his Father because, for the sake of our salvation, it has brought the gracious gift of conversion to the whole world"; in 12.7, the red cloth in the story

---

13. The divinity of Christ is also based on the phrase in 32.2, "From Jacob comes the Lord Jesus according to the flesh." The expression "the Logos" for Christ is not found in the letter, for the personified Logos is not in view in 27.4.

of Rahab is interpreted with the meaning that "through the blood of the Lord, salvation is given to all who believe in God and hope in him"; in 21.6 it is said that "the blood of Jesus has been given for us"; and in 49.6, it says, "For the sake of the love, which he has for us, Jesus Christ our Lord gave his blood for us according to the will of God, and his flesh for our flesh, and his spirit[14] for our spirit."

(8) In 24.1, the resurrection of Christ is mentioned as the beginning of the universal resurrection, and in 42.3 it says that the apostle-missionaries had been fully convinced by Christ's resurrection.[15]

(9) Christ is "the high priest of our offerings (prayers), the patron and helper of our weakness" (36.1) and this is repeated in chapters 61 and 64: ("The high priest and patron of our souls, through whom we praise God and through whom glory and majesty are offered to God.") Here, the whole thirty-sixth chapter is brought into consideration, wherein the work of Christ is described and praised (see below for details). Christ is also presented as an example (16.17), to whom the ancient men of God are added as models without any hesitation.

(10) Just as Christ is God's messenger, so also are the apostles on whom the establishment of the church of God on earth is based, the messengers of Christ (42.1). He has also equipped them with the gift of the foreknowledge of the future (44.1f).

(11) Just as the righteous Christian always has the sufferings of Christ before his eyes (see above), so also does he carry his words carefully in his heart (2.1). This means both the words which he spoke in Holy Scripture and those spoken on earth. But of the latter, only two are quoted (1 Clem 13.2; 46.8) with the introduction, "Above all,[16] bearing in mind the words of the Lord Jesus, which he spoke, teaching gentleness and patience" or "Remember the words of our Lord Jesus" (1 Clem 13.1; 46.7).[17] In our Gospels, these two citations are found in a slightly different version, such that it is unlikely that they were used, especially since there is no trace of the author's knowledge in the letter either. It is striking that Clement did not quote the

---

14. TN: The German "Seele" here can mean as many things as the Greek ψυχήν: spirit, soul, life.

15. Clement strongly felt the difficulty of belief in the resurrection and thus carefully underpinned it with a series of proofs (1 Clem 24–27).

16. Preceding Old Testament citations. The "most of all" (μάλιστα) is therefore to be taken into account. But it cannot possibly imply a super-ordination of the Lord's word over the word of Scripture. Instead, it is chosen because the Lord's word is particularly clear and striking.

17. This is followed by the invitation to take Paul's letter to the Corinthians into their hands.

words of the Lord more frequently.[18] This deficiency can hardly be explained except with the assumption that the tradition of teaching, which originally referred exclusively to the Holy Scriptures, only slowly allowed room for the words of the Lord to take place next to them, especially since these still existed in fluctuating formulations at the time or in books that had not yet received the reputation of being Holy Scripture. One is well aware of how difficult such school traditions are.[19] That, in principle, the authority of the words of the Lord were equal to that of the Scriptures cannot be doubted, which is also clear in Clement's quotations.

(12) It is said in 1 Clem 2.2 and 46.6 that the individual Christian and Christianity still continue to experience "the full outpouring of the Holy Spirit" and in 42.3 that the Spirit has given the apostles confidence in their missionary work. But a pneumatic-enthusiastic mood dominates neither the letter nor the congregation. Therefore, the prospect of the imminent end of the world, the new kingdom of Christ, and the Last Judgment also strongly recedes (see, however, 1 Clem 23).[20]

(13) The great congregational prayer, although built up according to the analogy and with the same means of ancient Judaism, moves Christ with and beside God into the center and has the character of a genuinely Christian prayer.

(14) The Holy Spirit, emanating from Christ, makes the church of God, or the flock of Christ, the site and the bearer of his efficacy and enables it to speak and act in his name. Spiritual enthusiasm authorized the church to write (1 Clem 63.2) that the Corinthians should "be obedient to what we have written through the Holy Spirit," "should not follow us but the will of God" (1 Clem 56.1), and "should submit to what God has said through us" (1 Clem 59.1). This expresses the authoritative identity of the Holy Spirit and the holy church, which can also be claimed by the individual congregation, since it is the local manifestation of the entire church.

This comprehensive complex of beliefs and convictions about Christ within the Roman congregation—it contains all possibilities of relations

18. Silently he may have thought of them in some places; so it is very probable to me, according to 13.1 combined with 16.17, that Clement had the saying from Matt 11:28f in mind.

19. Here, it is important to note the fact that, instead of the account of the Passion of Christ, the author cites Isaiah 53 *in extenso* because the Holy Scripture was more impressive to him than the historical account!

20. The Holy Spirit is not a spirit of miracles, not even, at least not primarily, a spirit of passionate excitement, but the spirit that leads to the performance of good deeds and strengthens moral order. Even the prospect of the imminent end of the world no longer dominates a congregation that sees its main task as the cultivation of a moral, orderly, and peaceful state of Christianity.

to Christ (Christ himself as acting God, as mediator, as the sacrament [the blood of Christ], etc. up to Christ as "model" in 16.17)—cannot be traced either in its totality or in individual parts to Paul or any other witness. Indeed, it does not suggest that even a single detail can be traced back exclusively to Paul, since it contains nothing specifically Pauline. Rather, one has the certain impression that behind this complex, there is an enormous stream of tradition from which it flows. This is of the utmost importance, for it teaches anew that tracing back ecclesiastical tradition to the writings of the New Testament or even to the "doctrinal terms" of the New Testament is erroneous. The tradition must have formed itself from an abundance of living testimonies, the basic features of which are unanimous.

Among these, the testimonies of Paul (and Peter) certainly played a major role, as our letter also proves (see 1 Clem 5). But also, in other places, the acquaintance with Paul or his influence is preserved. Not only does 1 Clem 47 explicitly refer to 1 Corinthians, which the addressees possess (and with several of Clement's remarks, it can be assumed that he is also dependent on Pauline sayings), but Clement has also taken the opportunity to explicitly reconcile himself with Paul at the important point of the doctrine of justification. In 1 Clem 32.3f, it says, "Therefore, even we who are called by God's will in Christ Jesus are not justified by ourselves, nor by our wisdom or insight or piety or works which we have done in holiness of heart, but by the faith by which the Almighty God justified all from the beginning (ἀπ' αἰῶνος)." Pauline theology cannot be expressed more clearly and correctly in a negative way than within this passage; but it is overturned by the positive statement, for the faith through which God justifies men according to Clement even before Christ is not the faith described by Paul, which is given only through, with, and in Christ, but is instead a faith of obedience through which Abraham and Rahab were justified in connection with their hospitality (1 Clem 10.7; 12.1) and which makes room for the statement within the context of justification by faith that "Lot was saved because of his hospitality and piety " (1 Clem 11.1). The author could believe himself to be in agreement with Paul because, as numerous passages prove, he too derives all good from God and also speaks of salvation. But the great difference between them is that Paul subordinates under justification the thought that "everyone receives in judgment according to his works," whereas Clement makes it superordinate.[21] Furthermore, what Paul means by "faith" in itself is something quite different from what Clement means by "faith." Therefore, this passage demonstrates how much

---

21. Clement basically does not know the idea of justification at all, but only has the word and a poor concept of redemption. Even the thought of guilt is only weakly provable with him.

4. THE SOURCES OF CLEMENTINE-ROMAN CHRISTIANITY 63

the author is interested in reconciling himself with the Great Apostle, but also how far away he is from him,[22] for his main slogan is Ἐξ ὅλης τῆς ἰσχύος ἡμῶν ἐργασώμεθα ἔργον δικαιοσύνης (33.8).

Let us return to the main point: We have noted from the letter an extensive complex of specifically Christian traditions, but it is not, or almost not, thoughtfully, theologically processed. Instead it is simply reproduced and thetically pronounced,[23] and is hardly connected[24] with the series of thoughts which we detailed in the first chapter ("The Old Testament"). This is most evident with the phrase, "blood of Christ." Certainly, Clement must have placed the highest value on the blood of Christ—it seems that the blood of Christ was the characteristic of Christianity—but what value can the suffering and death of Christ have in principle when God offered the possibility of repentance (change of mind) from the beginning, and his

---

22. The formula that he used twice before for Abraham shows this particularly clearly, "Was he not blessed because he practiced righteousness and truth through faith?" (1 Clem 31.2). Is it possible to distance oneself further from Paul? There is yet a second noteworthy passage in which Clement again takes up a word of Paul. He quotes (Rom 4:7) Ps 32:1 ("Blessed are those for whom lawlessness has been forgiven") and then he asks, Ὁ μακαρισμὸς οὖν οὗτος ἐπὶ τὴν περιτομὴν ἦν καὶ ἐπὶ τὴν ἀκροβυστίαν. Afterwards, he answers it in favor of ἀκροβυστία. Clement cites the same verse in 1 Clem 50.6 and then continues—at the beginning also with the words of Paul—with the assertion: Οὗτος ὁ μακαρισμὸς ἐγένετο ἐπὶ τοὺς ἐκλελεγμένους ὑπὸ τοῦ θεοῦ διὰ Ἰ. Χρ. Therefore, he, certainly intentionally, leaves aside the difference between περιτομή and ἀκροβυστία in favor of an indiscriminate universalism. Of older Christian writings, only the use of the Epistle to the Hebrews is quite clear in Clement. On this, see 1 Clem 36 (also other places in reminiscences). But even this use shows that it is sufficient for Clement to adhere to the wording of the letter without penetrating into its spirit and appropriating it, for he neither shows an understanding of the exegetical and theological attitude of the letter, nor has he received the high priest terminology for Christ, which he took from the letter, according to its sense. In the Epistle to the Hebrews, the concept of the high priest is closely related to the great idea of sacrifice; however, it is sufficient for Clement that Christ is the high priest, because he is our patron before God, who offers our prayers to him.

23. The Christian virtues of obedience, joy, unity of soul (in contrast with διψυχία), humility, gentleness, solidarity (1 Clem 38) and fraternity, love, etc. may have sprung up or been strengthened from here, but it is difficult to prove that. What is however clear is that for Clement, the *finis religionis* on earth is represented in them. Not in a correct doctrine—Clement has no sense for correct doctrine yet—nor in mysticism (he does not practice mystical contemplation), but instead he recognizes for his age the yield of religion to be found in a perfect moral *habitus*.

24. Or so connected that it is deprived of its meaning. If the meaning of Isa 53 in 1 Clem 16 and 17 is reduced to Jesus as an example, and if the ancient men of God are similarly placed in line with this example *par excellence*, and if according to Ps 51 the conclusion is drawn that David and other men of God "made us and the former generations better" by their example (1 Clem 18; 19), then religion is abandoned and morality takes its place.

mercy followed thereafter? What could redemption through Christ mean, indeed why did Christ appear at all, if God's mercy and forbearance have been effective at all times? A very modest answer to this question can be found in the author's explanations: the universalism of divine mercy has only become a fact through Christ's death (see 1 Clem 7.4; 12.7). Previously, God had held back from making salvation easily accessible to the whole human race (but that however means only those elect in him!). Now, the blood of Christ, which is so dear to him, has brought about universalism, which was previously only present in individual examples (Jonah and the Ninevites).[25] There is no need to doubt that Clement had a deeper or different sentiment for Christ and his death. After all, the affectionate words in 49.6 bear witness to just that: "For the sake of the love, which he has for us, Jesus Christ our Lord gave his blood for us according to the will of God, and his flesh for our flesh, and his spirit for our spirit." Nevertheless, conceptually he was incapable of grasping it,[26] because he could not rid his mental-theological framework of ancient Judaism.

Only from ancient Judaism? Here we must return to the passage in 1 Clem 35 quoted above and bring it into conversation with a second passage (1 Clem 36), wherein Clement speaks about the fruit of Christ's appearance:

First Clement 35.1–3: "How exhilarating and wonderful are the gifts of God, beloved, life in immortality, joy in righteousness, truth with candor, faith with confidence, self-control with holiness, and all these things lie within the realm of our understanding. But what then are the good things that will only be prepared for those who have endured? The craftsman and Father of the eons, the Most Holy one, he alone knows their greatness and their beauty." First Clement 36.2a: "Through Christ, we look into the heights of the heavens, through him we see as in a mirror God's blameless and most venerable face, through him the eyes of our hearts have been opened, through him our darkened mind blossoms again into the light, through him the Master has made us taste immortal knowledge." Is this really ancient

---

25. Here we are now able to answer the main question posed above (see 4.1: "The Old Testament"), by what power was Clement and Roman Christendom enabled to eliminate the national Judaism and the ceremonial law, while fully maintaining the old, ancient Jewish piety and doctrine: If the universality of salvation has only become a fact through Christ, although in principle it was always present, then it logically follows that his appearance and his word have given him the right to remove the national Jewish and ceremonial/legal barriers. Through him they have fallen away, and that must have been a success of Christ's mission that was conceptually bright and clear to Clement. This view is much simpler and straightforward than Paul's view as it relates to the abolition of the law. Here, again, we see that Clement was not a true disciple of Paul.

26. An attempt appears in 1 Clem 36.1, "Christ the helper of our weakness."

Judaism, or rather, exclusively ancient Judaism? Certainly not. There is yet another element that is most clearly visible here.

3. The Rational-Moralistic Idealism of the Age and Its Literary and Aesthetic Forms

Anyone who has read the characteristics of the letter given in chapter 3 must have already come to the realization that there is a third element in the letter which competes with the ancient Jewish, Old Testament element and with the specifically Christian element, and the nature of that element cannot be in doubt: It is rational moralism (as it was especially developed in more contemporary forms of Stoicism[27]), embedded in the literary and aesthetic forms of the age. Because it was involved in the formation of the branch of ancient Judaism, to which our letter belongs, it is not always distinguishable from it. Nevertheless, it permeates the substance and form of the entire letter, even leaving its mark upon it. In this twofold respect, it clearly emerges in 1 Clem 35 and 36, which were just cited. If the first begins with "life in immortality," the second concludes with "immortal *gnosis*," this is pure Hellenism. The same is true of the "beauty" of God's future gifts (cf. the expression in 49.3: τὸ μεγαλεῖον τῆς καλλόνης τῆς ἀγάπης), while the other splendors mentioned are a Hellenistic and Jewish mix (λαμπρότης ἐν δικαιοσύνῃ, ἀλήθεια ἐν παρρησίᾳ, ἐγκράτεια ἐν ἁγιασμῷ, and the great contrast between darkness and light). But formally, too, the letter is a print in two colors: the Hebrew color (LXX) and the color of philosophical, poetic artistic prose. The stronger color is that of Semitic poetry in Greek dress. In addition to the numerous quotations, the author's own explanations are, wherever possible, formally modelled on the poetic sections of the Septuagint. This model had to be chosen, for what had to be written to the brothers in Corinth was the will of God and had to be spoken by the Holy Spirit. But the Holy Spirit speaks the language of the Holy Scriptures. Mixed with it is the rhetorical, philosophical artistic prose, which is not written at a high level. Stylistically speaking, this mixture is not enjoyable. Those who approach the letter from reading the better Greek speakers will find this rhetoric, which embroiders the colorful flowers of Asian eloquence on the canvas of Hebrew poetic prose, daunting. It is teeming with sonorous figures—the letter was to be read aloud—external and internal rhymes, anaphoric references, rhetorical questions, carefully constructed rhetorical gems and rhythmic or artistically symmetric prose. The church does not want to be a part of this world, but the world enters it through the side gate!

---

27. However, a Platonic element is not altogether absent.

Furthermore, the entire layout of the letter is Hellenistic. Despite its psalmic character, it reads like an admonitorial diatribe about "peace and harmony." A *laudatio* is properly placed before the diatribe, which is formally and materially quite un-scriptural, and with its exaggerations, in addition to its good expositions, it is also unchristian. In this *laudatio* (1 Clem 1.2–2.8) alone one can already best study the whole syncretistic character of the letter! Then expositions are inserted such as 1 Clem 5—where the two apostles Peter and Paul are treated like ancient heroes, or like gladiator fighters, and the idea of reward is transferred into the idea of glory (see also 1 Clem 54)—and 1 Clem 20 (on the order of the divine cosmic governance) and 1 Clem 33 (God's order of creation and his joy in creation), which grow beyond the purpose of the letter and connect religion and nature such that it threatens to displace them. And at the end, where the author summarizes the main points of the letter that have been discussed, he lists *"sophrosyne"* alongside faith, change of mind, and love.

The Hellenistic-Roman character of the writing becomes even clearer in a long series of *termini technici* and reminiscences. At the beginning of the first chapter, the μεγαλοπρεπὲς τῆς φιλοξενίας of the Corinthians is praised (1.2). It should be recalled that it is said of Polydamas in Xenophon's Hellenica: ἦν καὶ ἄλλως φιλόξενός τε καὶ μεγαλοπρεπὴς τὸν θετταλικὸν τρόπον (6.1.3). The double parallel is remarkable.[28] It appears to be ancient when the calamity, which is caused by ζῆλος καὶ φθόνος, is presented in broad rhetorical expositions by means of biblical examples and certain examples from the recent Christian past, and then concludes with the words: ζῆλος καὶ ἔρις πόλεις μεγάλας κατέστρεψεν καὶ ἔθνη μεγάλα ἐξερίζωσεν (1 Clem 6.4). The interpreters have rightly compared this text not only with Sirach 28:14 (πόλεις ὀχυρὰς καθεῖλε καὶ οἰκίας μεγιστάνων κατέστρεψε), but also, and even better, with Horace, *Saec.* I.16f. (*Irae Tyesten exitio gravi stravere, et altis urbibus ultimae stetere causae cur perirent funditus*). Clement must have indeed had this secular story in mind here, and this is explicitly and objectively found in 1 Clem 55.1: "Ἵνα δὲ καὶ ὑποδείγματα ἐθνῶν ἐνέγκωμεν· πολλοὶ βασιλεῖς καὶ ἡγούμενοι, λοιμικοῦ τινὸς ἐνστάντος καιροῦ, χρησμοδοτηθέντες παρέδωκαν ἑαυτοὺς εἰς θάνατον, ἵνα ῥύσωνται διὰ τοῦ ἑαυτῶν αἵματος τοὺς πολίτας. πολλοὶ ἐξεχώρησαν ἰδίων πόλεων, ἵνα μὴ στασιάζωσιν ἐπὶ πλεῖον.

If recourse to ancient stories is evident—and indeed approved of—then one may perhaps also assume that in the preceding chapter (1 Clem 54.1–2), Clement remembers Cicero, *Mil.* 93 (*tranquilla republica cives mei—quoniam mihi cum illis non licet—sine me ipsi, sed per me perfruantur; ego cedam*

---

28. Μεγαλοπρεπής is one of Clement's favorite words, but is otherwise only used for God (1 Clem 9.1, 2; 19.2; 45.7; 60.1; 61.1; 64.1).

4. THE SOURCES OF CLEMENTINE-ROMAN CHRISTIANITY

atque abibo). Clement writes: Τίς ἐν ὑμῖν γενναῖος . . . εἰπάτω· εἰ δι' ἐμὲ στάσις καὶ ἔρις καὶ σχίσματα, ἐκχωρῶ, ἄπειμι οὗ ἐὰν βούλησθε, καὶ ποιῶ τὰ προστασσόμενα ὑπὸ τοῦ πλήθους· μόνον τὸ ποίμνιον τοῦ Χριστοῦ εἰρηνευέτω. It is an ancient thought that the patriot should exile himself if he can thereby return peace to the fatherland.

Ancient is also the inclusion of the legend of the phoenix (1 Clem 25) as a proof for immortality. A born Jew or a narrow-minded Christian would hardly have chosen this example (see however Hesiod, Herodotus, Antiphanes, Manilius, Tacitus, and Solinus), just as he would not have mentioned the previously discussed examples from secular history and would not have spoken approvingly of "our" soldiers, their exemplary discipline, and their ranks. However, Clement writes, "our father, Jacob," "our Lord Christ," "our apostles," and "our soldiers" (1 Clem 37.2). Clement also shows evidence of ancient, scientific knowledge, when he speaks of the μετὰ τὸν ὠκεανὸν κόσμοι (1 Clem 20.8).[29] Alexander von Humboldt collected the opinions from antiquity about them (see Strabo, Plutarch, and the famous prophecy of Seneca, *Med.* II.375, which was known to Columbus).[30] Furthermore, only an educated man writes (*loc. cit.*): ἥλιός τε καὶ σελήνη ἀστέρων τε χοροὶ ἐν ὁμονοίᾳ δίχα πάσης παρεκβάσεως ἐξελίσσουσιν τοὺς ἐπιτεταγμένους αὐτοῖς ὁρισμούς (20.3).

Jacobson and Lightfoot have pointed out that the sentence οἱ μεγάλοι δίχα τῶν μικρῶν οὐ δύνανται εἶναι, οὔτε οἱ μικροὶ δίχα τῶν μεγάλων· σύγκρασίς τίς ἐστιν ἐν πᾶσιν, καὶ ἐν τούτοις χρῆσις (1 Clem 37.4)—aside from the play on words with σύγκρασις, χρῆσις—is composed of plagiarisms; see Sophocles, *Aj.* 158: καίτοι σμικροὶ μεγάλων χωρὶς σφαλερὸν πύργου ῥῶμα πέλονται κτλ.; Plato, *Leg.* 902 E: οὐδὲ γὰρ ἄνευ σμικρῶν τοὺς μεγάλους φασὶν οἱ λιθολόγοι λίθους εὖ κεῖσθαι; and Euripides, *Frag. Aeol.* 2: ἀλλ' ἔστι τις σύγκρασις ὥστ' ἔχειν καλῶς. This is probably the case, but it is not certain; σύγκρασις could have also come from 1 Cor 12:24: ἀλλὰ ὁ θεὸς συνεκέρασεν τὸ σῶμα. Clement continues immediately: λάβωμεν τὸ σῶμα ἡμῶν. After that, he alone contributes: ὁ πλούσιος ἐπιχορηγείτω τῷ πτωχῷ, ὁ δὲ πτωχὸς εὐχαριστείτω τῷ θεῷ, ὅτι ἔδωκεν αὐτῷ δι' οὗ ἀναπληρωθῇ αὐτοῦ τὸ ὑστέρημα (38.2) and with Euripides, among others, one reads: ἃ μὴ γάρ ἐστι τῷ πένητι, πλούσιος δίδως· ἃ δ' οἱ πλουτοῦντες οὐ κεκτήμεθα τοῖσιν πένησι χρώμενοι θηρώμεθα (*Fragm.* 21).[31]

---

29. TN: This clause has been freely translated. The original "Antike Wissenschaft ist es auch, wenn er von den μετὰ τὸν ὠκεανὸν κόσμοι" literally means "It is also ancient, scientific knowledge when he speaks of the μετὰ τὸν ὠκεανὸν κόσμοι."

30. Photius (*Lex.* 126) rebuked Clement's use of both the phoenix and the worlds beyond.

31. Many things in Clement are reminiscent of the use of words by the Tragedians, such as τὰ νέρτερα in 1 Clem 20.5.

One senses the antiquity of the words ἁγνὰς καὶ ἀμιάντους χεῖρας αἴροντες πρὸς θεόν (1 Clem 29.1). Wettstein (on 1 Tim 2:8) compared the tragedian Heliodorus at Galen, *de Antid.* II.7: ὁσίας μὲν χεῖρας ἐς ἠέρα λαμπρὸν ἀείρας.

However, more important than all this is the fact that no small part of the letter is reminiscent of philosophical language, especially of the range of thoughts that are designated as of Seneca, Epictetus, and Plutarch.[32] Here, one may expect the preference for terms like σώφρων and σεμνός, ἐπιεικής, εὐσέβεια, in addition to τὰ ἐφόδια (1 Clem 2.1), ὁ κῆρυξ (1 Clem 5.6, used for the spiritual leaders), ἡ δικαιοπραγία (1 Clem 32.3), ὁ δισταγμός (1 Clem 46.9), ἡ ματαιοπονία (1 Clem 9.1), ἡ παλιγγενεσία (1 Clem 9.4), ἀρχεγόνος (1 Clem 59.3), ἀτμὶς ἀπὸ κύθρας (1 Clem 17.6), ἀόργητος of God (1 Clem 19.3), πολιτεία and πολιτεύεσθαι (1 Clem 2.8; 3.4; 6.1; 21.1; 44.6; 51.2; 54.4), διακοσμεῖν and κοσμεῖν Stoic (1 Clem 33.3 and in other places), χῶρος εὐσεβῶν (1 Clem 50.3), ἑτεροκλινής (1 Clem 11.1; 47.7), παμμεγεθέστατος (1 Clem 33.3), κοινωφελής (Clem 48.6), ἀμεταμέλητος (frequently), ἀπροσδεής of God (1 Clem 52.1), ὁ δημιουργός (1 Clem 20.11 and in other places), παντεπόπτης (1 Clem 55.6), ἐπόπτης (1 Clem 59.3), the ethical application of the growing vine (1 Clem 23.4), ἥδιον διδόντες ἢ λαμβάνοντες (1 Clem 2.1, where the ἥδιον points to Epicurious: τοῦ εὖ πάσχειν τὸ εὖ ποιεῖν οὐ μόνον κάλλιον ἀλλὰ καὶ ἥδιον. Seneca, *Ep.* 81.17: *errat si quis beneficium accipit libentius quam reddit*), and the figurative use of σκάμμα and κανών (1 Clem 7.2). But beyond the individual terms, the concept of God, the view of nature as an ordered and purposeful whole, the joy in the regular movement of the world and in the providence that dominates everything, the resounding interest in ὁμόνοια (1 Clem 9.4; 11.2; 20.3, 10, 11; 21.1; 30.3; 34.7; 49.5; 50.5; 60.4; 61.1; 63.2[33]), and finally the moralism, all these features bear witness to its Stoic imprint.[34] The Stoic tones here are fused with the psalmists' view of nature and testamentary ethics. In some places, the hands are Esau's hands, but the voice is Jacob's voice; in others, it is the other way around. A sure distinction is often impossible.

If one holds that Clement mainly writes according to the instructions of the Old Testament texts, then the above is sufficient proof of his Hellenistic education and of a substantial influence from the philosophical-rhetorical

---

32. But these philosophers penetrate deeper than our author into several moral-religious problems. In the following, I provide as important samples a series of colorful words, as colorful as they appear in the letter itself without a scholastic context.

33. TN: Harnack misses ὁμόνοια in 65.1.

34. What is quite remarkable, however, is that the Stoic pride of virtue is far removed from the author, despite his high esteem of works. The insight "What do you have, which you have not received" confronts pride of virtue.

4. THE SOURCES OF CLEMENTINE-ROMAN CHRISTIANITY   69

culture. That language, as far as I can see, is correct, but the vocabulary is varied. This is a necessary consequence of the heavy use of the LXX, liturgical reminiscences, and some popular, philosophical expressions.[35] Undoubtedly the letter, behind which lies a strong and clear will, though lacking a pronounced literary individuality, made a strong impression from the very beginning: this strong impression was first based upon its contents, but then also on the judgement Photius (*Lex.* 126) made about its style, which was probably already valid in the second century: ἐγγὺς τοῦ ἐκκλησιαστικοῦ. Of course, Photius also finds the letter ἁπλοῦς κατὰ τὴν φράσιν καὶ ἀπεριέργου χαρακτῆρος. Compared to the Byzantine church rhetoric and to the rhetoric in general, he has to appear "simple"; but the περίεργον is not missing. Photius did not perceive it as such, but as a free swing of the spirit of the ancient church. If, according to a "history" reported by Origen (Eusebius, *Hist. eccl.* V. 25.14), some have considered Clement the author of the Epistle to the Hebrews, then perhaps in it lies only a judgment about the style of the letter. Nevertheless, it is possible that the hypothesis arose from the observation of the objective relationship of both documents[36] or from the report that the Epistle to the Hebrews came from Rome.

Our letter is not only a print of two hues, but of three:[37] The Old Testament religion as understood in ancient Judaism, Hellenistic-moral idealism, and the reality of Christ's appearance (together with the *kerygma* and the new commandments for life, which it had given as imperatives, delivered as powers) forms the content of the letter. This trinity constitutes Christianity as it occurred to Clement and to the Roman congregation. But with it, Catholicism was also given as a religion; no essentially new element was needed.[38]

---

35. The vocabulary of the letter is not very rich, but has some ἅπαξ λεγόμενα or words that may be found here for the first time: ἀβαναύσως (44.3), ἁγιοπρεπής (13.3), ἀνατυλίσσειν (31.1), ἀτημελεῖν (38.2), αὐτεπαινετός (30.6), ἀφιλοξενία (35.5; see Sib. Or.), δωδεκάσκηπτρον (31.4), ἐνοπτρίζεσθαι (36.2), ἐπικαταλλάσσειν (48.1), εὐπρόσδεκτος (40.3), μεταπαραδιδόναι (20.9), πανάγιος (35.3), πανάρετος (1.2, and elsewhere), παντεπόπτης (55.6; 64.1; see Sib. Or.), παντοκρατορικός (8.5), προδημιουργεῖν (32), ὑπερεκπερισσῶς (20.11), χρησμοδοτεῖν (55.1). Other rare words include ἀνεξιχνίαστος (20.5) and ἀνεκδιήγητος (20.5).

36. As a side note, the relationship of the letter with Hebrews in terms of stylistic terms or in terms of content is not substantial.

37. TN: Markschies translates this sentence, "Unser Brief ist nicht nur ein Zwei, er ist ein Dreifarbendruck" as "Our Letter is not only influenced by two, but by three literary tones." See Markschies, "Harnack's Image of 1 Clement," 67.

38. Another word can be said about the significance our letter attributes to the concept of humility (ταπεινοφροσύνη). It must be judged to be a primary and specifically Christian virtue; it precedes even the virtue of abstinence (ἐγκράτεια), which entered into the church in part on the bridge of humility. It is instructive that more than one

Excursus: The Political Stance

It has been pointed out above that, in addition to his Stoic view of nature, Clement unabashedly and profusely referred to secular history (1 Clem 55) and called the Roman soldiers "our soldiers" (1 Clem 37). However, one would probably conclude too much from this to say that therein lies a doubtless form of Roman patriotism. On the other hand, not only does unconditional reverence for authorities and willing obedience to them arise from the great prayer at the end of the letter, but one must also judge that Clement saw in the secular authorities a divine institution that parallels the reign of God in heaven. This is the only way to understand the broad and penetrating statement in 61.1f. The divine mandate of the authorities is taken seriously, and firmly established is the consequence that the subject is not entitled to any right of contradiction, but that, even in distress and death, there remains only one thing to ask God: that he turn the will of the authorities to good. Whether this attitude, which so strongly contradicts that of a large part of Judaism, is judged to be exclusively a consequence of Paul's Epistle to the Romans (Rom 13) may be left open, though it probably is not solely responsible for this attitude. However, the fact that our Roman congregation's letter represents this attitude despite the Neronian and Domitianic persecutions must have been of utmost importance. It established the church's position on the Roman state, which led to the victory of the church. Recognition of the right of the authorities and a passive attitude were alone able to protect the political existence of the church until such time as it became a positive factor also for the state. Additionally, by so firmly standing up for the authorities and law on earth as divine institutions, the church prepares for what it will need in a later development. When she herself became an authority on earth and needed an earthly law, it was already there for her (in the closest connection with the divine law that reigns in heaven.). The sixty-first chapter of our epistle to the Romans stands not only above the subsequent development of the law of the state-church, but also above that of the law of the church-state!

---

hundred years later, the Christian concept of humility still created difficulties for those coming from paganism. Origen writes, "*Dicat aliquis: intelligo quomodo deus iustitiam ancillae suae sapientiamque respiciat, quomodo autem intendat humilitatem non satis liquet. considere, qui quaerit talia, quoniam proprie in scripturis una de virtutibus humilitas praedicetur* [Matthew 11:29 follows]. *quod si vis nomen huius audire virtutis, quomodo etiam a philosophis appelletur, ausculta eandem esse humilitatem quam respiciat deus, quae ab illis ἀτυφία sive μετριότης dicitur*" (*Hom. Luc.* 8; *Die Homilien zu Lukas*, 58). The question is more instructive than the answer given by Origen, who, as a Hellenist, does not understand early Christian humility itself.

Furthermore, as the following will demonstrate,[39] the letter prepares for the future development in another respect. It begins to develop the ecclesiastical offices analogously with the secular offices. Finally, the recognition of the law of the authorities and their political orders means much more than that of bowing under the criminal law of the state. It also means the recognition of civil law as God's order (as far as it does not commit sinful acts). With this, however, the *ecclesia* of God places itself beside the Holy Scripture and also on the ground of imperial culture as a divinely willed institution. This premise, however, implicitly contained the death sentence for all apocalypticism, insofar as it negates its very soil.

---

39. TN: See chapter 5, "The Struggle in Corinth about the Ecclesiastical Officials and the Order of the Office."

5. The Struggle in Corinth over the Ecclesiastical Officials and the Order of the Office

I WILL NOT GO into the extremely extensive literature, among which Wrede's *Untersuchungen* stands out,[1] or into the great controversy about the nature and right of canon law, which Sohm has created,[2] but instead I will limit myself to the presentation and explanation of the main facts. The controversy which has involved the deepest and highest questions of the doctrine of faith and the principles of the life and organization of the church has not yet come to an end. It is highly desirable that it be resumed (I hope that this wish will soon be fulfilled). The purpose which I am pursuing of introducing Clement's letter and through it the early church in elementary form does not permit this, however there will be clues for solving the controversy.

Section I

(1) No passage in the letter suggests differences in the organization and consideration of ministry between the churches in Rome and Corinth.

(2) Because the local congregation is a manifestation of the whole congregation, the church of God—in which all are equally called and chosen, and which is filled with the Holy Spirit—it represents a pneumatic democracy in which nothing can happen without the will of the whole. See

---

1. Wrede, *Untersuchungen zum ersten Klemensbriefe*.

2. In addition to the first volume of Rudolph Sohn's *Kirchenrecht*, see Sohm's treatise *Wesen und Ursprung des Katholizismus*. See also my own book, Harnack, *Entstehung und Entwicklung*.

5. THE STRUGGLE IN CORINTH

1 Clem 44.3: συνευδοκησάσης τῆς ἐκκλησίας πάσης; and 1 Clem 54.2: ποιῶ τὰ προστασσόμενα ὑπὸ τοῦ πλήθους.³

(3) The congregation has an office in its midst, the office τῆς ἐπισκοπῆς (44.1, 4). But there is no monarchial office.⁴

(4) The bearers of this office are called "bishops and deacons" (42.4, 5; God himself is called ἐπίσποκος in 59.3; ἡ ἐπισκοπὴ τῆς βασιλείας τοῦ Χριστοῦ in 50.3).

(5) Those who occupy this office are also bearers of the title "presbyter" (44.5; 47.6: στασιάζειν πρὸς τοὺς πρεσβυτέρους; 54.2: τὸ ποίμνιον τοῦ Χριστοῦ μετὰ τῶν καθεσταμένων πρεσβυτέρων; 57.5: ὑποτάγητε τοῖς πρεσβυτέροις).⁵

(6) The congregation owes these presbyters (bishops [and deacons]) not only reverence like the "old ones," but also obedience. This is demanded or presupposed by the letter writer (1.3; 21.6; 57.5), and thus pneumatic democracy is fractured and is pressed down.⁶ If this commandment is consistently applied, the congenial expression of the will of the congregation

---

3. The formal democratic sovereignty of the community is even more evident in the address and the whole attitude of the letter, from the first page to the last. Not one bishop writes to another bishop, not clerics to other clerics, not the congregation with its clerics to another congregation with its clerics, but simply the whole congregation to the whole congregation. It is filled with the Holy Spirit, and it speaks on his behalf. It admonishes, frightens, demands, delegates emissaries, etc. But the fact that this sovereignty (TN: of the democracy) had already been penetrated is demonstrated in what follows.

4. Not only is it missing, but the letter also excludes a monarchical office. The fact that its author, who was certainly an *episcope*, is indeed *primus inter pares* (see chapter 2 above), does not change this.

5. In 1.3; 3.3; 21.6, a sharp distinction is made in the congregation between the old (πρεσβύτεροι) and the young (νέοι) and a fitting honor awarded to them. We do not know how to master the nominal difficulty—it can be found also in later times and in other congregations—that there were two varieties of πρεσβύτεροι side by side (the presbyter according to age and the presbyter who bore the office). — The term οἱ ἡγούμενοι (προηγούμενοι), which is used twice to refer to the congregation, is as little a *terminus technicus* as our expression "the leaders." See 1.3: ὑποτασσόμενοι τοῖς ἡγουμήνοις ὑμῶν; 21.6: τοὺς προσηγουμένους ἡμῶν αἰδεσθῶμεν. This refers to the appointed presbyters, who are not so-called here (but rather ἡγούμενοι) because, in the same place, there is mention of those presbyters who are only presbyters on account of their age. If "teachers" were also present in the congregations, they are also included, but nowhere is there a mention of apostles, prophets, and teachers within the letter. — The fact that deacons, like bishops, also had the title presbyter at that time could be assumed on the basis of formal consistency. Perhaps this was the practice for a short period of time. Nevertheless, it is sufficient to assume that deacons (these executive officials in addition to the leading bishops) were also entitled to the honorary rights of the presbyters, that is, the old ones.

6. TN: "Suppressed" may be a better translation for "heruntergedrückt" here, but it carries too much the connotation that democracy is nowhere to be found within the congregation. Harnack's point is aimed more at the idea that democracy is splintering and slowly being replaced by another form of ecclesiastical governance.

will become a mere decoration, and a divergent one is no longer permitted.[7] We do not know how far the development in this direction had progressed in Corinth at that time. But in Rome, the office had already broken through the democracy.

(7) The nature of the office (ἐπισκοπή) is determined by the fact that its bearers are designated as those who (a) provide for the building up of the congregations that have been formed (42.4), who (b) "serve" the local flock of Christ (44.2ff: λειτουργεῖν, λειτουργία), and (c) offer the gifts (44.4; προσφέρειν τὰ δῶρα, namely in worship). From this, it can be concluded that the tasks of the office were very extensive and significant—for the edification of the congregation in every sense—and that they consisted especially in leading the congregation's main worship service, for the offering of the gifts must be understood as the gifts at the celebratory Lord's Supper. Whoever is not yet sure of this from 44.4 should consult 1 Clem 40f. (see below). The appointed presbyter functions as cult official, who at the same time served the congregations spiritually and both disciplined them and kept them in order. Why else the demand of obedience? It is best to imagine the figure of the presbyters (bishops), what they should do and how they should be, according to the posture of the letter itself. Although the congregation speaks here, in truth the presbyter (bishop), Clement, speaks and shows how he understands his office.

Section II

In the sentences compiled above, it has been explained what can be said about the organization of the congregation. What happened in Corinth? What was the "riot" that filled the Roman congregation with the deepest concern and caused them to take extreme counter measures?

(1) One must begin with the success of the rebellion: Some presbyters in Corinth, even though they had allegedly performed their office blamelessly, had been removed by the instigation of troublemakers. Since their appointment to office is assumed to have been carried out, at least the majority of the congregation must have agreed to it. The Romans address the removal from office; this was the impetus for its letter.

(2) The removal from office cannot have been the result of a fight against the office as such on the part of the troublemakers. Only a portion of the presbyters had been removed. "Spirit, not office" could not have

---

7. The strict demand of obedience to the office is thus older in Rome than the monarchical episcopate.

5. THE STRUGGLE IN CORINTH

been the general slogan of the troublemakers. After all, other presbyters had been left in office.

(3) In determining the cause and the nature of the dispute and the intentions of the troublemakers, one must refrain from Clement's moral assessment and condemnation. If he warns against bellicosity and arrogance, against ambition, pompousness and self-conceit, if he characterizes the troublemakers as πρόσωπα προπετῆ καὶ αὐθάδη (1.1) and the division as μιαρὰ καὶ ἀνόσιος (1.1c), then we should not take these things into consideration. For such reproaches are self-evidently aimed against a division that had broken out. However, it is also at the least quite doubtful whether the troublemakers can be regarded as particularly outstanding Christians (who unfortunately lack only a community spirit and humility), because the author writes in 48.5: ἤτω τις πιστός, ἤτω δυνατὸς γνῶσιν ἐξειπεῖν, ἤτω σοφὸς ἐν διακρίσει λόγων, ἤτω ἁγνὸς ἐν ἔργοις· τοσούτῳ γὰρ μᾶλλον ταπεινοφρονεῖν ὀφείλει, ὅσῳ δοκεῖ μᾶλλον μείζων εἶναι, καὶ ζητεῖν τὸ κοινωφελὲς πᾶσιν, καὶ μὴ τὸ ἑαυτοῦ. This admonition is quite general and is addressed to all Christians. He does not even have in view professional charismatics who only accepted their own *charisma*. Otherwise, he would not have been at ease when writing 38.1 (ἕκαστος . . . καθὼς ἐτέθη ἐν τῷ χαρίσματι αὐτοῦ). If one assesses the fact that concrete allegations of a dogmatic or ethical nature are not raised by Clement at all, that conversely Clement does not have to refute such accusations, that there is no talk of avarice, slander, etc.—the otherwise never missing companions of internal church disputes—and finally that Clement proposes to the troublemakers a heroic, noble act to settle the dispute (see below), and considers them capable of performing this act, it becomes more and more certain that the dispute, no matter how bad its effects, was not a fundamental[8] dispute at all, but merely represents a full-fledged squabble between cliques.

(4) This is confirmed by 1 Clem 47, for here the dispute, placed in its closest parallel with 1 Corinthians, is called πρόκλισις, and the only difference between that dispute in the apostolic age and the current dispute is seen only in the fact that at that time—which was excusable—the Corinthians' formed cliques around apostles and a famous man (Apollos), with whom the present leaders do not compare.

(5) It was, therefore, a matter of the management of personal cliques, without any basic background (as is so often the case in the aftermath of community disputes), and the course of events was as follows: Some prominent individuals (see 1.1: ὀλίγα πρόσωπα; 47.6: ἓν ἢ δύο πρόσωπα; 51.1:

---

8. TN: "Prinzipieller" ("fundamental") should be understood in light of Harnack's qualifications earlier in the sentence relating to "dogmatischer oder sittlicher Art" ("of a dogmatic or ethical nature").

ἀρχηγοὶ στάσεως; 57.1[9]) were hindered by the standing of some acting presbyter-bishops for their own (perhaps legitimate) purposes[10] of influencing the church. They succeeded in gaining so much influence over the church that the majority decided to dismiss the acting presbyter-bishops.[11] One consequence of this was that the church's unity in worship was destroyed (see 1 Clem 40f), for now there were two groups of *episkopen* in office, and there were two local centers.[12]

Section III

This was the situation in Corinth when the Roman congregation decided to intervene and to concentrate all its force on one point: the deposition of the *episkopen*. Therein, the dispute obtained its fundamental significance! How did the Roman congregation proceed? With the greatest care! But she gives the argument fundamental significance!

(1) It prefaces the theme with the exposition (1 Clem 37) that every organism (e.g., the military, the body) exists in a superior and inferior order of noble and baser parts, and that obedience must reign throughout the organism (1 Clem 37). The author then applies this exposition to the church (1 Clem 38).

---

9. TN: Whether Harnack intentionally or unintentionally left off the Greek text to which he refers in 57.1, it is now provided in this note: οἱ τὴν καταβολὴν τῆς στάσεως ποιήσαντες.

10. We do not know their purposes.

11. That numbered among the majority were especially many younger elements and that women also asserted themselves here is very probable according to 1.3; 3.3; 21.6, and according to 1.3; 21.7 (note the strong irony) respectively. The expression προσκλίσεις in 21.7 should especially be noted.

12. However, there is no information as to who took the place of the removed presbyter-*episcopen*, whether the troublemakers themselves—though that would have to be said—or their confidants. It is also possible that everything was still in limbo and that the reorganization was only a threat. It is also possible that the troublemakers had succeeded in keeping the deposed away from further exercise of their office.
In any case, the fact that the machinations of the troublemakers resulted in the deposition of the *episcopen* is a new proof of how influential this office had already been at that time. It must also be assumed that the spiritual edification, as performed by the deposed presbyters, was not sufficient for the opposition party, for the opposition is not to be considered so corrupt that it pursued the dismissal of the spiritual leaders, although they did not find fault in them. So even if the dispute was not a matter of principle, it is likely that the troublemakers and those they won would have wished for a different (higher) form of edification, and that the *charismen* may have had a role to play in it. Unfortunately, it is not possible to provide any further details on the matter.

5. THE STRUGGLE IN CORINTH

The Corinthians are presented with the terrible fate that awaits the "foolish" (i.e., the disobedient and conceited troublemakers) by the use of scriptural passages (1 Clem 39).

Sacred Scripture decrees that worship services are to be performed according to established orders, determined once and for all, concerning the times, place (only one), and persons (a high priest, priests, Levites, laity), and imposes the death penalty upon the disobedient. Clement does not dare say and cannot claim that this ceremonial law is still valid, but it is his clear opinion that one must proceed within the church in a corresponding and analogous manner with regard to worship. For God's will demands order (1 Clem 40; 41). These remarks (1 Clem 37–41) form the introduction.

(2) The following is an historical account of the origin of the office: It was created by the apostles who appointed their first converts as bishops and deacons. But since God sent Christ and Christ sent the apostles, the appointment of bishops and deacons must be analogous to the fact that it is just as firmly established and unassailable as the appointment of Christ and the apostles, which it continues (42.1–4).

(3) But Clement did not pronounce this conclusion dryly, but instead left his readers to infer it. However, in order to insinuate this conclusion, he returns to Holy Scripture with which (a) he proves with a corrected quotation from Isaiah that the appointment of bishops and deacons was prophesied under this name (42.5) and (b) with a miracle which God performed in the selection of Aaron and his tribe for the priesthood he shows that God identifies the officials he desires and then protects them against being contested (1 Clem 43).

(4) Now, after these strong safeguards have been put into place, the historical account is once again taken up, namely with a twofold assertion: (a) the apostles had foreseen, through the Lord Jesus Christ, the dispute over the office, (b) therefore they not only appointed officials themselves (see above), but also arranged that, after the death of these men, others should take their place, appointed by respected men[13] with the consent of the congregation. From here the Romans draw the conclusion: If this has taken place and these officials have served the congregation blamelessly for a long time, their deposition is a violation of the law. The Corinthians are guilty of violating this law, and the expression "great sin" is also used (1 Clem 44).

(5) What should happen now? First, an extensive admonition begins on the basis of the Holy Scriptures (1 Clem 45), a word of Jesus (1 Clem 46),

---

13. Who are they? How are they to be discovered? The author provides no further clarification.

and with reference to the divisions in Corinth at the time of Paul (1 Clem 47). Then, a lofty song about love is sung (1 Clem 49; 50). After this, the letter addresses the authors of the disputes directly, with threats from the Holy Scriptures, with appeals to their community spirit and nobility, and with reference to the brilliant example of Moses, who wanted to sacrifice himself for his people (1 Clem 51–55). After this preparation, the admonition culminates in the proposal to the troublemakers to submit themselves to the non-deposed presbyters or the congregation—thus the changed opinion of the congregation is presupposed—and to depart, namely to a place to be determined by the congregation. Whether they agree or disagree with the proposal, the final word comes in 57.1, "You who have laid the foundation of the rebellion, obey the presbyters and, bowing the knees of your heart, let yourselves be chastised to repentance." The letter concludes (1 Clem 62–65) with the hope that the Corinthian church will obey the reproaches inspired by the Holy Spirit and with the statement that the Roman church, together with this letter, will send an emissary of highly respected old members (not called officials) to Corinth, "who are to be witnesses between you and us" (63.3). The statements—the most important foundational documents (*Urkunde*) for the oldest constitutional history of the church—contain four undoubtedly fateful fictions (that Isaiah prophesied the appointment of bishops and deacons, that the Old Testament order of the worship service and priests have a similar analogous application in the church, that the apostles [the Twelve and Paul] foresaw the dispute over the office, and that they made a general arrangement about the succession of the officials appointed by them); however they have for themselves the right of what had already happened, and even more the right of what was becoming. If they demand obedience for the office, if they establish (consciously?) an ecclesiastical law (succession!) pertaining to offices on the basis of laws related to civil offices, if they closely link the mission of the apostles, and if they limit the possibility of deposing the officials to only cases where the officer is guilty, then they move away from the original state of the church, but instead promote what was already inexorably in the process of becoming.[14] It is not yet claimed that the officials are priests and that the Old Testament priestly orders are also valid for the church; there is still no monarchial bishop; there is still no claim by any official of the congregation that the apostolic ministry continues in him; nor is the irremovability of the officials of the congregation motivated only by the fact that they have carried out their ministry for many years. It is still true in theory that the congregation possesses the Holy Spirit and

---

14. TN: It is clear that what Harnack has in mind here is hierarchical ecclesiastical system to be fully developed in the Catholic system of (mono)episcopacy.

is sovereign. But what the Roman congregation already presupposes with regard to office and teaches on the basis of an alleged apostolic resolution is of fundamental importance for the emergence of Catholicism with respect to organization. For the most original and absolutely unique thing in the account is the alleged order of the apostles regarding the deaths of the officials they appointed, namely that new officials should be appointed by selected men with the participation of the congregation. This determination seems self-evident, but by being made by those appointed by the apostles themselves, the second generation of officials, and those that follow, are drawn into the divine system of the "*missio*," which goes from God to Christ, from Christ to the apostles, and from the apostles to the first generation of officials. Their ministry is therefore also stabilized by the will of God and thus exalted to heavenly heights. That the deposed officials belong to this second generation is expressly stated; yes, one may without hesitation assume that the singular and most striking instruction of the apostles was constructed precisely for the purpose of protecting the officials of the second generation, just as the officials of the first generation were protected by apostolic selection, that is, to raise up in general the offices above the congregation as divine institutions implemented by the apostles. Clement draws the conclusion only for the irremovability of the officials, and this conclusion is still cautiously and conditionally made.[15] But the justification—divine will and apostolic order have created the office—goes beyond this purpose. The subsequent development must have been inevitable by this justification, and the noiseless way in which the monarchical bishop (though he cannot yet be directly connected to 1 Clement), the theory of apostolic episcopal succession, and the approval of the phrase "*ecclesia in episcopo est*" have now made their way into the imperial church proves that it really was inevitable.

Finally, it should be noted that Clement, as certainly as he is to be claimed as the origin of the ecclesiastical theory of succession, does not yet think at all of the continuation of the specific apostolic office, such that the significance of this title has not yet come to his attention. What he wants and offers is partly less, partly more than the continuation of the apostolic office. It is less because it is not said at all what authoritative content the ministry of bishops and deacons has; it is more because these officials are all to be regarded as a part of the legitimate continuation of the line that reaches from God to Christ, and from Christ to the apostles. Therefore, nothing prevents the assumption that they are not inferior to the apostles.

15. From this, it follows that there was no legal provision concerning the irremovability of officials. But how can one expect such a provision in the earliest of times, since everything was determined by the spirit and *charisma* and by the corresponding competence of the officials?

But this assumption, which, incidentally, did not necessarily have to be made, did not and could not come to fruition. The theory of the apostolic office of the monarchical bishop had the effect of inhibiting this development and also must be acknowledged from here on. It immediately subordinates all other office bearers.

Excursus: Is the Attitude of the Letter Specifically Roman?

If the question is, "Does the letter, despite all its Hellenism and its Greek garb, also breathe a Latin spirit?" then I answer absolutely in the affirmative. Not only do some parts of the letter read as if they had been translated from Latin—although I find it difficult to give an account for why that is the case—also present is the sense of a closed, strict unity and the sense of authority, order, law, and obedience that runs through the whole letter in its fourfold composition cannot, in my opinion, be explained by Stoicism or Christianity alone. In the whole letter, a political dignity emerges, which we tend to judge as a sign of higher Roman civil service. If, however, the question is formulated as it is in the title of this excursus, then one must hesitate in offering an affirmative answer. At first glance, there is much to be said for the fact that the ruler, Rome, speaks and acts here. She mixes herself up unasked into the in-house quarrel of the Corinthian community; she has in mind what is of public benefit to the church; she consistently presents the word like a pedagogue and teacher, even if she speaks with the first person *pluralis*; she knows the laws of God, the Corinthians have misjudged them; she dares to make a proposal to settle the dispute, which entails the complete submission and defeat of one party; she expects the Corinthian congregation to be absolutely obedient to her directives, inspired by the Holy Spirit; and she sends a delegation to Corinth, which comes very close to an act of arbitration. And yet, according to original Christian principles, every church can and should do all this in sisterly love and care,[16] and nowhere is it motivated by a particular or even local claim. So it can

---

16. The Jerusalem congregation had also written in Acts 15:28: Ἔδοξεν τῷ πνεύματι τῷ ἁγίῳ καὶ ἡμῖν. The early Christian conviction that the Holy Spirit could be used in spiritual matters for the decisions of the congregations had an effect later on in the conviction of the infallibility of the councils, most recently in the West, in the doctrine of papal infallibility. One can also express the development in this way: Papal infallibility, after the teaching of the Spirit had been limited to the councils as its place and after the identification of the church and the pope had taken place in the East, is the residual product of that moving religious certainty of the most ancient Christendom that the Holy Spirit is always present for the church and guides its decisions.

only be said that no reference in the letter points with certainty to specific Roman claims; everything can be purely religious and fraternal. But the fact that no other imperial church or congregation or bishop (not even Ignatius) spoke and acted like this in the beginning of church history remains to be explained, and therefore the assumption cannot be suppressed that here, on Christian soil, the spirit, the claim, and the power of Rome have already asserted themselves: The Roman congregation dared to ascend the throne, which was accessible to every Christian congregation. Already in this letter, the Roman congregation has revealed the peculiar and interlocking understanding of the terms "order, law, obedience, charity, harmony, unity, and peace," which is characteristic of it and which, in the end, transformed the federation of brothers into an absolute monarchy.

6. Problems That Have Not Yet Been Conclusively Investigated Posed by 1 Clement, Which Can Also Be Addressed in Seminars[1]

- The history of the letter in the church.
- The manuscript tradition of the letter and the citations of Clement of Alexandria.
- Compile and assess ecclesiastically or dogmatically valuable variants.
- The author of the letter, in history and legend.
- Was there a particularly close relationship between Rome and Corinth in earlier times?
- The structure and disposition of the letter.
- The Old Testament citations in the letter and the Septuagint.
- Does the letter demonstrate a preference for certain Old Testament books and for certain Old Testament concepts?
- The apocryphal citations in the letter.
- What is the nature of legalism in the letter, and how does the letter understand the phrase δικαίωματα τοῦ θεοῦ?
- Is it possible that the author has more to say or something different to say than the assessment made about the Jewish people in 4.1?
- Should the absence of terms such as τὸ εὐαγγέλιον and ἡ βασιλεία τοῦ θεοῦ (Χριστοῦ) in the letter be regarded as accidental?

---

1. Some of the problems listed in chapter 7 are also suitable for seminar topics.

6. PROBLEMS THAT HAVE NOT YET BEEN CONCLUSIVELY INVESTIGATED

- Can we speak of a Pauline character of the letter, and to what extent? Has the letter used Pauline letters other than Romans and 1 Corinthians, and which ones?

- Did the letter use 1 Peter and the Pastoral Epistles? What influence does Hebrews have on the letter, and how strong is its influence?

- Is the concept of God directly dependent upon the Stoic concept of God or is its reliance on ancient Judaism sufficient? The same question must also be asked in relation to cosmology.

- What position does the letter take on culture? Does it go beyond the boundaries of Christianity here? Is it too comfortable in the world,[2] and does it explain the emergence of Montanism as a counter-movement?

- Does the letter show Platonic influences?

- The rhetorical style of the letter demands a closer investigation and assessment.

---

2. TN: The German term is "weltfreundlich," lit. "world-friendly." An alternate expression might be "is it too friendly with the world."

7. A Look at the Development of Church History That the Letter Grants and That Should Be Studied

THE MOST IMPORTANT PREVIEWS into the development of church history that the letter grants are as follows:

(1) Its attitude towards "Scripture" and the "law" offers the best starting point for the study of the immediate application of the widely divergent and conflicting views and teachings on the "Scriptures" and the "law" of the second century. See my treatise "Das Alte Testament in den Paulinischen Briefen und in den Paulinischen Gemeinden."[1]

During the investigation, it is particularly important to pay attention to the concepts of humility and meekness in the letter and to determine whether they were taken up subsequently with the sense in which Clement used them.

(2) The doctrine of God and the statements about God and the world, God and the moral order lead directly to the explanations of the apologists of the second century.

(3) The problem of God as the sole giver of all good or as the legislator of all good is clearly determined in the letter and will come to life in the future.

(4) The problem of Christian perfection, whether to conceive of it acosmically-ascetically or evangelically, cannot be underestimated in the letter and becomes operative in the era that follows.

(5) The letter is particularly important for the rapid and drastic weakening of the eschatological, realistic hopes within the church, and

(6) equally important for the retreat of enthusiasm, the quieting of the Holy Spirit in the church, and the emergence of anti-Montanist maxims.

---

1. Harnack, "Das Alte Testament," 121–41.

(7) The christological content of the letter is so rich that the development of the Christology of the Gentile church in the following period should be linked to it.

(8) The sacramentalism of the Gentile church in its beginnings should be studied with respect to the conception of the blood of Christ in Clement.

(9) Also, there are indications in the letter of the beginnings of the creation of the New Testament.

(10) The development of the constitution of the Gentile churches must begin with the study of the letter. Does the letter imply the practice of apostolic succession? Does it establish "canon law"?

(11) The history of the persecution of the church can conveniently take its starting point from the information provided in the letter about the persecutions under Nero and Domitian.

We can recognize how suitable the letter is for the purposes of introducing the study of the history of the most ancient forms of Gentile Christianity and the imperial church.

(12) Only one substantial line of development in its beginnings cannot be studied in the letter: the origin and development of Gnosticism.[2] Although it is instructive to examine the use Clement makes of the term *gnosis*, this does not lead to *Gnosticism*. This shortcoming is striking. Is it to be traced back to the fact that "in Rome itself, never a heresy arose" and that the congregation "shows no foreign color" (according to what Ignatius says about the Roman congregation)? Is it a coincidence or is it on purpose that Clement never touches upon heretical movements in the churches in his sixty-five chapters? This facet of the letter will have to be investigated.

---

2. The situation is different with Marcionism: Clement's position on the Old Testament (bibliolatry) could—indeed, had to—sooner or later cause a revision and a reaction even among Pauline Christians.

8. Concluding Word

WHAT THE ROMAN CHURCH considered to be the essence of Christianity, which pieces were decisive for it, what the core of the spiritual structure of a large part of Christendom was in the transition from the first to the second century, and what appears to be more or less insignificant in comparison with it, albeit attractive and interesting, is to be learned from this letter. No matter how much one takes into account the particular situation in which 1 Clement was written and declares the judgment of the Corinthian riots clerical and unjust, the main elements of Christianity, as they were perceived by the Roman congregation, remain unaffected. Here one has to learn that the ecclesiastical Christianity that has experienced a lasting history, made history, and produced reformations, was not everything that one so often today wants to make it out to be. It was not the playground for holy enthusiasts for whom there were no contemporary tasks; it was not an a-logical religion; it did not have to first laboriously and gradually gain a firm structure from a colorful plethora of gnostic clusters and syncretisms, but rather despite its disparate and complicated foundations—despite its synthesis with the philosophical culture of the age—it was a closed and firm moral movement in the sure consciousness of knowing the living God and of living as the redeemed in Christ. Compared with other religions, it was the religion of inwardness and the spirit,[1] and at the same time a fraternal covenant that was as comprehensive as human life and as deep as human need. It was a continuation of Jewish synagogual propaganda in the empire, deepened and purified, individualized and expanded, but again firmly united by the realization that brotherhood makes any national bond unnecessary. The "continuation" therefore nullified itself, for through the spiritual transformation something new emerged against Judaism: the flock

---

1. TN: The original reads "Religion der Innerlichkeit und des Geistes," which could be translated "the religion of inwardness and the *spirit*" or "the religion of inwardness and the *mind*."

of Christ from all peoples of the earth, which, chosen, seized, and guided by God, found eternal life and prepared itself in holy seriousness for this life. Everything that did not fall within these limits was peripheral and secondary, might not always be felt that way even by those involved, and could only express their deepest possessions in stammering or borrowed words. Neither apocalyptic, nor Gnostic, nor romantic, nor inhuman Christianity can be studied in this Roman writing, but one can learn from it classical (in the two-fold meaning which accompanies this word) Christianity for the imperial church of that time. And one can recognize in this letter that which is to the Roman church's credit at the beginning of the history of the church: A strong and pure will for good and for the construction of a new humanity lived in it energetically devoting itself to the brotherhood, despite its attachment to the Old Testament and despite the shadows darkening its own being, fell upon the new proclamation and the new faith. Finally, if one compares what the Roman congregation has written here with the rallies of cities, communities, associations, schools, and the like of the age, the tremendous difference between them is unavoidable,[2] and one remembers the words of the Apostle Paul to the Philippians, "You are children of God, blameless in the midst of a crooked and twisted generation, among whom you shine as lights in the world." The new beginning which the Gospel describes was still alive in this variation.

---

2. TN: The original German phrase is "springt der ungeheure Unterschied in die Augen" and literally means "the tremendous difference jumps into the eyes."

Notes

THE SALUTATION IS BUILT upon that of Paul's First Letter to the Corinthians, perhaps with the use of 1 Peter (on παροικούσῃ, see 1 Peter 1:17; on πληθυνθείη, see 1 Peter 1:2). With this address, the author expresses the idea that the congregation on earth feels itself to be a stranger, and this results from the peculiar self-confidence, probably attributable to Paul, that in it, as in every Christian congregation, the church of God is represented locally, which is not an earthly, but rather a pneumatical-heavenly greatness (it is paradoxical that today, *Parochie*[1] almost has the opposite meaning in comparison with the meaning of παροικεῖν). The author of the letter does not mention himself either here or elsewhere in the letter. The letter should, therefore, be understood in the strict sense as a congregational letter. The fourfold mention of God and the double reference to Christ as the mediator is stylistically clumsy, but objectively impressive (in the salutation of Paul's 1 Corinthians, as it reads today, "God" is mentioned three times and "Christ" four times). Παντοκράτωρ is often found in the letter. Paul, however, avoided the use of this word; the reason why he avoids it is unknown.

1.1. It is quite unusual and against all the rules of polite style that the author immediately indicates the topic of his letter, which is not very honorable for the addressee (but is similar to Paul's epistle to the Galatians). After he has introduced his topic with very strong expressions, however, he permits the usual *laudatio* to follow (1.2ff). — The "misfortunes and adversities" of the Roman community refer to the Domitian persecution. For from 1 Clem 5f, it follows that the Neronian persecution dates back some time, and the Trajan persecution cannot be meant, since the whole letter demonstrates that the situation which created it did not yet exist. The few testimonies that we have for the Domitian persecution (also the testimonies from the catacombs) have been collected several times.[2] The

---

1. TN: *Parochie* is the German word for a parish.
2. See Lightfoot, *Clement of Rome*, 1:104ff; Preuschen, *Analecta*, 1:11.

persecution was not yet a general persecution of all Christians throughout the empire, but rather originated from the suspicious arbitrariness and the fiscalism[3] of the emperor (during the final years of his reign). On "sudden," see Suetonius *Domitianus* 11: *inopinata saevitia*. — The Roman congregation was not called upon by the Corinthians to intervene in its affairs by a message, but instead does so of its own free will. However, our passage and the final chapters of the letter teach that the Roman congregation believes it is obliged to do so. That is very noteworthy. — The Roman congregation not only immediately takes sides, but the expressions it uses for the "dissension" are extraordinarily strong. They are by no means completely covered[4] by what it specifies about the dissension in the letter itself. — Only a few ringleaders; but they have apparently won the majority of the congregation! — The conclusion of the paragraph at least leaves it open that non-Christians in Corinth have also noticed the division and that this has resulted in disadvantages for the congregations. On this, see below (the reading βλαφθῆναι is to be preferred as the unusual form of βλασφημηθῆναι or βλασφημεῖσθαι; LS > AHC).

1.2—2.8. *Laudatio*: In this section, the character of the writing is already expressed in content and form as a synthesis of the high (Stoic) intellectual and moral culture of antiquity (Cicero, Seneca) and Christianity. The *laudatio* itself is "ancient," even already in its form: It is first put in the mouth of a guest who has just arrived and rises in rhetorical momentum, which offers up bad rhymes and is not exemplary in any other way. By comparing the content of Paul's *laudationes*, one can immediately see how this statutory *laudatio* differs from the truly Christian. On the other hand, one must not underestimate its valuable Christian elements and its excellent practical purpose. We do not know how much of this *laudatio* is to be taken at face value in relation[5] to the Corinthian community. But here, Roman Christians unmistakably represent their ideal of a church of God.

1.2. The epithet πανάρετος (here beside faith and πολιτεία) is just as characteristic for the author as σώφρων καὶ ἐπιεικὴς εὐσέβεια. Not only did he add ἐν Χριστῷ here, but also the often repeated ἐπιεικής (πραύς, ταπεινός) is based upon a gospel tradition (Matt 11:29). — The fact that after "faith and piety" and before "knowledge" stands "hospitality" proves how shallow the author thinks, but also how necessary this virtue was to youthful Christianity

3. TN: "Und dem Fiskalismus des Kaisers" is likely a reference to the *Fiscus Judaicus*, a taxation on the Jewish inhabitants of the empire.

4. TN: The sense of "vollkommen gedeckt" could be well represented with the translation "fully justified."

5. TN: The colloquial expression "für bare Münzen zu halten ist" could also be translated as "cash in the hand."

within the realm (see 1 Clem 10–12). — Safeguarded "knowledge": There is no mention of heretical *gnosis* anywhere in the writing.

1.3. God's "statutes" (see 1 Clem 3.8) and otherwise; religion is obedience to the law. — "Leaders" (ἡγούμενοι) as in the letter to the Hebrews (see 1 Clem 21.6f).

2.1. See Acts 20:35; however the author did not have this passage in mind, but rather a moral-philosophical commonplace. — The provisions of Christ (Χριστοῦ HLSC > θεοῦ A) is to be understood spiritually. "Words" and "sufferings" of Christ are side by side in the passage instead of the frequently attested formula "words and deeds of Christ." It will become apparent that the author frequently, unexpectedly jumps forward to the suffering (blood) of Christ. It was for him the characteristic note of the Christian religion.

2.2. Though the Holy Spirit is not forgotten, he is not the principle of the new life. Instead, he is considered an accessory. However,

2.3. for the life of prayer (the ancient attitude of prayer must be observed) and the forgiveness of sins, possession of the Spirit is the prerequisite. With regard to sins, it is true that Christians sin only involuntarily.

2.4. Each brother is responsible for the other and for the salvation of the brotherhood (in the NT only in 1 Peter 2:17; 5:9), that is, for the whole. "The number of his elect" is an early Christian expression of predestination. The words μετ' ἐλέους (Η δέους) καὶ συνειδήσεως are difficult to understand. Knopf translates them, "Through (your) compassionate disposition and sympathy." But can συνείδησις be understood in this way and should it not in any case be μετὰ συνειδήσεως καὶ ἐλέους? I suspect that συνειδήσεως is an ancient mistake.

2.5–8. The conclusion of the *laudatio* is a praise of the morals of the Corinthian congregation in contrast to the present situation. The former solidarity is once again emphasized.

3.1. "That which is written has been consummated": The entire letter, with its hundred quotations of and innumerable allusions to the OT, proves that the Roman congregation knows that it is as dependent on the OT as it is on Christ. These two dimensions are not differentiated in favor of Christ, but the OT is the absolute written revelation of God given to the church, to which the appearance of Christ (i.e., his words and his death on the cross) has been added.[6] Thus, the synthesis which underlies this Christianity is formed by Stoic idealism, the ancient Jewish religion resting on the OT, and the original tradition of Christ, which, as we will see, is hardly influenced by Paulinism.

---

6. See Wrede, *Untersuchungen zum ersten Klemensbriefe*.

3.2–4. Unfortunately, the letter does not say anything concrete about the outbreak of dissension and revolt; nor does it say anything concrete about the present terrible situation. Instead, it judges its aftereffects merely as a strong contrast to the former time. Thus, one can at most infer from the words of 1 Clement that young members of the congregation, who had previously had no reputation, were involved in the "revolt." The concluding expression, that in Corinth there is an evil zeal (jealousy) through which death once came into the world, cannot be surpassed in his dissuasive criticism. Whether the danger was really so great or whether the letter is the first document of clerical excessiveness towards opponents, we cannot judge for certain, but we must assume that it is a case of the later.

4.1–13. From Abel to David, there are seven examples of the bad consequences of evil zeal (be they for the pious or for the sinner) drawn from the OT (pagan examples are not given, see later). But only the story of fratricide is narrated in detail. Jacob (4.8) is called "our" father, thus demonstrating how strongly these Roman Christians feel that they are children of the Holy Scriptures! Only Miriam remained outside the camp (4.8). The addition of Aaron is a mistake by our author.

5. This chapter and the following are strongly rhetorical. This rhetoric is imprecise and is not at a sophisticated level: the apostles are presented as gladiators. The Jewish idea of wages has been transformed into the ancient idea of glory. — 5.1. The author considers the victims of the Neronian persecution to be among his generation. That this persecution is intended (also in chapter 6) should never have been denied.[7] 5.2. Already here, the author probably has only Peter and Paul in mind. For he would hardly have described all other martyrs as "the greatest pillars." This designation (οἱ μέγιστοι καὶ δικαιότατοι στῦλοι), which probably goes back to Gal 2:9, testifies to the outstanding esteem Peter and Paul enjoyed in Rome. — 5.3. Literally "the good apostles." However, the epithet ἀγαθός with ἀθλητής is to be understood as "brave," "hero."[8] — 5.4. The fact that Peter was also in Rome and suffered the martyr's death there (μαρτυρήσας does not in itself mean the martyr's death) is not clearly stated, but it follows from the context of chapters 5 and 6, and there are good testimonies to it from later times. — Afflictions from battle (πόνοι) is the specific term for the hero's deeds. The brevity of the statement about Peter in comparison to the one made about Paul must be noted. However, both the Romans and the Corinthians must have known facts that we do not know. — The "place of glory" is not to be understood as the general place for the departed pious. Rather, what is meant is a special place of honor

---

7. Lietzmann, *Petrus und Paulus in Rom*.
8. Norden, "Logos und Rhythmus," in his Berliner Rektoratsrede August 1928.

(see also with Paul). — 5.5f. The "endurance" (still thought of within an athletic context), emphasized twice in relation to Paul, also refers to the length of his heroic activity, with respect to which he must have been superior to Peter. βραβεῖον ἔδειξεν cannot mean, "He showed the (way to) the prize for the contest" (Knopf), but rather presented the prize (attained it). — The source which the author follows for the testimony about Paul is unknown to us. — "Magnificent glory of faith" is strange to us. — 5.7. "Piety": In Greek, it is δικαιοσύνη, but this also includes the idea of piety in ancient Jewish and Early Christian usage, and is likely the meaning here. The author, however, may also have had Rom 1:17 (δικαιοσύνη θεοῦ ἐν τῷ εὐαγγελίῳ ἀποκαλύπτεται ἐκ πίστεως) in mind, had he remembered "faith" shortly beforehand. — "The entire world": What Paul says about the triumph of the Gospel is here attributed to the effectiveness of that one Paul. — "The boundaries of the West" is the extreme West, and the term was then unmistakable in its reference to the "pillars of Hercules" in southern Spain. That Paul went to Spain is therefore the opinion of the Romans (see the Muratorian Fragment). That this opinion in Rome arose only from Paul's intention within his Epistle to the Romans to travel to Spain is very unlikely. — "The rulers" (ἡγούμενοι): The worldly authorities are meant here without a closer definition. — "He was liberated from the world" is to be understood poetically and not to be interpreted dogmatically. — "Taken up to the holy place": ἀνελήφθη, the reading in LSC, is to be preferred to ἐπορεύθη in AH. Whether it was deliberately erased and replaced by ἐπορεύθη (see what Clement previously said about Peter) because it grasped too high (see "ascension" in the Apostle's Creed) remains to be seen. — "The greatest example": Paul surpasses even Peter.

6.1f. "A great multitude": Since Tacitus (*Ann*. XV.44) speaks of an *igens multitudo* of the victims in the Neronian persecution, it is therefore proven that two apostle princes belonged among them. "Among us," that is, "us, Romans." Otherwise, the words would be superfluous. On the maltreatment and torture of those persecuted, see Tacitus *Ann*. XV.44 (*pereuntibus addita ludibria*) and Tertullian *Apol*. 15. The martyred women are particularly emphasized because to do such an abomination to women was outrageous; when Danaids (how?) and Dircae (tied to a bull) were exhibited, mocked, and murdered. — 6.3f. What facts does the author have in mind? He would have likely cited biblical facts by name: Jealousy and strife dissolve the foundation of human society and destroy its most powerful creations, cities.

7.1f. The author now gives his admonitions from fraternal diffidence in the communicative form[9] and repeats this form in the letter to the point

---

9. TN: The German original reads "kommunikativen Form," which is hardly descriptive since the author communicates through the letter in some communicative form/style or another. From the context, however, it is clear that Harnack is referring

of annoyance. — 7.2ff. ὁ κανὼν τῆς παραδόσεως = "*regula traditionis*," which is such an important term for the Roman Church at all times. It appears here for the first time, in the most comprehensive and in the highest sense (tradition as the epitome and the guide of all Christian being and life), but is not yet used as a technical term. The content of the term is determined by the immediate context: It is the will of God, the creator, and the blood of Christ. Thus, if the crucified Christ appears here next to the creator, then this Christ is reduced to the value that his shed blood has for God, who has thereby bestowed the "gracious gift" of conversion upon the whole world. But as soon as it said that such conversions had already taken place earlier at all times, even among the Gentiles, and since conversion is understood merely as an act of spontaneous obedience, then the blood of Christ is, in truth, deprived of any special significance, unless it is that conversion has now become more universal. The author is incapable of extracting a concept of faith from the formula about the blood of Christ that was handed down to him—apart from the fact that conversion is now proclaimed to the whole world—but he believes that he possesses such a concept. 7.5. The Master (δεσπότης), very rare in the NT, very frequent in our letter (also in other post-apostolic writings). Its usage here marks a characteristic difference! 7.6. Genesis knows nothing of the fact that Noah preached conversion. But the ancient Jewish tradition is aware of such a preaching (e.g., Josephus, *Ant.* 1.74; Sib. Or. 1.128f) and therefore also the post-apostolic tradition which depends upon it (see, e.g., 1 Clem 9.4; 2 Pet 2:5; Theophilus *Autol.* 3.19). Like the OT, ancient Jewish sacred texts penetrated into the churches, and thus also ancient Jewish *theologumena* and holy anecdotes.

8.1ff. This chapter, with its Old Testament quotations, testifies to what has just been said: The present situation with regard to conversion and salvation has always existed on God's side. — 8.3. This valuable saying is not found in the OT and comes from an apocryphon (of Ezekiel?). The author has often quoted apocryphal proverbs as if they were from the Old Testament. The books from which they come have not been preserved. In the synagogues of the Diaspora—perhaps also in Palestine—the third division of the OT was not yet closed. Here and there, various books of late origin were added to it, which were only gradually once again excluded. Certainly, the second division ("the Prophets") in some churches was not yet closed. The incomplete Bibles came into the churches from the synagogues. The view of the OT is simple and unambiguous: God, or the Holy Spirit, has written "Scripture." Therefore, there is no need to distinguish the individual books. Instead, it was sufficient to state, "It is written." The

---

specifically to Clement's use of the Greek term ἀγαπητοί ("brothers").

author almost never designates the book from which the quotation is taken. Of course, the Word of God remains valid and authoritative for all times and therefore also for Christians.

9.1. "Obey" (9.3 "obedience"): Faith is obedience (see chapter 10). — "Pointless toil" = ματαιοπονία, also in Plutarch and Lucian. — Enoch, Noah (doublet at 7.6), Abraham: The heroic ancestors (according to Heb 11:5ff, but also others). — 9.4. "New beginning" (παλιγγενεσία; often with Philo): Ancient Judaism taught the rebirth (new creation) of the second world after the flood, the third after a world fire. The Stoa speculated about successive worlds that would be replaced by catastrophes, but in which the events would be repeated. — "In harmony," a favorite term of Clement's.

10.1ff. The youthful Christianity, supported by Abraham, is already looking towards a great future. — 10.1. "Friend of God": a solemn Jewish epithet for Abraham (see Epiphanius, *Pan.* 78.6). — Faith and hospitality (see chapters 11–12): Christian hospitality at that time must have demanded such great costs, dangers, and sacrifices that it was considered a cardinal virtue and a specific test of Christianity (πίστις). The Bishop Melito of Sardis wrote a book on hospitality around 170 CE (Eusebius, *Hist. eccl.* IV.26.2).

11.1. "Hospitality and piety": This (εὐσέβεια) is therefore identical with faith (also with hope; see the following). — 11.2. Jewish legend about the woman. See Josephus, *Ant.* 1.11.4, who says he saw the pillar (Justin, *1 Apol.* 53; Irenaeus, etc.). The woman who is divided against her husband and doubts God's statement is presented to the Corinthians as a warning example. — "Double-minded people" (δίψυχοι, see James, Didache, Barnabas, and Hermas): lets the unambiguous character of the Christian bric-a-brac stand out.

12.1ff. The trade and lie of the woman are of little concern to Clement, just as it is of little to no concern for James, the author of Hebrews, and Justin Martyr (somewhat different is Irenaeus). — The "whore" according to A, but HLS add ἐπιλεγομένη. The believers should no longer judge Rahab as a whore. This addition can also be found in the biblical tradition. — 12.7f. Again the blood of the Lord is mentioned as the great means of redemption. 12.8. What Clement also subsumes under "faith" and how he imagines prophecy can be discovered here. Origen, *Adnot. Jes. Nav.* 111.4, writes: *Meretrix ex meretrice efficitur iam propheta.*

13.1f. "Humble" (ταπεινόφρων): the word does not occur in the NT,[10] but is very common in Clement (LXX) and is characteristic of his Christianity, along with "gentleness" and "understanding." It seems that

---

10. TN: While ταπεινόφρων may not have been in an edition of the Greek New Testament used by Harnack, it is present as a textual variant in 1 Peter 3:8 within the NA28.

only the Christian use of the term understood "lower mind" as "humble" mind. — 13.1. The deviations from the OT show that 1 Cor 1:31 has been used. — "Especially" is to be noted: Only here and in 46.8 are the Lord's words quoted next to "Scripture" (implied use likely several times), and here there is a strong emphasis placed upon the Lord's words. The citation formula (like Acts 20:35) is the oldest of its kind (the Lord's words are not yet a part of the decisively authoritative Scriptures and are therefore not γραφή; it is sufficient that they are the Lord's words). Whether Clement quoted the words from a gospel text or freely from memory is uncertain. The deviations from Matthew and Luke are significant (does Clement have a collection of Jesus's sayings in mind?).

14. The admonition to humility continues until 19.1. — 14.1. "Beloved brothers" (ἄνδρες ἀδελφοί); note the reception of this phrase. — 14.3. "Who created us": It is always God as the creator who stands in the foreground. — 14.3. "Greet one another" ἑαυτοῖς HLSC > αὐτοῖς A.

15.1. "Hypocritically": sharp accusation against the disturbers of the peace. — 15.2. Is Clement dependent on Mark (or Matthew) here in his deviation from Isaiah? — 15.5. The omission by homoeoteleuton is ancient (AHLC and Clement of Alexandria; the fact that S has the singular, correct reading is a testament to its value).

16.1. "Flock": The author also speaks of Christ as the shepherd (see 44.3). — 16.2. The pre-existence of Christ is presupposed; the world rule is enunciated through him. — "The majesty" (μεγαλωσύνης) is hard to maintain within the text because SC and Hieronymus do not attest to it. — 16.3ff. Already for the earliest Christians, Isaiah 53 was the gospel in the OT and was therefore frequently cited (the four gospels, Paul, 1 Peter, Acts, Barnabas, Justin Martyr, etc.). However, through his suffering and dying, Jesus is not only the Redeemer, but also the model[11] example (16.17; the "yoke of his grace" is hardly independent of the saying in Matt 11:29f; Barn. 2.6 knows nothing of a "yoke," but instead of the yoke of coercion of the law). — 16.15. Christ himself is the speaker here (see, e.g., 1 Clem 22).

17.1f. See Heb 11:37, compare in general with Heb 11:32–12.3. — Ezekiel is otherwise unknown. — Friend: See 1 Clem 10.1–17.6. The source of this saying of Moses is unknown; though the depiction is common in antiquity.

18.1. By repeating "the testimony" with reference to David, the author states that the distinction (17.1) between the prophets (three) and the

---

11. TN: "Model" has been used here on the supposition that "sondern auch das Vorbild" is used in a superlative sense, i.e., the perfect example, the model example, etc.

"testimonies" (four men) is important to him. — 18.12. The guiding spirit (πνεῦμα ἡγεμονικόν) was a particularly important concept for the Stoics.

19.1. Here, we find a review of the past generations like that in 7.5. The universal consciousness of solidarity is noteworthy. — Improved: Undisguised moralism despite Ps 51. — 19.2ff. The exemplary deeds of the biblical heroes should motivate us to set peace as our goal, which from time immemorial has been the goal set by God for believers. In the following, God, the all-giving creator, is celebrated as the God of great benefactions, that is, of order and peace. — 19.3. Free from anger (ἀόργητος): Specifically influenced by Stoicism.

20.1ff. According to Drews's work,[12] this piece is brought into connection with the liturgy of the Last Supper (probably correctly so; see on this 1 Clem 33ff), which in turn goes back to the Jewish liturgical practice ("Thanks for the Gifts of Creation"). However, this piece should not simply be claimed as liturgical. It is based on liturgical practice, but probably was in part the intellectual creation of the author. In favor of the fact that it is essentially Jewish, one could argue that neither Christ, nor the Logos, nor the Holy Spirit appear in it, but that Christ seems to be glued on afterwards (v. 11). The hymn is not Greek, although here again biblical and ancient mythology merge with Stoicism.

20.1. Were set in motion (σαλεύεσθαι): otherwise *in malam partem*. — 20.5. Courts (κρίματα): despite the unanimous tradition, the conjecture κλίματα is certainly to be preferred, if κρίματα cannot indeed be rendered "borders" (as the Coptic manuscripts translated it). — 20.8. Boundless (ἀπέραντος): According to the manuscripts and the quotations, except in Origen and S (ἀπέρατος). Worlds beyond the ocean: Antiquarians have written much about them. — 20.11f. Master craftsman (δημιουργός): this term occurs frequently in Clement (like δεσπότης); in the NT, only in Heb 11:10; in the OT, only in 2 Macc 4:1. The concept is platonic. — The doxology is to God, who is close to us through Christ. It is not a doxology to Christ. Doxologies occur in ten places within the letter (32.4; 38.4; 43.6; 45.7; 45.8; 50.7; 58.2; 61.3; 64; 65.2). There is no principle that explains how the author has distributed them.

21.1ff. This chapter is particularly vivid. — ἡμῖν LSC, πᾶσιν ἡμῖν A, σὺν ἡμῖν H. — 21.4. Christians are soldiers of Christ; see also 37.1. — 21.6. Another reminder of the blood of Christ; but at the same time Christ stands as the chief in the divided church. See 1 Clem 1.3 ("Haustafel" [household code]). — 21.7. "Silence" (σιγῆς) HLS and Clement of Alexandria, φωνῆς A (the bitter irony was incomprehensible or too strong for him; C omits

---

12. Drews, *Die clementinische Liturgie in Rom.*

διὰ τῆς σιγῆς). The women must have made themselves strongly felt in the quarrels. — 21.8. Our (ἡμῶν Clement of Alexandria, LSC > ὑμῶν AH) children. Ἡ ἐν Χριστῷ παιδεία: Even the mere title is important (see 1 Clem 22.1: ἡ ἐν Χριστῷ πίστις, and otherwise). — 21.9. Breath: Jews and Stoics alike share a common thought.

22.2. τίς ἐστιν to v. 7 (inclusive) is missing in H. — 22.8a is missing in ALC (H?), an easily understandable oversight.

22.2—27.7. This is really an excursus: the author also wants to testify to the highest gift of God and the greatest Christian hope, the resurrection, especially since it was always subject to doubt. Two themes are discussed: (1) the certainty of Christ's return, and (2) the resurrection of the body. — 23.3f. An unknown apocalypse, also mentioned in 2 Clem 11.2f. (the same saying, but increased by one verse at the end). Since it is quoted as "the Scripture," it was Jewish and not Christian. — 23.5. "The Holy One": LXX "the angel," a deliberate correction (Christ is higher than the angels).

24.1. Note that here, the resurrection of Christ can only be considered by the author as the first realization of the resurrection. — 24.2f. According to the author, the resurrection belongs to God's natural laws. There is evidence for this resurrection among living beings: the paradoxical story of the life of the phoenix (1 Clem 25), that ancient fable that has been known throughout the kingdom for centuries, comes from Egypt and is spread by Herodotus, and is also appropriated by the (Jews and) Christians (see the catacomb paintings). Photius rebukes Clement for including this citation (*Lex.* 126). The apparatus of proof of the resurrection is also familiar to the later Christian Apologists.

26.2f. Proof of the resurrection receives its firmest foundation from Scripture.

27. The author strongly feels the difficulty of belief in the resurrection, which is why he has written this chapter. — 27.3. "Faith in him": perhaps better "his trustworthiness."

28. The paraenesis is no longer directed against unbelief in the resurrection, but goes further. — 28.2. The Writings (γραφεῖον): Probably already the name for the third division of the Old Testament.

29. The author takes it for granted that the Christian people are God's chosen people.

30. The paraenesis continues, initially referring to the most grievous sins. However, the author keeps an eye on the Christian quarrels and provides a prelude (30.3) in connection with the admonition in order to find the right connection, which dominates the following chapters. — 30.1. Note the rhymes, like in 1 Clem 1. — 30.3. Presenting righteousness: this can also be translated as "justified."

31. Connection with the blessings of God, of which the three patriarchs are the original bearers. — 31.2. The formula chosen for Abraham clearly shows that Clement does not simply want to accept the Pauline formula. What he himself wants is likewise unclear (the combination of "righteousness and truth" does not call us to think of the Fourth Gospel's use of "truth"). — 31.3. Isaac prophetically foresaw Christ's sacrifice; the Jewish legend already claimed that he willfully went to be sacrificed (Jos, Ant. I.13.4).

32. Not only the three patriarchs, but also the priests and Levites, the Jewish kings and judges, as well as the tribes, all are regarded by Clement as glorious gifts of God for the Christians—so completely does this Christianity stand upon the ground of the Old Testament. The fact that Jesus stands among the ancient Jews does not improve upon this table of gifts. — 32.3ff. This repetition of Pauline thought comes as a surprise and is true in the negative; but the conclusion shows that Clement means something different with faith than Paul.

33. One must do good works according to the example of God's good works; good works are the ornaments of the righteous and make them joyful. To perform works of righteousness is the highest goal. Works do not belong to faith, but to love. — 33.1. ποιήσωμεν ASC > ἐροῦμεν (according to Paul) HL. — 33.3ff. The hymn is reminiscent of the hymn in chapter 20. It is not the Old Testament conception of the cosmos, though it is involved, that lies behind the first half, but rather the Greek conception; in the second half of the hymn, the situation is reversed. — 33.3. "Adorned" (διεκόσμησεν) is Stoic. — 33.3. "Prepared": προετοιμάσας HSLC > προδημιουργήσας A. — 33.4. "Most noble": παμμέγεθες LSC > παμμέγεθες κατὰ διάνοιαν AH (pedantically explanatory addition). — "Hands": Later Jewish concept. — 33.7. "Good" in the second place HSC; omitted in A; *nostris* erroneously in L. — 33.8. The connection with the will of God is temptingly suggested by the fact that one therefore comes to joy; for God himself rejoiced in the good works with which he adorned himself, which the author probably deduced from God's good judgement on creation. — "Join": προσέλθωμεν; particularly frequent in Hebrews.

34.3. "According to his work" in AHSC; plural in L and Clem. Alex. (according to the LXX). — 34.5. Renown (καύχημα) is Pauline. — 34.6f. Liturgical (see 1 Clem 20): The author writes as if he sees himself within a worship assembly together with the Corinthians. — 34.7. "Spiritually": τῇ συνειδήσει. — "Continuously" (ἐκτενῶς): Technical expression related to prayers. — 34.8. "Wait for him" (ὑπομένουσιν) > ἀγαπῶσιν in HS and Paul. Whether the author draws from the original source or from Paul is uncertain. The saying was probably familiar as the highest expression for the content of the divine promises in prayers.

35.1ff. Still the sublime language of prayer. — 35.2. "Life in immortality": Genuine Greek; the following gifts of God come from a syncretistic contemplation; the great, extensive words here have something chilly about them.[13] — 35. "Father of the eons, the Most Holy one" (πανάγιος appears here for the first time in Christian literature). These expressions do not belong to the private prayers of the heart, but to the common prayer celebrations, which received their momentum from Hellenism. — "Greatness and beauty (καλλονή) of the divine gifts": This is also Hellenistic. — 35.4. "Of those who persevere": A offers the reading "of those who expect him." — 35.5ff. Again, good works and the practice of turning away from bad ones; the vice catalogue of Romans 1:29ff. has an influence here (see especially v. 32); of greater importance is the addition of "inhospitableness" (cf. 1 Clem 1; 10–12). — "Lawlessness" (ἀνομίαν) in A, πονηρίαν in HLS, according to Romans.

36. The highest blessing we have found and should hold is Jesus Christ, in whom our salvation is decided. Clement enumerates the charity of Christ in a hymn, then he describes the dignity of his person according to Hebrews and its Old Testament citations. The *benefizia* are definitely not Pauline, but all fall under the term "immortal knowledge" mentioned at the end, so they are perceived to be of a Greek origin. But immediately at the beginning of this section, Christ is, according to Hebrews, named "the high priest of our prayers, the patron and helper of our weakness," whereby the intellectual schema is supplemented (but without consideration of his death on the cross and resurrection); one grasps that Photius (*Lex.* 126) missed the loftier statements about Christ. It is very likely that this chapter is also based on the liturgy, especially on account of the statement in the first verse. — 36.2a. It is difficult to speak of real mysticism here; rationalism is set in rhetorical momentum. — "Light" in LS and Clem. Alex.; the addition of "wonderful" (AH) comes from 1 Peter 2:9. — "Immortal knowledge": See 35:2, "To taste life in immortality." It is possible that the Lord's Supper is in mind here. — Remarkable is the following: 36.2 is better connected to 36.1 than to 36.2a. If one removes 36.2a, there is a coherent reproduction from the Epistle to the Hebrews. This shows that the piece in 36.2a was handed down to the author and that he inserted it in his text clumsily.

37. Transition to the treatment of the specific topic of the letter. — 37.2. It is noteworthy that the Roman Christians, who call themselves warriors of God, call Roman officers "our" officers. Both the image of the military and that of the body (for the purpose of depicting the need for unity, structured

---

13. TN: Harnack's meaning is unclear. The German reads: "Die großen weitschichtigen Worte haben etwas Frostiges."

by supra- and subordination) were familiar to the religious discipline of the age. — 37.3. "King" (βασιλεύς); the Roman Christian community, at the end of the first century CE, certainly consisted in large part of those from the east. As such, the use of the term "king" for the emperor would not have been objectionable to them. — 37.5. Clement has 1 Cor 12:12f. in mind, as the strong contact[14] proves.

38. Paraenesis on the basis of 1 Clem 37: In subordination marked by a readiness to serve, everyone should minister to the whole according to his *charisma*. This attitude is genuinely from Early Christianity, pious, and sensible all at the same time. The "body" is the church, which is represented in every congregation. — 38.2. The Roman community, therefore, included not only the strong and the weak, the rich and the poor, as well as the "wise," but also the virtuosos of humble submission and sexual ascetics. All boasting in oneself has been cut off from them. — 38.3. Meaning: How can there be rivalries and boasting when we have all been lifted up from the lowest dust by God's work! *Nostra merita = dei munera*.

39.1. One should think of the troublemakers in Corinth. The following long quotation is extremely sharp. The argument and refutation that 1 Clem 40 begins is introduced by the same; the adversaries should know from the outset what lies ahead of them from God's side.

40.1. "The insight into the depths of the divine knowledge" consists precisely in the knowledge of the judgment that threatens the troublemakers, which is drawn from Holy Scripture. By using the most sublime expression from the mystery language (τὰ βάθη τῆς θείας γνώσεως; see 1 Cor 2:10; Rev 2:24; Dan 2:22) for this and for the following construction, the author wants to emphasize strongly his narrow and miserly undertaking. "Order" is the main *Stichwort*: in the small section, the word (τάσσειν) with its derivations appears six times, and the general cult is the area which is alone in view here: According to the Holy Scriptures, there must be (1) a general order, (2) firmly established times and hours, (3) a firmly established place, (4) firmly determined individuals (high priests, priests, Levites, laity). The extent to which this should apply to Christian worship is not yet clear from this chapter. — 40.5. The word "laity" (λαϊκοί) is not found in the LXX, but λαός is used therein with the sense of λαϊκοί (in contrast to the priests or leaders respectively). Clement of Alexandria and Tertullian testify after Clement of Rome to the use of the term "laity" in the Christian sense of the term.

---

14. TN: "Starke Berührung" ("strong contact") is a reference to the strength of the parallels in language and content between this passage in 1 Clem and 1 Cor 12:12f.

41.1ff. It follows from this chapter that the author demands the following with respect to the Christian worship service: (1) general order, which prescribes the proper place for each person, (2) a certain place, (3) certain leaders (I cannot share Wrede's opinion that the passage for the Christian congregation can only be taken from the necessity of order), indeed he does not hesitate to assert the death penalty threatened in the Old Testament as still valid (41.3). Yet a twofold observation is noteworthy: (1) He reveals in v. 4 that he is aware that he is presenting new knowledge (or a new argument) which has heretofore not been very common. (2) He does not claim that the law of Moses is still valid as a law for the church, but he let it be known that God—of course—is delighted in order, though it remains open why the worship service is bound to a certain place and to certain individuals also within the Christian congregation. Thus the last clarification remains open. — 41.1. The reading εὐαρεστείτω (> A εὐχαριστείτω) is the correct reading, for the so-called Apostolic Church-Ordinance also testifies to it.

42.1ff. The beginning of the clarification is marked by a great review of history: God sent Christ and entrusted him with the gospel; he sent the apostles. God—Christ—the Apostles: this is the basic order on which the church rests. But a fourth member is added to it: the apostles, after having pneumatically tested their first fruits, appointed them as bishops and deacons for the continuation of the mission. So—this is the necessary conclusion—this fourth member is just as necessary as the first three and is just as firmly established. This member is also appointed "in an orderly manner according to the will of God." This is not said with barren words, but something more important is said: In the Holy Scriptures it was prophesied, "I will appoint their bishops in righteousness and their deacons in faithfulness." This prophetic word excludes all doubt: The institution of bishops and deacons belongs just as much to the fundamental history of revelation, foundation, and sending as the institution of the apostles and the institution of Christ. However, the prophetic word is a forgery! Isaiah 60:17 reads (as Irenaeus IV.26.5 also cites it): Δώσω τοὺς ἄρχοντάς σου ἐν εἰρήνῃ καὶ τοὺς ἐπισκόπους σου ἐν δικαιοσύνῃ. And yet the word "forged" is too harsh. Since the word of Isaiah states the mission of the bishops, the author could have heard therein, according to a higher (i.e., alchemical) exegesis of that time, the desired prophecy. But then he could have also clarified the prophecy himself with his change, for the Holy Spirit sometimes speaks in the Holy Scripture with half-hints, which the enlightened reader may and should supplement. Examples of this can be found in the works of Philo and Origen. — 42.2. This proposition can be verified from the Gospel accounts. — 42.3. An important effect of the resurrection of Christ, properly observed. — Jesus Christ, God, Holy Spirit: take note of the Trinity. — The apostolic, missionary proclamation of the coming of the kingdom of God is an expression of the earliest forms of Christianity. — 42.4. "And those who obeyed the will of God, baptizing" is present only in L. The archetype of the other manuscripts omitted the phrase due to homoeoteleuton. (It is hardly an addition by L.) — The oldest testimony for the existence of the bishops and the deacons can be found in the prescript of Philippians. On the question why the author does not name the presbyters (Acts 14:23; Pastoral Epistles), see later.

43.1ff. In addition to the passage from Isaiah, however, there is also a process in the Holy Scripture that is perhaps even more convincing than that prophecy, and which the author therefore adds before he concludes his refutation of the troublemakers and his positive argumentation: Since Moses recorded in the Holy Scriptures everything that God has prescribed for him, and the other prophets followed him, testifying to what he had recorded as laws—here, the term "law" is used—Moses also told of the great miracle that took place in his time, when a dispute arose over the priesthood and the tribes jealously fought over that same office. Meaning and application: God himself stands behind the choice of priests. Moses knew this, and he also knew that Aaron was the chosen one, and he could have simply proclaimed this. But, in order to suppress the threatening discord in the most certain manner possible, God demonstrated his will through the miracle *ad oculos*. Now this miracle applies to all analogous cases, and the apostles are just as authorized in their right to choose as Moses. — 43.6. (Towards the end:) reminiscent of John 17:3; the text, however, is not entirely certain.[15]

44.1ff. Now everything is prepared, and the decisive statement can be given. — 44.1. "Our apostles" cannot be Peter and Paul, but the twelve (along with Paul); see 42.1ff. — "Through our Lord Jesus Christ": it was a wonderful prophetic (see 44.2 πρόγνωσιν τελείαν) epiphany. — "About the office of bishop" (ἐπὶ τοῦ ὀνόματος τῆς ἐπισκοπῆς) refers back to 43.2 περὶ τῆς ἱερωσύνης; it is all the more important that the author did not simply identify both. The development was not there yet. — 44.2. Where and when this decision was made, the author does not say and could not say. — The first effect of the prophetic preventive knowledge was the establishment of the "firstfruits" (bishops and deacons); the second was the decree (ἐπινομήν in A and L [*legem*], ἐπιδομήν H, ἐπὶ δοκιμήν S, ??C; ἐπινομήν is otherwise not attested but must be retained [= ἐπινομίς]) that after the death of the first fruits (relationship with the apostles is impossible; some of the aforementioned—τινες in HSC; τινες omitted in AL—are in view, for the author cannot have

---

15. TN: That is to say, there are text critical problems at this point in the text, and the evidence for the text decided by Harnack is not overwhelmingly convincing.

thought that all the aforementioned will be sentenced to death in the court) other proven men should follow them in their service. With regard to their selection, the author provides two details: (1) that those selected are respected men [this is a very vague statement], (2) that the whole local church gives its consent. If they then have served the church blamelessly, humbly, peaceably, and not in pettiness, and have received a good testimony from all over the course of several years, it is certain that they are in their place according to God's will, and it is therefore a violation of righteousness, that is, it is a sin, to depose them (the general question of when individuals can be deposed is not discussed). This took place in Corinth; Accordingly, the congregation there was severely mistaken.

45.1ff. Could this biblical retrospective really make an impression in Corinth? It is entirely meaningless with respect to the question of who is wrong in Corinth and who is right. Nevertheless, the words could awaken a shiver of fear. — 45.8. αὐτοῦ HSC > αὐτῶν A (L, lacking).

46.6. Note the Trinitarian formula (see 42.3; 58.2) but also the addition: "A calling." — 46.7f. See 13.1f: the modest citation formula seems to have been of a solemn sort. It is unlikely that our gospels are the text quoted, but rather another source. — 46.8. ἕνα τῶν ἐκλεκτῶν μου διαστρέψαι LSC and Clem Alex. > ἕνα τῶν μικρῶν μου σκανδαλίσαι AH (see the gospels). — 46.8. Here, one sees that the author knows more about the conditions in Corinth than he mentions in the letter. What is important is that the division has caused sorrow far beyond Corinth.

47.1. The words of Paul follow after the words of the Lord! — "The letter" (τὴν ἐπιστολήν): It does not follow from this that Clement only knew 1 Corinthians, nor is it to be thought that ἐπιστολή does not always mean a single letter. — 47.2. How (*quemadmodum* = τίνα τρόπον) L > AHSC τί πρῶτον. — "At the beginning of the proclamation of the Gospel": This is how Clement refers to the time of the letter compared to the present. — "Truly pneumatic": the Spirit has not testified in the Holy Scriptures alone. — 47.4. Clement does not know of any "Christ-party" in Corinth. Note also the sharp distinction between the apostles and Apollos. — "Certified" (μεμαρτυρημένοις); one could probably translate with "have become martyrs." — 47.5f. So the number of ringleaders was small. It was not necessary for them to have enjoyed a special reputation beforehand, and they did not have a single presbyter as a leader. — "The secure and ancient church of Corinth": See 1 Clem 1f. The majority of the congregation allowed itself to be swept away. — "Against the presbyters," that is, against the bishops and deacons who are called "presbyters" (see 44.5). — 47.7. The news has not only reached foreign Christian congregations (see 46.8), but also non-Christians (Jews and pagans). This led to the damage of the reputation of

Christ's name (the fame, the acknowledged, Christian brotherly love, was in danger), and even in Corinth it seems that the police at least threatened to interfere (house-search as a result of the quarrels?). It is unlikely that "danger" is to be understood here as divine punishment.

48.1. Paraenesis is given in the first person to make the exhortation more emphatic through solidarity. It gains in momentum until it crosses over into a hymn in chapter 49. — 48.2ff. No relationship with the Lord's words. — 48.5ff. The fact that there were important individuals among the troublemakers cannot be concluded with certainty from these verses. The author only sets this out as a possibility. — "To have faith" (πιστός), used here in the emphatic sense. — 48f. Besides the rhymes, the double μᾶλλον (the second time before μείζων) can be explained by the author's rhetorical intentions.

49.1ff. This hymn is pieced together (also from 1 Cor), and it is not understood that the author dared to rival Paul. — 49.1. John 14:15; 1 John 5:3. — 49.5. (50.1). On "love" and "perfection," see 1 John 2:5. — 49.6. Again the author feels the need to remember the blood of Christ. When he thinks of the Lord's Supper, the addition of the "soul" is proof that a Greek is the author here.

50.1ff. Paraenesis. — 50.3. "Place of the pious" (χῶρος εὐσεβῶν) is Greek. — 50.3. Χριστοῦ LC and Clement of Alex. > θεοῦ HS (A omits). — 50.4. The "opportune" (ἀγαθός) day will be brought about by God. — 50.6. Paul also quotes this verse in Rom 4:9, but Clement trumps the apostle by referring the saying directly to the Christians.

51—59.1. Clement addresses the troublemakers directly in a particularly carefully elaborated reminder. First, he demands that they repent. — 51.1. διά τινας παρεμπτώσεις LC and Clem. Alex. > διά τινος τῶν AH. — 51.3ff. Two terrible examples of what happened to the rebellious (see 4.12). — θεράποντα ALSC > ἄνθρωπον H (perhaps correct).

52.1. Ἀπροσδεής: Greek *theologumenon*.

53.1ff. Preparation for the advice for the ringleaders to emigrate: Moses was willing to sacrifice himself for the good of the congregation. But the appeal is not addressed directly to them ("beloved" can only be the name for the whole congregation). In the congregation, Clement wants to awaken the necessary mood as a prerequisite for the decision of the troublemakers. He suggests the idea that the Corinthians themselves could suffer badly if the conditions continue. — 53.5. One should take note of the momentum of the speech.

54.1ff. The challenge to the ringleaders shows (1) how serious the situation was (living together no longer seems possible), (2) that Clement by no means considers the opponents to be feral Christians, but believes them capable of a substantial moral act, (3) that he assumes that the congregation will now declare itself against them. — 54.2. He should not only declare his willingness to emigrate, but also his willingness to be prescribed a new place of residence. — Do whatever the congregation (πλῆθος) commands": The churches are ultimately, that is according to the religious theory, still democratically constituted (though see 57.1). — "The appointed presbyters": That is, the bishops and deacons. Here it becomes particularly clear that the appointed presbyters, and not the presbyters as such, have an office. — 54.3. "Great glory in Christ": Greek! The council itself is "Greek." — "Every place will receive him": This confidence is based on God's reign, as the scriptural passage proves. When Chrysostom was threatened with banishment, he strengthened himself with the same saying. — 54.4. The emphatic conclusion reinforces the appeal; but we do not know what cases Clement has in mind (in the Bible? in the congregations?).

55.1. It is also uncertain which examples of voluntary exile he has in mind from secular history (there have been enough famous cases, and they have been told again and again). It is important in itself that he thinks of them at all. — 55.2. Important for the sacrificial activity of Christian love (see 1 Cor 13:3). Unfortunately, concrete examples are not given (not even in v. 4). — 55.4f. Oldest mention of the story of Judith and the book. — 55.6. τοῦ ἔθνους τοῦ Ἰσραήλ SLC > τοῦ Ἰσραήλ AH. — "All-seeing": Magic word.

56.1ff. Context: Through our intercessions, we wish to make it such that sinners become meek and humble and come to the right decision to yield. — 56.1. "To the will of God": the Roman church is aware (see 59.1; 63.2) that the Holy Spirit or God speaks through them and that, therefore, their admonition reflects the will of God. — "The saints" could be the angels, but also ideal Christianity. There is no thought of "the saints" in the later sense. — 56.2–59.1. "Discipline": The congregation leaves no doubt that it demands no small thing from its opponents, but something substantial: they must bow down.

57.1. Here we find the clear designation of those who were ultimately involved. Leaders and seducers are sharply separated. "Obey the presbyters": This makes a comparison with 54.2 ("do whatever the congregation commands") difficult. The solution lies in the fact that the congregation's formal request to the troublemakers to repent and to yield is made by the presbyters, that is the "appointed" presbyters, that is the bishops and deacons. Furthermore, it is found in the fact that the intention was in fact to subject oneself to the will of the reinstated by withdrawing the deposition, and that the officials were certainly already at that time the really authoritative and acting ones, and that the relationship with the congregation was a formality. — 57.3ff. These are severely threatening words with which

Clement closes his appeal. — 57.3. "All-virtuous Wisdom" (πανάρετος): The epithet is typical for Solomon's sayings. — 57.7. Confidently (πεποιθώς) LSC > omitted in H and LXX (lacking in A).

58.1. Liturgically ornate. The tradition has increased: ἁγίῳ LS > παναγίῳ H, ὅσιον LS > ὁσιώτατον H (is lacking in A, is doubtful in C). — 58.2. One should take note again (42.3; 46.6) of the threefold formulation, here in the solemn formula and with the important addition with which Ignatius, *Smyrn.* 10 can be compared: ἡ τελεία πίστις Ἰησοῦς Χριστός. The formula reproduces the Jewish formula "Chi Ihvh," but also on the sanctuary of the famous Gothic Nabataean king Obodath it is written, "Chi 'bdth." — "Laws and commandments": According to Clement, everything religious belongs to this category, which is connected with the early Christian, eschatological scheme. — "Those saved (Gentiles)": σωζομένων ἐθνῶν LC > σωζομένων HS. The reading of LC is quite unusual, but can it simply be deleted? Ancient dittography up to . . . ενων?

59.1. See 56.1: The congregation speaks in the name of God. — 59.2ff. Here begins the final part of the letter, which, as the countless parallels and testimonies (from the second century onwards) prove, goes back to the solemn prayers in the worship service, which in turn were modelled on the prayers of the synagogue (based on the LXX) under the influence of the spirit of the Greek mystery cults. By concluding with this great prayer, the letter takes seriously the fiction that when the Corinthians read this letter in worship, they form a congregation with the Roman brothers to hear God's instructions and to praise and implore him together. Even the letter of the bishop Julius I to Alexandria runs into a prayer, and the bishop expressly says, "Now we wish to add a prayer." — 59.2. "The number of the elect": This is the alpha and omega of all prayers. — "Through his servant (παῖς)": This is the oldest christological formula that has been preserved in the liturgy (even Clement only uses it liturgically). See my treatise "Die Bezeichnung Jesu als Knecht Gottes" in *Sitzungsberichte der preussischen Akademie der Wissenschaften.*[16] The addition "beloved" to "servant" is important, for it identifies the "servant," who has nothing to do with the Messiah (Son of God), with him. — 59.3. The hard transition from the third to the second person should not be corrected. — "Which contains the archetypal principle of all creation" (ἀρχεγόνος): Philosophical and gnostic. — "Name" in the sense of being and nature. — "In the highest . . . among the holy ones": perhaps, "Among the highest . . . among the holy ones." — "And heals" (καὶ σώζοντα) LS > omitted in HC. — "Watches

---

16. Harnack, "Die Bezeichnung Jesu als 'Knecht Gottes.'" Translated in this volume under the title "The Epithet 'Servant of God' Used of Jesus and Its History in the Ancient Church," 169–202.

over" (ἐπόπτης) LXX and Hellenistic. — "Savior" (σωτήρ): Occuring only here in the letter. — 59.3. Conclusion: The Jewish people stand here in the Jewish prayer. — 59.4. (We ask you) σε LSC > omitted in H. — "The weak" (ἀσθενεῖς) LSC > ἀσεβεῖς H. "Prisoners": It is not necessary to think of them as prisoners on account of their faith.

60.1ff. Praise of God as creator and giver of all good gifts. — 60.1a. "For" (γάρ) LS > omitted in HC. — 60.1a. Greek view of the cosmos. — "In what is seen": Unanimous reading (ἐν τοῖς ὁρωμένοις), perhaps σωζομένοις. — "Friendly" (χρηστός) LSC > πιστός H. — 60.2. The explicit mention of women is noteworthy. — καθάρισον LSC > καθαρεῖς H. — "Rulers" (ἄρχοντες) are the worldly leaders (see 1 Clem 61). — 60.3 (towards the end): The request for salvation for those who hate us is not connected with a request for revenge. — 60.4. "Our fathers" are the testimonies of the Holy Scriptures. — "Pious" (ὁσίως) LSC > omitted in H. — The grammatical style in this verse is monumentally incorrect. — "Glorious" (ἐνδόξῳ) LSC > παναρέτῳ H; see Herm., Vis. III.3.5: τοῦ παντοκράτορος καὶ ἐνδόξου ὀνόματος.

61.1. LS place the first clause of chapter 61 in 61.4. HC start a new sentence. A certain decision is not possible. In favor of LS is 60.2 (towards the end). — This prayer for the authorities, placed here in this context, shows not only loyalty, but also the conviction and the disposition that the Godhead in heaven corresponds to the authorities on earth, and that, therefore, their authority is conferred by God and is inviolable, and that their health and strength is the prerequisite of all earthly peace and wellbeing. But the emperor is the authority ("power of royal rule"). He is the *basileus* of the eons. But since the prayer consistently speaks of authority in the plural, all imperial officials are, according to him, holders of imperial authority (emperor ruled state[17]). — 61.2b. It is noteworthy what Clement believes the authorities to be capable of with regard to what is good and what he expects from God in relation to a good authority. — On the gross forgery involving L's church politics in 1 Clem 60.4 and 61, see the discussion in Harnack[18] and Knopf.[19] The forgery probably belongs to the eleventh century. — 61.3. "For us" (μεθ' ἡμῶν) omitted in C. — "From generation to generation" omitted in L.

17. TN: "Kaiser Obrigkeitsstaat" could also be translated with "imperial dictatorship."

18. Harnack, "Über die jüngst entdeckte lateinische Übersetzung"; "Neue Studien zur jüngst entdeckte lateinische Übersetzung." Both articles have been translated in this volume under the respective titles, "The Recently Discovered Latin Translation of 1 Clement," 109–122; "New Studies on the Recently Discovered Latin Translation of 1 Clement," 123–143.

19. Knopf, *Der erste Clemensbrief*, 55f.

62.2. Clement is aware of having given a complete practical doctrine of religion. — "Every subject" (τόπον) HL, τόπον τῆς γραφῆς CS. — "Father": Old Testament. — 62.3. If this is not mere flattery, the gloomy description in chapter 3 is very exaggerated. — "Especially distinguished men" (ἐλλογιμωτάτοις) H, *doctis* S, *probatis* L, questionable in C.

63.1. "To bend the neck": Clement knows that he demands something difficult. — "To fill" (ἀναπληρῶσαι) HLC; S reads ἀναπληρώσαντας προσκλιθῆναι τοῖς ὑπάρχουσιν ἀρχηγοῖς (or better γενομῆνοις ἡγουμένοις) τῶν ψυχῶν ἡμῶν, which would be the original. The officials removed from office by the majority receives thereby a special satisfaction. — 63.2. It is difficult to refer "by the Holy Spirit" to "to exterminate" (see 59.1).[20] — Clement himself describes his writing as *admonitio de pace et concordia*. — 63.3. These men have probably experienced, like Clement himself, the work of Peter and Paul in Rome (see 65.1). — "Witnesses." The mission of the men who are to determine whether the Corinthian congregation will carry out the exhortation of the Romans makes them appear as superiors. Such a conclusion, however, would be incorrect, because the Holy Spirit, in whose power the Roman congregation sends its admonition, can and should be claimed by every congregation in such an event. But how many congregations have had the solidarity and courage to do this? "Furthermore" and "also" are doubtful. — 63.4. Once again, it is clear that the Roman congregation experiences the discord of the sister congregation as if it were her own.

64. Liturgical blessing; take note of the splendid design. — Christ as "chosen one" ("servant" is lacking here); the same word applies to the Christians. — "High priest and patron," see 1 Clem 36.

65.1. The two Roman envoys belong to the other imperial "families" (Phil 4:22) of the Claudians and the Valerians (Messalina belonged to the latter). They are Greeks, and were probably freedmen. Whether Fortunatus belonged to the deputation or was a Roman Christian who was already living in Corinth cannot be decided. — 65.2. At the end, the Roman Christians turn once again to the whole church. — "And" (through him) is defective AS > HL. — "Eternal reign" (θρόνος αἰώνιος) is unusual in doxologies (reproduced in Mart. Pol. 21). One cannot stress the goal of making peace more urgent than by the threefold use of "as soon as possible." — The last words of the letter function like blasts from a trumpet.

---

20. TN: Reference to 59.1 does not seem to be accurate since Harnack does not use "ausrotten" ("to exterminate") in his translation of this passage. The term however appears in both 15.5; 53.3.

Appendix I

The Recently Discovered Latin Translation of 1 Clement

1894

Introduction

NINETEEN YEARS AGO, FOR the first time, the metropolitan Bryennios published the complete text of 1 Clement, the oldest post-apostolic writing, on the basis of a Constantinopolitan manuscript (written in 1056 = Codex H).[1] Up until this point, this text—damaged and incomplete—existed only in an ancient biblical manuscript, Codex Alexandrinus (fifth century = Codex A). A few months after the Metropolitan's publication had become known to us, it was discovered that, in the library of the late Orientalist J. Mohn of Paris, there was a Syriac biblical manuscript (written in 1169 = Codex S), which also contained the complete text of the letter. The Cambridge University Library purchased this manuscript, H. H. Bensly and Lightfoot examined it, and in 1877 Lightfoot gave a full report of its contents and relationship to Codex A and H. In the same year, von Gebhardt—who in 1876 reviewed the letter according to Codex A and H—published an investigation of Codex S[2] and corrected his edition accordingly. Finally, Lightfoot (afterwards H. H. Funk and Hilgenfeld also published editions of the letter) summarized all the research on Clement of Rome in his large edition *S. Clement of Rome* and presented, among other things, a new edition of the letter.[3]

---

1. TN: This manuscript is also known as Codex Hierosolymitanus. In the previous work, Harnack used the abbreviation H for this codex, and although he uses C as the abbreviation for this manuscript in this and the following essay, the abbreviation has been changed to H in conformity with the *Introduction* in order to avoid confusion.
2. Gebhardt, "Review of 'S. Clement of Rome.'"
3. Lightfoot, *Clement of Rome*, vols. 1–2.

On the basis of three witnesses (AHS) that were independent of one another, the text of the letter was secure in the majority of the passages. Lightfoot proved that, where they agree, they shared an archetype that belongs to at least the end of the second century, thereby making it at most a hundred years younger than the letter itself. With respect to text-critical principles (A is the most important witness; S is to be preferred to H), he is in complete agreement with von Gebhardt. Accordingly, the editions of the two scholars only differ in 95 places, even if one includes minor differences. The number of instances where one had to assume that there was already a mistake in the archetype behind AHS were small, and therefore only the most moderate use of conjectures was needed. Uncertainty only remains insofar as the rather frequent quotations from the letter by Clement of Alexandria do not agree throughout with the common testimony of AHS. It was believed that in most cases these discrepancies had to be explained by the assumption that Clement of Alexandria did not quote Clement of Rome precisely.

Towards the end of last year, we were surprised by the news that an ancient Latin translation of our letter in a manuscript from the eleventh century had been found in the seminary library at Namur, and it was presented to us a few weeks ago by the lucky finder, Morin, priest and monk, order of Saint Benedict in Maredsous.[4] The discovery was all the more surprising since the existence of a Latin translation of the letter—apart from a hidden note, which I will discuss below—had remained unknown since the sparse and short Latin citations of our letter in Hieronymus and John Diaconus (sixth cent.?) did not guarantee that a complete translation of the letter existed. Apart from these witnesses, the entirety of the East had remained silent about this most ancient letter of the Roman congregation. As much as the ancient church and the church of the Middle Ages was occupied with the persona of Peter's disciple, Clement, no one in the East mentions the real letter attributed to Clement (except the church history of Eusebius-Rubin, where the letter is mentioned), while fake letters of the most diverse kind circulated under the name of Clement, received a wider and greater reputation, and were aggrandized by Pseudoisidori in the ninth century.

That the now discovered translation of the letter belongs to the second century has already been recognized by Morin[5] and has been strengthened by a number of observations:

(1) In AHS, the letter already is positioned next to the pseudo, so-called 2 Clement. The coupling of the two letters had already been known before

---

4. Germain, *Anecdota Maredsolana*, vol. 1.
5. Germain, *Anecdota Maredsolana*, 1:xif.

the time of Eusebius and to our knowledge was not thereafter dissolved. Our manuscript, however, only contains the real letter, so it agrees with the fathers before Origen, who all know of only one letter of Clement.

(2) The language used within the translation is that of the vulgar Latin[6] from the second and third centuries and agrees with the language of ancient Italy in general (the biblical citations are not given according to the Vulgate); solecisms and Graecisms are exceedingly numerous, such that the translator understood Greek better than Latin.[7]

(3) The translation of individual terms points to the second century and probably to the first half of the second century. Thus, the translator renders ἐπίσκοποι καὶ διάκονοι with *episcopi et ministri*. Since ἐπίσκοπος is translated with *visitator* in 1 Clem 59.3 (174 [3] of Lightfoot's edition),[8] where it is used of God, there can be no doubt that the translator used the word *episcopus* in the other instances because the Latin congregations in his age called their rulers *episcopi*. But why does he not then use the term *diaconi*? This can hardly be explained apart from the assumption that at that time *diaconi* had not yet become a common title within the Latin congregations. However, at the end of the second century, *diaconus* was used no less within the Latin Church than *episcopus*.[9] Therefore, he must have translated before this time.[10] Furthermore, πρεσβύτεροι is translated as *seniores*; however, in one passage (1 Clem 54.2 [158 (8)]), the expression μετὰ τῶν καθεσταμένων πρεσβυτέρων is translated as *cum constitutis presbuteris*. This change is entirely accurate, for in all other places of the letter, πρεσβύτεροι really is a designation for the *seniores*, and in this case, however, the *seniores* are invested with an office, that is, presbyter. A later translator, however, can no longer be trusted with the understanding required for this fine distinction, because for him, he would have not considered *seniores* to be a definition of the term but instead would have only had "presbyter" in the sense of the ecclesiastical order in mind.[11] In 1 Clem 42.4 (128 [7]), it says

6. TN: That is, the common Latin tongue.

7. See the index compiled by Morin in the section entitled *Orthographica, Lexica et Grammatica* (*Anecdota Maredsolana*, 1:64f).

8. Lightfoot, *Clement of Rome*, vol. 2. TN: Harnack's citation of 1 Clement in this essay is heavily dependent on Lightfoot's edition where he provides the page number and line from Lightfoot. The translation maintains that practice.

9. See Tertullian, *Bapt.* 17; *Praescr.* 41. The Latin translation of Hermas, on the other hand, also offers *episcopi et ministri* (contra the Latin translation of the letters of Ignatius and Polycarp).

10. Also, it is important to note that the translator renders ὁ λαϊκὸς ἄνθρωπος as *plebeius homo* (40.5).

11. The Latin translation of Hermas offers *seniores* for οἱ πρεσβύτεροι. Tertullian writes (for particular reasons) *seniores probati* (*Apol.* 39), but otherwise *episcopus*,

that the apostles preached the gospel κατὰ χώρας καὶ πόλεις. The translator writes, *secundum municipia et civitates*. This is a strange translation, which would have made much less sense in the third century than it would have in the second century, in which one had the impression that Christianity was a religion of the cities, just as the expression "in all cities" takes the place of "in the whole of Christendom."[12]

(4) The translation proves its great age by the excellent original on which it is based, and which the translator has reproduced word for word as far as possible.[13] Admittedly, the translation of the second century—attested in the manuscript of the eleventh century, which has been marred by many mistakes—is not to be recognized as any more reliable than the others. Furthermore, many things have been omitted in the manuscript due to homoeoteleuton. However, wherever the foundational text (*Grundschrift*) can be established with certainty, this translation proves that its *Vorlage* was a Greek manuscript, which itself was not free from error in all places, but even surpasses Codex A not infrequently, is in agreement with S in many places against A and H, often confirms the readings of Clement of Alexandria against all three other witnesses, and in some places alone preserves the correct reading. However, since the archetype of L is completely independent of each of the three other witnesses and of Clement of Alexandria, it often is the deciding witness in the previous disputes between AH > S and HS > A, and thereby we come very close to the time of the composition of the letter itself. Today, on the basis of four (five) witnesses, the text of this most ancient letter of the Roman congregation can be reconstructed with

---

presbyteri, diaconi (*Bapt.* 17).

12. One could suppose that instead of χώρας, the translator had read χώρους and recalled that he translated ἔχουσιν χῶρον εὐσεβῶν in 1 Clem 50.3 (151 [8]) with *habent municipium religiosorum*. However, Clement of Alexandria, who cites this passage of our letter (*Strom.* IV.8.112) gives the reading ἔχουσι χώραν εὐσεβῶν. First Clement 25.3 (88 [9]), however, translates ἀπὸ τῆς Ἀραβικῆς χώρας with *e regione Arabiae*. Yet, in this case, *regio* was necessary and the translator is in any case inconsistent in his rendering. For example, he translates five different Greek words with the Latin *contumacia* while also translating the same Greek word in five to six different ways.

13. The fact that it has been translated from Greek and not, for example, Syriac is evidenced, if evidence is indeed necessary, by the following: In 1 Clem 47.5 (144 [3]) νυνὶ δε = *nunc vitae*, i.e., = *nunc vide* = νῦν ἴδε and in 1 Clem 50.3 (150 [7]) ἀλλ' οἱ = *alii* (see Morin on these passages).

greater certainty than that of any other early Christian monument,[14] with the exception of some Pauline letters.[15]

---

14. TN: Here, Harnack uses the word "Denkmäler," which could be translated as monuments, memorials, statues, etc. In his address at the *Studentenkonferenz* in Aarau, Switzerland, Harnack uses the same term and clarifies his meaning. He writes, "There are the monuments from all epochs of the last two thousand five hundred years and beyond. By monuments, I mean all that which is still extant from bygone ages, be it buildings, statues, inscriptions, coins, documents, handwriting, etc." (Harnack, "What Has History to Offer," 48).

15. Here, it is not my intent to debate the text-critical value of L. The results of the revision of the text belong within a new edition, which, however, will not differ significantly from the earlier ones since A and S were already excellent witnesses. However, a few observations are to be permitted. In the ninety-five instances where Lightfoot's and Gebhardt's editions differ, L supports Lightfoot's text forty-one times and Gebhardt's twenty-five times (in twenty-nine cases, L is not able to settle the dispute). From 1 Clem 22 (79 [20f]), there is the interesting fact that AL and Clement of Alexandria share the same defect, which therefore must be ancient. Instances in which L alone is judged to have the correct reading are the following: In 1 Clem 17.5 (64 [1ff]), AHS read: Μωϋσῆς πιστὸς ἐν ὅλῳ τῷ οἴκῳ αὐτοῦ ἐκλήθη, καὶ διὰ τῆς ὑπηρεσίας αὐτοῦ ἔκρινεν ὁ θεὸς Αἴγυπτον διὰ τῶν μαστίγων καὶ τῶν αἰκισμάτων αὐτῶν. The αὐτῶν is very conspicuous. L, however, offers the reading *poenis et tormentus saevis*, therefore read δεινῶν, if Morin supposes correctly. In 1 Clem 27.5 (90 [11ff]) AHS offer the reading: τίς ἐρεῖ αὐτῷ· τί ἐποίησας; ἢ τίς ἀντιστήσεται τῷ κράτει τῆς ἰσχύος αὐτοῦ; ὅτε θέλει καὶ ὡς θέλει ποιήσει πάντα, κτλ; instead of ὅτε, L reads *quia cum*; without doubt, read ὅτι ὅτε as the correct reading. In 1 Clem 42.4 (128 [6ff]), AHS read κατὰ χώρας οὖν καὶ πόλεις κηρύσσοντες καθίστανον (*scil.* οἱ ἀπόστολοι) τὰς ἀπαρχὰς αὐτῶν; L, however, reads *secundum municipia ergo et civitates praedicantes, eos qui obaudiebant voluntati dei baptizantes praeponebant primitiva eorum*. This can be an interpolation, but if we consider that the phrase *obaudre voluntati dei* is one of the most familiar to Clement, that the expression is a very old fashion, undogmatic one, and finally that the words, which conclude with βαπτίζοντες, could have easily been omitted after κηρύσσοντες because of homoeoteleuton, then we do not consider it unlikely that the words are original. In 1 Clem 43.6 (131 [23f]), H reads τοῦ ἀληθινοῦ καὶ μόνου κυρίου, S reads τοῦ μόνου ἀληθινοῦ θεοῦ, A lacks the phrase, but L reads *veri et uni*. In 1 Clem 47.2 (143 [9]), AHS include τί πρῶτον in the sentence ἀναλάβετε τὴν ἐπιστολὴν τοῦ μακαρίου Παύλου τοῦ ἀποστόλου. τί πρῶτον ὑμῖν ἐν ἀρχῇ τοῦ εὐαγγελίου ἔγραψεν; ἐπ᾽ ἀληθείας πνευματικῶς ἐπέστειλεν ὑμῖν περὶ αὐτοῦ τε καὶ Κηφᾶ τε καὶ Ἀπολλώ; for the interpreters, this was too much to accomplish. L gives the reading *quemadmodum* (τίνα τρόπον) for τί πρῶτον. With one stroke, the sentence is repaired; the following πνευματικῶς corresponds to τίνα τρόπον. — In the previous cases, L alone preserved the correct reading; in the following he will vote with Clement Alexandria against all other witnesses: In 1 Clem 1.2 (10 [1]), AH read ὑμῶν πίστιν, but Clem. Alex. and L (uncertain) read πίστιν ὑμῶν. In 1 Clem 1.3 (10 [5]), AH read νόμοις, but Clem. Alex. and L read νομίμοις. In 1 Clem 7 (35 [13]), AHS read ἡμῶν, but it is omitted in Clem. Alex. (uncertain) and L. In 1 Clem 15.6 (57 [10]), A reads ἐν σωτηρίᾳ, it is omitted in H, and dubious in S, but L and Clem. Alex. read ἐν σωτηρίῳ. In 1 Clem 17 (63 [10]), AHS read ἔτι δὲ καὶ, but L and Clem. Alex. read τε. In 1 Clem 21.5–6 (76 [7]), AHS read τῷ θεῷ, τὸν κύριον, L reads *deum aut dominum*, but Clem. Alex. also does not begin the new clause with τὸν κύριον. In 1 Clem 21.8 (78 [6]), AH read διανοίᾳ, Clem. Alex. has καρδίᾳ, and L reads *corde et cogitatione*. In 1 Clem 21.9 (78 [6]), AH

Let us now, however, leave aside the text of the old translation and turn to the present text, that is, to the eleventh-century copy. Morin did not wish to do away with all of the manuscript's errors but desired to improve the obvious spelling mistakes within the text. Nevertheless, as he himself notes in the preface, he was careful not to correct the author. Of course, he did not succeed everywhere: In some places, one wishes to read the transmitted text and not the corrections, which are only apparently evident. It is true that Morin indicates—as it seems, in all cases—where he deviates from the manuscript and where it was corrected by the first or a later hand. Yet, he does not seem to have asked himself the question of whether some of the errors are not deliberate deviations from the original text. And yet, the question is an urgent one. To put it briefly, Morin has not noticed a large forgery found at the end of the sixtieth and at the beginning of the sixty-first chapter. These chapters contain an extensive prayer (the Roman congregational prayer of that time). In this prayer, the intercession for the authorities occupies a large amount of space. Now, let us look at how Clement (according to Codex H and S; A lacks the prayer) wrote, and how the manuscript of Namur from the eleventh century claims he writes:[16]

---

read ἐστιν, while Clem. Alex. and L omit it. In 1 Clem 22.6 (79 [17]), A reads πρός, deficient in H, and Clem. Alex. and L read εἰς. In 1 Clem 22.7 (79 [20]), AS read αὐτοῦ, deficient in H, and omitted in both Clem. Alex. and L. In 1 Clem 22.8 (79 [22]), AH read τοῦ ἁμαρτωλοῦ, but Clem. Alex. and L read τῶν ἁμαρτωλῶν. In 1 Clem 28.3 (92 [3]), AHS read ἀφήξω, but Clem. Alex. and L read φύγω. In 1 Clem 28.3 (92 [6]), AHS read καταστρώσω, but Clem. Alex. and L read καταβῶ. In 1 Clem 34.1 (104 [6]), AHS read τὸ ἔργον, but Clem. Alex. and L read τὰ ἔργα. In 1 Clem 34.8 (106 [3]), AH read ὅσα, it is omitted in S, Clem. Alex. reads ἅ, and L reads *quae*. In 1 Clement 38 (116 [7]), Clem. Alex. and L read μόνον, whereas AHS omit it. In 1 Clem 38 (116 [9]), AH read ἑαυτόν, but Clem. Alex. and L read αὐτόν. In 1 Clem 40.1 (121 [6]), AH read ἡμῖν ὄντων, but Clem. Alex. and L (not certain) read ὄντων ἡμῖν. In 1 Clem 48 (146 [4]), AHS read ἥ, it is omitted in Clem. Alex. (in a citation; he cites this passage twice) and (probably) in L. In 1 Clem 50.3 (151 [8]), AH read χῶρον, but Clem. Alex. and L [?] read χώραν. In 1 Clem 51.1 (153 [8]), AHS read διὰ τινος τῶν τοῦ ἀντικειμένου, and Clem. Alex. and L read διὰ τὰς [τινας] παρεμπτώσεις τοῦ ἀντικειμένου. That is the correct reading. One can see, therefore, how AL and Clem. Alex. have the same errors, as is also true of AHS. The situation with our letter is like that of the writings of the New Testament. Already in the second century, the text had been copied many times and a series of errors can be followed back to this time. But so much is clear from L that the citations in Clement of Alexandria—not only where they are attested to by L—are to be considered of greater value than the editors have considered so far. The authority of Codex H is devalued with greater certainty because of L. A special investigation will require the interesting relationship between the Latin and Syriac versions. In any case, SL and Clem. Alex. are to be seen as superior to AH (see, e.g., 1 Clem 36 [112 (1)]). But even S and L, without the agreement of Clem. Alex., is of the highest value.

16. It is of the luckiest coincidence that the beautiful facsimile that Morin added to his publication contains precisely these chapters.

ὑπηκόους γινομένους [scil. ἡμᾶς = we Christians] τῷ παντοκράτορι καὶ παναρέτῳ ὀνόματί σου, τοῖς τε ἄρχουσιν καὶ ἡγουμένοις ἡμῶν ἐπὶ τῆς γῆς. Σύ, δέσποτα, ἔδωκας τὴν ἐξουσίαν τῆς βασιλείας αὐτοῖς διὰ τοῦ μεγαλοπρεποῦς καὶ ἀνεκδιηγήτου κράτους σου, εἰς τὸ γινώσκοντας ἡμᾶς τὴν ὑπὸ σοῦ αὐτοῖς δεδομένην δόξαν καὶ τιμὴν ὑποτάσσεσθαι αὐτοῖς, μηδὲν ἐναντιουμένους τῷ θελήματί σου· οἷς δός, κύριε, ὑγείαν, εἰρήνην, ὁμόνοιαν, εὐστάθειαν, εἰς τὸ διέπειν αὐτοὺς τὴν ὑπὸ σοῦ δεδομένην αὐτοῖς ἡγεμονίαν ἀπροσκόπως. σὺ γάρ, δέσποτα ἐπουράνιε, βασιλεῦ τῶν αἰώνων, δίδως τοῖς υἱοῖς τῶν ἀνθρώπων δόξαν καὶ τιμὴν καὶ ἐξουσίαν τῶν ἐπὶ τῆς γῆς ὑπαρχόντων· σύ, κύριε, διεύθυνον τὴν βουλὴν αὐτῶν κατὰ τὸ καλὸν καὶ εὐάρεστον ἐνώπιόν σου, ὅπως διέποντες ἐν εἰρήνῃ καὶ πραΰτητι εὐσεβῶς τὴν ὑπὸ σοῦ αὐτοῖς δεδομένην ἐξουσίαν ἵλεώ σου τυγχάνωσιν.	*oboedientes facti* [scil. *Nos* = we Christians] *omnia potenti et mirifico nomini tuo, principibus etiam et ducibus qui sunt super terram. Tu domine dedisti potestatem regni per magnificum et inenarrabile imperium tuum et cognito datam nobis a te gloriam et honorem subditi sint nihil resistentes voluntati tuae, quibus das nobis salutem et pacem et concordiam tranquillitatem: ut agant quod a te illis datum est regnum sine offensione. Tu enim dominator caelorum rex seculorum das filiis hominum gloriam et honorem et potestatem eorum quae* [pr. man. *qui*] *sunt super terram. Tu ordine dirige consilium eorum iuxta te bonum et placitum coram te, ut et gentes cum pace et mansuetudine pie possideant quae a te illis data est postestas, propicio illis.*

This, then, is the text of the manuscript and indeed, with the exception of the *qui* which has been replaced by the manufactured *quae*, proceeds smoothly without any correction. Morin, however, corrected *et* in line 8 with *ut* as an obvious spelling mistake; replaced *ordine* in line 21 with *Domine*; in line 24 *et gentes* with *agents* (indicating the change and the reading of the manuscript in his annotations). Furthermore, he noticed in line 6 that the translator omitted αὐτοῖς; in line 8f, he offered a translation that deviates from the foundational text; in line 12, he notes that the insertion of *nobis* was a *manifestus error*; that in line 22 *te* was superfluous; that in line 25 there was a wrong construction in the translation; and finally that in line 27 *te* was to be supplemented and did not correspond to *illis* in the original.

Am I finished with these remarks? Only if you isolate every "variant" and every "mistake."[17] But as soon as one looks at the Latin text in its entirety, the situation is quite different. While the Greek text calls for the most perfect obedience to the authorities, who are expressly recognized as established by God and described as our authorities, the Latin text offers a completely different picture, admittedly a confused one, but nevertheless a completely different one, indeed an opposite one: First, the ἡμῶν in line 4 has been removed; thus ἄρχοντες καὶ ἡγούμενοι are not called our authorities. Second, αὐτοῖς in line 6 is omitted, so that at the least it is not clear to whom the *potestas regni* are given. Third, and this is the main issue, line 8f. is translated in such a way, as if it said εἰς τὸ γινώσκοντας[18] αὐτοὺς τὴν ὑπὸ σοῦ ἡμῖν δεδομένην δόξαν καὶ τιμὴν ὑποτάσσεσθαι. That is, the translation reads as if it is prayed that the authorities may be obedient to us. But who wrote the letter? Clement the First, according to the medieval view, was the Roman pope and the disciple of Saint Peter. He prays, therefore, that the authorities may be subject to him and his own, that is, he prays the exact opposite of what the true Clement has prayed. And yet the forgery is not yet completed. In the original text, an urgent intercession for the authorities follows: οἷς δός, κύριε ὑγίειαν κτλ. (line 12f). But in the translation, *nobis* is inserted. Admittedly, this causes confusion (*quibus nobis*), but in the main the meaning is clear: "Pope" Clement does not pray for the authorities, but for himself and for his own, for the church.[19] But the following demonstrates, just like

---

17. Morin is right that in line 8 *et* is only a spelling mistake for *ut*, as *subditi sint* in line 10 demonstrates.

18. *Cognito* is used as an absolute participle in the customary manner since the time of Livius. Vergl. Liv. XXXVII.13.5: *ex agrestibus cognito, hostum naves ad Aethaliam stare, consilium habitum*.

19. "*That*" must have been turned into "*of that*"; otherwise, it would not be a request.

quibus left standing, that *nobis* is only inserted into a correct translation; for, if *nobis* were not there, the translation would continue: *ut agant quod a te illis datum est regnum sine offensione*. With the inclusion of *nobis*, this final clause is intolerable, or is only tolerable in case of emergency; without *nobis*, however, everything is appropriate. The correction *quae* from *qui* I will leave to the side, as well as the deviating construction at the end of the last clause. But is *ordine* for κύριε in line 21 really only a coincidental transference, along with the use of *et gentes* in line 24 for *agentes*? The possibility, indeed the probability that they are coincidental must be conceded, for similar transferences like *et gentes* = *agentes* occur frequently[20] in manuscripts and σύ, κύριε, τὴν οἰκουμένην ἔκτισας in 1 Clem 60.1 (176 [2]) is translated as *tu ordinem orbis terrae creasti*.[21] But the question is whether we can assume in the two places where *domine* is represented by *ordine* (*ordinem*) that it was only an oversight. *Ordo* is the priesthood (the spiritual state);[22] *ordo* is also the rule of the monk. How—if it is what the author wished to say—might God direct the council of authorities to what is best through the priesthood (or through the rule of the monks, that is, those called monks?)? Does this *Cluniac* appeal fit perfectly into the context the translator has created? And did he not really write it that way? Cannot *ordo* also be formulated in this way in the other passage: *Tu enim perpetuan mundi stabilitionem per opera manifestasi, tu ordinem orbis terrae creasti*? The Catholic priesthood, which is spread all over the world, is similar to how Hermas once set the structure of the world and the church in parallel! Since, however, this interpretation is highly questionable because *ordine* could easily arise from *domine* by change and because *et gentes* looks like a scribal error, I break off from this interpretation of the passage. Nevertheless, it is certain that in our manuscript the passage pertaining to obedience to the authorities has been forged in a pseudoisidorical sense and has been transformed into the opposite of its original sense.[23] In this case, we cannot resort to explaining the differences by accidental spelling errors.[24]

---

20. In 1 Clem 15.6 (56 [8]), *gentium* is written instead of *egentium* (Greek: τῶν πτωχῶν).

21. In 1 Clem 7.5 (37 [7]), *omnibus* is written instead of *dominus* (ὁ δεσπότης).

22. Thus already frequently in Tertullian. See, for example, *de exhortat. cast.* 7: *differentiam inter ordinem et plebem constutuit ecclesiae auctoritas*. The same difference would be assumed here: *ordo—gentes*; for *gentes* is *homines*.

23. The forgery, of course, has not been carried out consistently. It is, so to speak, only a strong attempt. The old text is still recognizable.

24. A noteworthy coincidence is, however, that very similar variants are found in the manuscript as real spelling errors. For precisely this reason, it is understandable that Morin did not recognize the mistakes here as tendentious.

If this is indeed certain, then the question arises whether the manuscript does not also contain other tendentious corrections. In fact, there is still a lot to be observed. In chapter 37, the real Clement relates his doctrine to the example of the soldiers in terms of obedience and order, and he calls the secular ἡγούμενοι "our leaders" (113 [17]): κατανοήσωμεν τοὺς στρατευομένους τοῖς ἡγουμένοις ἡμῶν, πῶς εὐτάκτως κτλ (37.2). All of the other three witnesses offer the reading ἡμῶν, but L omits it. No one would contend that this is a coincidence, since 1 Clem 60.2 (179 [8]) also omits ἡμῶν in connection with ἄρχοντες καὶ ἡγούμενοι. It could not be permitted that "Pope" Clement calls the leaders and rulers "his" leaders. The insertion of *vos* in 1 Clem 63.1 (183 [13]) is probably also tendentious. In the foundational text, Clement says, "we should bend the neck and be obedient"; however, L writes, "you should." However, he then continues in the purpose clause with the first person plural. Nevertheless, it is not probable to assume that this is a scribal error, after all that has already been detailed. Similarly, this will be judged to be the case for the missing ὑμῶν καί in 1 Clem 63.3 (185 [11]). The translation in 1 Clem 21.6 (77 [8f]) is also striking: ἐντραπῶμεν τοὺς προηγουμένους ἡμῶν = *vereamur eos qui pro nobis sunt*. But it may be harmless and ancient.[25] Finally, there is still a mystery in the idiosyncratic reproduction of ὁ δεσπότης with *pater familias* (so only in 1 Clem 40, that is, in the cultic section, otherwise countless times correctly translated by *dominus, dominator, deus*). I cannot completely suppress the suspicion that this is to mean the pope; but this cannot be proven. The possibility must remain that the translator found in his *Vorlage* οἰκοδεσπότης instead of δεσπότης, which is present in all other witnesses.[26] The question is, on whose account are these corrections to be made, on those of the scribe of the Greek *Vorlage*, or of an older copyist, or of the one who wrote our manuscript? The first two can easily be excluded, for (1) tendentious

---

25. Furthermore, both the strange treatment of the phoenix story in 1 Clem 25 (the translator, anxiously concerned about the real resurrection, does not allow a new bird to emerge, but the old one to renew itself), and the eradication of the "worlds behind the Ocean," of which the real Clement spoke (1 Clem 20.8 [73 (5)]), are to be regarded as an ancient correction. This idea has also been objectionable to others for dogmatic reasons. The translator has written *omnis orbis terrarum*. One could think of a tendency when, in the *inscriptio*, L writes simply *ecclesia consistens Romae* instead of ἡ ἐκκλησία ἡ παροικοῦσα Ῥώμην. See, however, the ancient Latin translation of the *Epistle of Polycarp*.

26. I know nothing to begin with the incomprehensible sentence (it may at the same time be regarded as an example of the barbarisms of translation) in 1 Clem 41.2 (126 [2f]): *sed contra aedem iuxta altarium prolatione expiator illud quod offertur pro pontifice et illarum predictorum ministrorum* = ἀλλ' ἔμπροσθεν τοῦ ναοῦ πρὸς τὸ θυσιαστήριον, μωμοσκοπηθὲν τὸ προσφερόμενον διὰ τοῦ ἀρχιερέως καὶ τῶν προειρημένων λειτουργῶν. Thus, we must ask, Did the translator speak of the order of the monks when he translated ἐνάρετος βίος in 1 Clem 62.1 (181 [16]) with *perpetua vita*? The context makes it probable.

APPENDIX I: THE RECENTLY DISCOVERED LATIN TRANSLATION   119

corrections of this kind have never been made in the second century, and (2) the disorder in which the clauses in 1 Clem 61 have fallen demonstrate that a Latin original has subsequently been corrected. But even the final copyist is most likely to be ruled out. As the facsimile shows, he smoothly copied a text before him.

Therefore, we assume that the tendentious corrections took place in the time between the original of the translation and our copy. But we can go one step further. Before Pseudoisidor, to our knowledge, forgeries that amount to all kings and princes being subject to the pope and his priests were not known. Thus, the forgery could not have come earlier than the middle of the ninth century. But it also could be later: It could belong to the time of the movement of *Cluniac* reforms and the Gregorian disputes and forgeries.

We must go into the provenance of the manuscript in more detail here. It is written in the eleventh century (the beginning of the twelfth probably cannot be excluded) and, according to Morin's statement *in fronte*, it bears the inscription *Liber Santi Johannis Baptiste Florinensis Cenobii*. The Florennes monastery, located in the dioceses of Liège (but not much further from Cambrai than from Liège), was founded by Gerhard I, originally the Domherr in Reim, then by 1012–1049 Bishop of Cambrai, and placed under the direction of the famous Abbot Richard of Verdun. On this influential personality, H. H. Wattenbach and Giesebrecht make the following remarks:

> He was educated in Reim as a secular clergyman, but was so taken by a monastic spirit that he entered the monastery of St. Vannes (S. Vitoni) in Verdun, where under the Abbey Fingan, seven Scottish monks of loose connection live. In vain, he attempted to imbue his ideas here, and therefore he went to Cluny, to the Abbey of Odilo. After some time, however, the latter sent him back to his monastery. After Fingan's death in 1004, he himself inherited the responsibilities of the abbey, and began by first reforming it. Then, he gradually reformed twenty other monasteries in Lorraine and France, which were subordinated to him. Until his death in 1046, he was held in high esteem. Emperor Henry III, who took care of the monastery reform himself, praised him very much and no less the King of France. It is easy to see that such an esteemed man also had to exercise a significant political influence. Just as the abbots of Cluny mediated between the pope and the emperor on the noblest stage, so also the abbots of Cluny were often able to bring about

the preservation or establishment of peace in the countryside through their personal prestige rather than through external means.[27]

Richard had also been to the Holy Land.[28] The fact that these *Cluniac* minded abbots were also intent on procuring books for their monasteries is illustrated by the example of Abbot Olbert von Gembloux (1012–1048), an admirer of Richard and one who was like-minded. Sigebert notes about him that he had taken care of the library like a second Philadelphus and had brought together one hundred volumes with spiritual content and fifty volumes of secular content. The unified ecclesiastical and political importance of the pioneers of strict monastic discipline in Lorraine, who were closely associated with Cluny and Dijon, their influence on central and northern Germany, and the no less hostile but *Cluniac* attitude of a man like Wago of Liège are well known.[29]

If our manuscript originates from the eleventh century, then it goes back to the beginnings of the Florennes monastery. But even more, its content suggests that either the manuscript itself or its nearest *Vorlage* is directly related to Richard of Verdun. The manuscript contains (1) the so-called Clementines, that is, the Pseudoclementine writings (Recognitions and the Letter to James), then (2) the real 1 Clement, and thereby presents itself as a *Corpus Clementinum*, but then it contains—by the same hand—(3) *Libellus Bedan presbiteri de locis sanctis quem de opusculis maiorum adbreviando composuit*, then (4) by another hand the well-known *Passiv S. Longini (militis centurions)*. Both pieces refer to Palestine, respectively to the holy sites and the holy history. We do know that Richard made a journey to the holy land. After this, it may be considered probable, which is probable in any case, that at his behest our manuscript or its nearest *Vorlage* was written or compiled. In the preface of his edition of the Pseudoclementine homilies, de Lagarde gave important hints as to how interest in the Roman "Pope" Clement I increased in the early Middle Ages due to the widely read Recognitions. The best proof of this is that Suitger von Bamberg, who ascended the papal throne after the Synod of Sutri in 1046, called himself Clement II. It must have been primarily the Cluniacs who—due to the Pseudoisidoric letters—were particularly interesting for the most ancient papal history and

---

27. Wattenbach, *Deutschlands Geschichtsquellen*, 2:104f. On Richard's students, see 104f.

28. The fact that he did not bring 1 Clement (Greek) to Lorraine from there does not need to be proven first; see what has been noticed above about the age of the Latin translation.

29. On the School of Liège, see Wattenbach, *Deutschlands Geschichtsquellen*, 1:305ff.

kept alive the (forged) memory of it. The names that the Cluniac and Gregorian oriented popes have taken for themselves since the middle of the eleventh century is the most significant evidence of this. Our manuscript, or its nearest *Vorlage*, is, if it was written at Richard of Verdun's behest, older than Clement II's ascension to the throne; for Richard himself died in 1046. So, it belongs to the series of apparitions that explain how Suitger came to name himself after the ancient, Roman Clement.

But from where did Richard obtain the real 1 Clement? That seems like a hopeless question, and yet we are not completely helpless against it. Junius, the editor of the *editio princeps* of the Greek 1 Clement (Oxford, 1633), writes in his Προσημείωσις (p. 3) that he hopes that the old Latin translation of the letter will be discovered again (he himself mistakenly believed that Hieronymus had written one): *spem (enim) nobis facit catalogus codicum Fratrum Lobiensium, quem domi habemus, scriptum ante 400 annos, ad calcem operum Fulgentii*. Junius read in a catalog attached to the *Opera Fulgentii*[30] of the Monastery of Lobbes, written in the thirteenth century, that in the monastery library there is the real letter of 1 Clement. Now, the Monastery of Lobbes is close to the Monastery of Florennes and was donated during the lifetime of King Pippin.[31] The assumption is therefore not far away that in the old famous Lobbes, a copy of the ancient Latin translation of 1 Clement has been preserved and that our manuscript flowed from it. However, one must wait to see if this copy of Lobbes does not come to light.[32] The ancient monastery could also have taken a copy of a manuscript of the younger monastery. In any case, we may regard it as a fact that there were two copies of our letter in the Middle Ages in that region, and that Junius was not mistaken. But then, it is probable that, where there were two exemplars, several more might have been copied. For the copies of the Pseudoclementinian Recognitions with which our letter is related in the manuscript of Florennes are exceedingly numerous. Especially the Northern French and Belgian manuscripts of the Recognitions from the dioceses of Cambray, Reims, and Liège will have to be examined, and the hope cannot be given up that we will find a second copy of the

30. Most likely, the *Opera* of Fabius Planciades Fulgentius are meant. Of the *Expositio sermonum antiquorum*, 9172 and 10083 copies can be found in Bruxell. Sigebert of Gembloux proved the *Expositio* to be known. Perhaps T. Gottleib, who has a copy of the Lobbes catalog according to his message (*Über mittelalt. Bibl.*, 280) can offer an explanation.

31. See Hauck, *Kirchengeschichte Deutschlands*, 1:281; Wattenbach, *Deutschlands Geschichtsquellen*, 1:108. On the significance of the monastery, see *Deutschlands Geschichtsquellen*, 1:11.

32. Of course, according to Gottlieb, among others, by far the greatest part of the old library was destroyed by fire.

translation. Finally, as to whether the Florennes forgeries come from the ninth or the eleventh century, whether they are Pseudoisidorian or Gregorian, I must refrain from making a decision. The time of Pseudoisidor is especially to be considered; but it could have also arisen at the end of the eleventh (beginning of the twelfth) century. In this case, our copy would not be the one made by Richard of Verdun, but a copy of it, and both he and his agents are innocent of the forgery. But a forgery from the first half of the eleventh century is hard to imagine.

I cannot conclude without congratulating Morin on his discovery and to express the best thanks for his edition of the same.

Appendix II

New Studies on the Recently Discovered Latin Translation of 1 Clement

1894

I.

CONCERNING LOBBES'S CATALOG, WHICH I mentioned in the session report from March 8, 1894, I can now provide information. This catalog, which Junius (1633) viewed, still exists, and Mr. Omont has edited it in the *Revue des Bibliothèques* (1891) 2:3–14. It is dated to 1059 CE bears the inscription, "*Anno dominicae incarnationis IXLVIIII. fratres Lobienses suum recensentes armarium hanc sibi reppererunt haberi summam librorum*"; is, as Junius correctly stated, "*ad calcem operum Fulgentii*" (not Fabius Planciades Fulgentius, but rather of Ruspe), that is, in a manuscript of Fulgentius that was once in Lobbes; and is now in London (British Royal Library 6AV). This manuscript is described in the catalog by Casley (1734) and notes that the ancient catalog (fol. 120ᵛ–124) is from the same hand that copied the preceding *Opp. Fulgentii*. A facsimile of the first page of the catalog has been published by the Palaeographical Society (I tab. 61).[1]

The numbering (147) system originated from Omont. He begins a new number where a new line begins in the manuscript. Obviously, the writer proceeded arbitrarily. Sometimes, he began a new line after a piece, sometimes he registered several pieces continuously without a new line, indeed

1. As far as we know, only this manuscript of the state library owned by the Lobbes Monastery in 1049 CE has been preserved for us (although Mr. Omont points out that the Bruxell. 14923 may be identical with #129 of the ancient catalog). Most of it was destroyed by a great fire in 1546. It is the most fortunate coincidence that the whole catalog of the library was listed in the preserved manuscript, or rather, this manuscript was probably kept in a special place for the catalog's sake and thereby escaped the fire.

even several volumes. There is often information about the volumes, and this is of course of importance. Unfortunately, however, it is not generally clear which pieces constitute an individual volume. In some places (partly deliberately, partly for brevity) no information is given.[2] The author of the catalog has put together works with similar content, and therefore did not shy away from making references between volumes. Numbers 1–8 (Omont) contain works of Ambrose; numbers 9–51 works of Augustine; numbers 52–71 works of Hieronymus (along with Gennadius and Isidor), etc.

The section of the catalog of interest to us has the following content: (Number 108 concludes with Isidor Hispal., Etymol.) Number 109 *Ejusdem de astrologia lib. I. vol I. Ejusdem sinonima l. II. Ejusdem de conflictu rationis et animae et de conflictu vitiorum atque virtutum, require in libro Institut. Patrum. Fulgentii episcopi de predestinatione, ad Monimum l. III.*

No. 110: *Contra XI. objectiones Trasamundi regis l. 1, De misterio mediatoris l. I, De immensitate filii dei l. I.*

No. 111: *De sacramento dominicae passionis l. I.*

No. 112: *Ad quendam familiarem epistola I. Ad Galliam ep. I. Ad Probam de virginitate epp. II. Ad Eugipium presb. ep. I. Ad Theodorum senatorem ep. I.*

---

2. Numbers 1–3 (Omont) = 1 vol; 4 = 1 vol.; 5 = 1 vol.; 6–7 = 1; 8 = 3 vols.; 9 = 1; 10 = 3 vols.; 11 = 2 vols.; 12 = 3 vols.; 13 = 1; numbers 14–25 have no volumes listed; 26 = 1; 27^a = 1; 27^b–29 = 1; 30 = 1; 31 and 32 = 1; 33 = 2 vols.; 34 = 1; 35^a = 1; 35^b–36^b = 1; 36^c–39 = 1; 40–43 = 1; 44–46^a = 1; 46$^{b, c}$ = 1; 47–49 = 1; 50 = 1; 51 contains only a referral; 52 and 53 = 1; lines 54–65 have no volumes listed; 66 = 2 vols.; 67 = 1; 68 = 2 vols.; 69^a = 1; 69^b–71 = 1; 72 = 2 vols.; 73 = 1; 74 = 1; 75 = 1; 76 = 2 vols.; 77 = 1; 78–80 = 1; 81 = 1; 82 = 1; 83 = 2 vols.; 84 = 1; 85 = 6 vols.; 86 = 1; 87 = 2 vols.; there are also extensive commentaries by Origen without volume numbers; 88 Origen's Homilies on Jeremiah without the number of volumes; 89 whose Homilies on Ezekiel have volume numbers; 90 = 1; 91 = 4 vols.; 92–106 = 2 vols.; 107 = 3 vols.; 108 = 2 vols.; 109^a = 1; 109$^{b, c}$ without specification, though 109^c is only a reference, specifically to number 128; 109^d–113^b = 1 [here, the catalog is attached]; 113$^{c, d}$ are references, specifically to number 114; 113^e = 1; 113$^{f, g, h, i}$ = 1; 113^k = 1; 113^l–114^d = 1; 114^e–116^a = 1; 116^b–117^a = 1; 117^b–118^e = 1; 118^f–119^c = 1; 119^d–120^b = 1; 1120^c = 1; 120^d = 1; 120^e = 1; 121 = 3 vols.; 112–123^d = 1; 123^e = 1; 124 = 1; 125 = 1; 126 = 3 vols.; 127 = 6 vols.; 128^{a-g} = 1; 128^h = 1; 128^i = 1; 128^k = 1; 128^l–129^b = 1; 129$^{c, d}$ = 1; 129$^{e, f}$ = 1; 129^g = 1; 130 = 2 vols.; 131 = 2 vols.; 132 = 1; 133, 134 = 1; 135 = 1; 136, 137^a = 1; 137^b = 1; 138^a = 1; 138^b = 1; 138$^{c, d}$ = 1; 138^e–140^a = 1; 140$^{b, c}$ = 1; 140^d–141^a = 4 vols.; 141^b = 1; 141^c = 1; 141^d = 1; 142 = 3 vols.; 143 = 1; 144 = 1; 145^{a-d} = 4 vols.; 145^e–146 = 1; 147 is without specification. Therefore, there are 143 volumes that are distinguished in the catalog. But in a number of places, doubt remains as to whether the pieces specified really are in one volume while in other cases one is amazed that such small works would have formed their own volumes. In any case, the library consisted of more than 160 volumes of manuscripts. It included translations of works of Origen, Basil, Gregory of Nazianzus, Chrysostom, Dionysius of Areopagite, as well as the works of some classical authors (e.g., Seneca, Eutropius, etc.), and finally an exemplar of *Lex Salica*.

No. 113: *Ad Venantiam ep. I. Absque litteris lib. XIIII. vol. I. Ejusdem de remissione peccatorum. Ejusdem de quinque quaestionibus Ferrandi diaconi, require in libro Ticonii de septem regulis. Clementis papae historiarum libri X, a Rufino translati, vol. I. Ejusdem epistola ad Corinthios. Cipriani expositio in orationem dominicam. Cassiodori senatoris de anima l. I. Enchiridion Syxti martyris vol. I. Cirilli archiepiscopi de Aepheseno concilio vol. I. Ejusdem de incarnatione unigeniti l. I.*

According to this list, it must be considered probable that a new volume begins at *Fulgentii ep. de praedestinatione*. Before this, there is a reference that refers to No. 128, and even further back it says *Ejusdem (Isidori) de astrologia lib. I. vol. I*. Here, therefore, the volume is concluded. The only consideration that must remain doubtful is where the title *Ejusdem sinonima l. II.* belongs, or whether the work constitutes its own volume.

But how far did the volume that began with the text of Fulgentius's *de praedestinatione* extend? It is highly probable that it extended to No. 113^b because it is not until there that one first finds the note "*vol. I.*" This is followed by another double reference, for "*require*" refers to both texts (No. 113$^{c,\,d}$), which is proven by the following No. 114, where both texts are listed. Therefore, the Recognitions of Clement of Rome formed a special volume (No. 113^e). The next volume, however, consisted of four pieces:

No. 113^f *Ep. Clementis ad Corinthios.*

No. 113^g *Cypriani expositio in orationem dominicam.*

No. 113^h *Cassiodori senatoris de anima l. I.*

No. 113^i *Enchiridion Sixti martyris.*

After these four pieces, we finally encounter the note "*vol. I.*"

The details concerning the pieces, as they are put together in various volumes, is in fact partly confirmed by the London Codex Lobiensis. It begins in fact with *Fulgentius de praedestinatione*, consists of—according to the precise description of Casley—all the pieces up until No. 113^b, concludes with this piece (*Absque litteris l. XIIII*), and contains the catalog on the remaining free leaves (fol. 120^v–124). So what was in any case the most likely scenario is confirmed by the still extant Codex Brit. Mus. 6AV: the volumes close where *vol.* stands.

Now then, there is no doubt about the fact that the exemplar of 1 Clement in Lobbes's manuscript was not handed down behind the manuscript of the *Recognitions*. It can be asserted, though not with the same degree of confidence, that 1 Clement stood at the head of the three other pieces (No. 113^{g-i}) mentioned above, united within a single volume. The cause of uncertainty is the fact that, as noted previously, the author of the catalog omitted information about the volumes in some places. It can only be assumed that they existed together because (1) it is not likely that the small letter of 1 Clement formed its own "volume" and it is not noted in the catalog as forming its own volume, and (2) the information about the volumes in section No. 108ff. is very brief.

If we therefore follow the not insignificant probability that those four writings stood together in the Lobbes manuscript, several important observations emerge:

(1) The possibility that the Florennes manuscript was the same as the Lobbes manuscript itself has now been excluded. One could have come to that conclusion when superficially looking at the catalog. One might assume that the first half of the Codex, comprised of the works of Fulgentius, had been preserved, while the second half, containing the Recognitions and the letter, had been moved to Florennes and from there to Namur. The comparison of the manuscripts (see the facsimile by Morin and the notice board of the Paleographical Society), can only provide a negative result, and the formats would not have allowed for a confident conclusion. Only the different position decides the matter.

(2) It is improbable that the Lobbes manuscript was taken from the Florennes manuscript. It cannot be foreseen why, in Lobbes, the natural connection between the Recognitions and the letter should have been dissolved, if the *Vorlage* offered such a connection, in order to reconnect it in the manner in which we find it in the catalog.

(3) Conversely, however, there is nothing to be said against the idea that the Florennes manuscript was not taken from the Lobbes manuscript. But there is nothing in particular that can be said about it either, except for the observation that in Florennes the connection between Recognitions and the letter, which the Lobbes catalog has made (because its author put together what belongs together), was now also carried out in a manuscript.

(4) The sequence *Ep. Clementis ad Corinthios* and *Cypriani expositio in orationem dominicam* is instructive because it provides an indication of its later estimation and the use of the letter in the Western Church. Cyprian's tractate on the Lord's Prayer is one of the oldest devotional works in the Western Church, and therein Cyprian's reputation, before Augustine, was second only to the Bible. Nevertheless, Clement's letter is not attached to Cyprian's work, but precedes it.[3] Also, the connection with Rufinus's translation of the Sentences of Sextus, that is the Sentences attributed to Sextus the Pope and martyr, does not need to be viewed as odd. On the other hand, I cannot

---

3. If our letter was not or no longer connected to the NT in the West, the connection with a Cyprian work was the highest estimation that could be given to it.

explain its compilation with Cassidor's tractate. I suspect, therefore, that only the connection with Cyprian's work is important. The other was added later; but that connection may very well belong to the fourth century.

After the sad fate experienced by the Lobbes library, it is difficult to hold on any longer to the hope of discovering the manuscript contained therein. But it is important to know that there were at least two Latin manuscripts of 1 Clement in Belgian monasteries, and that the letter, before it was connected with Rufinus's Recognitions, had been connected with a tractate of Cyprian's.

II.

Sanday demonstrated in the journal "The Guardian" (March 28, 1894) that the recently discovered Latin translation of 1 Clement was probably used by Ambrose:

Ep. Clem. 25.1[4]

Ἴδωμεν τὸ παράδοξον σημεῖον, τὸ γινόμενον ἐν τοῖς ἀνατολικοῖς τόποις, τουτέστιν τοῖς περὶ τὴν Ἀραβίαν. ὄρνεον γάρ ἐστιν ὃ προσονομάζεται φοῖνιξ· τοῦτο μονογενὲς ὑπάρχον ζῇ ἔτη πεντακόσια· γενόμενόν τε [δὲ HS] ἤδη πρὸς ἀπόλυσιν τοῦ ἀποθανεῖν αὐτό, σηκὸν ἑαυτῷ ποιεῖ ἐκ λιβάνου καὶ σμύρνης καὶ τῶν λοιπῶν ἀρωμάτων, εἰς ὃν πληρωθέντος τοῦ χρόνου [vitae suae + S] εἰσέρχεται καὶ τελευτᾷ [in illo + S]. σηπομένης δὲ [τε H] τῆς σαρκὸς σκώληξ τις γεννᾶται [ἐγγεννᾶται HS, + illic S], ὃς [ὅστις S] ἐκ τῆς ἰκμάδος τοῦ τετελευτηκότος ζώου ἀνατρεφόμενος πτεροφυεῖ·

Interpret. Vet. Lat.

Videamus et hanc rem miram, quae fit in regione orientis, in loco Arabiae. avis enim, quae vocatur fenix, et est unica, haec vivit annis D. quaecum appropiaverit finis mortis eius, facit sibi thecam de ture et myrra et ceteris odoribus, et impletum scit esse sibi tempus vitae, ibi intrat et moritur. et de umore carnis eius nascitur vermis, qui ibi enutritur, et tempore suo fit pinnatus in avem qualis ante fuerat.

Ambrose, Hex. V.23

Phoenix quoque avis in locis Arabiae perhibetur degere, atque ea usque ad annos D. langaeva aetate procedere. quae cum sibi

---

4. S = Syriac translation; H = Codex Hierosolymitanus (Constantinople).

> *finem vitae adesse adverterit, facit sibi thecamde thure et myrrha et ceteris odoribus, in quam, impleto vitae suae tempore, intrat et moritur. de cuius umore carnis vermis exsurgit paulatimque adolescit, ac processu statuti temporis induit alarum remigia atque in superioris avis speciem formamque reparatur.*

The fact that Ambrose also knew the foundational text may be inferred from *in quam* = εἰς ὅν, which is not present in the Vet. Lat. Only the conclusion is in itself uncertain and it becomes even more so if one assumes with Morin that the text in L (Vet. Lat.) is corrupt here.[5] However, the fact that Ambrose—whether he knew the foundational text or not—used L is not only probable, it is a necessary assumption. Of course, *in locis (loco) Arabiae* could be coincidental; *quae cum* could be coincidental; it could also be a coincidence that Ambrose knew of a Greek text in which τῆς ζωῆς αὐτοῦ was written after τοῦ χρόνου. But what cannot be a coincidence is (1) that ἀπόλυσις is translated as *finis*, (2) that, although in different places, both note that the bird foresees its end, and (3) that *facit sibi thecam* (σηκὸν ἑαυτῷ ποιεῖ) and the almost literally identical clause up to *moritur* are present. However, the following considerations are decisive: (a) both leave out the words τις up to σκώληξ, (b) both reproduce σηπομένης τῆς σαρκὸς ... ἐκ τῆς ἰκμάδος simply with *de [cuius] umore carnis [eius]*, (c) both have *tempore suo* (or *processu statuti temporis*), (d) both finally say that a retransformation takes place with *in avem qualis ante fuerat, in superioris avis speciem formamque*, respectively. Regardless of whether one of these expressions is stronger than the other, neither were offered within the original text. The original text speaks of a "dead" bird. L avoided this expression, as did Ambrose. Accordingly, I view it as an inevitable assumption that Ambrose had L in front of him and did not reproduce it word for word.

There are two other passages in the works of Ambrose that mention the phoenix. One of these (Expos. in Psalm. CXVII, sermo 19 c. 13) is not useful for our purposes; though the other one (*de fide resurr.* 59) is of significance.

> *Avis in regione Arabiae, cui nomen est Phoenix, redivivo suae carnis umore reparabilis, cum mortua fuerit reviviscit; solos non credimus homines resuscitari? atqui hoc relatione crebra et scripturarum auctoritate cognovimus, memoratam avem D. annorum spatia vitalis usus habere praescripta, eamque cum sibi finem vitae adesse praesaga quadam naturae suae aestimatione cognoverit, thecam sibi de thure et myrrha et ceteris odoribus*

---

5. *Exsurgit* in Ambrose is probably only a free reproduction of *nascitur* and has nothing to do with the variant ἐγγεννᾶται (HS).

adornare, completoque opere pariter ac tempore intrare illo atque emori. ex cuius umore oriri vermem paulatimque eum in avis eiusdem figuram concrescere usumque formari, subnixam quoque remigio pennarum, renovatae vitae officia munere pietatis ordiri. nam thecam illam vel tumulum corporis vel incunabulum resurgentis, in qua deficiens occidit et occidens resurgit, ex Aethiopia in Lycaoniam vehit, atque ita resurrectione avis huius locorum incolae completum D. annorum tempus intelligunt . . . plerique etiam opinantur quod avis haec rogum sibi ipsa succendat, et rursus de favillis suis et cineribus reviviscat.

It is obvious that this passage, in which Ambrose is also dependent on other legends about the phoenix, is under the influence of 1 Clem 25, and here again the Latin translation comes into consideration, as the above cited text proves.[6] The clause *thecam illam vel tumulum corporis* offers a paricularly clear proof. The original text here reads τὸν σηκὸν ἐκεῖνον ὅπου τὰ ὀστᾶ τοῦ προγεγονότος ἐστίν, and therefore does not contain the word σῶμα. L, however, offers the reading *thecam illam, in qua ossa prioris corporis illius sunt*. What is particularly striking is that Ambrose writes *ex Aethiopia in Lycaoniam*. The original text offers the reading ἐκ τῆς Ἀραβικῆς χώρας ἕως τῆς Αἰγύπτου εἰς τὴν λεγομένην Ἡλιούπολιν; L reads *e regione Arabiae usque in Aegiptum, in colonia(m) quae vocatur Solis civitas*. The unsubstantiated *in Lycaoniam* cannot be explained from the original text, but probably from the Latin version. It seems to have originated from *colonia*, which the Latin version offers. Perhaps Ambrose used a copy in which the words *in Aegiptum* and *quae vocatur Solis civitas* were illegible and the scribe conjectured *colonia* from the partly legible *Lycaonia*, perhaps our text of Ambrose is corrupted, and *colonia* has been used instead of *Lycaonia*. Whatever the mistake may be, *colonia* of the Latin text perhaps offers an explanation for its origin, while the original text leaves an explanation missing. It is tempting to interpret Ambrose's expression *scripturarum auctoritas*, which refers (at least) to our letter in a concise sense and to conclude accordingly that Ambrose attached a canonical or quasi-canonical prestige to the letter. The mere contrast between *crebra relatio* and *scripturarum auctoritas* makes it much more probable, if not certain, that this expression is to be understood only as the authority of written testimonies as distinct from mere oral tradition.[7] Ambrose's testimo-

---

6. One can conclude from *ex cuius umore oriri vermem* that no weight is to be placed on *exsurgit* in the passage from Hexaem. V.23 (L *nascitur*); see above. *in avis eiusdem figuram concrescere* does not correspond exactly with *ris avis speciem formamque reparatur* nor with *in avem qualis ante fuerat* and can only be explained from the latter and not from the original text.

7. Irenaeus (III.3.3) also calls 1 Clement *scriptura*. But here, too, one does not need

ny that 1 Clement enjoyed canonical or quasi-canonical prestige somewhere in the West in the fourth century was entirely isolated.

The citations by Ambrose prove that the Latin translation given to us again was available before the last third of the fourth century.[8] In addition, though, there is external evidence that pushes us further.

Lactantius's poem *de phoenice*, whose authenticity in my opinion does not seem to be shaken, has several points of connection. In most of these cases, it cannot be determined whether the Greek or the Latin text of the letter was used. But there are three passages that demonstrate Lactantius's use of our Latin translation:

I.

Greek: σκώληξ

Latin: *vermis tempore suo fit in avem qualis ante fuerat.*

Lactantius (v. 102): *vermis emenso sopitur tempore certo . . . (105) inde reformatur qualis fuit ante figura.*

II.

Greek: τὰ ὀστᾶ τοῦ προγεγεονότος

Latin: *ossa prioris corporis illius.*

Lactantius (v. 117f): *quidquid de corpore restat ossaque.*

III.

Greek: ταῦτα (scil. τὰ ὀστᾶ) βαστάζων διανύει . . . εἰς τὴν λεγομένην Ἡλιούπολιν καὶ . . . ἐπιπτὰς ἐπὶ τὸν τοῦ Ἡλίου βωμὸν τίθησιν αὐτά.

Latin: *portat illiam (scil. thecam, in qua ossa insunt) . . . in colonia quae vocatur Solis civitas, et . . . advolat et consedet super aram solis et ibi ponit eam.*

Lactantius (v. 121f): *portat illam (scil. formam, in quam ossa etc. conglobavit) gestans contendit Solis ad urbem inque ara residens ponit*[9] *in aede sacra.*

---

to understand the word in a constrictive sense. In our passage, the plural *scripturae* does not in itself exclude the interpretation of 1 Clement as Holy Scripture, but rather probably does not do so because it is obvious that Ambrose did not think at all of a single writing here, but of several, among which our letter stood at the head.

8. If Ambrose became aware of the letter from the comments by Origen or another Greek author, his dependence not on the original text but on the Latin translation testifies that he himself had the Latin version of the letter in his hands.

9. All the editions offer this reading. Only H. Brandt gives the reading *promit* according to the manuscript, but even he doubts the correctness of this reading. In my opinion, one may confidently correct the reading in accordance with L, which even

Lactantius's text can only be explained on the basis of L in these three passages. In v. 102ff, Lactantius offers the addition about which the Greek and the Syriac text know nothing, but which L contains. In v. 117f, *corpus* is a peculiarity of the Latin text. In v. 121f, the fact it "settles" on the altar is also peculiar to the Latin text.[10] The assumption that our translation is dependent on the poem would likely not be supported by anyone. Thus, we can assume that Lactantius read our letter in the Latin translation that has been passed down to us,[11] and that this translation therefore already existed at the end of the third century.

As far as I can see, the external evidence does not lead us any further back, for even if Tertullian *de resurr.* 12, 13 is dependent upon 1 Clem 24, 25, it is not possible to determine whether the original text or the Latin translation is the basis.

III.

The question of the age and origin of the Latin translation of 1 Clement is of great significance in four regards: (1) for the history of the letter itself, (2) for the history of the New Testament canon, (3) for the history of the Latin translations of the Bible, (4) for the history of the Latin language, especially of vulgar Latin. In my preliminary report,[12] I spoke out in favor of the second century ("more in favor of the first half than in the second") and with this estimate I joined with Morin, the editor. Von Gebhardt is of the same opinion,[13] and Hilgenfeld seems to agree with this opinion.[14] Von Wölffin attempts to show that the translation belongs to the time of Tertullian;[15]

---

makes a contribution to the text-critical problems in Lactantius. A confusion of *pomens* and *promens* is also found in Pseudo-Tertullian *adv. omn. haer.* 14 (Oehlfr o. 1170, 9). See Kunze, *De Historiae Gnosticismi Fontibus*, 62.

10. An involuntary reminiscence of 2 Thess 2:4 is probably not present, although in L there are some strange influences from the New Testament texts. For example, in 1 Clem 7.2 ἔλθωμεν ἐπὶ τὸν εὐκλεῆ καὶ σεμνὸν τῆς παραδόσεως ἡμῶν κανόνα is reproduced in L, under the influence of Rom 6:17 (εἰς ὃν παρεδόθητε τύπον διδαχῆς), by *veniamus ad exornatum et sanctum doctrinae exemplum.*

11. That Lactantius knew the original (Greek) text on the basis of its reading *contendit* = διανύει, which is absent in L, is in my opinion a weak argument, especially since it does not reproduce ἐπιπτάς.

12. Harnack, "Über die jüngst entdeckte lateinische Übersetzung," 262. Translated in this volume under the title "The Recently Discovered Latin Translation of 1 Clement," 109–122.

13. Gebhardt, "Review of 'Germain Morin,'" 545–47.

14. Hilgenfeld, "Review of 'Germain Morin,'" 425–29.

15. Wölffin, "Die lateinische Übersetzung," 9:81ff.

Haussleiter counts it among the oldest Latin translations, though without any further specification. Sanday alone considers such approaches to be too early or too precise and recommends the provisional timeframe of 200–350. "For ourselves," he writes, "we do not think that the version falls within the second century. The limits we should be inclined to propose for it would be 200–350 CE. Further investigation might enable us to draw these somewhat closer." Zahn goes even further in an article in the *Theologische Literaturblatt*.[16] He claims that the translation could very well have been written in the fifth century. Only, he has provided no basis for this late estimation—one has to take his attempt to discredit the value of the translation as a reason—and his assumption was already disproved when he pronounced it, since Sanday had already proven the use of the translation by Ambrose four weeks earlier. However, Sanday's estimation is no longer correct. Since Lactantius already knew the translation, the first half of the fourth century also falls away as the timeframe for the translation. The question can only be whether our translation is from the third or the second century.

The attempt is to answer this question on the basis of the biblical passages quoted in the letter (in its relationship to the remains of the Old Latin Bible that we possess) and the linguistic character of the translation. Also, von Wölfflin, Haussleiter, and Sanday have already begun investigations in this direction. What is certain is that the biblical citations do not yet show any influence on the part of the Vulgate, and that they partly deviate considerably from Cyprian's Bible, and partly agree with it. It is probable that they contain a European and not the ancient African text. But whether this text is older or younger than Cyprian will not be easy to determine.[17] The chronology of the remains of the Old Latin Bible, although we have a fixed point in Cyprian's quotations, is still so much in the dark that from here it is difficult to find a reliable answer to the question of the age of the translation of 1 Clement. Even such an excellent expert of vulgar Latin as von Wölfflin has so far only been able to produce probabilities,[18] indeed it is questionable whether his observations can be described as such. When he remarks that according to Tertullian one must expect that the translator would have rendered διαθήκη with *ostensio* (not by *testamentum*), if his translation had been made around 150, Zahn has already refuted the misunderstanding that according to Tertullian *testamentum* is a younger translation of the

---

16. Zahn, "Review of 'Germain Morin,'" 197–200.

17. Even if it can be established that the biblical text available in the translation is closer to that used by Augustine than to Cyprian's, nothing has yet been decided about its age.

18. Wölfflin, "Die lateinische Übersetzung," 97f.

word διαθήκη.[19] If he considers the time before ca. 200 to be excluded because of the "unabashed appearance" of the words *salvier* and *salvator* in the translation, because Tertullian was still very reserved with the use of these words (this is also the judgment of Haussleiter), it can be objected that Tertullian was reserved with regard to the use of some words which did not yet have citizenship in scriptural Latin. If he notices that the resolution of the *Accus. cum. inf.* with *quoniam* after *Verbis dicendi et sentiendi* speaks against the second century, since Tertullian first used this form and only twice in biblical citations (in our letter, it occurs three times), then one could argue the reverse: In the Latin Bible, written in vulgar Latin, the *quoniam* already existed before Tertullian, but Tertullian himself did not yet want to use it, while in the vulgar (biblical) language, written pieces, such as our letter, already offered it. No certainty can be obtained here, not even about the place of origin of our translation. While Haussleiter, a student of von Wölfflin's, wants to conclude the translation is of an African origin, von Wölfflin himself does not consider the proof to have been furnished. Sanday also doubts it, and Zahn finds no reason to dispute the assumption that the translation was made in Italy or Gaul.

So if, for objective reasons, it is not possible to determine the time and place of the writing of the translation, we will at best have to wait a very long time until it has been established from the biblical citations and the translation's linguistic character. There is at least no lack of objective reasons for the decisive questions. I have already hinted at it in my preliminary report[20] and will elaborate on it here because of the importance of the matter. If they prove to be sufficient, a great deal is gained. For in the translation of 1 Clement we then have a secure basis and a starting point for the evaluation of the other Old Latin translations whose age and origin are still doubtful.

1. In the three manuscripts A (Alexandrinus), H (Hierosolymitanus/Constantinople), and S (Syriac), our letter has been connected with a fake, so-called 2 Clement, and this connection is also testified to by the Church Fathers from Eusebius onwards. Directly, however, it cannot be shown that the compilation already belongs to the second century—for we do not possess any quotation today nor any certain allusion to 2 Clement before Eusebius's time—but indirectly it can be shown very likely to have been carried out already at that time.

Lightfoot, in his edition of the letter,[21] has provided good reasons why the archetype of AHS should not be set later or not much later than the end of

---

19. Zahn, *Geschichte des neutestamentlichen Kanons*, 1:52.
20. Harnack, "Über die jüngst entdeckte lateinische Übersetzung," 262ff (109-122).
21. Lightfoot, *Clement of Rome*, 2:116-47.

the second century. In this archetype, however, our letter and the so-called 2 Clement were already connected, and this connection has not been dissolved later, as far as we know. In L, however, the real letter still stands alone.[22] In addition to the text-critical reasons Lightfoot gave, there are also reasons from the history of the canon. The fact that the second letter has gained a canonical or quasi-canonical reputation has, according to all probability, not only taken place in the third but already in the second century.[23] But it only gained this status by being attached to 1 Clement. So this assignment, which L does not yet presuppose, belongs to the second century.[24]

2. We only owe the preservation of 1 Clement (in the original and in the Syriac translation) to the New Testament, for it was copied because of its connection with the New Testament.[25] That 1 Clement was numbered among the New Testament writings has its origin in the second century. Already at the beginning of the third century, the reputation of the letter in the Greek churches had already weakened in extent and intensity. The fact that the letter is in the biblical codex A (fifth century) is to be judged to be a relic of an older order. This is already true of Eusebius's judgment (although he held the letter in high esteem and also testifies to its general acceptance in antiquity) and Athanasius cut every connection 1 Clement had with the New Testament. Should the Latin translation of 1 Clement have been produced quite

---

22. Also a certain Johannes Diaconus Romanus (sixth century?), who uses a Latin quotation from our letter (Pitra, *Spicil.*, 1:293), also seems to know only of one letter. For he introduces the quotation with the words *In epistola S. Clementis ad Corinthios*. It cannot be proved that he used our translation, but if we consider that Lactantius and Ambrose knew it and that the quotation from Johannes is apparently very free, indeed can only be one cited from memory, it is noticeable that there are quite a few similarities with our translation in these few words. Compare *sciebat, virga, floritura, convocavit, honorabilis, inveniretur* (1 Clem 43). What is important is that this deacon Johannes, who incidentally has not yet been identified with certainty, was in any case a member of the Roman congregation.

23. This assumption is based on an idea of the beginnings of the formation of the New Testament canon, which to my knowledge is not disputed by anyone.

24. Eusebius writes of 2 Clement: Ἰστέον δ' ὡς καὶ Δευτέρα τις εἶναι λέγεται τοῦ Κλήμεντος ἐπιστολή· οὐ μὴν ἔθ' ὁμοίως τῇ προτέρᾳ καὶ ταύτην γνώριμον ἐπιστάμεθα, ὅτι μηδὲ τοὺς ἀρχαίους αὐτῇ κεχρημένους ἴσμεν (*Hist. eccl.* III.38.4.4). These words are not entirely clear. Eusebius says 2 Clement is not (any longer?) as well known as 1 Clement because, as far as he knows, even the ancients did not mention it. One may well conclude from this that Eusebius found the letter in older Bible directories or in older Bibles, but that he himself, in agreement with others, does not wish to acknowledge it any longer because the fathers did not mention it. By the way, one may conclude from *Maximus Confessor Prolog. in Opp. S. Dionysii*, xxxvi, that Origen knew the letter (edited by Corder). The critical doubts of Eusebius did not have the power to separate the second letter from the first. Instead, the letters remained together.

25. Also in Codex H, the letter is contained among the New Testament *Antilegomena*.

independently of the Latin Bible? At first, this seems to be the case because (1) we know absolutely nothing about a canonical or quasi-canonical reputation of our letter in the West and (2) the Latin translation has not been handed down to us like that of the epistle of Barnabas or Hermas, together with one or more biblical books,[26] but rather with Cyprian's treatise *De oratione* or with the pseudo Clementine literature. Nevertheless, it can be argued that the translation is not independent of the Latin Bible. As we have demonstrated above, it dates from the last decades of the third century at the latest. If it were younger, if it belonged to the fourth or the fifth century or even later, there would certainly be no reason to think of the Latin Bible. The most diverse interests could have made the translation desirable.[27] Only a translation of an early Christian document that is older than Lactantius has the prejudice for itself that it is made for church purposes, that is to say, for the purposes of reading aloud in the congregation. The burden of proof is on the one who denies this fact, not on the one who claims it.[28] But if our letter has been translated for the purpose of being read out loud in the congregation, it is more likely that this happened in the second century than in the third. Towards the end of the second century and at the beginning of the third, the Roman Church reduced the stock of its ecclesiastical reading material. At that time, the Apocalypse of Peter, the letter of Barnabas to the Hebrews, and soon also the Shepherd of Hermas fell away. At that time also 1 Clement must have been excluded, and indeed earlier than the Shepherd. The African Church likely continued to accept the Shepherd of Hermas, but not 1 Clement from the Roman Church. Since we now find nothing of an ecclesiastical reputation or use of 1 Clement in the literature of the West that is accessible to us, which begins with Tertullian, and since no Bible or Bible index contains the letter, it makes more sense to assume that it was translated in the second century and soon disappeared from church usage, than to assume that it was sent to the Latin church only in the third century. That assumption also agrees with the findings established in section I, that 1 Clement was translated alone, that is, translated without the so-called 2 Clement. But as far as this is concerned, there is simply nothing at all that speaks for Africa

26. The Latin translation of the epistle of Barnabas has been handed down to us together with the Latin translation of the epistle of James.

27. Also, the letter could have returned from the East to the West along with other writings only at that time.

28. The general linguistic character of the translation is similar to that of the Old Latin Bible and, as far as I can see, does not deviate from it in any way. (What Zahn, "Sancti Clementis," 198, has asserted against it—the translation is supposed to be freer than for the biblical books—does not apply as far as I am aware.) Therefore, Wölfflin was also correct in his description and treatment of the language of the letter as "biblical Latin" ("Die lateinische Übersetzung," 81ff).

as the location of its translation because no trace of its usage has been proven in any African author.[29] The translation first appears in Milan, where we find it used by Ambrose. Where it became known to Lactantius, unfortunately, cannot be said. Then, we find it in the old, Belgian monastery of Lobbes, and then in Florennes. The theory that, if it was made in the second century, it would have been produced in Gaul or Milan, is highly unlikely. The most obvious assumption is that it was translated in Rome itself.[30] I am unaware of any arguments against this assumption.[31]

29. Tertullian mentions Clement as Bishop of Rome (*Praescr.* 32), but not his letter. On the other hand, Irenaeus mentions him in connection with the Roman list of bishops and without mention of 2 Clement. In my treatise "Die ältesten christlichen Datierungen und die Anfänge einer bischöflichen Chronographie in Rom," 617ff, I proved that Irenaeus had obtained the numbered list of bishops from Rome, and that this list also contained brief historical information, including a note about 1 Clement and the Shepherd of Hermas. In Rome, therefore, the letter was so highly esteemed at the time of Bishop Soter (166/7–174/5) that he was mentioned in the catalog alongside the Shepherd (which was certainly one of the early Christian texts read aloud), while nothing was known at all of 2 Clement. If it now turns out that the ancient translation of the Shepherd is internally related to the translation of our own translation, then it is very likely that both texts were translated in Rome and that they were both translated as late as the second century.

30. In the previous note, I pointed out that in Irenaeus, with respect to the oldest catalog of Roman bishops, our letter is mentioned. It is missing in the Catalogus Liberianus, whereas Shepherd is mentioned. On the other hand, in the first edition of the *Liber pontificalis* (Felicias and Cononianus), there is the strange note at "Clement": "*et fecit duas epistolas*" (Duchesne, 1:52, 53). This note has passed into the final edition with the addition "*quae catholicae nominantur*" (Duchesne, 1:123). Lightfoot and I, in our editions of 1 Clement, have related this information to the two pseudo-Clementine epistles; Duchesne relates it to the genuine and the false Corinthian Letters of Clement. In favor of Duchesne's assumption are the following: (1) that in what follows, a pseudo-Clementine letter is spoken of in such a way that it does not seem to be included under the aforementioned *duae epistolae*; (2) that the statement may have flowed from Hieronymus's treatise *De viris illustribus*, which the editor of *Liber pontificalis* also used; (3) that the pseudo-Clementine letters cannot be called *catholicae*. The *quae catholicae nominantur* alone can also, as Duchesne himself admits, be a thoughtless repetition of the indication in the letters of Peter, and from Hieronymus the note does not explain itself well because he repeated Eusebius's unfavorable judgment of 2 Clement. But even if we were to admit that the Corinthian letters are intended here, not much is gained. The mention of two letters makes it probable that the statement is no longer connected with the older one made by Irenaeus, and it does not testify to a present possession of the Roman church, but rather simply reproduces a testimony that comes from the East.

31. One might object, not to the origin of the translation in Rome, but to its use in the worship service there, that the congregation would not have included its own letter among its readings. Certainly a canonical meaning in any sense would never have been attached to it. But such a canonical meaning only developed later for Christian texts. The letter, on the other hand, was particularly suitable for the worship service, and was even made for the purpose of repeated readings because of the congregational prayer at the end of the letter. Furthermore, the following is to be taken into account. Although

3. As a strong argument for the antiquity of the translation, I have said that although the translator already uses the technical term *episcopus*—where God is called ἐπίσκοπος, he uses *visitator* (1 Clem 59.3)—he still uses the term *minister* instead of *diaconus*.[32] Already during Tertullian's time, this expression was no longer in use in Africa. Instead, one would have said *episcopus et diaconi*.[33] Also, in chapter 3 of the Acts of Perpetua and Felicitas, it says *diaconi, qui nobis ministrabant* and in chapters 6 and 10 Pomponius is called a *diaconus*. In the Freising *Italafragmente*,[34] the translation *episcopi et diaconi* is given for Philippians 1:1.[35] In the translation of the Polycarp's epistle, *minister* is only used as a translation when διάκονος is not used in a technical sense, otherwise *diaconus* is used; see Pol. *Phil.* 5: ὁμοίως διάκονοι . . . ὡς θεοῦ καὶ Χριστοῦ διάκνοι = *similiter diaconi . . . sicut dei et Christi ministri*. As far as I know, there is only one parallel to the expression in our letter, namely the two translations of the Shepherd of Hermas, which can be considered to be one here and also offer the reading *episcopi et ministri*. But precisely this ancient translation of Shepherd has the prejudice for itself that it belongs to the second century and comes from Rome. In later Latin translations, of course, the translation *minister* for διάκονος appears more often. But I do not know of any place where the word appears next to *episcopus* in the technical sense. If the technical διάκονος is translated once with

---

the letter begins like an occasional letter, it progresses and develops into a homiletical address that encompasses all the main points of the Christian religion, and even designates itself as such at the end of the letter: Περὶ μὲν τῶν ἀνηκόντων τῇ θρησκείᾳ ἡμῶν, τῶν ὠφελιμωτάτων εἰς ἐνάρετον βίον τοῖς θέλουσιν εὐσεβῶς καὶ δικαίως διευθύνειν, ἱκανῶς ἐπεστείλαμεν ὑμῖν, ἄνδρες ἀδελφοί. περὶ γὰρ πίστεως καὶ μετανοίας καὶ γνησίας ἀγάπης καὶ ἐγκρατείας καὶ σωφροσύνης καὶ ὑπομονῆς πάντα τόπον ἐψηλαφήσαμεν, ὑπομιμνήσκοντες δεῖν ὑμᾶς ἐν δικαιοσύνῃ καὶ ἀληθείᾳ καὶ μακροθυμίᾳ τῷ παντοκράτορι θεῷ ὁσίως εὐαρεστεῖν, ὁμονοοῦντας ἀμνησικάκως ἐν ἀγάπῃ καὶ εἰρήνῃ μετὰ ἐκτενοῦς ἐπιεικείας, καθὼς καὶ οἱ προδεδηλωμένοι πατέρες ἡμῶν εὐηρέστησαν ταπεινοφρονοῦντες (1 Clem 62.1ff). Furthermore, the letter explicitly claims the inspiration of the Holy Spirit (1 Clem 59.1; 63.2). Such a homiletical work (see Wrede, *Untersuchungen*, 55–60), rich in material and at the same time useful as a compendium of the most important contents of the Old Testament, will not have been left unused by the Roman congregation itself for its own edification in subsequent times. After all, it was only formally written to the Corinthian congregation, but in truth it was also in the eyes of Rome the work of the celebrated teacher, Clement.

32. Also, he translates ἐπισκοπή in the three places it occurs with "*episcopatus*" and διακονία like ὑπηρεσία with "*ministerium*." He makes no difference between διάκονος and λειτουργός in his translation. He reproduces θεράπων with both "*servus*" and "*famulus*."

33. See *Bapt.* 17; *Praescr.* 3, 41; *Fug.* 11; *Mon.* 11. Cyprian (*Ep.* 52.1) already offers the word *diaconium*.

34. Ziegler, *Italafragmente*.

35. I know of no Latin translation of the Bible that translates διάκονος in Phil 1:1 with *minister*.

minister, then, to my knowledge, there are always special circumstances for it. If one reads, for example, in the Latin translation of Origen's commentary on Romans: "*Sunt et multi vocati magistri per omnes ecclesias dei, et vocati ministri; sed nescio, qui in his electi magistri sint et electi ministri*,"[36] then everyone is able to see why the word *minister* was chosen and not *diaconus*. Commodianus offered four poems in his *Instruct*. II.26–29 with the headings "*Lectorius—Ministris—Pastoribus—Maioribus natis*." He deliberately chose only Latin terminology and therefore avoided the word *episcopus*. But the poem dedicated to the *ministri* begins with the words "*Mysterium Christi, Zacones, exercite caste, Idcirco ministri facite praecepta magistri*." Thus, *zacones* is a *terminus technicus* for him. It is possible, after all, that someone attests to the use of the language *episcopi et ministri* into the third century. But provided this has not happened, the pre-Tertullian origin of texts that use this expression should be maintained.[37]

Except for *ministri*, I have also referred to the translation of *seniores* for πρεσβύτεροι. The letter offers the translation *seniores* in all places except one, where it translates μετὰ τῶν καθεσταμένων πρεσβυτέρων with *cum constitutis presbiteris* (1 Clem 54.2). Thus, the technical term *presbyteri* was already known to the translator, just as it was known to Tertullian.[38] The subtlety alone, which cannot be attributed to another cause, lies in the fact that he so sharply and correctly distinguishes between "elders" as a position of honor in the communities (*seniores*) and the "elders" as officers in the congregation (*presbyteri*).[39] The old Latin translation of Irenaeus also offers at times the translation *presbyter* and sometimes *senior* (or a synonym). However, one cannot say that the decision for one or the other proceeded consistently according to a determined principle. By way of contrast, both the translations of Shepherd of Hermas and the Laudianius Oxoniensis translation of Acts avoid the word *presbyteri* (but not the old Latin translation of the Letter of James in Codex Corb., nunc Petropol., nor the translation of Acts in the *Gigas librorum*, which, for example, offers *presbyteri* in chapter 15 and then *seniores* for no apparent reason), so that with regard to the naturalization of the same into the language of the Western Church,

---

36. Lommatzsch, *Origenis*, 5:15.

37. Also, the Latin translation of Irenaeus translates διάκονος with *diaconus*, not only in I.13.5 where it is used as a *terminus technicus*, but even in I.14.7 where it is not used in this sense: *Usus est autem diacono septem numerorum magnitudine*. Immediaely afterwards, διακονεῖν is translated with *ministrare*.

38. See the passages listed on the previous page. In addition to *episcopus et diaconus*, Tertullian constantly makes use of *presbyter*. *Seniores* alone is found in *Apol*.

39. In 1 Clem 44.5, the translator could have also represented οἱ πρεσβύτεροι with *presbyteri* instead of *seniores*, but it was not necessary.

the translation of Shepherd of Hermas, 1 Clement, and Tertullian (with which the Latin Irenaeus stands together) form three stages.[40] In chapter 13 of the Acts of Perpetua and Felicitas, it says "*Aspasius presbyter doctor.*" Our translator provides the rendering "*eos, qui prae* (manuscript likely corrupt '*pro*') *nobis sunt*" for the *terminus technicus* οἱ προηγούμενοι ἡμῶν. The Vulgate version of Hermas provides the same translation (Vis. II.2.6; III.9.7: οἱ προηγούμενοι τῆς ἐκκλησίας = "*qui praesunt ecclesiae*"), while the Palatina version offers *priores*. Ἡγούμενοι (Christian leaders) in 1 Clem 1.3 are represented with *praepositi*, while the secular ἡγούμενοι (rulers, officers, etc.) are called *potentes, duces, principes*, and once even *praepositi* (1 Clem 5.7; 32.2; 37.2; 51.5; 55.1; 60.4).

It should be mentioned that in 1 Clem 39.4, 7, within the citation of Job, ἄγγελος is translated by *nuntius*. However, because of the fact that it is within a citation, the passage cannot carry any weight within the discussion. Additionally, even in Commodian's *Carm. apolog.* v. 99 we find *nuntius = angelus.*"[41] On the other hand, Sanday rightly pointed out[42] that the translation of κατὰ χώρας with *secundum municipia* (1 Clem 42.4) and ἔχουσιν χῶρον εὐσεβῶν with *haben municipium religiosorum* (1 Clem 50.3), which I

---

40. In Irenaeus I.15.6, πρεσβύτης is reproduced with *senior* (2x); II.22.5: πάντες οἱ πρεσβύτεροι μαρτυροῦσιν = *omnes seniores*; III.23.3: *ex veteribus quidam* (the original text is missing); IV.32.1: *senior apostolorum discipulus*; V.17.4: *quidam de senioribus* (ἔφη τις τῶν προβεβηκότων). This is correct, and it is equally understandable that in III.2.2, the translator writes *successiones presbyterorum* and *non solum presbyteris sed etiam apostolis* because here οἱ πρεσβύτεροι = οἱ ἐπίσκοποι (the same also applies to IV.32.1: *in ecclesia sunt presbyteri, apud quos est apostolica doctrina*). On the other hand, it is incorrect when he writes in IV.27 *a quodam presbytero* and *sicut dixit presbyter* respectively. Here, *senior* would have been the appropriate translation, and in fact the translator renders ὁ πρεσβύτερος as *senior* only a few lines later (the expression refers to the same man). Also, in IV.28.1; 30.1, 4 (here the expression is *de antiquis presbyter*); V.5.1; 33.3; 36.1 (2x), the translation *presbyteri* is given when one would have expected *seniores*. The Vulgate version of Hermas reproduces *presbuteroi* in three places where it occurs with *seniores*. The Palatina version offers *priores* in the first instance and *seniores et maiores natu* in the second. Only when the context itself calls for the distinction between the elders in regard to age and elders on account of their office can a sharp distinction be found in later times. See, for example, the translation of Origen, *Select. in Psal.* (on Ps 36 hom. 4 c. 3 Tom. XII p. 212 ed. Lommatzsch): *Unde et nos optare debemus non pro aetate corporis neque pro officio presbyterii appellari presbyteri et seniores, sed pro interioris hominis perfecto sensu et gravitate constantiae*. Ambrose (on Ps 36, c. 60) writes: *Ioannes senex coepit scribere . . . epistolas, qui cum refugeret apostolorum se scribere, seniorem scripsit.*

41. It is also significant that παντοκράτωρ is translated once as "*omnia potens*" (1 Clem 60.4). Wölfflin, however, thinks that *omnipotens* must have been manufactured here ("Die lateinische Übersetzung," 85). On λαϊκός = *plebeius*, it is not necessary to refer back to the second century, since it is already used in chapter 1 of *Vita Cypriani*.

42. *Guardian*, March 28, 1894. 457.

had noted, provides an important hint: "The use of *municipium* is specially characteristic of the text of Cod. Vercellensis,"[43] that is, the foundational Latin text of the Gospels, and certainly the European text as opposed to the African text.[44] The translation of 1 Clement seems to point us towards Europe, that is, towards Rome. As a side note, there is a unique relationship between the Vercellensis text and our own translation. That codex is the only witness to the striking translation *"homo paterfamilias"* in Luke 19:12 (ἄνθρωπος εὐγενής). Both the Vulgate and the pre-Hieronymian tranlsation correctly provide the translation *nobilis*. The translation of 1 Clement alone offers the rather unexpected translation *paterfamilias* (for ὁ δεσπότης) in chapter 40.[45] Accordingly, the relationship of our translation to the translation of the Gospels in Vercellensis and to the Old Latin translation of Hermas will have to be examined. These works seem to belong closer together. The translation of 1 Clement, however, points to the second century, and I have found no reasons to oppose this estimate.

4. This estimation is not proven, but it is reinforced by the excellent original, which the translation is based upon and which, as I have shown earlier, in some places agrees with Clement of Alexandria against all other witnesses while in other places alone preserved the correct reading.[46] Now a later translator may certainly have come across an ancient manuscript, but the most obvious assumption is not this assumption, but that the ancient translator lived nearer to the time of the manuscript from which he translated. If, for the reasons offered above, one is convinced of the high probability that our translation belongs to the second century, then this is an extraordinary gain for the evaluation of other Old Latin translations, for the history of the Latin Bible, and for the history of vulgar Latin. We now have a second fixed point, in addition to the works of Cyprian.

---

43. Sanday, *Old-Latin-Biblical Texts*, 2:ccccvii; Belsheim, *Codex Vercell.*

44. In Mark 6:6, 36; 8:23, 26; 11:2; Luke 5:17; 9:6; 24:13, κώμη is translated with *municipium*.

45. I do not maintain the suspicion that *paterfamilias* only came into the text of the translation at a later date. On the word, see Tertullian, *Apol.* 34: *Etiam familiae magis patres quam domini vocantur.*

46. Zahn does not wish to include τίνα τρόπον (*quemadmodum*) in 1 Clem 47.2, where the other witnesses offer the hardly understandable τί πρῶτον. He thinks that the translator simply left πρῶτον untranslated. But how could he have thought of translating τί with *quemadmodum*? In any case, τίνα τρόπον is attested elsewhere in the letter (1 Clem 24.4).

IV.

In my first treatise,[47] I believe I proved that there is a forgery in the manuscript of the translation of 1 Clement since the passage concerning the obedience to worldly authorities is transformed into its opposite (1 Clem 60–61). Wölfflin recognized "the arbitrary corruption (interpolation) in the decisive sentence";[48] Gebhardt writes that the hypothesis would be unchallengeable if *nobis*, appearing on p. 37, line 4 between *das* and *salute* within the manuscript was not found there but rather in line 3, after *subditi*;[49] Zahn rejects any thought of clerical forgery for the purpose of strengthening the power of the papacy over the worldly authorities, for "priests who want to deceive tend to speak more clearly and to forge more thoroughly." Furthermore, the "we," to whom God is to give all good things, "because of *concordiam*" can only be the Christians as a whole, and the worldly rulers, the holders of the royal power endowed by God and given to them are to submit without resistance not to the Christians, but rather to the will of God.[50]

The first argument made by Zahn is irrelevant. The one who proves a forgery exists is not obligated to give an account of why it was not more audaciously and thoroughly forged. Also, the assumption that deceptive priests usually forged more thoroughly is highly contestable.[51] It is true that this is an instance of meddling, the consequences of which have not all been drawn, but that does not mean that the meddling is unclear. Zahn's second argument coincides, for instance, with the remark by Gebhardt. However, it is not really a counter-argument either. Nevertheless, it deserves closer consideration.

Indeed, one expects to find *nobis* after *subditi sint* and not after *quibus das*. But is it at all tolerable after the words that follow? It is hardly likely that someone wrote *Quibus das nobis salutem* on purpose. But now Wölfflin has

---

47. Harnack, "Über die jüngst entdeckte lateinische Übersetzung," 266ff (109–122).

48. Wölfflin, "Die lateinische Übersetzung," 97.

49. Gebhardt, "Sancti Clementis."

50. Zahn, "Sancti Clementis," 199. But Zahn basically concedes the essential part of the argument when he writes, "The reverent attitude towards the pagan state, which found such a strong expression in that great congregational prayer [in the original], is alien to the translator." If a translator expresses a different attitude towards the state than its original, then he mostly likely falsifies it.

51. I did not think it necessary to give examples to prove such small and yet large, imperfect and yet effective forgeries of text in the manuscripts—one may say—of all time. But since the treatise "über den *liber decretorum* Burchard's von Worms," by a contemporary of the scribe of the Florennes manuscript, read by Hauck in the K. Sächsischen Gesellschaft on May 5, 1894, has come into my hands, I would like to refer to it here. The corrections Burchard makes to his texts are—objectively speaking—of a different kind, but nevertheless relevant for comparison. If one wants to find parallels in terms of content, one should study the manuscripts of the Concilia and Synodal Resolutions.

already pointed out that the later insertion of *nobis* could still have been likely.[52] In the original, it says οἷς δὸς ὑγιείαν.[53] Accordingly, the translator wrote QUIBUSDASALUTEM. When *nobis* was inserted into these letters, the S of SALUTEM got stuck on the DA and was of course repeated at SA-LUTEM. It now reads *quibus das* (instead of *da*) *nobis salutem*. From this, it follows that *nobis* was originally given only in the margin or above the line and was only included in the text by the next scribe. But we must go one step further: this *nobis* was not originally intended to be here at all, but was supposed to replace *illis*, which preceded it and was objectionable. That this is the case becomes clear as soon as one recalls that a line previously undoubtedly had *nobis* not simply inserted, but had taken the place of *illis* and thus changed the meaning into its opposite. Thus *nobis* was not above the line where it should have been inserted, but on the edge, and the copyist—the copyist of Codex Florennes is, as should be expected, not himself the forger—inserted it in the wrong place.

The following summary proves the stages of text falsification:

... εἰς τὸ γιγνώσκοντας ἡμᾶς τὴν ὑπὸ σοῦ αὐτοῖς δεδομένην δόξαν καὶ τιμὴν ὑποτάσσεσθαι αὐτοῖς μηδὲν ἐναντιουμένους τῷ θελήματί σου· οἷς δός, κύριε, ὑγιείαν ...

Original Translation:

... UTCOGNITODATAMATEILLISGLORIAMETHONOREMSUBDITI SIMUSILLISNIHILRESISTENTESUOLUNTATITUAEQUIBUSDASA LUTEM ...

First Instance of Meddling:

... UTCOGNITODATAMATEILLISGLORIAMETHONOREMSUBDITI   NOBIS
SIMUSILLISNIHILRESISTENTESUOLUNTATITUAEQUIBUSDASA   NOBIS
LUTEM ...

Current Shape:

... ET[54] COGNITO DATAM NOBIS A TE GLORIAM ET HONOREM SUBDITI
    SINT NIHIL RESISTENTES
UOLUNTATI TUAE QUIBUS DAS NOBIS SA
LUTEM ...

One can see that the first NOBIS also did not appear exactly at the place that the Greek original demands, and that the second NOBIS, just like the first, must have taken the place of *illis*. The fact that the second scribe placed it after

---

52. Wölfflin, "Die lateinische Übersetzung," 97.

53. I do not include κύριε from the original because the translator either did not read it or left it untranslated.

54. This is only a scribal error.

DA and did not give it the decisive position after SUBDITI SINT, which his predecessor obviously had in mind, is proof that he proceeded thoughtlessly, was therefore not interested with the content,[55] and thus did not deliberately falsify the text. The deliberate falsification is the responsibility of the previous scribe,[56] namely the one who made the marginal notes. That these marginal notes are a *lusus ingenii* of a harmless nature would not be assumed by any judicious individual, for they invert the sentence into its opposite which coincides with well-known high church tendencies of those times. But the remark by Zahn, that this "we" could only be the Christians as a whole because of the subsequent *concordiam*, would be correct if the forger had wanted to take the trouble to correct the whole text systematically and to think through and draw out all the consequences of his alterations. But it was only the decisive sentence that was of relevance to him, and here the meaning of the desired words, "the worldly rulers should be obedient to us," can only mean that they may be obedient to the author of the letter—that is, to Pope Clement or the Roman Church—but not to Christians as a whole.

A certain relief, however, is that the forgery was originally only done *in margine* and everything else then apparently took place in a mechanical manner and without malicious intent. The relief becomes even greater when one considers that no good Roman Catholic Christian at that time could believe that "Pope" Clement had really written of the authorities as he had written. But this is not at all a question of the degree of responsibility of the scribe who wanted to see the meaning of the text transformed into its opposite, but only of the statement of facts.

---

55. For this very reason not only he, but also his predecessor, would have changed *sumus* into *sint*.

56. The assumption that it was the scribe of the direct *Vorlage* of Codex Florennes is not necessary.

Appendix III

The First Letter of Clement

A Study to Determine the Character of the Oldest Form of Gentile Christianity

1909

PARTLY BECAUSE OF THE discovery of new sources, partly as a result of a sharper interpretation of those sources long known, and finally because of a courageous and fruitful combination of them, the image of pre-Catholic Christianity has been extraordinarily enriched and expanded within the last twenty years. We could speak of the conquest of entire provinces for ancient church history and of a condominium, which lies between it and philology, that in former times was held by the insecure footing of the lonely theologian. A new sun shines to illuminate the darkness that had covered them recently: the "history of religions" method penetrates even the most remote and darkest ravines; indeed, it shines especially into these places and seems to reveal that they are blooming gardens and groves, much like Latomia of Syracuse. One gift after another is brought to the friend of ancient church history, and sometimes they are truly figs among the thorns and grapes among the thistles. Nevertheless, the joy of these gifts is not undivided and pure. It cannot be denied that the new discoveries are often presented in such a way that, because not everything is equally present to the researchers, the facts are not properly weighed and unalterable guidelines are pushed aside. Sometimes, the apocalyptic-enthusiastic elements are unduly exaggerated; sometimes, superstitions that have been dragged away are now treated as the main elements of the history of the Christian religion. In sum, peripheral matters are brought into focus, and the central issues are overlooked. In this way, it can sometimes seem that the oldest form of Gentile Christianity was a kind of folkloristic religion and that its conventions differed from pagan ones only in differently named *sacra*. As far as tradition is concerned, the subterranean-insidious tradition is preferred to the obvious one; from the literature, texts, whose readership we know almost nothing about, are given precedence over that which is in everyone's hands. In the end, even in the great works of published literature, the small in the meagerest are selected with love and care and placed in a light that would almost make the truly valuable jealous.

Everything that is done here in devoted work is useful and beneficial. However, it becomes alarming when what we already possess and have long been acquainted with is forgotten, and when it is misunderstood that the guidelines that we have received from there in order to understand the whole are generally unchangeable. Also, is it really a new insight, if we now are able to see that the ancient Christians were clothed in Hellenism when we knew long ago that Hellenism filled their heads and hearts? No one can be reproached here: We hardly have any unmethodical workers, and fortunately no one has brought a rough account of the general picture of nascent Catholicism into the public sphere in recent years. But there are numerous works which, in their excellent investigations, shift the center of gravity a little, and since the shift usually goes in the same direction, the cumulative effect distorts the picture and gives the impression that the overall picture of the ancient history of the church and of dogma must be replaced by another one. Such impressions are irrefutable and may be warranted because they stimulate research. However, it is their duty to keep in force the certain facts that, at the same time, mark the limits within which progress must move if it is not to become like Icarus's flight.

To illustrate this, I have chosen a document which, in terms of its time and its origin, form and validity, is one of the most distinguished—if not the most distinguished—among the post-apostolic writings, namely the so-called First Letter of Clement. As is well known, it is an official letter that the Roman congregation addressed to the Corinthian congregation around the years 93–95 CE. We possess it not only in the original, but also in Syriac, Latin, and Coptic translations. One of the two Greek manuscripts, in which it is found, is the famous Codex Alexandrinus. Furthermore, since it is included in the Syriac New Testament manuscript, it is even divided into liturgical pericopes. This tradition alone already makes it stand out from the mass of early Christian literature, for one can count on one's fingers, with the exception of the NT writings, the number of early Christian writings that are contained in those four languages and that have been handed down to us from antiquity. This letter likely received this honor precisely because at times and in some churches it stood within the New Testament. Furthermore, shortly after its publication, the famous Bishop Polycarp of

Smyrna, in his Epistle to the Philippians, not only used it, but virtually looted it. He silently exploited it alongside "1 Peter" and used both texts equally as the basis of his paraeneses.[1] Therefore, there can be no doubt that the letter was considered to be a classical Christian foundational document (*Urkunde*) within the ancient Gentile church, and that the church, with its ideals and powers, had found these things once again in the letter. If one now adds to this the fact that it was written from the main congregation in the West to the most important congregation in Greece and that, at the end of the letter, the Roman congregation noted that it had spoken in sufficient detail about everything that "belongs to our religion," for it had left nothing unmentioned with regard to faith, repentance, genuine love, abstinence, *sophrosyne*, and patience, then there is no other document in the entire field of the oldest, post-apostolic literature that can be compared with this one in terms of its significance.[2] When one approaches the let-

---

1. It is also very important that Irenaeus interrupts his reproduction of the list of Roman Bishops (III.3.3) when he reaches Clement (the interruption probably belongs to the source itself) and writes (the beginning is preserved in its original in Eusebius *Hist. eccl.* V.6): Ἐπὶ τούτου τοῦ Κλήμεντος στάσεως οὐκ ὀλίγης τοῖς ἐν Κορίνθῳ γενομένης ἀδελφοῖς, ἐπέστειλεν ἡ ἐν Ῥώμῃ Ἐκκλησία ἱκανωτάτην γραφὴν τοῖς Κορινθίοις, εἰς εἰρήνην συμβιβάζουσα αὐτούς, καὶ ἀνανεοῦσα τὴν πίστιν αὐτῶν, καὶ ἣν νεωστὶ ἀπὸ τῶν ἀποστόλων παράδοσιν εἰλήφει. *annuntians, annuntiantem unum deum omnipotentem, factorem coeli et terrae, plasmatorem hominis, qui induxerit cataclysmum et advocaverit Abraham, qui eduxerit populum de terra Aegypti, qui collocutus sit Moysi, qui legem disposuerit et prophetas miserit, qui ignem praeparaverit diabolo et angelis eius* [the last clause is not covered within the content of the letter!], *hunc patrem domini nostri Jesu Christi ab ecclesiis annuntiari ex ipsa scriptura* [just as in the letter] *qui velint discere possunt et apostolicam ecclesiae traditionem intelligere, cum sit vetustior epistula his qui nunc falso docent.*

2. 1 Clement 63: Περὶ μὲν τῶν ἀνηκόντων τῇ θρησκείᾳ ἡμῶν ... ἱκανῶς ἐπεστείλαμεν ὑμῖν, ἄνδρες ἀδελφοί. περὶ γὰρ πίστεως καὶ μετανοίας καὶ γνησίας ἀγάπης καὶ ἐγκρατείας καὶ σωφροσύνης καὶ ὑπομονῆς πάντα τόπον ἐψηλαφήσαμεν, ὑπομιμνήσκοντες δεῖν ὑμᾶς ἐν δικαιοσύνῃ καὶ ἀληθείᾳ καὶ μακροθυμίᾳ τῷ παντοκράτορι θεῷ ὁσίως εὐαρεστεῖν, ὁμονοοῦντας ἀμνησικάκως ἐν ἀγάπῃ καὶ εἰρήνῃ μετὰ ἐκτενοῦς ἐπιεικείας. This is a perfect description of the content of the letter, which in 1 Clem 63.2 is abbreviated to ἔντευξις περὶ εἰρήνης καὶ ὁμονοίας. That it is not as incoherent as it seems at first sight has been demonstrated by Wehofer, *Untersuchungen*.

1. Greeting; *Laudatio* as a Preliminary Strophe (1–2)
2. Ζῆλος, μετάνοια, πίστις, ὑπακοή (3–13).
3. Contact only with Friends of Peace (14–30).
4. The Way of Blessing (31–36).
5. The Actual Center of the Letter; The Rectification of the Disturbers of the Peace; The τάθις among the λειτουργία (37–47).
6. The High Praise of Love; Blessed Are Those Who Love (49; 50).
7. Alternative: Departure or Subjugation of the Disturbers of the Peace (51–58).
8. The Prayer as the Climax of the Edifying Admonition (59–61).

ter from antiquity, its significance for ecclesiastical and dogmatic history is naturally at odds with its significance to literary history. This alone is only one of the many instances in which, in the appreciation of early Christian literature, the historian and the literary historian, judging by the standards of antiquity, part ways. The latter more or less disparagingly pushes aside a document whose artistry is not able to impress him and whose originality as a document of the church he does not need to appreciate; the former views every line as precious because even those lines that have been borrowed are now placed within a new historical context.[3]

We may, therefore, hope that the extensive letter of sixty-five chapters will enlighten us about how Christianity was constituted as a possession of the Gentile church at the end of the first century, where the various accents fell, how the various functions of the religion were ordered, how the

---

9. Concluding Paraenesis and Doxology (62–65).

The realization that the explanations have all flowed out of the topic does not yet settle the question raised and carefully discussed by Knopf whether the author used his own older sermons (*Der erste Clemensbrief*, 177ff). It does, however, exclude the idea of a mechanical transfer (see also Wehofer, *Untersuchungen*, 143ff).

It is remarkable and increases the significance of the letter as a foundational document (*Urkunde*) for the knowledge of the oldest form of Gentile Christianity that Clement does not at any point present the reader with special knowledge, but is instead conscious—except in one case (1 Clem 41)—of only bringing to light and introducing what is already known.

It is possible, indeed not improbable, that the letter was also intended to be distributed further. The author's careful literary construction of the letter as well as the reference in the letter that the irksome disputes in Corinth had become notorious everywhere and even bring about the dishonor of Christianity among the Gentiles (1 Clem 1; 47) speak in favor of this. However, I would not make this claim as certainly as Wehofer (*Untersuchungen*, 201). However, his thesis (on the basis of αὕτη ἡ ἀκοή in 1 Clem 47.7) is baseless.

3. For more details about the literary historical dimensions of the letter, see Excursus I. In order to appreciate the historical significance, the following is especially important: How close was the danger that the new religion might lose itself in the misery and barbarism of the base people, or be transformed into the magical mysteries, or perish in the embers of the ascetics and prophets! That this did not happen, and by what attitude and by what means it was prevented, is taught to us by our letter, whose author is worthy of veneration precisely in those places, by his sobriety and discipline, he does not charm us. On the prudent nature of the letter, see Lightfoot, *Clement of Rome*, 1:95ff, 396ff. He rightly emphasizes the following as the three most important elements: "(1) the comprehensiveness, (2) the sense of order, (3) the moderation" (however, ἐπιείκεια is not without strong shadows in comparison with the schismatics). As far as "teaching" is concerned, he also correctly says, "In short there is no dogmatic System in Clement. This, which might be regarded from one point of view as a defect in our epistle, really constitutes its highest value. It exhibits the belief of his church as to the true interpretation of the Apostolical records." Instead of "Apostolical," it would be better to call it "the apostolic age."

essence of religion was conceived, what moral impulses it produced, and how the cult and the relationship between the authoritative and dormant elements interacted with the pneumatic and tumultuous ones. Only in the latter respect will we have to be reserved if we wish to make generalizations, for since the purpose of the letter is to settle a serious dispute that has broken out in the Corinthian congregation against the ecclesiastical office in favor of that very office, it naturally strongly emphasizes the authoritative moments and is almost entirely silent about the scope of the pneumatic and the individual.[4] Meanwhile, as far as we know, the subsequent period never criticized these statements—Polycarp was happy to follow them—and very shortly thereafter even went beyond them.

The strongest impression one gets from the letter is that the new religion was not first and foremost a cult, not even an enthusiastic religion, still less a Gnostic or speculative-mystery religion, but was a moral movement, one that was founded upon monotheism and was felt with the utmost seriousness and liveliness. From the first to the last leaf, this fundamental character is strongly expressed in the letter, and one must descend to Calvin, to the resolved morality of the Puritans of England and the New England states, in order to find in the common religion the sovereignty of God's holy laws so naturally as the Alpha and Omega of all living things. But the conviction that those who have received this salvation owe it to the election of God, which cannot be fathomed any further, who has provided a fixed number as the people of his property, also can be found here. Ultimately the content of the moral law is hardly different: for there and here it is by no means antithetically directed towards the world, as if the world itself was the evil principle, but directs itself towards the positive ideals of moral purity and spiritual and corporate unity gained through humility, love, and service, and that presents itself in corporate unity. The moral ideal is not escapism and asceticism—it is rarely mentioned, and where it

---

4. Wrede has taken up and rejected unfounded interpretations related to the claim of earlier researchers that the Corinthian dispute was simply a contention between the Pneumatics (*Untersuchungen zum ersten Klemensbriefe*, 30ff). Knopf has rejected the assumption entirely (*Der erste Clemensbrief*, 170f). He is correct that the letter does not appeal to the enthusiastic motives of the "troublemakers." However, if one does not wish to simply accept the egoistic and vulgar motives of the "troublemakers," only these remain. And they are indirectly confirmed within the letter. If, apparently, the cult was the main area in which the opponents clashed, and if the "troublemakers" did not want to commit themselves to certain times and places, and even wanted to act in place of the presbyters, and had already partly affected their removal, one must conclude that they had enthusiastic motives. The striking fact, however, that Clement does not fight his opponents as Pneumatics can probably be explained by the fact that they could not be apprehended as such.

is once conceived of, ascetics receive a warning against arrogance[5]—but the complex of all the virtues that guarantee a holy and pure, a peaceful and charitable life with others. It is, in a word, simple morality, illuminated by the presence and power of God, which is what matters to these Christians. The natural forms of existence and the differences between one another on the basis of possessions and education are taken for granted and should be regarded as gifts from God and used for the good of the whole. In the sense and in the style of the *Haustafeln* (household codes) of the later Pauline epistles, warnings are repeatedly given to parents concerning the proper upbringing of children; to women concerning their conjugal duties, discipline, modesty, and domestic service;[6] but especially to the younger generation concerning reverence and obedience to the elderly. Clement writes, "May our entire body remain safe in Christ Jesus and may each one submit to his neighbor in accordance with his own *charisma*. Let not the strong underestimate the weak; let the weak respect the strong. Let the rich support the poor; let the poor thank God that he has given them someone to help them overcome their deficiencies. Let the wise man show his wisdom not in words but in good deeds. Let the humble man not testify to his own humility, but let someone else do it."[7] The admonitions build to the climax of the letter within a hymn to love, composed according to the model in 1 Cor 13, though naturally without attaining the achievement of the model.[8] It is easy to draw parallels to all these moral exhortations from the OT, even from the moral-philosophical diatribes. But behind the words here there is a closed community which, by its actions and obedience, strips moral commonplaces of their triviality and, with energetic implementation, makes the basis of its communal life what was elsewhere often only inconsequential words. It is aware that it has a new sociological principle in its relationship with God, but the application of this principle is left entirely to the lively mind of the individual. The diversity of the social classes disturbs the spiritual and religious sense of unity so inconsequentially that no thought is given to a balancing of the class differences. This

---

5. 1 Clement 38.2: ὁ ἁγνὸς ἐν τῇ σαρκὶ μὴ ἀλαζονευέσθω, γινώσκων ὅτι ἕτερός ἐστιν ὁ ἐπιχορηγῶν αὐτῷ τὴν ἐγκράτειαν.

6. In 1 Clem 21.7, we find the lovely oxymoron that women should τὸ ἐπιεικὲς τῆς γλώσσης αὐτῶν διὰ τῆς σιγῆς φανερὸν ποιεῖν. The author, like Paul in Corinth, had probably had his own experiences, and apparently even now women played a great and not always pleasant role within the congregation. Incidentally, tradition has it that the oxymoron attested in the later Greek, Syriac, Latin, and even Clement of Alexandria witnesses has been corrected. Codex Alexandrinus reads φωνῆς instead of σιγῆς, and the Coptic simply leaves out διὰ τῆς σιγῆς.

7. 1 Clem 38.1–2.

8. 1 Clem 49.

community feels the contrast in which it stands with the world around it and its endangered situation without harboring any bitterness or resentment. Indeed, when reading the letter, one can sometimes think that there is no fundamental contrast, and that it is only the inevitable opposites of evil and good, slackness and moral strength, and such enmities that never end. The request is necessary: "Lord, deliver us from those who unjustly hate us; free our prisoners."[9] However, everything is limited to this request. No morbid addiction to martyrdom, no ostentation, and no complacent reflection disturbs the serene and simple seriousness of the letter's entire attitude. To such a degree, all *échauffement* is missing—such unbiased ancient examples of self-sacrifice in the service of the whole are given;[10] with such contentment the exemplary discipline of "our" (i.e., the Roman soldiers) is pointed out;[11] so sincerely and heartily is a prayer offered for the authorities and their welfare;[12] so matter of fact, it seems, that the congregation does not lack the freedom to truly carry out that which is good in its midst—that we are permitted to have before us a letter from a time when Christianity has already completed its assimilation into the world, without, however, abandoning or reducing its ideals. The pneumatic element is just as present as the expression of a living and objective awareness of a nearness to God, and also the expectation of the imminent end of the world is confidently sharpened.[13] But all this is only to strengthen the inner moral attitude and to strengthen trust in God. Impatient and stormy emotions are not at all present within these Christians, and even the religious imagination is not stimulated by the "Spirit" and by eschatology towards colorful productions or reproductions.[14]

9. 1 Clem 60.3; 59.4.

10. 1 Clem 55.1: "Ἵνα δὲ καὶ ὑποδείγματα ἐθνῶν ἐνέγκωμεν· πολλοὶ βασιλεῖς καὶ ἡγούμενοι, λοιμικοῦ τινὸς ἐνστάντος καιροῦ, χρησμοδοτηθέντες παρέδωκαν ἑαυτοὺς εἰς θάνατον, ἵνα ῥύσωνται διὰ τοῦ ἑαυτῶν αἵματος τοὺς πολίτας. πολλοὶ ἐξεχώρησαν ἰδίων πόλεων, ἵνα μὴ στασιάζωσιν ἐπὶ πλεῖον.

11. 1 Clem 37.2. Wrede has correctly said, "In his relationship to paganism, Clement has inherited something of the broad-minded humanism that is characteristic of Hellenistic Jews" (*Untersuchungen zum ersten Klemensbriefe*, 100f).

12. Wehofer's attempt to interpret the authorities, for whom the prayer in 1 Clem 61 is offered, as presbyters instead of the secular authorities is mistaken (*Untersuchungen*, 207ff). Admittedly, the Latin manuscript that has been handed down to us wishes the prayer to be understood in this manner; see my essays on this matter in these meeting reports: Harnack, "Über die jüngst entdeckte lateinische Übersetzung"; Harnack, "Neue Studien." These essays are also contained within this volume under the titles "The Recently Discovered Latin Translation of 1 Clement," and "New Studies on the Recently Discovered Latin Translation of 1 Clement," respectively.

13. 1 Clem 23.

14. It is instructive to see in what context the πλήρης πνεύματος ἁγίου ἔκχυσις is

This makes the testimony of the one living God, the creator, all the more multifaceted and moving; indeed, we do not possess any text from the post-apostolic period that is expressed with such inwardness and with such a wealth of relationships. A large number of the statements in the letter serve him. Here, one can clearly see what the former pagans experienced and felt first and foremost about the new religion, which brought them into an indissoluble relationship with the living source of all things. Everything else receded behind this ongoing experience. God in nature, his creative will, his lawful administration, and his orders are praised; God in his work in history, establishing an end and determining boundaries; God as the power that has foretold and prepared everything; God who peers into that which is hidden; God as judge; God as the redeemer and as the giver of all good gifts;[15] God as the force that alone leads to himself, *a deo per deum ad deum*. All convictions and sentiments awakened by living theism are offered here in astonishing reverence and joy. Again, parallels to these statements can be found in abundance from the most diverse and obvious texts, and it can also be said of each of them individually that they show little originality; but he who is unable to feel the joy and the full seriousness of the simple knowledge of God in these testimonies[16] which are constantly springing up in the letter, and to distinguish them from religious stylistic exercises, must be denied the ability to distinguish the articulation of sincere religious life from the semblance of such a life. But if it is argued that the poetic prose and the rhetorical clothing of most passages cast doubt on that sincerity, it must not be forgotten that it was caused by the example of the Psalms, which was an indispensable garment that could not be missing from a document that went from one cosmopolitan city to another and was to be read out aloud publicly. One can argue about the artistic taste of the letter's author, but the purity and strength of his dispositions remain unaffected. It is this purity in particular that evokes the highest admiration. No polytheistic sub-tone and no selfishness disturbs the articulation of a living knowledge of the purest view of God. It is only through the author's

---

mentioned; Πάντες τε ἐταπεινοφρονεῖτε, μηδὲν ἀλαζονευόμενοι, ὑποτασσόμενοι μᾶλλον ἢ ὑποτάσσοντες, ἥδιον διδόντες ἢ λαμβάνοντες, τοῖς ἐφοδίοις τοῦ χροστοῦ ἀρκούμενοι. καὶ προσέχοντες· τοὺς λόγους αὐτοῦ ἐπιμελῶς ἐνεστερνισμένοι ἦτε τοῖς σπλάγχνοις. καὶ τὰ παθήματα αὐτοῦ ἦν πρὸ ὀφθαλμῶν ὑμῶν· οὕτως εἰρήνη βαθεῖα καὶ λιπαρὰ ἐδέδοτο πᾶσιν καὶ ἀκόρεστος πόθος εἰς ἀγαθοποιΐαν, καὶ πλήρης πνεύματος ἁγίου ἔκχυσις ἐπὶ πάντας ἐγίνετο (2.1–2). Similarly on *"charisma"* in 1 Clem 38.1.

15. They are summarized in 1 Clem 35.1–2: Ὡς μακάρια καὶ θαυμαστὰ τὰ δῶρα τοῦ θεοῦ, ἀγαπητοί. ζωὴ ἐν ἀθανασίᾳ, λαμπρότης ἐν δικαιοσύνῃ, ἀλήθεια ἐν παρρησίᾳ, πίστις ἐν πεποιθήσει, ἐγκράτεια ἐν ἁγιασμῷ. Notice which gift comes first and how completely all fleshly goods are abandoned.

16. The warmest of theses is the great prayer into which the letter flows.

care for the unity and order of the church, which is increased to the point of harshness, that the letter is marred. But who can say today how much importance was then attached to this strict unity?

The author has the highest admiration for God as a God of order. But it is hardly likely that this is related to the fact that he almost never speaks of miracles. This entire, great chapter in the history of ancient Christianity is almost completely omitted by him. Neither do miraculous phenomena have a place where he draws the ideal picture of a Christian community (1 Clem 1; 2), nor where he describes God's work. He certainly is not "afraid of miracles." He reminds his readers of Old Testament miracles, and he bases the hope of the resurrection—in addition to a rational argument—on the miraculous resurrection of Jesus and on the legend of the phoenix (1 Clem 24; 25). The choice of this pagan legend, which tells the story not as a miracle but as a natural phenomenon, is significant. He is either unaware of contemporary Christian miracles, which would be applicable here (how different is he in comparison to Irenaeus), or he is afraid to use such singularities. Nor does he even touch upon the vast field of miraculous healings and demon exorcisms, as the author hardly has anything to do with demons, Satan, or the devil anywhere.[17] But even the "angels" only occur once (outside of quotations) within the letter.[18] The living God, the virtues, and the sins:[19] these are the factors that determine the inner and outer life.

The organ that establishes the connection with God is faith. But this is only clear to the author as an active obedience of faith. In the few places where the author betrays a deeper understanding, he is so dependent on Pauline sayings that one may doubt whether he has arrived at this deeper understanding on his own accord.[20] Alone, this somewhat flatter concept of faith is the general one present in the nascent Gentile church and corresponds to its overall moralistic attitude, which is best described as σώφρων

---

17. The devil appears as "the adversary" only once; see 1 Clem 51.1 (ὁ ἀντικείμενος).

18. 1 Clem 34.5. Very characteristic—they too must serve to inculcate the idea of order and obedience: κατανοήσωμεν τὸ πᾶν πλῆθος τῶν ἀγγέλων αὐτοῦ, πῶς τῷ θελήματι αὐτοῦ λειτουργοῦσιν παρεστῶτες!

19. ἁμαρτία, ἁμαρτάνειν, ἁμάρτημα, ἁμαρτωλός are found around thirty-four times within 1 Clement (twenty-four of which appear within citations).

20. The most Pauline passage comes from 1 Clem 32.4 (justification by faith). But it is not quite Pauline because it does not have ἔργα νόμου in opposition to it but its own σοφία. Σύνεσις, εὐσέβεια, and the works which we have done ἐν ὁσιότητι καρδίας. That the question of justification of the apostolic age is no longer of any importance for the author is shown by the observation that the following three formulas on justification are peacefully juxtaposed: (1) justification οὐ δι' ἔργων, ἀλλὰ διὰ τῆς πίστεως, 1 Clem 32.4; (2) ἔργοις δικαιούμενοι καὶ μὴ λόγοις, 1 Clem 30.3; (3) justification διὰ πίστιν καὶ φιλοξενίαν, 1 Clem 10.7; 11.1.

εὐσέβεια and as subordination to νόμιμα or δικαίματα καὶ προστάγματα τοῦ θεοῦ. This obedience of faith is intimately bound up with humility[21] and breathes the fear of the judge, but does not yet bear the heavy stamp of the restless and terrible fear of lacking something and thereby forfeiting the bliss that makes, for example, 2 Clement and the Shepherd of Hermas such an embarrassing read. Rather, the author is aware of God's boundless mercy, which looks at and forgives mistakes. Admittedly, Christians can only sin involuntarily and have temporary weaknesses in the face of the adversary's attempts against them, for the author shares the conviction with the whole of the most ancient form of Christianity that Christians have been removed from the realm of sin and are therefore capable of being and are obliged to be sinless. He alone differs from the judgment of most in that even serious sins committed by Christians fall under the concept of involuntary sin or seduction and that he, therefore, does not doubt the possibility that all these sins can be forgiven the Christian. However, it requires a hard and constant struggle by the brothers for the brother in sin, but above all the repentance and penance of the sinner himself. But repentance always seems to be available: God's mercy for forgiveness is won over and over, proving God's love.[22] The proof that χάρις μετανοίας has been give is close

---

21. Ταπεινοφρονεῖν (ταπεινός, ταπεινοφροσύνη, ταπεινόφρων, ταπεινοῦν, ταπείνωσις) is now of the central concept of the letter; see 1 Clem 2.1; 13.1, 3; 16.1, 2, 7, 17; 18.8, 17; 19.1; 21.8; 30.2, 3, 8; 31.4; 38.2; 44.3; 48.6; 53.2; 55.6 (2x); 56.1; 58.2; 59.3 (3x), 4; 62.2. Through it, the letter gains a close relationship with the sayings of Jesus and his ethics. This becomes all the more obvious as here and there the later traits of ascetic self-denial are still entirely missing (in Tertullian, *Jejun.* 12 ταπεινοφρόνσις is a technical term and describes ascetic exercises. The first passage in 1 Clem 2 shows how ταπεινοφροσύνη should be understood: ἐταπεινοφρονεῖτε μηδὲν ἀλαζονευόμενοι (also, according to 1 Clem 13 and 16, ἀλαζονεία is contrasted with humility), ὑποτασσόμενοι μᾶλλον ἢ ὑποτάσσοντες. ἥδιον διδόντες ἢ λαμβάνοντες, τοῖς ἐφοδίοις τοῦ χριστοῦ ἀρκούμενοι καὶ προσέχοντες. According to 1 Clem 13.3, it is the humble one who acts according to the saying, "He who wants to boast, boast in the Lord." According to 1 Clem 16, as in Philippians, Christ himself is the model of humility. According to 1 Clem 19.1, humility and obedience belong together. Μαθέτωσαν, he exclaims in 1 Clem 21.8, τί ταπεινοφροσύνη παρὰ θεῷ ἰσχύει. It is also the stipulation of ὁμόνοια (1 Clem 30.3) and virtue, which is proper to those who lead the church (1 Clem 44.3) and it says in 1 Clem 48.6: ἤτω τις πιστός, ἤτω δυνατὸς γνῶσιν ἐξειπεῖν, ἤτω σοφὸς ἐν διακρίσει λόγων, ἤτω ἁγνὸς ἐν ἔργοις—τοσούτῳ γὰρ μᾶλλον ταπεινοφρονεῖν ὀφείλει, ὅσῳ δοκεῖ μᾶλλον μείζων εἶναι, καὶ ζητεῖν τὸ κοινωφελὲς πᾶσιν, καὶ μὴ τὸ ἑαυτοῦ. In 1 Clem 30.8, 56.1, and 62.2, humility is linked to ἐπείκεια, and the final admonition of the letter leads to the remark that all Old Testament pious people have gained God's favor because they were humble πρὸς τὸν πατέρα καὶ θεὸν καὶ κτίστην καὶ πάντας ἀνθρώπους. But behind the call to humility is the beautiful confession in 1 Clem 38.3: ἀναλογισώμεθα, ἀδελφοί, ἐκ ποίας ὕλης ἐγενήθημεν, ποῖοι καὶ τίνες εἰσήλθαμεν εἰς τὸν κόσμον. ἐκ ποίου τάφου καὶ σκότους ὁ πλάσας ἡμᾶς καὶ δημιουργήσας εἰσήγαγεν εἰς τὸν κόσμον αὐτοῦ.

22. See 1 Clem 2.3–4: ἱκετεύοντες θεὸν ἵλεων γενέσθαι εἴ τι ἄκοντες ἡμάρτετε· ἀγὼν

to the main purpose of the letter.²³ Thus, the tormenting and restless fear of God and the oscillation between fear and hope that we usually consider characteristic of Gentile Christian piety is absent here.

Knowledge (*gnosis*) is highly esteemed, indeed it belongs after and beside πίστις, εὐσέβεια, and φιλοξενία as the four foundational elements of the new religion.²⁴ However, it does not go over into foreign territories, but instead remains entirely within the understanding of the revelations of the creator God in nature and in the Old Testament, and receives its deepest content through Christ. Through him, the ἀθάνατος γνῶσις, that is, probably the knowledge that involves immortality, is made accessible.²⁵ But to depict this knowledge with fantasy, or to form it with philosophy, or with the means of some cultic wisdom is quite far away from the intent of the author. When he speaks in 1 Clem 40.1 of the βάθη τῆς θείας γνώσεως into which Christians gain insight, he means the correct understanding of the Old Testament, be it of the Mosaic regulations, be it of the prophets!²⁶ But he also

---

ἣν ὑμῖν ἡμέρας τε καὶ νυκτὸς ὑπὲρ πάσης τῆς ἀδελφότητος εἰς τὸ σῴζεσθαι μετ᾽ ἐλέους καὶ συνειδήσεως τὸν ἀριθμὸν τῶν ἐκλεκτῶν αὐτοῦ. Additionally, see 1 Clem 51.1: ὅσα οὖν παρεπέσαμεν καὶ ἐπταίσαμεν διά τινας παρεμπτώσεις τοῦ ἀντικειμένου, ἀξιώσωμεν ἀφεθῆναι ἡμῖν; and 1 Clem 50.5: μακάριοί ἐσμεν, εἰ τὰ προστάγματα τοῦ θεοῦ ἐποιοῦμεν ἐν ὁμονοίᾳ ἀγάπης, εἰς τὸ ἀφεθῆναι ἡμῖν δι᾽ ἀγάπης τὰς ἁμαρτίας. It is curious that the author has not yet been made aware of the fact that his view of the sins of Christians as merely involuntary and based upon seduction is untenable. Either his judgment is a particularly superficial one, or the Roman congregation must have been exemplary in its purity at that time. Incidentally, the author has obviously judged the evil revolutionaries in Corinth, whom he characterizes and threatens so severely, to be nothing more than involuntary sinners or temporarily seduced. For everywhere he considers the possibility of restitution. For more details, see Hans Windisch, whose statements, in my opinion however, require some correction with regard to Clement (*Taufe und Sünde*, 321ff).

23. Compare the passages on μετάνοια within the letter (1 Clem 7.4-6; 8.1-2, 5; 57.1; 62.2). According to 1 Clem 7.4, the blood of Christ shed for our salvation has brought about παντὶ τῷ κόσμῳ μετανοίας χάριν.

24. The compilation is not indifferent. The mention of φιλοξενία in this context is particularly noteworthy (cf. 1 Clem 10-12). It proves that under the circumstances of the time, this virtue was particularly necessary, that many virtues converged in it, as in a focal point, and that it must have formed a *nota confessionis*. Wehofer's assertion that φιλοξενία within the letter means ὑπακοή does not deserve any refutation (*Untersuchungen*, 161).

25. See 1 Clem 36.2.

26. It is strange that Clement not only likes to use the expression γνῶσις, but also the expression τὰ βάθη τῆς θείας γνώσεως. Indeed Paul had already spoken of τὰ βάθη τοῦ θεοῦ (1 Cor 2:10) and John of τὰ βάθη τοῦ Σατανᾶ (Rev 2:24), but in the second century the term is almost exclusively the property of the Gnostics. See Hippolytus, *Philos.* V.6: ἐπεκάλεσαν ἑαυτοὺς γνωστικούς, φάσκοντες μόνοι τὰ βάθη γινώσκειν. Tertullian, *Val.* 1: (*Valentiniani*) *suspenso supercilio "Altum est" aiunt.* Irenaeus II.28.9: *aliquis eorum qui altitudines dei exquisisse se dicunt*; II.22.3: *profunda dei adinvenisse se dicunt.*

knows that *gnosis* is a growing and varied one among Christians, and that increased knowledge means increased responsibility.[27] No line leads from his point of view to the speculations of the gnostics and the *mythologumena* of excited apocalyptics.[28]

What he has to say about Christ, he does not offer as his own *gnosis* but as an expression of a fact that he only has to remember. What comes to expression most often is the certainty that, for the Christian, everything is decided ἐν Χριστῷ. This age-old apostolic experience and confessional formula recurs in various applications and dominates the whole letter.[29] It surely expresses more certainly than any doctrine about Christ that the Christians had won their lives in him and that they knew they were in his sphere. The apostle Paul, through his preaching and letters, has certainly most strongly awakened the nature of this awareness and certainty—"mysticism" for any outsider, simple experience for the disciple of Christ—and so it is he, along with the author of the Letter to the Hebrews, who guides our author in his christological statements. He does not indulge in his own speculations. When he calls Christ ἀπαύγασμα τῆς μεγαλωσύνης τοῦ θεοῦ (1 Clem 36.2) or τὸ σκῆπτρον τῆς μεγαλωσύνης αὐτοῦ (1 Clem 16.2), occasionally presupposes his pre-existence and remarks that he could probably have appeared ἐν κόμπῳ ἀλαζονείας καὶ ὑπερηφανίας instead of in lowliness on earth if he had wanted to (1 Clem 16.2), then these are all statements which are simply copied from apostolic sayings.[30] He has no Christology of his own and has no interest in

---

However, one cannot grasp βάθη τοῦ θεοῦ as less "gnositc" than Clement.

27. 1 Clem 41.4; 48.5.

28. Also not to the apologists. It is strange that, in the letter, the aspect of apologetics withdraws completely and does not even casually assert itself.

29. 1 Clem 1.2: εὐσέβεια ἐν Χριστῷ; 1 Clem 21.6: παιδεία ἐν Χριστῷ; 1 Clem 22.1: πίστις ἐν Χρ; 1 Clem 32.4; 46.6: κλῆσις ἐν Χρ; 1 Clem 38.1: σωτηρία ἐν Χρ; 1 Clem 43.1: ἔργον πιστευθὲν ἐν Χρ; 1 Clem 47.6: ἀγωγὴ ἐν Χρ; 1 Clem 48.3: πύλη ἐν Χρ; 1 Clem 49: ἀγάπη ἐν Χρ; 1 Clem 46.7: the believers are τὰ μέλη τοῦ Χριστοῦ are ἴδιον σῶμα; 1 Clem 3.4: everything has to happen κατὰ τὸ καθῆκον τῷ Χριστῳ. The related formula is equally consistent and reliable: διὰ (τοῦ κυριου ἡμῶν) Ἰησοῦ Χριστοῦ; not only are Christians chosen, sanctified, saved, preserved, endowed with all the goods of God through Jesus Christ (Inscription; 50.7; 58.2; 59.2, 3; 64), but also χάρις and εἰρήνη proceed from God through Christ (Inscription); one flees to the mercy of God through him (20.11); one confesses his sins to God through him (61.3); indeed the apostles, when they saw the future, received this knowledge through him (44.1).

30. Σκήπτρον τῆς μεγαλωσύνης is, according to the wording, peculiarly but probably copied from Heb 1:8, where Ps 45:6 (ῥάβδος εὐθύτητος ἡ ῥάβδος τῆς βασιλείας σου) is applied to Christ. Much like Luke in so many places, Clement has only improved the expression linguistically. It is strange that the term "Son of God" is found only once (1 Clem 36.4), but that is only by chance, for 1 Clem 32.2 says, "The Lord Jesus comes

further speculative statements about the nature of the Redeemer. But an idea concerning Christ, the ἀρχιερεὺς τῶν προσφοσῶν ἡμῶν καὶ προστάτης καὶ βοηθὸς ἡμῶν,[31] completely fills him, and it is also the only one that, apart from ἐν Χριστῷ, breaks the rational structure of his religious thoughts—that is the idea of the blood of Christ and its inestimable value. Here too Paul has certainly been the guiding force, but our author does not follow him throughout. He is satisfied with the mere articulation of Pauline thought, for he did not feel that σκάνδαλον, which was what death on the cross meant for the Jews, and the "folly" is cancelled out by the consideration that many kings and leaders also saved their fellow citizens by their blood.[32] Only the words that the blood of Christ is τίμιον τῷ θεῷ indicate that it also has an important meaning with respect to God.[33] That it was "given for us" is a reminiscence of the Lord's Supper. But it is very noteworthy that in the description of the Christian as he is to be (1 Clem 2), it is emphasized that not only the words of Christ are deeply implanted in his heart, but also that the sufferings of Christ should also be before their eyes. This calls for a steady direction of the mind towards the death of Christ, which the church has only grasped through Bernardian piety. But the author does not carry out the thought in the Bernardian way. It is enough for him to have expressed it.[34] Like John, he states all the more definitively that Christ is the gate ἐν ᾗ μακάριοι πάντες οἱ εἰσελθόντες (1 Clem 48.4), and that love ἐν Χριστῷ must prove itself in the fulfillment of Christ's

---

from Jacob τὸ κατὰ σάρκα." The name ὁ παῖς θεοῦ is found at the end of the congregational prayer in 1 Clem 59 (3x). ὁ κύριος is used both for Christ and for God himself; for the latter, it also appears in the form ὁ κύριος ἡμῶν Ἰησοῦς Χριστός.

31. In 1 Clem 36.1–2 this is explained in the following way: "Through Jesus Christ, we look with certain eyes into the heights of the heavens; through him we see as in a mirror God's blameless and most venerable face; through him the eyes of our hearts have been opened; through him our darkened mind blossoms again into the light; through him the Master has made us taste immortal knowledge. 'He who is the reflection of his majesty, is so much greater than the angels because he has received a more excellent name.'"

32. 1 Clem 55.1 (see above).

33. In 1 Clem 7.4, it is also said that the blood of Christ was shed for our salvation and brought the grace of repentance to the whole world. In 1 Clem 12.7, one reads that it is through the blood of the Lord that λύτρωσις ἔσται πᾶσιν τοῖς πιστεύουσιν καὶ ἐλπίζουσιν ἐπὶ τὸν θεόν, and in 1 Clem 49.6 it says: διὰ τὴν ἀγάπην, ἣν ἔσχεν πρὸς ἡμᾶς, τὸ αἷμα αὐτοῦ ἔδωκεν ὑπὲρ ἡμῶν Ἰ. Χρ. ὁ κύριος ἡμῶν ἐν θελήματι θεοῦ, καὶ τὴν σάρκα ὑπὲρ τῆς σαρκὸς ἡμῶν καὶ τὴν ψυχὴν ὑπὲρ τῶν ψυχῶν ἡμῶν.

34. Strangely enough, the resurrection of Jesus is relatively restricted to the background, so it is certainly proclaimed and described as the ἀπαρχή of our resurrection (1 Clem 24.1) and as the means by which the apostles were filled with confidence (1 Clem 42.4). It has not inspired the author to a particular form of *gnosis*.

commandments (1 Clem 49.1). So his "Christology" and christological mysticism is essentially a practical one—even the old Trinitarian formula is repeated without any speculation[35]—and Christ remains superordinate with respect to it: ὁ παντεπόπτης θεὸς καὶ δεσπότης τῶν πνευμάτων καὶ κύριος πάσης σαρκός, ὁ ἐκλεξάμενος τὸν κύριον Ἰησοῦν Χριστὸν καὶ ἡμᾶς δι' αὐτοῦ εἰς λαὸν περιούσιον (64.1). The Christians, through Christ the people of God: this thought is still understandable to the author. However, "the kingdom of Christ" or "the kingdom of God" is almost only a reminiscence to him. The expression is only found twice in the letter, once in the formulaic expression that the apostles went out to proclaim the coming of the kingdom of God (1 Clem 42.3), then in the similarly formulated proclamation that the perfected ones will be revealed ἐν τῇ ἐπισκοπῇ τῆς βασιλείας τοῦ Χριστοῦ (1 Clem 50.3). All the more definite is the general resurrection and a resurrection of the flesh, which Clement teaches and provides evidence for (1 Clem 24) without sharp Pauline reservation. With this, the author precedes all the teachers of the second century who proclaimed the resurrection of the flesh as the real centerpiece of Christian doctrine in contrast to the pagans and the Gnostics.

Of the "mysteries" or the "sacraments" in general, the author seems to know nothing. Of course, we cannot doubt that he shares the common Christian view of baptism and the Lord's Supper—he mentions them once (1 Clem 42), which he presupposes[36]—but we do not know how to think about the holy acts.[37] In an intimate and detailed letter to Christians, this is striking, and one may at least assume from this silence that Christianity was not a mystery religion to him, but rather that he found its essence expressed in historical facts and in God's bright revelations. The sources of the author are primarily the texts of the OT. He does not presuppose any doubt about its dignity either, just as he does not make any distinction between the

---

35. The author uses the Trinitarian formula twice (1 Clem 46.6: ἕνα θεὸν ἔχομεν καὶ ἕνα Χριστὸν καὶ ἓν πνεῦμα τῆς χάριτος τὸ ἐκχυθὲν ἐφ' ἡμᾶς; and in 1 Clem 58.2: ζῇ γὰρ ὁ θεὸς καὶ ζῇ ὁ κύριος Ἰησοῦς Χριστὸς καὶ τὸ πνεῦμα τὸ ἅγιον, ἥ τε πίστις καὶ ἡ ἐλπὶς τῶν ἐκλεκτῶν; and there is also an allusion in 1 Clem 42.3). He does not comment upon it, certainly because he felt no more difficulties about this confession as did Paul. Beyond the Trinitarian confession, there is, as an allusion to the later Roman symbol, the formula ὁ θεὸς παντοκράτωρ and the resurrection of the flesh. — The ζῇ with the name of God has a Semitic origin. Cf. the formula חי יהוה and חי עבדת on the inscription HI on the recently discovered sanctuary of the deified Nabataean king Obodas (Compt. rend. de l'Acad. des inscr., January 1904, 63). See also Ael. Publ. Julius von Debeltus (ca. 190) in Eusebius *Hist. eccl.* V.19: ζῇ ὁ θεὸς ὁ ἐν τοῖς οὐρανοῖς.

36. Not only 1 Clem 21 (see above), but also 1 Clem 44, where the gifts of the Lord's Supper should at least be included within the τὰ δῶρα προσφέρειν.

37. Both actions also allowed for a rational evaluation that had nothing to do with magical mysteries.

books. Wrede has talked about the many ways Clement uses the book in his wonderful investigations about 1 Clement.[38] Wrede's investigations were so exhaustive that no further word is necessary. Almost all ways the OT could be used and has been used subsequently is applicable here. Indeed, the OT is so sovereignly in the foreground that, according to our letter, the Christian religion could be called a religion of the book, namely of the OT, which has been Christianized through its interpretation. But nothing is singular here either. Only five[39] of Clement's quotations cannot be identified and must have come from books that, together with the OT, came out of the synagogue as holy texts into the Christian congregations, but which were later eradicated. Such apocryphal quotations can also be found in the writings of the second century, indeed even later.

The Christian tradition is not yet available to the author as a written, holy one.[40] The gospels are not cited. What is told of the history of Christ, of the apostles, and of the apostolic times is so little that one does not have to accept written sources for it. The two rather extensive groups of sayings by Jesus (1 Clem 13.2; 46.8) do not coincide with any version in the gospels preserved for us and are introduced with the same old and direct formula[41] that Luke uses in the book of Acts where he quotes a word of the Lord. The author has carefully read some of Paul's letters and the Epistle to the Hebrews and has been shaped by them. But that these letters constitute or belong to a sacred codex is of course not in view. Most remarkable for our purposes is Clement's refrain from all foreign substances. There is nothing exotic and mysterious and there is no foreign cultic wisdom consulted.[42] On the other hand, a reminder is issued to adhere to the κανὼν τῆς παραδόσεως.[43] If the church subsequently restricts itself strictly to the

---

38. Wrede, *Untersuchungen zum ersten Klemensbriefe*.

39. In 1 Clem 8.3; 17.6; 23.4; 26.2; 46.2.

40. Εὐαγγέλιον is found once in the book (1 Clem 47), but only with the sense of the missionary preaching of the apostles. In 1 Clem 42.1, 3, εὐαγγελίζεσθαι is also written twice about the apostles who proclaimed the future kingdom of Christ.

41. 1 Clem 13.2: μάλιστα μεμνημένοι τῶν λόγων τοῦ κυρίου Ἰησοῦ, οὓς ἐλάλησεν διδάσκων ἐπιείκειαν καὶ μακροθυμίαν· οὕτως γὰρ εἶπεν; and in 1 Clem 46.8: μνήσθητε τῶν λόγων Ἰησοῦ τοῦ κυρίου ὑμῶν· εἶπεν γάρ.

42. The phoenix does not belong here, for in Clement's view, it belongs as a part of natural history. The unbiased use of examples from secular Roman history (1 Clem 55) and the Roman military (1 Clem 37) is also out of the question in this context.

43. 1 Clem 7.2: ἀπολίπωμεν τὰς κενὰς καὶ ματαίας φροντίδας καὶ ἔλθωμεν ἐπὶ τὸν εὐκλεῆ καὶ σεμνὸν τῆς παραδόσεως ἡμῶν κανόνα (cf. 1 Clem 19). The expression is not quite clear, but it can certainly be grasped in a very general sense, which has in view everything that belongs and is handed down to Christianity.

two Testaments and has suppressed or forbidden everything else, this is indeed already pronounced in our letter.

The local (Roman) church consciousness as well as the consciousness of the unity of all Christians is keenly developed by the author. Although the word ἐκκλησία is only used of the individual congregation, and although ecclesiastical speculation such as is found in Paul's letter to the Ephesians, 2 Clement, and the Shepherd of Hermas is not found within the sober author of 1 Clement, his interest in solidarity for "the whole fraternity" is strongly expressed in the letter, especially in the final prayer.[44] In truth, the theme "love and unity" and "unity and love"—the later, foundational, ethical schema of Catholicism—was not already brought to expression, but the same harsh and unpleasant use of the formula vis-à-vis the schismatics that characterizes later Catholicism is already evidenced. But what is even more instructive is that—in contrast to the Corinthian turmoil—for the worship service, which is at the center of Christian activity,[45] aspects such as order, time, space, and officers who are called and placed into a hierarchy are the most pervasive. As is well known, they are almost completely missing in the Pauline age, let alone at the center of attention. But here they almost seem to be the most important thing. In strict contrast to Paul, the Old Testament ordinances are applied to them, and there is even the reminder that, in the OT, violation of these laws resulted in the death penalty![46] Truly the "development" here has taken place quickly, and has indeed taken place in Rome![47] If we add

---

44. Terminology of the church's self-consciousness is Pauline, but it is most likely pre-Pauline (i.e., generally Christian terminology): Christians are called and chosen (6.1; 46.4; 49.6) by God through Christ (50.7; 65.2); they are the κλητοὶ ἡγιασμένοι (inscription); they represent the foretold number of the chosen ones (2.4; 58.2; 59.1, 3; 64); they are τὸ ἐκλογῆς μέρος (29.1) and the ἁγία μερίς (30.1), chosen from among the nations of the world (29.3); they are the army of God (21.4; 37.1; 41.1), but at the same time the flock of Christ (16.1; 44.3; 54.2; 57.2), indeed they are members of Christ (46.7), and Christ is their high priest, intercessor, overseer, and helper (vv.11). Furthermore, they are also Israel, and Abraham is their father (31.2); their fathers are the righteous ones in the Old Testament (30.7). Finally, the Christians are οἱ πολιτευόμενοι τὴν ἀμεταμέλητον πολιτείαν τοῦ θεοῦ (54.4) and are under the παιδεία of God (56).

45. Wrede rightly says that the cult must have been the field where the leaders of the turmoil and the presbyters met as rivals (*Untersuchungen zum ersten Klemensbriefe*, 48f). Knopf's objection is not conclusive (*Der erste Clemensbrief*, 173).

46. 1 Clem 41; 51. The author was aware of the fact that, in this disastrous application to the Christian, he had put forward something quite new—it is, apart from his theory of ministry, the only "new" thing the letter contains—and he concludes his explanation with the words: ὁρᾶτε, ἀδελφοί, ὅσῳ πλείονος κατηξιώθημεν γνώσεως, τοσούτῳ μᾶλλον ὑποκείμεθα κινδύνῳ (41.4).

47. The Roman local patriotism can be seen in 1 Clem 5 and 6, where the Roman examples (Peter, Paul, and the victims of the persecution of Nero) were pulled in by the hair.

that the author sets up a chain—"God sent Christ, Christ the apostles; the apostles appointed their first converts as bishops and deacons (δοκιμάσαντες ἐν πνεύματι) and, prophetically foreseeing later struggles, ordered that these should be followed by other tried and tested men (συνευδοκησάσης τῆς ἐκκλησίας πάσης) after their death"—then the roots of the whole later authority and theory of offices of Catholicism is already found here. For even if the author initially draws the conclusion that those who are thus appointed should not be removed, the reasoning behind this goes much further. If Christ has the authority of God, and the apostles have the authority of Christ, this suggests the conclusion that the officials appointed by the apostles also have the authority of the apostles.[48]

The most recent expositions of the letter are peculiar to it and could probably be left out here. However, they are also valuable within the circle of interests that concern us: the only particular and forward-looking exposition within the letter does not point in the direction of Gnosticism or mysticism or syncretism, but prepares the way for Roman Catholicism.

What had been considered to be the essence of Christianity, which pieces were decisive in determining what was the core of the spiritual structure of Christianity at the transition from the first century to the second century, and what, in comparison with it, must be considered more or less insignificant, even if it is attractive and interesting, has to be learned from this letter. No matter how much one takes into account the particular situation in which 1 Clement was written and declares the judgment of the Corinthian riots clerical and unjust, the main elements of Christianity, as they were perceived by the Roman congregation, remain unaffected. Here, one has to learn that the Christianity that has made history was not everything that one so often today wants to make it out to be. It was not a folkloristic, unreflected religion; it was not the playground for enthusiasts, who were nothing more than enthusiasts;[49] it did not have to laboriously gain a firm structure from a plethora of Gnostic distortions and syncretisms, but was a serious and deep, closed and firm moral movement in the consciousness of knowing the living God. Compared with other religions, it was the religion of inwardness and of the spirit.[50] This is how it appears in this letter. It was a continuation of Jewish synagogual propaganda in the realm, purified and

---

48. 1 Clem 40–44.

49. The letter testifies to the fact that there was a Christianity in broad, authoritative circles in which the enthusiastic element completely receded behind the mature, moralistic Christianity (see Wrede, *Untersuchungen zum ersten Klemensbriefe*, 106).

50. TN: The original reads "Religion der Innerlichkeit und des Geistes," which could be translated "the religion of inwardness and the *spirit*" or "the religion of inwardness and the *mind*."

deepened, expanded, individualized, but again firmly united by the knowledge of God in the κύριος Χριστός. The "continuation" therefore nullified itself, for through the transformation something completely new emerged, namely a brotherhood of those who were seized by God, who had found eternal life, and who prepared themselves for the same in holy joy and seriousness. Everything that did not fall within these limits was secondary and peripheral, even if it was not always felt that way by those involved, and even if they could only express their deepest possessions in stammering or borrowed words. For this reason, a real understanding of the nascent Catholic Church can only be won over by studying the history of the Christian faith and ethics, but not by efforts to bring the side and undercurrents to light. It may be a serious shortcoming of the letter that these side and undercurrents are almost entirely absent in it. It neither gives an idea of the richness and diversity of the expressions of Christian thought, nor does it teach about what has already been carried along by Christianity. But it is the very absence that proves that these colorful fabrics were only of minor importance at that time. "Folkloristic"[51] Christianity, such as existed then, cannot be studied by means of the letter. But the "folkloristic Christianity," that nest of tenacious and sluggish superstitions and indifferent habits, as a rule has only a very limited, even a negative value in the Christian religion: one experiences how the eternal yesterday clasps the new and the holy and pulls it down to itself. That too must be studied, but nothing significant can be learned there, neither for the *homo sapiens* himself nor for his actual history.

Excursus I

Connections between 1 Clement and Ancient Literature and Culture

From a literary point of view, 1 Clement is a work of art. When the author says at the beginning of the letter that unexpected and adverse circumstances had delayed the writing of the letter, he could have added that the preparation of the letter took a significant amount of time. Not a single paragraph is thrown out quickly and naturally, but everything is well thought out, formally and thoroughly executed, and stylistically filled out. Everything is laid out in artistic prose—even the historical passage about Peter and Paul—and it is difficult in many parts of the letter to distinguish the author's artistic prose from poetry.

---

51. TN: "Volkstümliches" can mean be "popular" or "folkloristic."

But the letter is a literary print in two hues. It is painted with the Hebrew hue (LXX) and the Greek hue of artistic prose.

The stronger hue is that of Semitic poetry in Greek dress. Not only do the numerous, largely poetic Old Testament quotations occupy a significant portion of the letter, but also the author's own statements are, wherever possible, formally modelled on the poetic sections of the Septuagint. Some passages read like portions of the Psalms, and where the replica is not so far advanced, the author demonstrates—by laying everything out in simple order, using *parallelismus membrorum* and *Isokola* incessantly, dissolving causal and conditional sentences into parataxis and forming concatenations—that he always has the sacred, biblical style in mind.

This model had to be chosen because what had to be written to the brothers in Corinth was the will of God and had to be spoken by the Holy Spirit, and the Holy Spirit speaks the language of the Old Testament. The letter explicitly says that the Corinthians should be obedient to "what we have written by the Holy Spirit" (1 Clem 63.2), should "not follow us but the will of God" (1 Clem 56.1), should "submit to what God has said through us" (1 Clem 59.1)[52]—then it was necessary to speak the language of God. But precisely because this was required in an objective sense,[53] one must be careful not to conclude from the reproduction of the language of the Psalms and the Prophets that the author of 1 Clement was a born Jew.[54] One can say only as much as can be said with regard to Luke, who also reproduces the Septuagint style. The abstract possibility that Clement was a Jew by birth should not be denied,[55] but it cannot be substantiated with the Septuagint style of the letter, nor is the virtuoso knowledge of the OT proof of it. On the other hand, there are strong observations that lead away from Judaism.

Stylistically speaking, the letter is, as noted, a mixed product, and it is a mixture that aesthetically sensitive critics critique. Those who come to the letter after reading the Greek orators, of course, cannot find themselves in this rhetoric, which embroiders the colorful flowers of Asian eloquence upon the canvas of the Hebrew poetic prose. It is teeming with sonorous figures—the letter is to be read aloud—external and internal rhymes,[56] with anaphoric references, rhetorical questions, carefully constructed rhetorical

---

52. In this sense also the Roman congregation is still an enthusiastic one. It is certain that it may and can speak through the Holy Spirit.

53. Wehofer in particular has shown how strongly the letter emulates the LXX, but he goes too far here and there.

54. See Lightfoot, *Clement of Rome*, vol. 1; Wehofer, *Untersuchungen*.

55. See Wrede, *Untersuchungen zum ersten Klemensbriefe*.

56. Whether the rhymes are always intentional is questionable; but in many cases there is no doubt about it.

gems and rhythmic or artistically symmetrical prose. In some places, one can ask whether Semitic influence is to be assumed here or whether it is emerging Greek rhetoric. But as is well known, this question is often asked in relation to later Hellenistic literature and cannot be answered with certainty. However, on the basis of a number of observations, it is clear that the author's eloquence cannot be explained exclusively by his imitation of the OT, but also by training in Greek rhetoric.

This is also taught by the entire construction of the "letter," which, despite its Psalmic character, reads like an admonitory diatribe about "peace and concord." It begins with a laudatory speech, then the theme follows; examples follow immediately, and at the end the laudatory speech resumes (1 Clem 62).

The Hellenistic-Roman character of the letter, in contrast to the Jewish character, becomes even clearer in a number of details. Some of them are listed here:

Immediately in 1 Clem 1.2, the μεγαλοπρεπὲς τῆς φιλοξενίας ἦθος of the Corinthians is praised. It should be recalled that it is said of Polydamas in Xenophon's Hellenica: ἦν καὶ ἄλλως φιλόξενός τε καὶ μεγαλοπρεπὴς τὸν Θετταλικὸν τρόπον (6.1.3). The double parallel is remarkable.[57] It appears to be ancient when the calamity, which is caused by ζῆλος καὶ φθόνος, is presented in broad rhetorical expositions by means of biblical examples and certain examples from the recent Christian past,[58] and then concludes with the words: ζῆλος καὶ ἔρις πόλεις μεγάλας κατέστρεψεν καὶ ἔθνη μεγάλα ἐξερίζωσεν (1 Clem 6.4). The interpreters have rightly compared this text not only with Sirach 28:14 (πόλεις ὀχυρὰς καθεῖλε καὶ οἰκίας μεγιστάνων κατέστρεψε), but also, and even better, with Horace, Saec. I.16f. (*Irae Tyesten exitio gravi stravere, et altis urbibus ultimae stetere causae cur perirent funditus*). Clement must have indeed had this secular story in mind here, and this is explicitly and objectively found in 1 Clem 55.1: Ἵνα δὲ καὶ ὑποδείγματα ἐθνῶν ἐνέγκωμεν· πολλοὶ βασιλεῖς καὶ ἡγούμενοι, λοιμικοῦ τινὸς ἐνστάντος καιροῦ, χρησμοδοτηθέντες παρέδωκαν ἑαυτοὺς εἰς θάνατον, ἵνα ῥύσωνται διὰ τοῦ ἑαυτῶν αἵματος τοὺς πολίτας. πολλοὶ ἐξεχώρησαν ἰδίων πόλεων, ἵνα μὴ στασιάζωσιν ἐπὶ πλεῖον.

If recourse to ancient stories is evident—and indeed approved of—then one may perhaps also assume that in the preceding chapter (1 Clem

---

57. Μεγαλοπρεπής in one of Clement's favorite words, but is otherwise only used for God (1 Clem 9.1, 2; 19.2; 45.7; 60.1; 61.1; 64.1).

58. Two parallels stand out, which are coincidental but not unimportant. Clement speaks of a πολὺ πλῆθος of the martyred Christians (1 Clem 6.1), and Tacitus speaks of a *multitudo ingens* (*Ann.* XV.44); Clement speaks of the suddenness of the blows under Domitian (1 Clem 1.1), and Suetonius of the *inopinata saevitia* of the emperor (*Dom.* 11).

54), Clement remembers Cicero, *Mil.* 93 (*tranquilla republica cives mei—quoniam mihi cum illis non licet—sine me ipsi, sed per me perfruantur; ego cedam atque abibo*). Clement writes: Τίς ἐν ὑμῖν γενναῖος; . . . εἰπάτω· εἰ δι' ἐμὲ στάσις καὶ ἔρις καὶ σχίσματα, ἐκχωρῶ, ἄπειμι οὗ ἐὰν βούλησθε, καὶ ποιῶ τὰ προστασσόμενα ὑπὸ τοῦ πλήθους· μόνον τὸ ποίμνιον τοῦ Χριστοῦ εἰρηνευέτω (54.1-2). It is an ancient thought that the patriot should exile himself if he can thereby return peace to the fatherland.

Ancient is also the inclusion of the legend of the phoenix (1 Clem 25) as a proof for immortality. A born Jew or a narrow-minded Christian would hardly have chosen this example (see however Hesiod, Herodotus, Antiphanes, Manilius, Tacitus, and Solinus), just as he would not have mentioned the previously discussed examples from secular history and would not have spoken approvingly of "our" soldiers, their exemplary discipline, and their ranks. However, Clement writes, "our father, Jacob," "our Lord Christ," "our apostles," and "our soldiers" (1 Clem 37.2). Clement also shows evidence of ancient, scientific knowledge, when he speaks of the μετὰ τὸν ὠκεανὸν κόσμοι (1 Clem 20.8).[59] Alexander von Humboldt collected the opinions from antiquity about them (see Strabo, Plutarch, and the famous prophecy of Seneca, *Med.* II.375, which was known to Columbus).[60] Furthermore, only an educated man writes (*loc. cit.*): ἥλιός τε καὶ σελήνη ἀστέρων τε χοροὶ ἐν ὁμονοίᾳ δίχα πάσης παρεκβάσεως ἐξελίσσουσιν τοὺς ἐπιτεταγμένους αὐτοῖς ὁρισμούς (20.3).

Jacobson and Lightfoot have pointed out that the sentence οἱ μεγάλοι δίχα τῶν μικρῶν οὐ δύνανται εἶναι, οὔτε οἱ μικροὶ δίχα τῶν μεγάλων· σύγκρασίς τίς ἐστιν ἐν πᾶσιν, καὶ ἐν τούτοις χρῆσις (1 Clem 37.4)—aside from the play on words with σύγκρασις, χρῆσις—is composed of plagiarisms; see Sophocles, *Aj.* 158: καίτοι σμικροὶ μεγάλων χωρὶς σφαλερὸν πύργου ῥῶμα πέλονται κτλ.; Plato, *Leg.* 902 E: οὐδὲ γὰρ ἄνευ σμικρῶν τοὺς μεγάλους φασὶν οἱ λιθολόγοι λίθους εὖ κεῖσθαι; and Euripides, *Frag. Aeol.* 2: ἀλλ' ἔστι τις σύγκρασις ὥστ' ἔχειν καλῶς. This is probably the case, but it is not certain; σύγκρασις could have also come from 1 Cor 12:24: ἀλλὰ ὁ θεὸς συνεκέρασεν τὸ σῶμα. Clement continues immediately: λάβωμεν τὸ σῶμα ἡμῶν (37.5). After that, he alone contributes: ὁ πλούσιος ἐπιχορηγείτω τῷ πτωχῷ, ὁ δὲ πτωχὸς εὐχαριστείτω τῷ θεῷ, ὅτι ἔδωκεν αὐτῷ δι' οὗ ἀναπληρωθῇ αὐτοῦ τὸ ὑστέρημα (38.2) and with

---

59. TN: This clause has been freely translated. The original "Antike Wissenschaft ist es auch, wenn er von den μετὰ τὸν ὠκεανὸν κόσμοι" literally means "It is also ancient, scientific knowledge when he speaks of the μετὰ τὸν ὠκεανὸν κόσμοι."

60. Photius (*Lex.* 126) rebuked Clement's use of both the phoenix and the worlds beyond.

Euripides, among others, one reads: ἃ μὴ γάρ ἐστι τῷ πένητι, πλούσιος δίδως· ἃ δ' οἱ πλουτοῦντες οὐ κεκτήμεθα τοῖσιν πένησι χρώμενοι θηρώμεθα.[61]

One senses the antiquity of the words ἁγνὰς καὶ ἀμιάντους χεῖρας αἴροντες πρὸς θεόν (1 Clem 29.1). Wettstein (on 1 Tim 2:8) compared the tragedian Heliodorus at Galen, *de Antid.* II.7: ὁσίας μὲν χεῖρας ἐς ἠέρα λαμπρὸν ἀείρας, and the series of good things in 1 Clem 35.2 sounds Hellenistic: ζωὴ ἐν ἀθανασίᾳ, λαμπρότης ἐν δικαιοσύνῃ, ἀλήθεια ἐν παρρησίᾳ!

However, more important than all this is the fact that no small part of the letter is reminiscent of philosophical language, especially of the range of thoughts that are designated as of Seneca, Epictetus, and Plutarch. Here, one can count τὰ ἐφόδια (1 Clem 2.1), ὁ κῆρυξ (1 Clem 5.6, used for the spiritual leaders), ἡ δικαιοπραγία (1 Clem 32.3), ὁ δισταγμός (1 Clem 46.9), ἡ παλιγγενεσία (1 Clem 9.4), ἀτμὶς ἀπὸ κύθρας (1 Clem 17.6), [τὸ πνεῦμα ἡγεμονικόν (1 Clem 18.12)], ἀόργητος (1 Clem 19.3), πολιτεία and πολιτεύεσθαι (1 Clem 2.8; 3.4; 6.1; 21.1; 44.6; 51.2; 54.4), ἑτεροκλινής (1 Clem 11.1; 47.7), παμμεγεθέστατος (1 Clem 33.3), κοινωφελής (1 Clem 48.6), ἀμεταμέλητος (1 Clem 2.7; 54.4; 58.2), ἀπροσδεής (1 Clem 52.1), the ethical application of the growing vine (1 Clem 23), ἥδιον διδόντες ἢ λαμβάνοντες (1 Clem 2.1, where the ἥδιον points to Epicurious: τοῦ εὖ πάσχειν τὸ εὖ ποιεῖν οὐ μόνον κάλλιον ἀλλὰ καὶ ἥδιον. Seneca, *Ep.* 81.17: *errat si quis beneficium accipit libentius quam reddit*), and the figurative use of σκάμμα and κανών (1 Clem 7.1). But beyond the individual terms, the concept of God,[62] the view of nature as an ordered and purposeful whole, the joy in the regular movement of the world and in the providence that dominates everything, the resounding interest in ὁμόνοια (1 Clem 9.4; 11.2; 20.3; 20.10, 11; 21.1; 30.3; 34.7; 49.5; 50.5; 60.4; 61.1; 63.2; 65.1), and finally the moralism, all these features bear witness to its Stoic imprint. The Stoic hues here are fused with the psalmists' view of nature and testamentary ethics.

If one holds that Clement mainly writes according to the instructions of the Old Testament texts, then the above is sufficient proof of a Hellenistic education and of a substantial influence from Hellenic culture.[63] That

---

61. Many things in Clement are reminiscent of the use of words by the Tragedians, such as τὰ νέρτερα in 1 Clem 20.5.

62. Just look at the names of God (ὁ μέγας δημιουργὸς καὶ δεσπότης τῶν ἁπάντων, etc.) and compare them with those in the New Testament. In the NT, ὁ δημιουργός occurs only once (Heb 11:10) and is never used (of God) in the whole of the LXX. Clement also speaks of the μεγαλεῖον τῆς καλλονῆς τοῦ θεοῦ (1 Clem 49.3).

63. The letter is completely devoid of "proletarian" traits. It is, therefore, suitable for thoroughly correcting the ideas that one has about the proletarian character of the oldest Christian communities. In any case, the leadership and resounding character of the Roman congregation has never been proletarian. Even such small traits carry weight, such as the fact that the church addresses the fellow Christians in Corinth not only as

language, as far as I can see, is correct, but the vocabulary is varied. This is a necessary consequence of the heavy use of the LXX, liturgical reminiscences, and some popular, philosophical expressions.[64] Undoubtedly the letter—behind which lies a strong and clear will, though lacking a pronounced literary individuality—made a strong impression from the very beginning. This strong impression was first based upon its contents, but then also on the judgement Photius (*Lex.* 126) made about its style, which was probably already valid in the second century: ἐγγὺς τοῦ ἐκκλησιαστικοῦ. Of course, Photius also finds the letter ἁπλοῦς κατὰ τὴν φράσιν καὶ ἀπεριέργου χαρακτῆρος. Compared to the Byzantine church rhetoric and to the rhetoric in general, he has to appear "simple"; but the περίεργον is not missing. Photius did not perceive it as such, but as a free swing of the spirit of the ancient church. If, according to a ἱστορία reported by Origen (Eusebius, *Hist. eccl.* V. 25.14), some have considered Clement the author of the Epistle to the Hebrews, then perhaps in it lies only a judgment about the style of the letter. Nevertheless, it is possible that the hypothesis arose from the observation of the objective relationship of both documents,[65] or from the report that the Epistle to the Hebrews came from Rome.

Excursus II

Ecclesiastical *termini technici*, Attested to for the First Time in 1 Clement

Inscription: ἡ ἐκκλησία ἡ παροικοῦσα] The next oldest passage can be found in the address of the inscription of the letter of Polycarp to the Philippians.

1 Clement 40.5: οἱ λαϊκοί] = for those who have no ecclesiastical office: the next oldest testimonies to my knowledge occur in Clement of Alexandria and Tertullian.

ἀγαπητοί and ἀδελφοί, but also as ἄνδρες ἀδελφοί. The contact with Greek culture, first appearing in the Lukan writings, has made further progress. Luke and Clement belong together. Paul stands for himself.

64. The vocabulary of the letter is not very rich, but has some ἅπαξ λεγόμενα or words that may be found here for the first time: ἀβαναύσως (44.3), ἁγιοπρεπής (13.3), ἀνατυλίσσειν (31.1), ἀτημελεῖν (38.2), αὐτεπαινετός (30.6), ἀφιλοξενία (35.5; see Sib. Or.), δωδεκάσκηπτρον (31.4), ἐνοπτρίζεσθαι (36.2), ἐπικαταλλάσσειν (48.1), εὐπρόσδεκτος (40.3), μεταπαραδιδόναι (20.9), πανάγιος (35.3), πανάρετος (1.2; 2.8; 45.7; 57.3; 60.4), παντεπόπτης (55.6; 64.1; see Sib. Or.), παντοκρατορικός (8.5), προδημιουργεῖν (32), ὑπερεκπερισσῶς (20.11), χρησμοδοτεῖν (55.1). Other rare words include ἀνεξιχνίαστος (20.5) and ἀνεκδιήγητος (20.5).

65. As a side note, the relationship of the letter with Hebrews in terms of stylistic terms or in terms of content is not substantial.

1 Clement 54.2: τὸ πλῆθος] = the entire congregation; the next oldest passage is in Hermas, *Mand.* 11.9. See Irenaeus in Eusebius, *Hist. eccl.* V.20.6.

1 Clement 44.3: συνευδοκεῖν of the congregation when appointing officials] see Cyprian, *Ep.* 33; 55; 67; 68.

1 Clement 41.1: τάγμα from the ranks in the congregation τάξις τ. προφητῶν in the fragment of a document from the second century that has been preserved for us only in fragments.[66]

1 Clement 40: The bishops and deacons, compared with the priests and Levites], see the ancient Catholic Fathers.

1 Clement 7.2: ὁ κανὼν τῆς παραδόσεως], see Polycarp, *ad Phil.* 7; Clement of Alexandria, *Strom.* I.1 (both of whom are dependent on our Clement).

1 Clement 2.3; (8.5); 32.4; 60.4; 62.2 and the Inscription: ὁ θεὸς παντοκράτωρ] are first here, along with Revelation, in terms of terminological usage.

1 Clement 2.1: τὰ ἐφόδια τοῦ Χριστοῦ (θεοῦ)], see Dionysius *Cor.* in Eusebius *Hist. eccl.* IV.23.

It is remarkable that the designation οἱ Χριστιανοί is not found in the letter (see however the Antiochian Ignatius), which confirms the old age of the letter.

Excursus III

The Dating of the Letter's Composition

Since the dating of the letter's composition—although it is one of the most certain in the history of early Christian literature—has recently been contested, apart from the excellent external evidence, which already begins with Polycarp, some observations about the internal evidence should be pointed out here, which are more hidden, but are no less conclusive.

(1) The letter still shows the same unbiased assessment of the Roman authorities as the Pauline epistles, 1 Peter, and Acts, which would be striking in both Trajan and post-Trajan eras.

(2) Where the author accumulates examples of the terrible consequences of ζῆλος καὶ φθόνος and finally comes up to Christianity, he only knows of the Neronian persecution in Rome, so he is not yet aware of more general persecutions.

---

66. See the meeting reports of the *Sitzungsberichte der preußischen Akademie der Wissenschaften* on July 14, 1898. See also Eusebius, *Hist. eccl.* V.19.2.

(3) It is also a sign of its old age (i.e., from the first century) that, at the time of this letter's composition, the sharp tension between the new religion on the one hand and the state and society on the other hand was still quite latent. The casuistic, constantly recurring conflicts with the world and with the secular professions only reach their threshold at the beginning of the second century and thus become a serious problem for the church. Previously, Christians were a small, little known flock, and withdrawal from the world was not difficult for the small group of people from middle and lower classes of society, who wanted little from the world. What I have proven in my treatise "Militia Christi"[67] about the Christian's relation to the military is also true of other professions. The crisis only begins in the second century.

(4) The author does not quote the words of the Lord written in the gospels, but simply the words of the Lord.

(5) The "Gnostic" movements could still be completely overlooked in the letter (in contrast to the Shepherd of Hermas, which was edited at the end of the first third of the second century).

(6) The deacons are still very close to the episcopates and even seem to belong to the circle of appointed presbyters, which is later nowhere attested.

---

67. Harnack, *Militia Christi*.

Appendix IV

The Epithet "Servant of God" Used of Jesus and Its History in the Ancient Church

1926

Introduction

The history of Christology can be illustrated by the names of Jesus. This has happened, but in doing so, the name *ebed YHWH* (Παῖς θεοῦ, *puer dei*) has almost always been passed over. What meaning and scope did this name originally have? Has this meaning changed over time? These questions will be examined in the following paper.[1] The word *ebed* ("servant," "slave"; in socio-political linguistic use "servant, official of a king" and a submissive self-designation) is used in Semitic languages to designate the worshippers of a deity.[2] Jews also followed this linguistic usage, and according to it the congregation (the people) of Israel is also called the *ebed YHWH* in the OT. But the word also became an honorary designation for those men whom God called into special service, or who distinguished themselves by their worship of God. Therefore, the patriarchs Moses, Joshua, Job, David, the prophets, etc. are called "servants of God" as well as the mysterious personality that God has chosen and will send in Deutero-Isaiah (in addition to the

---

1. Fifty years ago, in my commentary on 1 Clement, Barnabas, and the Didache, I collected some particularly important source texts on παῖς θεοῦ as an epithet for Jesus, and later in my textbook on the *History of Dogma* I briefly acknowledged the expression (Harnack, *Lehrbuch der Dogmengeschichte*, 1:205; see also Harnack, *Neue Untersuchungen*, 74). In my opinion, only Bousset has dealt with the problem in detail, but he did not do so exhaustively and did not, in my opinion, do so properly (*Kyrios Christos*, 54ff; among other places). A valuable hint can be found in Leitzmann, *Messe und Herrenmahl*, 8of. I am not aware of other studies.

2. For example, *eben Hauran* (Nabataean).

repeated designation of Israel and Jacob as "servants of God"). The *ebed* "of God" also means the Messiah in the Semitic originals of the Apocalypse of Ezra and Baruch,[3] which no longer exist but can in part be reconstructed. In the former, Noah, Abraham, and David are also called *ebed*. *Ebed* of God is not, in itself, a messianic designation, but only means that the person concerned has been taken by God into his service.[4]

The Septuagint has translated *ebed* haphazardly with δοῦλος, θεράπων, παῖς.[5] No proof is required to demonstrate the use of δοῦλος as an epithet of Israel and its men of God. God's Israel,[6] the faithful worshipper of God,[7] especially David[8] and Moses[9] are all called παῖς. Accordingly, the *ebed* in Isaiah is called παῖς in the LXX.[10] In one passage, however, he is called the δοῦλος.[11] Therefore, because of this passage (and the proven indiscriminate use in Isa 42:19), hardly any weight should to be attached to the fact that Israel is not called δοῦλος in Isa 46:3, 6, but the mysterious παῖς (both times as a translation of *ebed*). In the Greek translations of the apocalypses of Ezra and Baruch, which no longer exist in their originals, the *ebed YHWH Messias* is translated as παῖς θεοῦ (see the Latin translation *puer*).[12] Παῖς, as is well known, has a diverse meaning: the child as a son (or daughter), a boy (or girl), the follower (the disciple) with respect to the leader or master, and finally the lad, *puer*, servant, and in earlier and

---

3. See Bruno, *Die Apokalypsen des Esra und des Baruch in deutscher Gestalt*, 74, 182f, 187.

4. The facts of the case in the two Jewish apocalypses are more precise: The apocalypse of Baruch offers "my servant, the Messiah" (Violet, 308). In this way, he is also introduced in the Apocalypse of Ezra (Violet, 74, in two successive verses; in my opinion, incorrectly so, Violet considers "my servant" next to "Messiah" in the first passage as not original). Then, he is named simply "my servant" four times (Violet, 182, 183, 187, 191). One cannot conclude from this that "my servant" was an equivalent of "Messiah," but rather it is an addition to this epithet, which can also occur alone, however, if the context makes it clear who is intended.

5. The haphazard nature of the translation is particularly clear in Isa 42:19: τίς τυφλὸς ἀλλ' ἢ οἱ παῖδές μου . . . . καὶ ἐτυφλώθησαν οἱ δοῦλοι τοῦ θεοῦ. Both times the foundational text contains *ebed*. Nowhere is *ebed* translated as παιδίον except Judges 19:19, where the reading is uncertain.

6. See Isa 41:8f; 42:19; 44:1f, 21; 45:4. See also Psalms of Solomon 12:6; 17:21.

7. See Psalm 68 [69]:17; 85 [86]:16; 112 [113]:1; Wisdom 2:13.

8. See Isa 37:35; Psalm 17 [18] inscription.

9. See Neh 1:7.

10. See Isa 43:10; 44:26; 49:6; 50:10; 52:13.

11. Isa 49:5: ὁ πλάσας με ἐκ κοιλίας δοῦλον ἑαυτῷ τοῦ συναγαγεῖν τὸν Ἰακώβ. Immediately before, Israel is called δοῦλος.

12. See Bruno, *Die Apokalypsen des Esra und des Baruch*. A mere possibility is that he was referred to as δοῦλος at one point or another.

biblical Greek also the official (pl. servants) of the king (Gen 41:37f; 1 Sam 16:15ff; 18:22, 26; Dan 2:7; 1 Macc 1:6, 8; Ezra 2:16; 5:33, 35; Matt 14:2).[13] Παῖς θεοῦ has entered the religious parlance of the LXX exclusively via *ebed YHWH*, and both terms correspond in meaning with "the one called by God into his service, the servant of God." However, with the use of *ebed*, the baser meaning "servant, slave" resonates as well as the converse, higher meaning "son, child." *Puer*, which is provided in the Latin translation, does not quite match the meaning of παῖς, that is, does not achieve the intimacy that is found with παῖς. These differences had to be expressed in the history of the term in the church.

It is a secure historical fact that the relationship of Isa 42ff and 53 with Jesus belongs to the early church, for since it appears in Mark 15:28 (Luke 22:37); Matt 8:17; 12:27f; Acts 8:26ff; 1 Peter 2:23f; John 1:29; 12:38, and also, in my opinion, 1 Cor 15:3, it must be ancient. But it is also certain that παῖς θεοῦ is not a common name for Jesus in the NT Scriptures because, apart from the fact that it appears in Matt 12:17f in the evangelist's citation of Isa 42:1f, it is only found in one sermon (2x) and in one prayer in the whole NT (2x), which is present in the book of Acts (Acts 3:13, 26; 4:27, 30). Therefore, Bousset's assumptions and conclusions[14]—that παῖς θεοῦ is the original solemn designation of Jesus, that the voice at baptism might have originally said σὺ εἶ ὁ παῖς μου ὁ ἀγαπητός, ἐν σοὶ ηὐδόκησα, that the meaning and epithet of Jesus under the names παῖς and υἱός are incompatible and could not have originated within the same milieu, such that the epithet υἱὸς τοῦ θεοῦ is later, Hellenistic, and must be denied ancient Jewish Christianity—urgently need to be reviewed.[15]

13. Even earlier is παῖς in an erotic sense = "lovers."

14. Bousset, *Kyrios Christos*.

15. It is probably the boldest thing Bousset has undertaken by declaring the name ὁ υἱὸς τοῦ θεοῦ for Jesus as chronologically secondary and to deny it to the early church, although Paul and the synoptics testify to it, while they are completely silent about παῖς θεοῦ, apart from a quotation from Matthew. Even if it is correct that we cannot prove "Son of God" was used in the Jewish messianic dogmatics of the age—it is not the place to examine this question here—the testimony of the NT Scriptures leaves no doubt about its antiquity. After all, it did not require any special insight into the profession or the nature of Jesus in order to give him the title "Son of God," since Israel's king had long since been regarded as the Son of God, and—under the assumption of Jesus' role as messiah, the recognition of which cannot be denied to the early church—a new knowledge did not mean anything at all ("Son of God" does not say more than "the anointed one," "the chosen one," "the beloved one," "the only one"; it was only more suitable than these titles to be filled with new content in later times). It is incomprehensible to me how Bousset can write, "On closer consideration, we see clearly that the title 'the Son of God' does not at all correspond to the sensibility of Old Testament piety. It has a far too mythical sound that contradicts the rigid monotheism of the OT [but is the

The problem is this: Why has ὁ παῖς θεοῦ as an epithet for Jesus penetrated into the churches and their history, if according to the findings in the NT, it was not a common designation for Jesus (like "Christ" and "the Son of God")? To answer this question, it is necessary to present and examine all the material. But before that, there are two matters that must be noted here:

(1) The conception and designation of Jesus as "the heavenly child" in the mythological sense—whose origin Norden uncovered in a brilliant investigation and which, from Egyptian antiquity up to the present, has had such a rich history in the cult and in art—is to be abandoned. This predication, expressed by τέκνον or παιδίον, has nothing to do with παῖς θεοῦ, which goes back to *ebed*.[16]

(2) Likewise, the early reports about apparitions of Jesus in the form of a radiant boy or youth (καλός, εὔμορφος εὐειδής) are to be left aside. From the Acts of John onwards, they can be found in numerous apocryphal Acts of the Apostles, as Photius (Cod. 114) has already noted.[17] The oldest story of this kind belongs to Apelles, Marcion's disciple and sect founder: *eodem phantasmate eidem Philumenae*.[18] Apelles narrates the following with respect to a prophetess of his sect: *pueri habitu se demonstrante, qui puer apparens Christum se aliquando, aliquando assereret Paulum*.[19] Jesus also

---

OT alone in question here?]. When the OT speaks of the sons of God *par excellence* [but here it is a question of the Son of God who receives the predicate for the people of God], supernatural beings are meant and it is an echo of a mythical conception" (*Kyrios Christos*, 53). In fact, Old Testament monotheism was rigid, that is, so rigid that it could not even think of a physical or mythical sonship in relationship to God when it put "God" and "Son" together. But Bousset further asserts that Origen is an explicit testimony that Jews could not call the Messiah "the Son of God," because he corrects Celsus, who allows a Jew to say ὅτι προφήτης τις εἶπεν ἥξειν θεοῦ υἱόν, and replaces it with ὅτι ἥξει ὁ Χριστὸς τοῦ θεοῦ (see Celsus I.49). But he overlooks the fact that Origen does not take the Jewish sense of ὁ υἱὸς τοῦ θεοῦ as a standard here, but the Christian sense from the third century.

16. The few places where it can be asked whether the *bambino* or the *ebed-παῖς* is meant, or whether they flow together will be discussed below. As a rule, "the heavenly child" does not mean παῖς. Norden, therefore, had no reason to go into the history of the *ebed-παῖς-puer* formula in his monograph *Die Geburt des Kindes*, nor did Gressmann in his essay Hugo Gressmann, "Götterkind und Menschensohn," 1977ff.

17. See Lipsius, *Apokryphen Apostelgeschichten und Apostellegenden*, 1:8, 269, 464, 542, 551–56, 598, 602, 620; 2:171, 184, 265; 3:111f, 212.

18. See this in Augustine, *De haer.* 23, taken from the lost writing of Tertullian, *adv. Apell.*; cf. Harnack, "Neue Untersuchungen," 95ff; and my volume Harnack, *Marcion*, 408.

19. Perhaps even older, but probably apocryphal, and quite different, is an alleged experience of the heretic Valentin (in Hippolytus, *Refut.* VI.42): Οὐαλεντῖνος φάσκει ἑαυτὸν ἑωρακέναι παῖδα νήπιον ἀρτιγέννητον, οὗ πυθόμενος ἐπιζητεῖ τίς ἂν εἴη, ὁ δὲ ἀπεκρίνατο λέγων ἑαυτὸν εἶναι τὸν λόγον. This belongs to the "divine child." Very unclear is the word of Jesus quoted by the Naassers from the Gospel of Thomas (Hippolytus,

APPENDIX IV: THE EPITHET "SERVANT OF GOD" 173

appears to martyrs as a *puer*.²⁰ But these Christ-*puer*-appearances have a different basis than the *ebed*-παῖς θεοῦ designation for Christ. According to ancient mythological tradition, they are supposed to express eternal youth, that is, the divinity of Jesus, as is also present in the early pictorial representations of Jesus.²¹ Also, the *mythologumenon* of the "divine child" may have had an effect here, but *ebed*-παῖς-*puer* is not present.²²

I now turn to compile the source material for *ebed YHWH* (παῖς θεοῦ) as an epithet for Jesus.²³ The individual citation and treatment of the sources is justified because of their antiquity and because of the fact that they are relatively scarce. I have attempted to achieve a certain completeness as far as the history of the development of the expression goes, but I cannot guarantee it.²⁴ To my knowledge, the inscriptions lack this epithet entirely. This

---

Refut. V.7): Ἐμὲ ὁ ζητῶν εὑρήσει ἐν παιδίοις ἀπὸ ἐτῶν ἑπτά.

20. See, for example, the Acts of Xanthippe and Polyxena 66.30; 68.20; 74.8 [James].

21. One can express the "eternity" of a person through old age and youth, and both have happened in ancient times. In the Shepherd of Hermas, the Church first appears as an old woman, then as young and beautiful. She herself declares that she appears as an old woman "because she was created πάντων πρώτη" (Vis. II.4.1). She then gives a completely different explanation for her change in form into a young and beautiful woman (Vis. III.10ff), but this is secondary, as so often the case with Hermas when he interprets what has been handed down to him.

22. I have no reason to draw on parallels in the history-of-religions in the following description since the origin of the idea of the servant of God is irrelevant here, and since foreign religions with their speculations on this point have not penetrated into the Christian religion. Of course, one could make a long history-of-religions investigation into the term "the servant of God" in Isaiah, but to insert it here would only be misleading. I think that, with similar problems of ancient church history, some historians have not been reserved and careful enough. For by tracing back the prehistory of a *terminus technicus* of the Christian cult or dogma or an ancient religious narrative up to the grey prehistoric times or to neighboring religions and by determining its original meaning, they often enough leave the reader in doubt whether this meaning still has anything to do with the sense in which the new religion seized and appropriated the tradition. If, in addition to this, one is more or less indifferent to this in relation to the age of the sources from which they draw, then the result is that, in the best case, a confusing jumble arises, and in the worst case, what one attempted to illuminate is completely obscured by these "ancient" sources.

23. The name δοῦλος τοῦ θεοῦ for Jesus was mentioned by Origen in his enumeration of the names of Jesus (*Comm. Jo.* I.21), but only because of Isa 49:5. Δοῦλος τοῦ θεοῦ had not been an epithet for Jesus. Appeal cannot be made to Phil 2:7 or to the parable in Hermas's fifth Similitude (see below at #18) because, although Jesus is referred to in the parable as the δοῦλος of God, one cannot conclude from this that δοῦλος was his name for Jesus.

24. A passage here or there that might be missed is left aside because I do not see in them a certain testimony of παῖς as an epithet for Christ. Bousset (*Kyrios Christos*, 56f), based on Schmidtke (*Neue Fragmente*, 37.1:64, 108ff, 114), assumes that the Nazarenes called Jesus this because it says in Epiphanius (*Pan.* 29.7) that they called him ἕνα θεὸν

is a very important testimony against the exaggerated distribution of the expression! With regard to the Latin inscriptions, Diehl kindly wrote the following to me, "To my knowledge, the designation of Jesus as *puer* does not appear on Latin inscriptions. Even if the indices are only in their skeletal form, I believe I can answer your question with a clear conscience in the negative." Greek inscriptions with the designation παῖς θεοῦ as an epithet for Jesus are not attested either according to Dölger, as he has kindly made known to me. But he did point out to me the possibility that such inscriptions could be found on Syrian household inscriptions.

Textual Analysis

1

(1) Matthew 12:17f: ἵνα πληρωθῇ τὸ ῥηθὲν διὰ Ἡσαΐου τοῦ προφήτου λέγοντος· ἰδοὺ ὁ παῖς μου, ὃν ᾑρέτισα, ὁ ἀγαπητός μου, ὃν εὐδόκησεν ἡ ψυχή μου· θήσω τὸ πνεῦμά μου ἐπ' αὐτόν, καὶ κρίσιν τοῖς ἔθνεσιν ἀπαγγελεῖ· οὐκ ἐρίσει οὐδὲ κραυγάσει οὐδὲ ἀκούσει τις ἐν ταῖς πλατείαις τὴν φωνὴν αὐτοῦ· κάλαμον συντετριμμένον οὐ κατεάξει καὶ λίνον τυφόμενον οὐ σβέσει, ἕως ἂν ἐκβάλῃ εἰς νῖκος τὴν κρίσιν· καὶ τῷ ὀνόματι αὐτοῦ ἔθνη ἐλπιοῦσιν.

This passage, together with chapter 53, undoubtedly caused him to recognize Jesus as the παῖς prophesied here and accordingly to introduce him in prayer as the παῖς θεοῦ because what had been predicted in these two prophecies had been fulfilled in him. The other παῖς passages in Isaiah are not considered alongside them.

It is noteworthy that the evangelist did not cite the introductory words according to the LXX, where they are quite different (Ἰακὼβ ὁ παῖς μου, ἀντιλήψομαι αὐτοῦ· Ἰσραὴλ ὁ ἐκλεκτός μου, προσεδέξατο αὐτὸν ἡ ψυχή μου), but instead cites it according to the foundational Hebrew text. The source of the difference does not need to be discussed here.[25]

καταγγέλλουσι καὶ τὸν τοῦτον παῖδα Ἰ. Χρ. It is possible that Epiphanius here reproduced the words of the Nazarenes exactly. But more cannot be said because, in his time, the use of παῖς with the sense of υἱός as an epithet for Christ can easily be proven, and he himself writes: τὸν μονογενῆ παῖδα Ἰ. Χρ., τὸν υἱὸν τοῦ θεοῦ τοῦ ζῶντος (*Pan* 78.3). The reference to the fragments of Nazarite interpretations of Isaiah (in Jerome, *Comm. Isa.* on 29.20f; 31.6ff) is obsolete because it says *filius dei* (not *puer*) and Schmidtke's remark is not plausible that παῖς must have been the original, because the author of the interpretations is dependent upon those pericopes in Acts in which παῖς is found. However, dependence upon Acts is uncertain.

25. One cannot assume a Christian interpolation has taken place here, for how would this have come into the foundational text?

The ancient Latin manuscripts, including the Vulgate, unanimously translated παῖς with *puer*. This is how the ancient Greek Christians understood the word here (not as "son").

If in the following texts ὁ παῖς often appears to be connected with ὁ ἀγαπητός, the passage in Isaiah may be thought of as the starting point for this connection. The connection does not lead the term to a meaning beyond the Messianic connotations,[26] but only through the connection does it establish a secure expression since ὁ παῖς on its own does not clearly indicate a Messianic context but receives such a connotation when connected with ὁ ἠγαπημένος.

2–5

(2) Acts 3:13 (Peter's speech): ὁ θεὸς Ἀβραὰμ καὶ ὁ θεὸς Ἰσαὰκ καὶ ὁ θεὸς Ἰακώβ, ὁ θεὸς τῶν πατέρων ἡμῶν, ἐδόξασεν τὸν παῖδα αὐτοῦ Ἰησοῦν, ὃν ὑμεῖς μὲν παρεδώκατε καὶ ἠρνήσασθε κατὰ πρόσωπον Πειλάτου κτλ.

(3) Acts 3:26 (Conclusion of the speech): Ὑμῖν πρῶτον ἀναστήσας ὁ θεὸς τὸν παῖδα αὐτοῦ ἀπέστειλεν αὐτὸν εὐλογοῦντα ὑμᾶς ἐν τῷ ἀποστρέφειν ἕκαστον ἀπὸ τῶν πονηριῶν ὑμῶν.

(4) Acts 4:25f (in the congregational prayer, after the citation of Ps 2:1f, which is introduced with the words): διὰ [πνεύματος ἁγίου] στόματος Δαυεὶδ παιδός σου and concludes with the words: κατὰ τοῦ κυρίου καὶ κατὰ τοῦ Χριστοῦ αὐτοῦ): συνήχθησαν ἐπ' ἀληθείας ἐν τῇ πόλει ταύτῃ ἐπὶ τὸν ἅγιον παῖδά σου Ἰησοῦν, ὃν ἔχρισας, Ἡρῴδης τε καὶ Πόντιος Πειλᾶτος σὺν ἔθνεσιν καὶ λαοῖς Ἰσραήλ.

(5) Acts 4:30 (Continuation): ἐν τῷ τὴν χεῖρά σου ἐκτείνειν σε εἰς ἴασιν καὶ σημεῖα καὶ τέρατα γίνεσθαι διὰ τοῦ ὀνόματος τοῦ ἁγίου παιδός σου Ἰησοῦ.

For comparison: Luke 1:54 (in the "Magnificat"): ἀντελάβετο Ἰσραὴλ παιδὸς αὐτοῦ, μνησθῆναι ἐλέους, and in Luke 1:69 (in the "Benediction"): ἐν τῷ οἴκῳ Δαυεὶδ τοῦ παιδὸς αὐτοῦ.

From these passages, it follows (1) that Luke uses the same name παῖς for Israel, David, and Jesus;[27] (2) that in all passages he also had Isaiah in mind, like #4 with Ps 2;[28] (3) that he did not understand παῖς θεοῦ in a Messianic

---

26. Ὁ ἀγαπητός (ἠγαπημένος) was, in the days of Jesus and the apostles, a messianic designation, which does not need to be proven (see Eph 1:6). Valentinus writes (in Clement, *Strom.* VI.6.52): Ὁ λαός, ὁ τοῦ ἠγαπημένου, ὁ φιλούμενος καὶ φιλῶν αὐτόν.

27. From this it immediately follows that Luke (despite Luke 1) does not think of the "divine child" when he calls Jesus παῖς θεοῦ in the book of Acts in accordance with his sources.

28. See Isa 52:13: ὁ παῖς μου . . . δοξασθήσεται; on παῖς ὃν ἔχρισας, see Isa 42:1 (according to the foundational text): παῖς ὃν ᾑρέτισα; on ἴασιν, see Isa 53.

sense because otherwise he would not have added (#4) ὃν ἔχρισας; (4) that the addition of ἅγιος (#4 and #5) should ensure a messianic understanding, as well as the absolute use of ἐδόξασεν (#2); (5) and that constantly beside παῖς only Ἰησοῦς is written, such that one has to think that it is formulaic.[29] It is entirely impossible that Luke understood παῖς as "son."[30]

Beyond that, it is of greater importance that ὁ παῖς is found in Luke only in reference to Isaiah and in a solemn prayer, and that from #5 the conclusion is very obvious that miracles and exorcisms were performed at that time with the invocation of παῖς Ἰησοῦς or with the activity of God διὰ τοῦ παιδὸς αὐτοῦ Ἰησοῦ. I will return to this when I examine the related passages in the Acts of John.

Instructive are the old Latin versions. An overview shows that the original translation of *puer* was profuse, but that at an early stage offense was taken with the use of *puer* next to Jesus and was replaced with *filius*, though this is not the case for Israel and David! In Acts 3:13 (#2), only Codex d, e, gig, as well as Ambrosius have *puer*, while all the remaining witnesses (even the Vulgate) have replaced it with *filius*. In Acts 3:26 (#3), only Codex d offers the reading *puer*, while all the remaining witnesses have *filius*. In Acts 4:25, 27 (#4), all Latin witnesses translate παῖς with *puer* in reference to David, and the majority of the witnesses (including the Vulgate) conspicuously retain this word in reference to Jesus (perhaps because it was used shortly before with reference to David and they hesitated to translate it differently in its second occurrence); however, Codex e and gig, as well as Tertullian (*Bapt.* 7; *Prax.* 28), Hilary, Lucifer, and Irenaeus (III.12.5, 6) give the reading *filius*. Finally, in the last passage, Acts 4:30 (#5), the translations read, including the Vulgate, *filius*, with the exception of d, e, and p, as well as Beda—because of his knowledge of the foundational text and his criticism—who makes the noteworthy remark: *In Graeco habetur: "Per nomen sancti pueri tui Jesu" quod magis apostolorum votis congruere videtur* (*Retract.* 118).

The offense taken for *puer* as an epithet of Jesus is, as Tertullian's text teaches, almost as old in the Western Church as the translation itself![31] The Peshitta offers the translation *bar* (*filius*).

---

29. It is missing in #3 (Codex A and some other manuscripts offer this reading); but it started in the same speech.

30. On the other hand, it is not unimportant that those who pray call themselves δοῦλοι τοῦ θεοῦ (4:29) within the prayer. A difference between δοῦλος and παῖς is usually felt, even where παῖς was understood to mean "servant."

31. Corrections to παῖς as a Messianic name can also be found in the versions of the Apocalypse of Ezra, as Violet's apparatus demonstrates with reference to the above-mentioned passages (the manuscripts of these versions were all copied by Christians).

APPENDIX IV: THE EPITHET "SERVANT OF GOD" 177

6–9

The Ancient "Teaching of the Apostles" (Didache)

(6) Didache 9.2: Πρῶτον περὶ τοῦ ποτηρίου· Εὐχαριστοῦμέν σοι, πάτερ ἡμῶν, ὑπὲρ τῆς ἁγίας ἀμπέλου Δαβὶδ τοῦ παιδός σου, ἧς ἐγνώρισας ἡμῖν διὰ Ἰησοῦ τοῦ παιδός σου· σοὶ ἡ δόξα εἰς τοὺς αἰῶνας.

(7) Didache 9.3: Περὶ δὲ τοῦ κλάσματος· Εὐχαριστοῦμέν σοι, πάτερ ἡμῶν, ὑπὲρ τῆς ζωῆς καὶ γνώσεως, ἧς ἐγνώρισας ἡμῖν διὰ Ἰησοῦ τοῦ παιδός σου· σοὶ ἡ δόξα εἰς τοὺς αἰῶνας.

(8) Didache 10.2: Μετὰ δὲ τὸ ἐμπλησθῆναι· εὐχαριστοῦμέν σοι, πάτερ ἅγιε, ὑπὲρ τοῦ ἁγίου ὀνόματός σου, οὗ κατεσκήνωσας ἐν ταῖς καρδίαις ἡμῶν, καὶ ὑπὲρ τῆς γνώσεως καὶ πίστεως καὶ ἀθανασίας, ἧς ἐγνώρισας ἡμῖν διὰ Ἰησοῦ τοῦ παιδός σου· σοὶ ἡ δόξα εἰς τοὺς αἰῶνας.

(9) Didache 10.3: ἡμῖν δὲ ἐχαρίσω πνευματικὴν τροφὴν καὶ ποτόν καὶ ζωὴν αἰώνιον διὰ Ἰησοῦ [thus true to the copy] τοῦ παιδός σου.

The author calls Jesus "son" (υἱός) in the baptismal formula (Did. 7) and in the short sermon (Did. 16: υἱὸς τοῦ θεοῦ); he calls him "Lord" often; and he calls him "Jesus Christ" once (Did. 9.4), at the end of the first of the congregational prayers in the doxology.[32] It is all the more striking that he constantly writes in the prayer for the Lord's Supper: διὰ Ἰησοῦ τοῦ παιδός σου. Thus the words were a formula that had been handed down to him, precisely in these Eucharistic prayers of thanksgiving, but which did not lead him to mention Jesus as the παῖς θεοῦ within his little book.

That these prayers of thanksgiving are very old is now generally conceded, even if they may represent a second stage in development;[33] but even at this stage, they belong to the oldest form of Christianity, which is dependent on Jewish cultic customs and prayers, which I cannot prove here.[34] The perennial question,[35] however, whether speaking in Aramaic or Greek, which is so often raised today, also in connection with related problems, should be generally rejected because not only is our knowledge insufficient to answer it, but also it should not be overlooked that genuine, Aramaic speaking Judaism (thus also Jewish Christianity) in Jesus' age had arrived at concepts and cultic formulas influenced by Hellenism, the extent of whose influence can never be determined. Certainly ἐγνώρισας, ζωὴ καὶ γνῶσις,

---

Also here "son" has been used as a translation of *ebed*.

32. No one will be surprised to find along with it in the doxology: ὅτι σοῦ ἐστιν ἡ δόξα καὶ ἡ δύναμις διὰ Ἰησοῦ Χριστοῦ εἰς τοὺς αἰῶνας.

33. The prayers presuppose a certain spread of Christianity within the kingdom.

34. See Lietzmann, who has gone deeper here than his predecessor (*Messe und Herrenmahl*, 230ff).

35. TN: literally "doctoral question" ("Doktorfrage").

γνῶσις καὶ ἀθανασία and πνευματικὴ τροφὴ καὶ ποτὸς καὶ ζωὴ αἰώνιος may seem Hellenistic at first sight,[36] but who can claim that it could not have come from Palestine, not from Jerusalem, not from the oldest Jewish-Hellenistic Christian circles there (the followers of Stephen)?[37]

The antiquity of the prayers is also evident from the comparison with the passages from Acts discussed above. Here (#5) as well as there, it is already something formulaic, but with limited scope.[38] Here as well as there, the simple formula διὰ (τοῦ ὀνόματος) Ἰησοῦ τοῦ παιδός σου comes to the fore, which cannot be surpassed in simplicity, and it is postulated that it occurs within prayers. Here as there, Ἰησοῦς is found without Χριστός. Finally, here as there, David is also referred to beside Jesus, and he too is called παῖς θεοῦ.[39] These cannot be coincidences, and these observations justify a very early dating for the prayers of the Didache.

Although God is called "our Father" in these prayers, no one would claim that παῖς here means "son." On the contrary, both παῖς Δαβίδ as well as "our Father" speaks against it. What is intrinsic to Christianity here, as usual, lies in the phrase διὰ Ἰησοῦ. There could be no analogies to this in the Jewish prayer formulas.

10–12

1 Clement 59

(10) 1 Clement 59.2: ὅπως τὸν ἀριθμὸν τῶν ἐκλεκτῶν αὐτοῦ ἐν ὅλῳ τῷ κόσμῳ διαφυλάξῃ ἄθραυστον ὁ δημιουργὸς τῶν ἁπάντων διὰ τοῦ ἠγαπημένου παιδὸς αὐτοῦ Ἰ. Χρ., δι' οὗ ἐκάλεσεν ἡμᾶς ἀπὸ σκότους εἰς φῶς, ἀπὸ ἀγνωσίας εἰς ἐπίγνωσιν δόξης ὀνόματος αὐτοῦ.

---

36. Conversely, ἁγία ἄμπελος Δαβὶδ τοῦ παιδός σου, the formula διὰ Ἰησοῦ τοῦ παιδός σου, and ὄνομά σου, and οὗ κατεσκήνωσας ἐν ταῖς καρδίαις ἡμῶν seem to us to be strictly Jewish-Christian.

37. On ἀθανασία, see 1 Cor 15:53f. It is one of the most gratifying advances in criticism that clumsy references to Philo have ceased. They belong here as little as they do in the Gospel of John. An entirely different question is whether there is not an element in both that Philo also testifies to—oriental mystical speculation, taken up by Greek-speaking Jews. In my opinion, there is no Philonic thought in ancient church history before the Apologists, perhaps in the epistle to the Hebrews.

38. The limited scope results from the fact that neither Luke nor the author of the Didache know of or need the expression παῖς θεοῦ as a reference for Jesus outside of a very small area.

39. With the "son of David" as the name of Jesus, it has a similar relationship as with παῖς θεοῦ, and this formula therefore has a very similar history until its relative demise or until its quiescence. So far it has only been investigated in fragments.

(11) 1 Clement 59.3: ἐκ πάντων ἐκλεξάμενον τοὺς ἀγαπῶντάς σε διὰ 'Ι. Χρ. τοῦ ἠγαπημένου παιδός σου, δι' οὗ ἡμᾶς ἐπαίδευσας, ἡγίασας, ἐτίμησας.

(12) 1 Clement 59.4: γνώτωσαν σε πάντα τὰ ἔθνη, ὅτι σὺ εἶ ὁ θεὸς μόνος καὶ 'Ι. Χρ. παῖς σου καὶ ἡμεῖς λαός σου καὶ πρόβατα τῆς νομῆς σου.

Only in the great concluding prayer of this Roman letter do we find παῖς (but also ὁ υἱὸς τοῦ θεοῦ is found only once in the lengthy letter as the name of Jesus in 1 Clem 36.4, and there it obviously flowed out from the epistle to the Hebrews).[40] This prayer is, as is generally acknowledged, not a free creation of Clement, but a variant of parts of the great Roman congregational prayer, which even then had fixed forms (or a fixed schema). But this congregational prayer is not itself a free creation either, but instead rests upon synagogual prayers.[41]

A traditional ancient ecclesiastical foundation based on Jewish prayers, and the minor ingredient of Clement (or the Roman congregation) can be differentiated. Ancient is διὰ τοῦ παιδός σου (see the prayers in Acts and Didache); ancient is the combination of παῖς and ἠγαπημένος (2x)—it originates from Isa 42 (see #1), and will be encountered frequently—ancient is the combination of ἠγαπημένος and ἀγαπῶντες; ancient is combination of 'Ι. Χρ. παῖς σου and ἡμεῖς λαός σου κτλ.; ancient are the ἐκλεκτοί, the ἀριθμὸς τῶν ἐκλεκτῶν, and their κλῆσις; ancient is the combination of παῖς θεοῦ with the imparting of knowledge by him (see 1 Peter 2:9; the prayers of the Didache; and 2 Clement 2.1);[42] and ancient is δόξα ὀνόματος, because this is entirely Judeo-Christian thought and not at all Hellenistic. Hellenistic, on the other hand, is perhaps δημιουργὸς τῶν ἁπάντων, and the rhyming pattern created with ἐπαίδευσας, ἡγίασας, ἐτίμησας, which is also found elsewhere in Clement, is Greek. The formula διὰ παιδός σου Ἰησοῦ, also present in Acts and the Didache, is already clarified with Χριστοῦ, which is not insignificant.

Lightfoot (on these passages) assumes that Clement, because he connects παῖς with ἠγαπημένος, has understood the word in the sense of "son." In my opinion, one should not raise this question because it cannot be answered: Clement simply adopts the formula handed down to him compulsorily, in which ἠγαπημένος (Messiah)—whether he added it himself or received it from the congregation must remain an open question—says nothing about how the Messiah is conceived of. One has to be content

---

40. Even the Trinitarian formula in 1 Clem 58.2 does not offer υἱός, but rather ζῇ ὁ θεὸς καὶ ζῇ ὁ κύριος, 'Ι. Χρ. καὶ τὸ πνεῦμα τὸ ἅγιον.

41. This too is probably now generally accepted. Schermann's treatise should be used with caution (*Griechische Zauberpapyri*).

42. On this, cf. Const. App. VIII.11: ὁ διὰ Χριστοῦ κήρυγμα γνώσεως δοὺς ἡμῖν εἰς ἐπίγνωσιν τῆς σῆς δόξης καὶ τοῦ ὀνόματός σου. On ἀγνωσία, see 1 Peter 2:15; 1 Cor 15:34; and already in Job 35:16; Song 13:1; 3 Macc 5:27.

with the double insight that Clement, like Luke and the Didache, also felt bound in prayer to the formula διὰ παιδός σου and that in Clement's case ὁ ἠγαπημένος παῖς θεοῦ means the Messiah, which ὁ παῖς θεοῦ, as we have seen, does not in itself express.

The ancient Latin translator has translated παῖς with *filius* in three places. This is not surprising (see what was said about the Latin translation of Acts) and does not determine the meaning that Clement gave to the word.

13–15

Martyrdom of Polycarp 14.1, 3; 20.2

(13) Martyrdom of Polycarp 14.1 (Polycarp's Prayer): Κύριε ὁ θεὸς ὁ παντοκράτωρ, ὁ τοῦ ἀγαπητοῦ καὶ εὐλογητοῦ παιδός σου Ἰ. Χρ. πατήρ, δι' οὗ τὴν περὶ σοῦ ἐπίγνωσιν εἰλήφαμεν.

(14) Martyrdom of Polycarp 14.3 (Continuation of the Prayer): διὰ τοῦτο καὶ περὶ πάντων σὲ αἰνῶ· σὲ εὐλογῶ, σὲ δοξάζω διὰ τοῦ αἰωνίου καὶ ἐπουρανίου ἀρχιερέως Ἰ. Χρ., ἀγαπητοῦ σου παιδός, δι' οὗ σοὶ σὺν αὐτῷ καὶ πνεύματι ἁγίῳ δόξα κτλ.

(15) Martyrdom of Polycarp 20.2 (Final Doxology of the Letter): Τῷ δυναμένῳ πάντας ἡμᾶς εἰσαγαγεῖν τῇ αὐτοῦ χάριτι καὶ δωρεᾷ εἰς τὴν ἐπουράνιον αὐτοῦ βασιλείαν διὰ τοῦ παιδὸς αὐτοῦ τοῦ μονογενοῦς Ἰ. Χρ. δόξα κτλ.

That Polycarp's prayer (#13, #14) is closely connected with the Eucharistic prayer (of Smyrna) has long been recognized, and of course the final doxology (#15) has essentially been handed down. All three passages have παῖς, but all three determine its meaning: the first by ὁ πατὴρ τοῦ ἀγαπητοῦ παιδός σου Ἰησοῦ Χριστοῦ; the second by ἀγαπητός and the exalted expression ὁ αἰώνιος καὶ ἐπουράνιος ἀρχιερεὺς Ἰ. Χ.; the third by the addition of μονογενής. So the simple ὁ παῖς σου Ἰησοῦς could no longer be tolerated, and it was determined that παῖς should be understood as "son." For the first time, μονογενής[43] appears here next to παῖς, while ἀγαπητός (ἀγαπημένος) is already known to us. The fact that in none of

---

43. In the NT, this name for Jesus is exclusively Johannine and its usage here probably originates from there. It is not found within the Apostolic Fathers, but it is found in Valentine (surely following John), the "Docetism" of Hippolytus, and then in the letter of Diognetus (10.2). Jesus is not called μονογενής in John as the λόγος, but rather λόγος σαρκωθείς. The same applies for παῖς μονογενής. In what way and to what extent Jesus is said to be divine, μονογενής has no contributing role. It only claims that the historical Jesus came to be through a special act of God (and indeed only Jesus), and that therefore God is his Father in a special sense. αἰώνιος ἀρχιερεύς is also found in Polycarp's letter (Mart. Poly. 12). Thus it was also present in the Eucharistic prayer of the church of Smyrna.

the three passages υἱός appears instead of παῖς is proof that a liturgical setting prevailed here. παῖς had already become a sacred word within the liturgy. The fact that it is a tradition handed down through the liturgy is also evident from the connection of παῖς with the imparting of knowledge (see the prayers in the Didache and in 1 Clement).

The tradition behind these passages both within the Greek and Old Latin manuscripts remains of interest:

In #13, Codex Mosquensis has σου υἱοῦ for παιδός σου; the Latin manuscripts have *filii tui domini nostri Jesu Christi*! In #14, the Latin manuscripts leave out ἀγαπητοῦ σου παιδός, three Greek manuscripts correct δι' οὗ with μεθ' οὗ and therefore have to delete καὶ σὺν αὐτῷ![44] In #15, the Latin manuscripts have deleted παιδὸς αὐτοῦ τοῦ μονογενοῦς and written *per dominum nostrum Jesum Christum salvatorem, per quem ipsi est et cum ipso gloria*. Thus *puer* was not bearable for them.

16–17[45]

Letter of Barnabas

(16) Barnabas 6.1: Ὅτι οὖν ἐποίησεν τὴν ἐντολήν· τί λέγει; Τίς ὁ κρινόμενός μοι; ἀντιστήτω μοι· ἢ τίς ὁ δικαιούμενός μοι; ἐγγισάτω τῷ παιδὶ κυρίου.

(17) Barnabas 9.2: Τὸ πνεῦμα κυρίου προφητεύει· Τίς ἐστιν ὁ θέλων ζῆσαι εἰς τὸν αἰῶνα; ἀκοῇ ἀκουσάτω τῆς φωνῆς τοῦ παιδός μου.

Both passages offer difficulties. The first is a quotation from Isa 50:8, but this verse reads Ἐγγίζει ὁ δικαιώσας με· τίς ὁ κρινόμενός μοι; ἀντιστήτω μοι ἅμα· καὶ τίς ὁ κρινόμενός μοι; ἐγγισάτω μοι (LXX). How does Barnabas get παῖς κυρίου into it? A Jewish interpolation can hardly be assumed and it could hardly have been a lapse in memory (see the parallel in #17). Therefore, it is a Christian interpolation. Did the interpolation take place before Barnabas?

In #17, Ps 33:3 is quoted, but there the context is about life, not eternal life. This too is a Christian interpolation. The Christian is reminded of Isa 50:10: ὑπακουσάτω τῆς φωνῆς τοῦ παιδὸς αὐτοῦ (perhaps he also knew the singular [Christian] reading in Isa 42:43 from Sinaiticus εἰσακούσεται τῆς φωνῆς

---

44. One can ask if the original reading was not . . . ἀγαπητοῦ σου παιδός, δι' οὗ σοι σὺν [αὐτῷ καὶ] πνεύματι ἁγίῳ δόξα κτλ, and perhaps this is the right solution, since "the price through the Son to God and to the Son," though not unbearable, is striking, and since we will encounter something similar in Hippolytus. Even then, the corrections are quite remarkable.

45. Here, the Nazarenes would have to be inserted if they had named Jesus παῖδα θεοῦ. But this is doubtful (see the last note on the introduction above).

τοῦ παιδὸς αὐτοῦ; LXX: εἰσακούσατε [al. εἰσακούσεται] εἰς τὰ ἐπερχόμενα, the foundational text as well) and added the word to the passage. In Barnabas, there are also other falsifications in Old Testament quotations, for example, Barn. 8.5: ἡ βασιλεία Ἰησοῦ ἐπὶ ξύλου according to the known falsification in Ps 96:10: Ὁ κύριος ἐβασίλευσεν ἀπὸ τοῦ ξύλου.

The very old Latin translation offers *puer* in both passages.

18

The Shepherd of Hermas

In the complicated Similitude V in the Shepherd of Hermas, in which several parables, allegories, and interpretations that are not brought together in harmony but are nevertheless connected,[46] the following parable from Herm. Sim. V.2 can certainly be excluded from the discussion because it does not contain the word παῖς, but rather the synonym δοῦλος:

Hermas Similitude V.2: εἶχέ τις ἀγρὸν καὶ δούλους πολλοὺς καὶ μέρος τι τοῦ ἀγροῦ ἐφύτευσεν ἀμπελῶνα, καὶ ἐκλεξάμενος δοῦλόν τινα πιστὸν καὶ εὐάρεστον ἔντιμον, προσεκαλέσατο αὐτὸν καὶ λέγει αὐτῷ· Λάβε τὸν ἀμπελῶνα τοῦτον, ὃν ἐφύτευσα, καὶ χαράκωσον αὐτόν ἕως ἔρχομαι, καὶ ἕτερον δὲ μὴ ποιήσῃς τῷ ἀμπελῶνι· καὶ ταύτην μου τὴν ἐντολὴν φύλαξον, καὶ ἐλεύθερος ἔσῃ παρ' ἐμοί. ἐξῆλθε δὲ ὁ δεσπότης τοῦ δούλου εἰς τὴν ἀποδημίαν. ἐξελθόντος δὲ αὐτοῦ ἔλαβεν ὁ δοῦλος καὶ ἐχαράκωσε τὸν ἀμπελῶνα. καὶ τελέσας τὴν χαράκωσιν τοῦ ἀμπελῶνος εἶδε τὸν ἀμπελῶνα βοτανῶν πλήρη ὄντα. ἐν ἑαυτῷ οὖν ἐλογίσατο λέγων· Ταύτην τὴν ἐντολὴν τοῦ κυρίου τετέλεκα· σκάψω λοιπὸν τὸν ἀμπελῶνα τοῦτον, καὶ ἔσται εὐπρεπέστερος ἐσκαμμένος, καὶ βοτάνας μὴ ἔχων δώσει καρπὸν πλείονα, μὴ πνιγόμενος ὑπὸ τῶν βοτανῶν. λαβὼν ἔσκαψε τὸν ἀμπελῶνα, καὶ πάσας τὰς βοτάνας τὰς οὔσας ἐν τῷ ἀμπελῶνι ἐξέτιλλε. καὶ ἐγένετο ὁ ἀμπελὼν ἐκεῖνος εὐπρεπέστατος καὶ εὐθαλής, μὴ ἔχων βοτάνας πνιγούσας αὐτόν. μετὰ χρόνον [τινὰ] ἦλθεν ὁ δεσπότης τοῦ δούλου καὶ τοῦ ἀγροῦ καὶ εἰσῆλθεν εἰς τὸν ἀμπελῶνα. καὶ ἰδὼν τὸν ἀμπελῶνα κεχαρακωμένον εὐπρεπῶς, ἔτι δὲ καὶ ἐσκαμμένον καὶ πάσας τὰς βοτάνας ἐκτετιλμένας καὶ εὐθαλεῖς οὔσας τὰς ἀμπέλους, ἐχάρη λίαν ἐπὶ τοῖς ἔργοις τοῦ δούλου. προσκαλεσάμενος οὖν τὸν υἱὸν αὐτοῦ τὸν ἀγαπητόν (the Holy Spirit, according to Hermas, is the Son), ὃν εἶχε κληρονόμον, καὶ τοὺς φίλους, οὓς εἶχε συμβούλους, λέγει αὐτοῖς ὅσα ἐνετείλατο τῷ δούλῳ αὐτοῦ, καὶ ὅσα εὗρε γεγονότα. κἀκεῖνοι συνεχάρησαν τῷ δούλῳ ἐπὶ τῇ μαρτυρίᾳ ᾗ ἐμαρτύρησεν αὐτῷ ὁ δεσπότης. καὶ λέγει αὐτοῖς· Ἐγὼ τῷ δούλῳ τούτῳ ἐλευθερίαν ἐπηγγειλάμην, ἐάν μου τὴν ἐντολὴν φυλάξῃ ἣν ἐνετειλάμην αὐτῷ· ἐφύλαξε δέ μου τὴν ἐντολὴν καὶ προσέθηκε τῷ ἀμπελῶνι ἔργον καλόν,

---

46. Dibelius, *Der Hirt des Hermas*, 560–77.

καὶ ἐμοὶ λίαν ἤρεσεν. ἀντὶ τούτου οὖν τοῦ ἔργου οὗ εἰργάσατο θέλω αὐτὸν συγκληρονόμον τῷ υἱῷ μου ποιῆσαι, ὅτι τὸ καλὸν φρονήσας οὐ παρενεθυμήθη, ἀλλ' ἐτέλεσεν αὐτό. ταύτῃ τῇ γνώμῃ ὁ υἱὸς τοῦ δεσπότου συνηυδόκησεν αὐτῷ, ἵνα συγκληρονόμος γένηται ὁ δοῦλος τῷ υἱῷ.

One can doubt whether the "Son" (the Holy Spirit)—Hermas is a binitarian—originally belonged in the parable, which here is no longer present in its original form. But the following may also remain true: it is certain that this parable refers to Jesus. This is also how Hermas understood and interpreted it. Therein, Jesus is depicted as δοῦλος. It is therefore a certain proof of the idea of Jesus as the servant among other servants, but who has experienced an exaltation to glory and sonship because of his work.

Hermas himself did not invent this parable, but it was handed down to him. This is demonstrated by the fact that he received it because it was acceptable to him, but that he corrected it with the interpretation he gave it (Hermas V.5f). It was already unbearable to him that Jesus was thought of as δοῦλος. He, therefore, raises the question why Christ εἰς δούλου τρόπον κεῖται in the parable? The answer that follows is εἰς δούλου τρόπον οὐ κεῖται, ἀλλ' εἰς ἐξουσίαν μεγάλην κεῖται καὶ κυριότητα, and an explanation follows that can be left aside here, because it does not fit the parable at all, but rather comes from Hermas's own unclear Christology.

The narrative is therefore of great value in two respects, firstly because it still contains the pure Adoptionist Christology of the servant of God as its basis, and secondly because it shows that it was already offensive in this wording at the time of Hermas (ca. 140 CE).

19

The Docetists

(19) The Docetists, whom Hippolytus (*Haer.* VIII.10) refutes, spoke of μονογενὴς παῖς.[47] Since they also call him ὁ μονογενὴς υἱός[48] or simply ὁ μονογενής,[49] they have understood παῖς as υἱός (and he is παῖς αἰώνιος, so he did not appear to be just a son). Otherwise, I have not found παῖς as a name for Jesus either in the Gnostics or in Marcion.

---

47. Wendland, *Hippolytus Werke* 228.4; 230.8.
48. Wendland, *Hippolytus Werke* 229.22.
49. Wendland, *Hippolytus Werke* 231.5.

20

Celsus

(20) In his work, Celsus speaks a dozen times of παῖς θεοῦ and calls Jesus thus in the Christian sense (Origen, *Contra Celsum* I.67; II.9; V.52; VI.42, 74; VII.53 [ὑμεῖς κἂν Σίβυλλαν, ᾖ χρῶνταί τινες ὑμῶν, εἰκότως ἂν μᾶλλον προεστήσασθε ὡς τοῦ θεοῦ παῖδα]; VII.14, 39 [Χριστός, ὡς σὺ φής, ὁ τοῦ θεοῦ παῖς], 41). On his own initiative, he says: θεὸς καὶ θεοῦ παῖς οὐδεὶς κατῆλθεν (V.2). In spite of VIII.39, it must remain doubtful whether he has heard from the Christians at all or has heard often from them the use of παῖς θεοῦ for Jesus (they may also have used υἱός), or whether it is he himself who has preferred it (by analogy with θεῶν παῖδες). The passage in VII.9 does not decide the matter either, since it is only likely, but not certain, that Celsus put the words Ἐγὼ ὁ θεός εἰμι ἢ θεοῦ παῖς ἢ πνεῦμα θεῖον in the mouth of an ecstatic Christian or heard them from him. It could also be that a local prophet was meant. Bousset refers to Corp. Hermetic. XIII.14: Θεὸς πέφυκας καὶ θεοῦ παῖς (cf. XIII.2, 4).[50] From Origen's refutation (see below), one gets the impression that παῖς θεοῦ (for Jesus) was not a common name among Christians (see there).

21–25

The Apologists

The Apologists hardly use παῖς as an epithet for Jesus, and when they do use it (only Athenagoras and the Epistle to Diognetus), they understand it to mean "son." Justin knows the men of God from the OT as παῖδες θεοῦ, and he cites Isa 42:1f. (*Dial.* 123, 135, according to the LXX, not according to Matt 12) and Isa 52:10–54, 56 (*Dial.* 13) with the understanding that Jesus is παῖς. However, he himself never calls Jesus by this name.

Only five passages from the writings of the Apologists belong within this discussion.

(21) Athenagoras, *Suppl.* 10: In the explanation about the Logos and the Trinity, he always speaks of υἱός, but lets the pagan addressee ask questions about it: Ὁ παῖς τί βούλεται;

(22) Athenagoras 1.12: In the continuation of the discussion about the Trinity υἱός and παῖς alternate: Τίς ἡ τοῦ παιδὸς πρὸς τὸν πατέρα ἑνότης, τίς ἡ τοῦ πατρὸς πρὸς τὸν υἱὸν κοινωνία, τί τὸ πνεῦμα, τίς ἡ τῶν τοσούτων ἕνωσις καὶ διαίρεσις ἑνουμένων, τοῦ πνεύματος, τοῦ παιδός, τοῦ πατρός.

---

50. Bousset, *Kyrios Christos*, 56.

(23) Diognetus 8.9: ἐννοήσας (ὁ θεὸς) μεγάλην καὶ ἄφραστον ἔννοιαν ἀνεκοινώσατο μόνῳ τῷ παιδί.

(24) Diognetus 8.11: ἐπεὶ ἀπεκάλυψε διὰ τοῦ ἀγαπητοῦ παιδὸς καὶ ἐφανέρωσε τὰ ἐξ ἀρχῆς ἡτοισμένα.

(25) Diognetus 9.1: παντ' οὖν ἤδη πάρ' ἑαυτῷ σὺν τῷ παιδὶ οἰκονομηκὼς κτλ.

In all of these passages, παῖς is simply υἱός—the baser meaning of the word is no longer even thought of—and it is even probable that παῖς is used by the author of Diognetus because he was reminded of Homer and Plato (Timaeus p. 40 DE; Athenagoras, *Suppl.* 23) and attached something more archaic, noble, and more intimate to the term.[51] The Apologists also refer to the emperor's son as παῖς; see Justin, *2 Apol* 2: Οὐ πρέποντα Εὐσεβεῖ Αὐτοκράτορι οὐδὲ φιλοσόφῳ Καίσαρος παιδὶ οὐδὲ τῇ Ἱερᾷ Συγκλήτῳ κρίνεις; Athenagoras 1, 37: εὐχόμεθα ἵνα παῖς παρὰ πατρὸς διαδέχησθε τὴν βασιλείαν; Melito in Eusebius, *Hist. eccl.* IV.26.7 (to the emperor): οὗ σὺ διάδοχος εὐκταῖος γέγονάς τε καὶ ἔσῃ μετὰ τοῦ παιδός. It is remarkable (and it supports the already stated assumption) that Athenagoras has even included παῖς for υἱός in the Trinitarian formula, and he is not entirely alone in this (see #26). It is also remarkable that Diognetus needs ὁ ἀγαπητὸς παῖς where he speaks of the apocalypse through the Son (#24), which has probably been influenced by the prayers (see above). Otherwise, this author speaks of Jesus as υἱὸς θεοῦ (see 9.2, 4; 10.2; [7.4]), and he explicitly states that God did not send a servant (ὑπηρέτης) or an angel etc. to us, but the δημιουργὸς τῶν ὅλων himself (7.2). These are statements of exaltation in which he uses παῖς.

26

Acts of Justin

(26) In this Acts of a Martyr, Justin makes the following confession of faith before the judge: Εὐσεβοῦμεν εἰς τὸν τῶν Χριστιανῶν θεόν, ὃν ἡγούμεθα ἕνα [τοῦτον?] ἐξ ἀρχῆς ποιητὴν καὶ δημιουργὸν τῆς πάσης κτίσεως, ὁρατῆς τε καὶ ἀοράτου, καὶ κύριον Ἰ. Χρ., παῖδα θεοῦ, ὃς καὶ προκεκήρυκται (chapter 2).

That here παῖς is used for υἱός (a few lines later it says: προκεκήρυκται περὶ τούτου ὃν ἔφην θεοῦ υἱὸν ὄντα) can hardly be explained in any other way than the explanation offered above: παῖς seemed to be more intimate and sacred. But the process here and in Athenagoras of inserting παῖς into the confession (here it is written for the first time next to κύριος), to my

---

51. Or has the "divine child" perhaps also had an effect here, or the liturgical, sacred formula διὰ τοῦ παιδός σου?

knowledge, has not been found in any successors. The traditional υἱός could not be replaced at this point.

27–28

Acts of Paul and Thecla (Acts of Paul) 17 and 24

(27) Acts of Paul 17: Ἔπεμψεν ὁ θεὸς τὸν ἑαυτοῦ παῖδα, ὃν ἐγὼ εὐαγγελίζομαι.

(28) Acts of Paul 24 (prayer): Πάτερ, ὁ ποιήσας τὸν οὐρανὸν καὶ τὴν γῆν, ὁ τοῦ παιδὸς τοῦ ἀγαπητοῦ σου Ἰ. Χρ. πατήρ, εὐλογῶ σε κτλ.

The first passage is based upon the Pauline epistles. Nevertheless, the author uses παῖς for υἱός and risked that the reader would interpret it in its "baser" sense. This requires an explanation, and again it can only be found in the fact that παῖς was considered to be more intimate and sacred. Number 28 is the beginning of a prayer, and thus it is modelled on the liturgical prayers which have ὁ παῖς ὁ ἀγαπητος σου (see above), but although the prayers in the Didache tolerated the simple παῖς σου next to πατὴρ ἡμῶν, the author repeats the word πατήρ with παῖς σου (see already in #13)!

The Latin translators have stumbled here.[52] For #27, Codex aC and bC have *puerum suum*; the remaining manuscripts, however, have the reading *filium*. For #28, Codex cC reads *pueri tui*; the others omit the words (the prayer is translated rather freely by them).

29

Acts of John 11 (Bonnet[53])

(29) Acts of John 11: Ὁ θεὸς ὁ τῶν οὐρανῶν ποιητής, ὁ κύριος καὶ δεσπότης ἀγγέλων δοξῶν κυριοτήτων, ἐν τῷ ὀνόματι Ἰ. Χρ., τοῦ παιδός σου μονογενοῦς, δὸς τούτῳ τῷ τεθνηκότι κτλ.

It is an invocation of God at a raising of the dead. Immediately παῖς reappears in a prayer—also note the formula ἐν τῷ ὀνόματι (see above at #5)—but by the addition of μονογενής he is unmistakably designated as son.[54]

---

52. Gebhardt, *Die lateinischen Übersetzungen der Acta Pauli et Theclae*, 2.

53. Lipsius et al., *Acta apostolorum apocrypha*, vol. 1.

54. Martyrdom of Matthew 5 (Bonnet), where the pagan women call out to the apostle Ὁρῶμεν καὶ τὸν παῖδα Ἰησοῦν, τὸν υἱὸν τοῦ θεοῦ σὺν σοὶ ὄντα, does not belong here because in this passage παῖς means παιδίον (in this form Jesus appeared to the apostle and entered into conversation with him).

30–31

The Latin Bible translation in Tertullian and Latin Irenaeus

It should be recalled here (see #4) that Tertullian (*Bapt.* and *Adv. Jud.* 28) found (or wrote?) *filius* (for παῖς) in Acts 4:27, and that the Latin Irenaeus, whose dating is not fixed has *David pueri tui* in Acts 4:25, but *sanctum filium tuum* in Acts 4:27 (Iren. III.12.5) and repeats it in what follows.

32–36

Hippolytus and the Roman Church Orders of Hippolytus

(32) *De antichristo* 3: ὅπως ἃ πάλιν τοῖς μακαρίοις προφήταις ἀπεκάλυψεν ὁ τοῦ θεοῦ λόγος, νῦν αὐτὸς πάλιν ὁ τοῦ θεοῦ παῖς, ὁ πάλαι μὲν λόγος ὤν, νυνὶ δὲ καὶ ἄνθρωπος δι' ἡμᾶς ἐν κόσμῳ φανερωθείς κτλ. . . . εἷς ὁ τοῦ θεοῦ παῖς, δι' οὗ καὶ ἡμεῖς τυχόντες τὴν διὰ τοῦ ἁγίου πνεύματος ἀναγέννησιν.

(33) *De antichristo* 6: "καὶ ἔτεκεν," φησίν, "υἱὸν ἄρσενα, ὃς μέλλει ποιμαίνειν πάντα τὰ ἔθνη" (Rev 12), τὸν ἄρσενα καὶ τέλειον Χριστόν, παῖδα θεοῦ, θεὸν καὶ ἄνθρωπον.

(34) *Contra haeresin Noeti* 5: ὁρῶν τὸν θεὸν οὐδεὶς εἰ μὴ μόνος ὁ παῖς καὶ τέλειος ἄνθρωπος καὶ μόνος διηγησάμενος τὴν βουλὴν τοῦ πατρός; see *Noet.* 11: δύναμις μία ἡ ἐκ τοῦ παντός, τὸ δὲ πᾶν πατήρ, ἐξ οὗ δύναμις λόγος. οὗτος δὲ νοῦς, ὃς προβὰς ἐν κόσμῳ ἐδείκνυτο, παῖς θεοῦ (otherwise always within the treatise as υἱός).

(35) *Refutatio omnium haeresium* X.33: τὰ πάντα διοικεῖ ὁ λόγος θεοῦ, ὁ πρωτόγονος πατρὸς παῖς, ἡ πρὸ ἑωσφόρου φωνή.

That Hippolytus uses παῖς θεοῦ for Jesus, without any connection with *ebed* is obvious. In #32, it is clear that he uses this epithet of the human-born one (not the pre-existent Logos); see also the mention of humanity in #33 and #34; in #33 and #35, the line of the "divine child" intersects with the line of παῖς as υἱός. In #34, παῖς stands together with the revelation of the Father that comes through him (see the prayers of the Didache and others). Number 35 confirms that, in exalted speech, παῖς seemed to be particularly appropriate.

(36) However, the Church Orders of Hippolytus, once called the Egyptian Church Orders, still reflects the older sense of παῖς as *ebed* within the prayers because it records the ancient formula (but Hippolytus himself certainly understood the term παῖς as son).

(a) (Prayer for the consecration of a bishop): ἐπίχεε τὴν παρά σου δύναμιν τοῦ ἡγεμονικοῦ πνεύματος οπερ διὰ τοῦ ἠγαπημένου σου παιδὸς Ἰ. Χρ. δεδώρησαι τοῖς ἁγίοις σου ἀποστόλοις κτλ.[55] The old Latin version offers *filius*.[56]

(b) (Prayer for the consecration of a bishop, towards the end): ὀσμὴν εὐωδίας διὰ τοῦ παιδός σου Ἰ. Χρ., δι' οὗ σοι δόξα κράτος τιμὴ σὺν ἁγίῳ πνεύματι νῦν καὶ ἀεὶ κτλ. This corrected text had to be produced first, because the text in the *Diataxen* reads: διὰ τοῦ παιδός σου Ἰ. Χρ. τοῦ κυρίου ἡμῶν, μεθ' οὗ σοι δόξα κρ. τιμὴ σὺν ἁγίῳ πνεύματι, while the Latin text reads *per puerum* [here this word is retained!] *tuum Jesum Christum, per quem tibi gloria et potentia et honor, patri et filio cum spiritu sancto*. One can see that the genuine text was unbearable to both witnesses, and they helped each other in different ways. There, δι' οὗ was boldly transformed into μεθ' οὗ and τοῦ κυρίου ἡμῶν was added; here, *patri et filio* was inserted. It is precisely this situation in which, just like #14 (Mart. Poly.), the paradox arose that through the *puer* glory was offered to the *filius* and was accepted.

(c) (Prayer for the Lord's Supper, p. 42): *Gratias tibi referimus, deus, per dilectum puerum tuum J. Chr., quem in ultimis temporibus misisti nobis salvatorem*; (towards the end, p. 45): *ut te laudemus et glorificemus per puerum tuum J. Chr., per quem tibi gloria et honor [patri et filio] cum spiritu sancto in sancta ecclesia tua*. The words [*patri et filio*]—they create the same paradox that we have just encountered—are not present within the Ethiopian version;[57] it also does not have the reading *cum spiritu sancto*, and Lietzmann therefore also omits it;[58] but since it is witnessed in two texts (36b and also 36d), I will allow it to stand. The Ethiopian text omitted it because a binitarian doxology (Father and Spirit alone) was offensive to it, but the Son was already mentioned in δι' οὗ and he neither had the courage to change δι' οὗ into μεθ' οὗ nor did he want to take on the paradox as is created in the Latin text.

(d) (Prayer for the consecration of a presbyter, p. 48): *ut tibi ministremus in simplicitate cordis laudantes te per puerum tuum Christum Jesum, per quem tibi gloria et virtus, [patri et filio] cum spiritu sancto in sancta ecclesia*. For the third time we encounter in the Latin—the Greek foundational text is also missing here—the doxological paradox. Here, too, *patri et filio* should be omitted.

---

55. Schermann, *Die allgemeine Kirchenordnung*, 38ff. The Greek text is contained in Hippolytus's Διατάξεις περὶ χειροτονιῶν in Funk, *Didascalia et Constitutiones Apostolorum*, 2:77ff.

56. Hauler, *Didascaliae apostolorum fragmenta Veronensia latina*.

57. See Funk, *Didascalia et Constitutiones Apostolorum*, 2:200.

58. Leitzmann, *Messe und Herrenmahl*, 80.

(e) (Prayer at the offering of the fruits, conclusion, p. 88): *per puerum tuum J. Chr., dominum nostrum, per quem tibi gloria.*⁵⁹

Where these prayers were recited in the foundational text, παῖς could easily be read as υἱός and was certainly understood by Hippolytus as such at the time. But *puer*, which the Old Latin once replaced with *filius*, was not as tolerable. And yet, what could not be endured in traditional, ecclesiastical prayers!

37–39

Clement of Alexandria

(37) *Stromateis* VII.4.1: Ὁ θεὸν πεπεισμένος εἶναι παντοκράτορα καὶ τὰ θεῖα μυστήρια παρὰ τοῦ μονογενοῦς παιδὸς αὐτοῦ ἐκμαθών.

(38) *Quis dives salvetur* 42.10 (conclusion of the work): ᾧ (θεῷ) διὰ τοῦ παιδὸς Ἰ. Χρ., τοῦ κυρίου ζώντων καὶ νεκρῶν, καὶ διὰ τοῦ πνεύματος εἴη δόξα κτλ.

Παῖς is found sparsely in Clement (although he uses υἱός countless times). This makes these two passages all the more valuable because they clearly confirm for us that παῖς belongs to the liturgy and the doxology. Number 38 is a doxology, and here παῖς even appears in connection with a sentence of the confession of faith (see Athenagoras and the Acts of Justin), but at the same time it contains an expansion (διὰ τ. ἁγ. πν.). Number 37 also has usage within the worship service and its prayers (παντοκράτωρ, μυστήρια), and again παῖς is the mediator (however, it is no longer διά but rather παρά!) of the (mystery) knowledge. In #37, παῖς is marked by μονογενής and in #38 by the clause from the symbol of the lower sphere.

(39) Hymn at the conclusion of *Paedagogus* (V.58f):

μέλπωμεν ὁμοῦ
πέμπωμεν ἁπλῶς
παῖδα κρατερόν.

In these verses, wherein the absolute form παῖς κρατερός is used as a name for Jesus, a different explanation should perhaps be offered for παῖς than that given in #37 and #38. Clement may have had the "divine child" in mind, which is offered within mythology and of whom Rev 12 speaks. However, the absolute expression can also be understood on the basis of παῖς μονογενής, such that the relationship with the "divine child" remains questionable.

---

59. Also the evening prayer, which has been preserved only in Ethiopian and translated back into Greek by Goltz, would have begun with the words: Εὐχαριστοῦμέν σοι, θεός, διὰ τοῦ παιδός σου Ἰ. Χρ., τοῦ κυρίου ἡμῶν.

40

Origen uses the familiar, common names for Jesus and avoids παῖς θεοῦ, although Celsus (#20) prefers to use this name for Jesus in the Christian sense. Origen probably wanted to reserve the name for liturgical usage. But at the beginning of his *Ep. Afr.*, he writes: Ὠριγ. Ἀφρικανῷ, ἀγαπητῷ ἀδελφῷ, ἐν θεῷ πατρὶ διὰ Ἰ. Χρ. τοῦ ἁγίου παιδὸς αὐτοῦ εὖ πράττειν. It is not at all clear how we should explain the formula here which comes from Acts 4:27. Presumably he wanted to express a solemn seriousness by use of a liturgical formula, and thereby introduce the seriousness of the letter in a worthy manner.[60]

The critic Leo Castrius (in Wettstein's *editio prima*) found παῖς as an epithet for Christ so strange that he tried, by changing the text, to make παῖς to be a reference to Origen (with respect to Africanus).

41

Dionysius of Alexandria

(41) In Eusebius, *Hist. eccl.* VII.6, Dionysius writes in a letter about the Sabellian doctrine: βλασφημίαν περὶ τοῦ παντοκράτορος θεοῦ, πατρὸς τοῦ κυρίου ἡμῶν Ἰ. Χρ., ἀπιστίαν τε πολλὴν περὶ τοῦ μονογενοῦς παιδὸς αὐτοῦ, τοῦ πρωτοτόκου πάσης κτίσεως, τοῦ ἐνανθρωπήσαντος λόγου, ἀναισθησίαν δὲ τοῦ ἁγίου πνεύματος.

Here, παῖς is in the Trinitarian confessional formula (cf. #22, #26, #38), in which the second part is particularly rich and sublime. Also, once again we encounter μονογενής next to παῖς.

---

60. In Origen's long enumeration and discussion of the many names of Jesus, he does not list παῖς—which is remarkable—but instead δοῦλος τοῦ θεοῦ, which is striking (comments on John 1:21; Preuschen, *Origens Werke*, 4:25ff). He cites Isaiah 49:3 as evidence. Right after that, he cites Isa 49:6 for the name φῶς τῶν ἐθνῶν, in which παῖς also happens to occur, but he does not include it. He is also silent about παῖς in his discussion of υἱὸς τοῦ θεοῦ. That δοῦλος τοῦ θεοῦ is not given as a name for Jesus has already been explained at the end of the introduction. The same is true of numerous other names of Jesus, which have been determined by exegetical princely wealth ("*Plusmacherei*") from both Testaments. My colleague Mr. Dölger kindly drew my attention to a curiosity that belongs here: In Franz Diekamp's *Doctrina Patrum de Incarnatione Verbi*, among the 187(!) names for the Redeemer, in #73 [al. 39/40] Παῖς πένης is listed according to the arbitrary interpretation of Eccl 4:13 (Ἀγαθὸς παῖς πένης καὶ σοφὸς ὑπὲρ βασιλέα πρεσβύτερον καὶ ἄφρονα) as a name for Jesus (*Doctrina Patrum de Incarnatione Verbi*, 288). Thus, this author also leaves παῖς θεοῦ aside, like Origen, as an epithet for Jesus. Is that a coincidence?

42

Didascalia apostolorum

This work from the third century, which has survived in Latin and Syriac and is the model for the first 6 books of the Apostolic Constitutions,[61] offers the following works in the introduction:

(42) μέτοχοι τιμίου καὶ ἀθῴου αἵματος τοῦ Χριστοῦ, οἱ παρρησίαν εἰληφότες τὸν παντοκράτορα θεὸν πατέρα καλεῖν, συγκληρονόμοι καὶ συμέτοχοι τοῦ ἠγαπημένου παιδὸς αὐτοῦ (*dilecti pueri eius*).[62] Here also the exalted words are based upon the liturgical prayers. On παντοκράτωρ and παῖς, see #13, #37, and #41.

43–45

Sibylline Oracles I

(43) Sibylline Oracles I.324f: δὴ τότε καὶ μεγάλοιο θεοῦ παῖς ἀνθρώποισιν ἥξει κτλ.

(44) Sibylline Oracles I.330f: δὺ δ' ἐνὶ φρεσὶ σῇσι νόησον ἀθανάτοιο θεοῦ Χριστὸν παῖδ' ὑψίστοιο.

(45) Sibylline Oracles I.364: οὐρανίου ὅτι παῖδα θεοῦ διεδηλήσαντο.

The Christian revision of the first book of the Sibylline Oracles probably originates from the second half of the third century.[63] Note also here that παῖς is close to (four) high predications about God. Here too it can be recalled that the *mythologumenon* of the divine child has had an effect. But this assumption is not necessary. The liturgical prayers provide a sufficient enough explanation for choosing the word παῖς.

46

Pseudo-Cyprian, *De montibus Sina et Sion*

(46) Chapter 4: *Vero etiam et vitem veram se esse dixit, patrem suum agricolam* (John 15). *si ergo Christus est vitis vera, utique constat quia et nos qui in illo credimus et ipsum induimus sumus vitis vera quae est vinea dominica. et Christus custos vineae suae dicente Salomone:* "*Posuerunt me custodem in vineam*" (Song 1:6). *invenimus enim in conversu huius mundi in simili tudincm spiritalem figuraliter esse vineam habentem dominum et possessorem*

---

61. Funk, *Didascalia et Constitutiones Apostolorum*, 2:2ff.
62. Funk, *Didascalia et Constitutiones Apostolorum*, 2:4.
63. See Harnack, *Geschichte der altchristlichen Literatur bis Eusebius*, 2:184f.

suum. vero tempore maturo prope dies vindemiarum ponunt in mediam vineam custodem puerum in alto ligno media vinea confixo et in eo ligno facinnt speculum quadratum de harundinibus quassatis et per singula latera quadraturae speculi faciunt caverna terna, quae fiunt caverna duodecim: per quam quadraturam cavernorum custos puer omnem vineam perspiciens custodiat cantans, ne viator ingrediens vineam dominicam sibi adsignatam vexet vel fures viam (uvam?) vineae vestigent. quod si inportunus fur egens in vineaim voluerit introire et uvam demere, illic puer sollicitus de vinea sua deintus de speculo dat vocem maledicens et comminans, ne in vineam viator fur audeat accedere dicens: "Rectum arnbula." fur autem timens vocem pueri sibi comminantem refugit de vinea, speculun videt, vocem audit, puerum intus in speculo sibi comminantern non videt, timens post viam suam vadit.

Hic conversus saecularis similatus gratiae spiritali. ita est enim et in populo deifico, sicut in vinea terrena. vinea dominica spiritalis plebs est Christianorum, quae custoditur iussu dei patris a puero Christo in ligni speculum exaltato. quod si viator diabolus perambulans viam saecularem [si] ausus fuerit de vinea spiritale hominem de plebe dominica separare et vexare, statim a puero caeleste correptus et flagris spiritalibus emendatus exulans ad centesimum effugit in locis aridis et desertis. hic custos est puer filius dominicus, qui vineam suam sibi a patre commendatam salvandam tenet et reservandam.

This charmingly narrated parable of the *puer-Christus* by an unknown, moderately educated author writing during the time period of Cyprian, or even before him, in the common dialect is related in content and in its impartiality to the parable preserved in Hermas (#15), which admittedly—due to the Adoptionistic foundation on which it is based—indicates its antiquity. The author knows that the *puer Jesus* is the *filius dominicus* (*filius* because of *caro*). But the fact that he was able to invent this parable or, more likely, retell it testifies to the antiquity of his Christianity or to the continued effect of the translation of παῖς with *puer*, in its baser sense, within the Western Church.

47

Pseudo-Tertullian, *Carmen adv. Marcionem*
    (47) V.204: *Filius ipse dei, carissimus ipse minister.*

Ὁ ἀγαπητὸς παῖς is certainly the basis of the later expression. But παῖς is, to my knowledge, only represented here by *minister*, probably because the hexameter did not allow the usage of *puer*. Note the composition of *minister* (*puer*) and *filius*, as in #46. Both authors still felt the original meaning of παῖς. The time of the polemical poem is still controversial despite Holl's research;[64] see Erich Caspar's work *Die älteste römische Bischofsliste*, which has removed one of the main arguments in favor of the poem's later date.[65] I think it likely that a renewed study of the poem[66] will teach us that one should not date the composition of the text later than the beginning of the fourth century.

48–52

Eusebius and Eusebiana (Selection)

(48) *Vita Constantini* I.32: ὁ τοῦ ἑνὸς καὶ μόνου θεοῦ μονογενὴς παῖς (as an interpretation of the emperor's great vision).

(49) *De laudibus Constantini* XVII.13: θεοῦ παῖδα (as an epithet of Christ in a lofty apologetic speech).

(50) *Ad coetum sanctorum* IX.4: ὁ λόγος αὐτὸς θεὸς ὢν αὐτὸς τυγχάνει θεοῦ παῖς· ποῖον γὰρ ἄν τις ἄλλο ὄνομα αὐτῷ περιτιθεὶς παρὰ τὴν προσηγορίαν τοῦ παιδὸς οὐκ ἂν τὰ μέγιστα ἐξαμαρτάνοι; ὁ γάρ τοι τῶν πάντων πατὴρ καὶ τοῦ ἰδίου λόγου δικαίως ἂν πατὴρ νομίζοιτο.

(51) *De laudibus Constantini* XI.8: τάχα δ' ἄν τις εἴποι· πόθεν ἡ προσηγορία τοῦ παιδός, ποία δὲ γένεσις (γέννησις?), εἴπερ εἷς μόνος ὢν θεὸς τυγχάνει, πάσης δὲ μίξεως οὗτός ἐστιν ἀλλότριος;

(52) *Historia ecclesiastica* X.4.56 (in the highly rhetorical ceremonial address): αὐτὸς ὁ θεόπαις.

Eusebius has no recollection of the fact that παῖς (with or without μονογενής) ever meant "servant" when applied to Christ. For him, it is the loftiest epithet for the Logos and it would have been a gravest sin to swap it with another! The idea of the "divine child" could have had an influence here, but accepting its influence even here is not necessary because the liturgical prayers provide a sufficient enough basis. — Here, for the first time in Christian literature, θεόπαις appears, which appears more frequently later, but is also reserved for exalted speech.

53

Magical Papyri from Fayum (ca. 300 CE):

(53) Here, Christ is called ἠγαπημένος παῖς.[67]

---

64. Holl, "Zeit und Heimat," 514ff.
65. Caspar, *Die älteste römische Bischofsliste*, 213ff.
66. See Harnack, *Geschichte der altchristlichen Literatur bis Eusebius*, 2:442ff.
67. Schermann, *Griechische Zauberpapyri*, 3.

54

Epiphanius

Panarion 78.3: τὸν μονογενῆ παῖδα Ἰ. Χρ., τὸν υἱὸν τοῦ θεοῦ τοῦ ζῶντος.

I have singled out this passage from the literature because it apparently still demonstrates an understanding of the difference between παῖς and υἱός (like Pseudo-Tertullian #47 in the Latin literature). This alone is an aberration with regard to the unanimous understanding of παῖς in the Greek church already within the third century. Ephiphanius, on the other hand, explains the lofty expression μονογενὴς παῖς with the realistic one.

55

Pseudo-Athanasius, *De virginitate*

(55) *De virginitate* 13: "Ὅταν καθεσθῇς ἐπὶ τῆς τραπέζης καὶ ἐρχῇ κλᾶσαι τὸν ἄρτον . . . εὐχαριστοῦσα λέγε· Εὐχαριστοῦμέν σοι, πάτερ ἡμῶν, ὑπὲρ τῆς ἁγίας ἀναστάσεώς σου· διὰ γὰρ Ἰησοῦ τοῦ παιδός σου ἐγνώρισας ἡμῖν αὐτήν.[68]

The eucharistic prayer of the Didache functions as the basis here, and thus the simple διὰ Ἰησοῦ τοῦ παιδός σου ἐγνώρισας appears.

56–61

Apostolic Constitutions and Canons

In the first book of the Constitutions, ἠγαπημένος παῖς from the *Didascalia* (see #42) is picked up. In book 7 and 8, the prayers from the Didache and from the Church Orders of Hippolytus, which offer παῖς, are partly taken over verbatim, partly arranged, corrected, and reproduced (see VII.25, 26, 27;[69] VIII.5, 12, 14, 39, 40, 41). Highlighted are the following:

(56) VIII.5: διὰ τοῦ ἁγίου παιδός σου Ἰ. Χρ. τοῦ θεοῦ καὶ σωτῆρος ἡμῶν, μεθ' οὗ καὶ δι' οὗ σοι δόξα;[70] pay attention to μεθ' οὗ.

(57) VIII.12: ὁ θεὸς ὁ μέγας καὶ μεγαλώνυμος, ὁ μέγας τῇ βουλῇ καὶ κραταιὸς τοῖς ἔργοις, ὁ θεὸς καὶ πατὴρ τοῦ ἁγίου παιδός σου Ἰησοῦ, τοῦ σωτῆρος ἡμῶν.[71]

---

68. Migne, *PG*, 28:266.

69. The prayer found here in relation to anointing with oil, which also offers the formula διὰ Ἰησοῦ τοῦ παιδός σου, is not in the Didache itself, but is in the Coptic liturgical recension (see Schmidt, "Das koptische Didache-Fragment," 85, 94).

70. Lagarde, *Constitutiones apostolorum* 238.29.

71. Lagarde, *Constitutiones apostolorum* 259.2.

(58) VIII.14: δέσποτα, ὁ θεὸς ὁ παντοκράτωρ, ὁ πατὴρ τοῦ Χριστοῦ σου, τοῦ εὐλογητοῦ παιδός.[72]

(59) VIII.39: τῷ ἠγαπημένῳ σου παιδί, μεθ' οὗ σοι δόξα κτλ.[73]

(60) VIII.40: εὐχαριστοῦμέν σοι, κύριε παντοκράτωρ . . . διὰ τοῦ μονογενοῦς σου παιδὸς Ἰ. Χρ., τοῦ κυρίου ἡμῶν.[74]

(61) Apostolic Canons, conclusion: ὁ θεὸς καταξιώσει ἅπαντας ὑμᾶς τῆς αἰωνίου ζωῆς σὺν ἡμῖν διὰ τῆς μεσιτείας τοῦ ἠγαπημένου παιδὸς αὐτοῦ Ἰ. Χρ., τοῦ θεοῦ καὶ σωτῆρος ἡμῶν, μεθ' οὗ ἡ δόξα αὐτῷ.[75] Here, take note of μεθ' οὗ in addition to διὰ τῆς μεσιτείας τοῦ ἠγαπημένου παιδός (cf. the *Diataxeis* of the apostle περὶ χειροτονιῶν διὰ Ἱππολύτου [1. c. p. 7]: διὰ τῆς μεσιτείας τοῦ Χριστοῦ σου).

Results

From the beginning of the history of Christianity, the *ebed YHWH* of Isaiah has been interpreted as a prophecy about Jesus. Thus, it would have been expected that the *ebed YHWH* (παῖς θεοῦ) might have been a common name for Jesus. This however is not the case. These then are the results of our investigation:

(I) First, the findings, as they exist in the oldest passages, must be considered individually: In the entirety of Christian literature from 50 CE to 160 CE that has been preserved for us, παῖς θεοῦ has been handed down to us as an epithet for Jesus—apart from citations of Isaiah[76]—only fourteen times in only four texts (Acts; Didache; 1 Clement; Mart. Poly.).[77] This number is rather meager in comparison with the names Χριστός, κύριος, υἱὸς τοῦ θεοῦ, which have been handed down to us from this time period more than 2,000 times. Παῖς θεοῦ was therefore not a common name for Jesus at that time. The scarcity of usage in only a few texts (only in two chapters of Acts) is applicable for all Christian writings up until the middle of the second century, that is, for the entire period itself, thus making the hypothesis of

---

72. Lagarde, *Constitutiones apostolorum* 260.9.
73. Lagarde, *Constitutiones apostolorum* 273.31.
74. Lagarde, *Constitutiones apostolorum* 274.4.
75. Lagarde, *Reliquiae Juris Ecclesiastici Graece*, 35.
76. Once in Matthew (#1), twice in Barnabas (#16 and #17).
77. It must remain an open question whether the Nazarenes (Epiphanius, *Pan.* 29.7) called Jesus *ebed YHWH*; see above at the last note to the "Introduction." Even if Epiphanius has quoted verbatim, it remains questionable whether the Nazarenes were familiar with the term *ebed*.

Bousset invalid.[78] The reason for this almost entirely negative finding can only be that, although the *ebed* of Isaiah had to be interpreted messianically at that time, there were doubts about using it as an epithet for Jesus because of its base meaning, and because of the fact that παῖς did not exclude understanding the term according to is baser meaning.

(II) All four texts, which contain παῖς θεοῦ as an epithet for Jesus use it in prayers twelve times, such that it only occurs outside of prayers twice (only in Acts). Within the prayers, it appears ten times in the δία formula (#5–#11, #13–#15): διὰ Ἰησοῦ τοῦ παιδός σου. Originally, therefore, it existed exclusively within a prayer formula,[79] and Luke took it out of the formula and used παῖς θεοῦ independently as an epithet for Jesus.

(III) But the prayer formula was in the eucharistic prayer, which very probably, though perhaps in a somewhat older form, also underlies the passages in Acts, and originally read without any further addition: διὰ Ἰησοῦ τοῦ παιδός σου. It was this formula that first made the eucharistic prayer of the new community, which had grown out of synagogual prayer, a Christian one. The keyword παῖς θεοῦ (*ebed YHWH*) came from Isaiah— a name was not to be given through the same Jesus, but was, as the context teaches, originally a functional name: Jesus is the servant (attendant),[80] through whom the almighty creator God manifested the new, great gifts, knowledge of God, and eternal life.[81] To my knowledge, we have here the only instance of a word, which later—albeit in a very limited way—became an epithet for Jesus, that we can trace not only to a source but also to a

---

78. See above in the Introduction.

79. Thus the prayer formula remains, even if it can be demonstrated with great probability from #5 (Acts 4:30) with respect to #29 (Acts of John) that even in the most ancient days of Christianity healings and miracles were performed under the invocation of God διὰ τοῦ παιδὸς αὐτοῦ Ἰησοῦ; invocations are also prayers. We could perhaps go one step further: Is not the healing and exorcism formula the starting point and the basis on which παῖς has been taken up into prayer? Even if Matt 7:22 etc. and Mark 9:38 (Luke 9:49) may be a *hysteron-proterone* (Διδάσκαλε, εἴδομέν τινα τῷ ὀνόματί σου ἐκβάλλοντα δαιμόνια)—though this assumption is by no means necessary—it is certain that this practice is ancient and perhaps even older than the invocation of Jesus' mediation in prayer to God. Thus, it is not impossible that the formula διὰ Ἰησοῦ τοῦ παιδός σου has its ultimate root in an invocation of incantation or healing. — It is perhaps remarkable that in the entirety of Christian literature up to ca. 160 CE one finds neither in prayers, prayer-like sentences, or doxologies the formula διὰ Ἰησοῦ τοῦ υἱοῦ σου (outside of these passages, διὰ τοῦ υἱοῦ is not rare).

80. TN: The translation of "Knecht (Diener)" with "servant (attendant)" is not adequate, but it must suffice.

81. Such great gifts from such a great giver require a serving mediation. — It is not a paradox that these gifts do not consist of the forgiveness (or removal) of sins, but in the knowledge of God and eternal life, if one acknowledges the oldest history of the Lord's Supper. This cannot be discussed here. See Lietzmann, *Messe und Herrenmahl*, 211–63.

APPENDIX IV: THE EPITHET "SERVANT OF GOD" 197

specific liturgical use, and from which we recognize anew the importance of liturgical formulas for terminology.

(IV) Already in these four texts a development can be seen quite clearly. The first stage is marked in the Didache. There, one has not yet felt the need to define παῖς in further detail within the formula διὰ Ἰησοῦ τοῦ παιδός σου.[82] But within the Acts of the Apostles, it is already distinguished from Δαβὶδ ὁ παῖς σου and is refined by reference to its glorification (#2), respectively by the addition of ὃν ἔχρισας (#4) and by the addition of ἅγιος (#4 and #5), which otherwise only the "Spirit" (or the church) receives, that is, it unambiguously designates the "servant" as the Messiah. Clement also expresses this through the additions Χριστός (#10–#12) and ἠγαπημένος (#10 and #11). The latter of these was also supplied by Isaiah. Finally, the letter about the martyrdom of Polycarp goes a step further and explicitly refers to Almighty God as the Father of the beloved παῖς Jesus Christ (#13), and therefore to Jesus himself as the μονογενὴς παῖς (#15). In this way, the "servant" is made out to be, in the clearest possible way, the "Son of God." Only at this point did the functional designation for Jesus become a name, that is, it flowed together with the name "Son of God." In this development nothing was more welcome than the double meaning of the word παῖς, which the Hebrew word *ebed* did not have. One could retain the ancient formula handed down in prayer for the Lord's Supper διὰ Ἰησοῦ τοῦ παιδός σου, because παῖς could be and was understood as a "son."[83] Also, παῖς θεοῦ could not be used outside of the formula as a name of Jesus—which only Luke had heretofore attempted—and, be it with or without additions, become independent in the sense of "Son." But the meaning of "the chosen and glorified servant of God" was still expressed by Hermas (#18) in the parable of the slave adopted as a son (without needing the word παῖς), and his book, which was read in churches a great deal and for a long time and with reverence, brought him close to the believers, and it was a source of embarrassment for them.[84]

---

82. A new proof of the antiquity of the eucharistic prayers in the Didache.

83. Did Paul take offense at the formula? A definite answer cannot be given, but it is likely. If one considers how often he uses the formula διὰ Ἰησοῦ Χριστοῦ (διὰ τοῦ κυρίου), but never our formula, then it is very likely that he deliberately avoided it. The assumption that he did not know it is impossible.

84. Since it has been asserted that παῖς exclusively had the meaning "Son" from the very beginning within Christian congregations and in the Christian literature (Wernle contra Bousset), I compile the reasons against it here: (1) A formula that is found in the Didache's prayers for the Lord's Supper, which grew out of the Jewish prayers, and in the book of Acts must belong to the most ancient of usage, that is, it must have already been spoken in Hebrew (Aramaic). Here, however, the word used would have been *ebed*, which has nothing at all to do with "son"; (2) the use of παῖς for Jesus next to παῖς

(V) The main development was already finished around the middle of the second century, but the following period still offers numerous and varied observations of interest regarding παῖς θεοῦ as an epithet for Jesus:

(1) The epithet παῖς θεοῦ for Jesus still remains sparse in the following centuries, especially if one compares the enormous frequency of other epithets. Furthermore, it is notable that Origen did not include παῖς among the names of Jesus (#40).[85] The fact that it might have been understood according to its baser sense must have been the cause of this.[86]

(2) Still, παῖς θεοῦ is found relatively often in prayers, doxologies, etc. and with the old additions such as ἀγαπητός, ἠγαπημένος, and especially μονογενής.[87] The continued use of the oldest formula is also evident in

---

Δαβίδ and similar contexts could have only meant "servant" and received its peculiarity only through additions such as ἅγιος and ὃν ἔχρισας, which would have been entirely superfluous if παῖς in itself meant "son" and therefore "Messiah"; (3) parables like the aforementioned parable of Hermas and *puer custos* (#46) indicate that παῖς originally (according to the Isaiaic source) also meant "servant" within the church; (4) the history of παῖς in church parlance or the general reluctance towards the use of this term and its use only in liturgical and exalted speech are not understandable if παῖς had been understood from the beginning as "son." However, this history is understandable if παῖς originally had the meaning of *ebed* with reference to Jesus.

Conversely, there is probably no longer any need to refute the assertion that παῖς, with the meaning of *ebed*, must therefore have been the original, common name for Jesus, but which was soon eradicated because it was testified to by Acts and the Didache. Terms that are not found either in the Synoptics or in Paul could never have been common.

85. It should be remembered that when Celsus lets Christians speak and has them speak of Jesus as the παῖς θεοῦ, we should not assume that this is an indication of Christian usage of the name (#20).

86. In the fragments of the writings of the Adoptionists (of both Theodosius', Paul of Samosata, etc.), the epithet παῖς (*puer*) for Jesus is not found. — Novatian, in his great argument against the Adoptionists (in his work *De Trinitate*), dealt in detail with the epithet *angelus* for Christ and he refuted the Adoptionist view (he also referred to Phil 2:7), but he did not at all consider παῖς (*puer*). In the controversy between Hilary and the Adoptionists (*De Trinitate* XI.10.13f) about whether the Redeemer has in common with human beings both creation and bondage, because God is also his God and Lord, the discussion is not about *puer dei*, but *servus*. Certainly the expression παῖς (*puer*) had to be a welcome one for the Adoptionists (since they even called the Redeemer δοῦλος), but we do not know whether they used it. In the great christological struggles, neither παῖς nor *puer dei* play a role. They disappear from the ecclesiastical and theological language to such an extent that even the name of David as *puer dei* appears as a singularity in Optatus II.25 (Carolus Ziwsa, *S. Optati Milevitani Libri VII*, 63.15).

87. See #28, #29, #36a-e, #37, #38, #55-61. On μονογενής, see #19, #29, #37, #41, #48, #60. Epiphanius must have regarded παῖς μονογενής as a hierarchical formula, since he provides an explanation of it (see #54). It is possible that the additions to the expression in Dionysius Alexandria (#38) are meant to function as an explanation of the old formula: ὁ μονογενὴς παῖς θεοῦ, ὁ πρωτότοκος πάσης κτίσεως, ὁ ἐνανθρωπήσας λόγος.

the fact that παῖς still seems to be connected with διά, that it still is often connected with παντοκράτωρ (or with the solemn designation of God as the creator),[88] and that the mediation of the knowledge of God by the παῖς is also still in mind.[89]

(3) Also, the observation is valuable that παῖς appears—except in prayers—almost only in exalted, poetic, sacred speech.[90] Indeed, compared with υἱός, it must have been perceived as the more distinguished word (just like our word "woman"[91]), in spite of the possible baser meaning of the word (possibly also as the more intimate, heartfelt word that can only be proven from antiquity).[92] Did the idea of the "divine child" have a role in this? The question of an effect is obvious in #33 (Hippolytus on Rev 12), 35 (Hippolytus: ὁ πρωτόγονος παῖς), 39 (Clement of Alexandria: παῖς κρατερός), 43–45 (Sibylline Oracles: παῖς οὐρανίου), 46 (Pseudo-Cyprian: *puer caelestis*), 52 (Eusebius: θεόπαις). But as far as I can tell, it cannot be answered definitively in the affirmative.

Eusebius calls out, Ποῖον ἄν τις ἄλλο ὄνομα Ἰησοῦ περιτιθεὶς παρὰ τὴν προσηγορίαν τοῦ παιδὸς οὐκ ἂν τὰ μέγιστα ἐξαμαρτάνοι! Who would have thought that the Isaianic *ebed*, translated, could ever become the highest epithet for Jesus! The last shall be first! But despite Eusebius's exclamation, it was not παῖς but rather υἱός that was the common word and that soon displaced its rival completely.

(4) Παῖς did not penetrate into dogmatic usage: υἱός belonged to the symbolic and dogmatic linguistic usage, and παῖς to the liturgy and elevated speech. But a few signs of penetration—even into the Trinitarian formula—have been demonstrated. Athenagoras writes (#22): ἕνωσις . . . τοῦ πνεύματος, τοῦ παιδός, τοῦ πατρός, and Dionysius Alexandria (#41) offers: βλασφημίαν περὶ τοῦ παντοκράτορος θεοῦ . . . ἀπιστίαν περὶ τοῦ μονογενοῦς παιδὸς αὐτοῦ . . . ἀναισθησίαν τοῦ ἁγίου πνεύματος. In Justin (#26), the following words are put in his mouth: εὐσεβοῦμεν εἰς τὸν . . . θεόν . . . ἕνα ἐξ ἀρχῆς ποιητὴν καὶ δημιουργὸν τῆς πάσης κτίσεως . . . καὶ κύριον Ἰ. Χρ., παῖδα θεοῦ,[93] and Clement of Alexandria (#38) connects παῖς Ἰ. Χρ. with κύριος ζώντων καὶ νεκρῶν. However, these approaches remained isolated.

---

88. See #26, #28, #29, #37, #41–45, #57, #58, #60.

89. See #24, #34, #37, #55.

90. See #23–27, #32, #33, #37, #39–41, #43–45, #48–52, #54.

91. TN: Harnack uses the word "Weib" here (not "Frau") as a way to illustrate his point.

92. Characteristic here is #40: Origen does not usually call Jesus παῖς, but in a solemn address he has chosen the liturgical word.

93. On this, cf. Epiphanius, *Pan.* 29.7: ἕνα θεὸν καταγγέλλουσι καὶ τὸν τούτου παῖδα Ἰ. Χρ.

(5) The sparse use of the word παῖς proves that the baser meaning was still felt. But there is also positive evidence of this: Codex Mosquensis of the Martyrdom of Polycarp (#13) has transformed παιδός σου into σου υἱοῦ.[94]

(6) Unlike the Greek Church, the Latin Church was opposed to the use of (παῖς)-*puer* because *puer* could not be understood as "son" as easily as παῖς, even though there is no lack of evidence for this meaning. The Latin reader must have felt more and more reminded of the term "fellow" or "servant" with the term *puer* than the Greek term παῖς.[95] This is the only way to explain first the numerous substitutions of *filius* for *puer* in the manuscripts or removal of this word (in its use for Jesus), where it originally appeared in the texts; see #2-5, #10-#12, #28, #30, #31, #36. Let us recall again the enlightened remark by Beda on Acts 4:30 (#5; *filius*): *In Graeco habetur: "Per nomen sancti pueri tui Jesu," quod magis apostolorum votis congruere videtur.* —Beda still knew or again came to the knowledge that παῖς θεοῦ Ἰησοῦς originally meant "servant of God." Second, it is the only way to explain the observation that the old meaning *peur = minister* in the West still quietly continued to have effect on the conception of Jesus. Proof of this is found both in Pseudo-Tertullian (#47), who unbiasedly writes, *Filius ipse dei, carissimus ipse minister*, thus ὁ ἀγαπητὸς παῖς is translated as *carissimus minister*, as well as in Pseudo-Cyprian (#46), who tells the charming parable, reminiscent of the parable in Hermas (#18), of the *custos puer* of the vineyard, which he interprets with reference to the *filius dominicus* (*puer caelestis*). Here, as with Pseudo-Tertullian, both possible interpretations of παῖς are expressed in Latin in a differentiated and parallel manner.

After the Clementine liturgy and since the fifth century, if I am not mistaken, παῖς and *puer* as an epithet for Christ disappear completely from the liturgies and prayers. Mistakenly, I have looked for them in the Greek and Latin masses. David is probably παῖς τοῦ θεοῦ (Liturgia Marci), but not Jesus. The absolute use of μονογενής and *unigenitus* is found in the Sacramentarium Serapionis and in the Latin masses, and since it is striking, it can

---

94. This exchange is at least harmless compared to the bad one in Codex Constantinople on 2 Clement 9.5 where, in the sentence Χριστὸς ὢν μὲν τὸ πρῶτον πνεῦμα ἐγένετο σάρξ, the word λόγος is used for πνεῦμα. — It soon became unbearable that, according to the oldest doxology, the God of creation (the Father) was offered glory and honor by the παῖς, while these also belong to the παῖς himself. This led to corrections: δι' οὗ was transformed into μεθ' οὗ (or added to it), or "the son" was inserted and resulted in the paradoxical reading in the doxology that one offered glory and honor through the Son (God and) to the Son and to the Holy Spirit (or with the Son and with the Holy Spirit); see #14, #36b-d, #56, #59, #61.

95. *Pueri* ("slaves") is not uncommon. Tertullian writes in *Apol.* 14: *pueris vel canibus*, that is, "slaves and dogs." The Greek would probably read δούλοις τε καὶ κυσίν. Also, the intimacy that παῖς can express is, in my opinion, missing in the word *puer*.

be assumed that παῖς (*puer*) once stood next to it and was later omitted. But this remains a mere supposition.

The use and non-use of the name *ebed* (παῖς, *puer*) for Jesus in the church, which is exclusively attributed to Isaiah, is of equal interest in liturgical and dogmatic-historical terms. An ancient liturgical formula has been the only source for the sparse use of the name, but even this formula was not able to protect the name in the end. Indeed, it was completely eradicated in ancient ecclesiastical times. This is reason enough not to forget it! In general, however, one can learn here that liturgical formulae have the power to protect the obsolete for centuries, but that in the end they lose this power and they themselves have to leave the field.

Bibliography

Bakke, Odd. *"Concord and Peace": A Rhetorical Analysis of the First Letter of Clement with an Emphasis on the Language of Unity and Sedition*. WUNT 2/141. Tübingen: Mohr Siebeck, 2001.

Barclay, John M. G. "There Is neither Old nor Young? Early Christianity and Ancient Ideologies of Age." *New Testament Studies* 53 (2007) 225–41.

Bardy, Gustave. "Expressions stoïciennes dans la 1e Clementis." *Récherches de Science réligieuse* 12 (1922) 73–85.

Bousset, Wilhelm. *Kyrios Christos: Geschichte des Christusglaubens von den Anfängen des Christentums bis Irenaeus*. 2nd ed. Göttingen: Vandenhoeck & Ruprecht, 1921.

Breytenbach, Cilliers. "Civic Concord and Cosmic Harmony, Sources of Metaphoric Mapping in 1 Clement 20:3." In *Encounters with Hellenism: Studies on the First Letter of Clement*, edited by Cilliers Breytenbach and Laurence L. Welborn, 182–96. Arbeiten zur Geschichte des antiken Judentums und des Urchristentums 53. Leiden: Brill, 2004.

Breytenbach, Cilliers, and Laurence L. Welborn, eds. *Encounters with Hellenism: Studies on the First Letter of Clement*. Arbeiten zur Geschichte des antiken Judentums und des Urchristentums 53. Leiden: Brill, 2004.

Bruno, Violet. *Die Apokalypsen des Esra und des Baruch in deutscher Gestalt*. Leipzig: Hinrichs, 1924.

Bumpus, H. B. *The Christological Awareness of Clement of Rome and Its Sources*. Cambridge: Cambridge University Press, 1972.

Caspar, Erich. *Die älteste römische Bischofsliste. Kritische Studien zum Formproblem des eusebianischen Kanons sowie zur Geschichte der ältesten Bischofslisten*. Berlin: Deutsche Verlagsgesellschaft für Politik und Geschichte, 1926.

Dibelius, Martin. *Der Hirt des Hermas*. Handbuch zum Neuen Testament. Ergänzungs-Band: Die apostolischen Väter 4. Tübingen: Mohr Siebeck, 1923.

———. *Rom und die Christen im ersten Jahrhundert*. Heidelberg: Winter, 1942.

Diekamp, Franz. *Doctrina Patrum de Incarnatione Verbi*. Münster: Aschendorff, 1907.

Drews, Paul. *Untersuchungen über die sogen. clementinische Liturgie im VIII. Buch der apostolischen Konstitutionen. I. Die clementinische Liturgie in Rom*. Studien zur Geschichte des Gottesdienstes und des gottesdienstlichen Lebens II und III. Tübingen: Mohr (Paul Siebeck), 1906.

Fischer, Joseph. *Die Apostolischen Väter. Schriften des Urchristentums Part I*. Darmstadt: Wissenschaftliche Buchgesellschaft, 1964.

Funk, F. *Didascalia et Constitutiones Apostolorum*. Vol. 2. Paderborn: Schöningh, 1906.

Gebhardt, Oskar von, and Adolfus Harnack. *Patrum Apostolicorum Opera: Clementis Romani ad Corinthios quae dicuntur Epistulae: Textum ad fidem codicum et Alexandrini et Constantinopolitani nuper inventi.* 2nd ed. Leipzig: Hinrichs, 1876.

Gebhardt, Oskar von. *Die lateinischen Übersetzungen der Acta Pauli et Theclae: Nebst Fragmenten, Auszügen und Beilagen.* Texte und Untersuchungen zur Geschichte der altchristlichen Literatur 22. Leipzig: Hinrichs, 1902.

———. "Review of 'Germain Morin: Sancti Clementis Romani ad Corinthios epistulaeversio latina antiquissima.'" *Deutsche Literaturzeitung* 18 (1894) 545-47.

———. "Review of 'S. Clement of Rome. An Appendix, Containing the Newly Recovered Portions by J. B. Lightfoot.'" *TLZ* 13 (1877) 354-63.

Germain, Morin. *Anecdota Maredsolana; Seu, Monumenta Ecclesiasticae Antiquitatis en Mss. Codicibus nunc Primum Edita.* Vol. 1. Maredsoli: Monasterio S. Benedicti, 1894.

Grant, Robert M., and Holt H. Graham. *First and Second Clement.* The Apostolic Fathers: A New Translation and Commentary 2. New York: Nelson, 1965.

Gressmann, Hugo. "Götterkind und Menschensohn." *Deutsche Literaturzeitung* 39 (1926).

Hagner, Donald. *The Use of the Old and New Testaments in Clement of Rome.* Novum Testamentum Supplements 34. Leiden: Brill, 1973.

Harnack, Adolf von. "Das Alte Testament in den Paulinischen Briefen und in den Paulinischen Gemeinden." *Sitzungsberichte der Preussischen Akademie der Wissenschaften* (1928) 121-41.

———. "Ansprachen in der Festsitzung des Kirchenhistorischen Seminars zum Feier des sechzigsten Geburtstages (1911)." In *Aus der Werkstatt des Vollendeten,* 7-15. Giessen: Töpelmann, 1930.

———. "Die Bezeichnung Jesu als 'Knecht Gottes' und ihre Geschichte in der alten Kirche." *Sitzungsberichte der preußischen Akademie der Wissenschaften* 28 (1926) 212-38.

———. *Einführung in die alte Kirchengeschichte: Das Schreiben der römischen Kirche an die korinthische aus der Zeit Domitians (1 Clemensbrief).* Leipzig: Hinrichs, 1929.

———. *Entstehung und Entwicklung der Kirchenverfassung und des Kirchenrechts in den zwei ersten Jahrhunderten: Nebst einer Kritik der Abhandlung R. Sohm's: Wesen und Ursprung des Katholizismus und Untersuchungen über "Evangelium," "Wort Gottes" und das trinitarische Bekenntnis: Verfassung u. Recht d. alten Kirche.* Leipzig: Hinrichs, 1910.

———. "Der erste Klemensbrief: Eine Studie zur Bestimmung des Charakters des ältesten Heidenchristentums." *Sitzungsberichte der preußischen Akademie der Wissenschaften: Philosophisch-historische Klasse* (1909) 38-61.

———. "Fünfzehn Fragen an die Verächter der wissenschaftlichen Theologie unter den Theologen." *Christliche Welt* 37 (1923) 6-8.

———. *Geschichte der altchristlichen Literatur bis Eusebius.* 2 vols. Leipzig: Hinrichs, 1893-1904.

———. *Lehrbuch der Dogmengeschichte.* 3 vols. Freiburg: Mohr (Paul Siebeck), 1886.

———. *Lehrbuch der Dogmengeschichte.* Vol. 1. 4th ed. Tübingen: Mohr (Paul Siebeck), 1909.

———. *Marcion: Das Evangelium vom fremden Gott.* 2nd ed. Leipzig: Hinrichs, 1921.

———. *Militia Christi: Die christliche Religion und der Soldatenstand in den ersten drei Jahrhunderten.* Tübingen: Mohr (Paul Siebeck), 1905.

———. "Neue Studien zur jüngst entdeckte lateinische Übersetzung des 1 Clemensbriefs." *Sitzungsberichte der preußischen Akademie der Wissenschaften* 27 (1894) 601–21.

———. *Neue Untersuchungen zur Apostelgeschichte und zur Abfassungszeit der Synoptischen Evangelien*. Beiträge zur Einleitung in das Neue Testament 4. Leipzig: Hinrichs, 1911.

———. "Review of Heinrich Hoffmann, *Der neuere Protestantismus und die Reformation*." *Deutsche Literaturzeitung* 45 (1924) 409–10.

———. "'Sanftmut, Huld und Demut' in der alten Kirche." In *Festgabe für D. Dr. Julius Kaftan zu seinem 70. Geburtstage, 30. September 1918*, 113–29. Tübingen: Mohr (Paul Siebeck), 1920.

———. "Das Schreiben der römischen Kirche an die korinthische aus der Zeit Domitians (1 Clemensbrief)." In *Encounters with Hellenism: Studies on the First Letter of Clement*, edited by Cilliers Breytenbach and Laurence L. Welborn, 1–103. Arbeiten zur Geschichte des antiken Judentums und des Urchristentums 53. Leiden: Brill, 2004.

———. "Über die jüngst entdeckte lateinische Übersetzung des 1 Clemensbriefs." *Sitzungsberichte der preußischen Akademie der Wissenschaften* 26 (1894) 261–73.

———. "What Has History to Offer as Certain Knowledge Concerning the Meaning of World Events?" In *Adolf von Harnack: Liberal Theology at Its Height*, edited by Martin Rumscheidt, 45–62. London: Collins Liturgical Publications, 1989.

Hauck, Albert. *Kirchengeschichte Deutschlands*. Vol. 1. Leipzig: Hinrichs, 1887.

Hauler, Edmundus, ed. *Didascaliae apostolorum fragmenta Veronensia latina*. Leipzig: Hinrichs, 1900.

Hilgenfeld, Adolf. "Review of 'Germain Morin: *Sancti Clementis Romani ad Corinthios epistulae versio latina antiquissima*.'" *Wochenschrift für klassische Philologie* 16 (1894) 425–29.

Holl, Karl. "Über Zeit und Heimat des pseudotertullianischen Gedichts adv. Marcionem." *Sitzungsberichte der preußischen Akademie der Wissenschaften* (1918) 514–59.

Jaubert, Annie. "Thèmes lévitiques dans la Prima Clementis." *Vigiliae Christianae* 18 (1964) 193–203.

Knopf, Rudolf, ed. *Der erste Clemensbrief untersucht und herausgegeben*. Texte und Untersuchungen zur Geschichte der altchristlichen Literatur 20. Berlin: de Gruyter, 1899.

———. *Die Lehre der Zwölf Apostel. Die Zwei Clemensbriefe*. Die Apostolischen Väter 1. Tübingen: Mohr/Siebeck, 1920.

Kunze, J. *De Historiae Gnosticismi Fontibus*. Leipzig: Hinrichs, 1894.

Lagarde, P. de. *Constitutiones apostolorum*. Leipzig: Teubner, 1862.

———. *Reliquiae Juris Ecclesiastici Graece*. Leipzig: Teubner, 1856.

Lietzmann, Hans. *Geschichte der Alten Kirche*. Vol. 1. Berlin: de Gruyter, 1932.

———. *Messe und Herrenmahl. Eine Studie zur Geschichte der Liturgie*. Arbeiten zur Kirchengeschichte 8. Berlin: de Gruyter, 1926.

———. *Petrus und Paulus in Rom: Liturgische und archäologische Studien*. 2nd ed. Arbeiten zur Kirchengeschichte 1. Berlin: de Gruyter, 1927.

Lightfoot, J. B. *S. Clement of Rome*. 2nd ed. 2 vols. The Apostolic Fathers 1. New York: Macmillan, 1890.

Lindemann, Andreas. *Die Clemensbriefe*. Handbuch zum Neuen Testament 17. Tübingen: Mohr Siebeck, 1992.

Lipsius, Richard Adelbert. *Die Apokryphen Apostelgeschichten und Apostellegenden.* 2 vols. in 3. Braunschweig: Schwetschke, 1883–1887.
Lipsius, Richard Adelbert, et al., eds. *Acta apostolorum apocrypha.* Vol. 1. Leipzig: Hinrichs, 1891.
Löhr, Hermut. *Studien zum frühchristlichen und frühjüdischen Gebet.* WUNT 160. Tübingen: Mohr Siebeck, 2003.
Lommatzsch, C. H. E., ed. *Origenis Opera Omnia Quae Graece vel Latine Tantum Exstant et Ejus Nomine Circumferuntur.* Vol. 5. Berlin: Haude et Spener, 1831.
Lona, Horacio. *Der erste Clemensbrief.* Kommentar zu den Apostolischen Vätern 2. Göttingen: Vandenhoeck & Ruprecht, 1998.
Markschies, Christoph. "Harnack's Image of 1 Clement and Contemporary Research." *ZAC* 18 (2013) 54–69.
Marsh, Charles. *Strange Glory: A Life of Dietrich Bonhoeffer.* New York: Knopf, 2014.
Mikat, Paul. *Die Bedeutung der Begriffe Stasis und Aponoia für das Verständnis des 1. Clemensbrief.* Arbeitsgemeinschaft für Forschung des Landes Nordrhein-Westfalen 155. Cologne: Westdeutscher Verlag, 1969.
Origenes. *Die Homilien zu Lukas in der Übersetzung des Hieronymus und die griechischen Reste der Homilien und des Lukas-Kommentars.* Edited by Max Rauer. Leipzig: Hinrichs, 1930.
Paget, James Carleton. "1 Clement, Judaism, and the Jews." *Early Christianity* 8 (2017) 218–50.
Preuschen, Erwin. *Analecta: Staat und Christentum bis auf Konstantin.* Vol. 1. 2nd ed. Tübingen: Mohr (Paul Siebeck), 1909.
———. *Origens Werke.* Vol. 4 of *Der Johanneskommentar.* Leipzig: Hinrichs, 1903.
Rösch, F. *Bruchstücke des 1 Clemensbriefs.* Strassburg: Du Mont Schauberg, 1910.
Rothschild, Clare K. "Reception of 1 Corinthians in 1 Clement." In *New Essays on the Apostolic Fathers,* by Clare K. Rothschild, 35–60. WUNT 375. Tübingen: Mohr Siebeck, 2017.
Sanders, Louis. *L'Hellénisme de Saint Clément de Rome et Le Paulinisme.* Louvain: Universitas Catholica Lovaniensis, 1943.
Schermann, Theodor, ed. *Die allgemeine Kirchenordnung, frühchristliche Liturgien und kirchliche Überlieferung.* Vol. 1. Studien zur Geschichte und Kulture des Altertums. Ergänzungsband 3. Paderborn: Schöningh, 1914.
———. *Griechische Zauberpapyri und das Gemeinde- und Dankgebet im I. Klemensbriefe.* Texte und Untersuchungen 34.2b. Leipzig: Hinrichs, 1910.
Schmidt, Carl. "Das koptische Didache-Fragment des British Museum." *Zeitschrift für die neutestamentliche Wissenschaft* 24 (1925) 81–99.
Schmidtke, Alfred. *Neue Fragmente und Untersuchungen zu den judenchristlichen Evangelien: Ein Beitrag zur Literatur und Geschichte der Judenchristen.* Texte und Untersuchungen zur Geschichte der altchristlichen Literatur 37.1. Leipzig: Hinrichs, 1911.
Smith, Jonathan Z. *Drudgery Divine: On the Comparison of Early Christianities and the Religions of Late Antiquity.* Chicago Studies in the History of Judaism. Chicago: University of Chicago Press, 1990.
Sohm, Rudolph. *Kirchenrecht: Die geschichtlichen Grundlagen.* Vol. 1. Leipzig: Duncker & Humblot, 1892.
———. *Wesen und Ursprung des Katholizismus.* Berlin: Teubner, 1912.

Tomson, Peter J. "The Centrality of Jerusalem and Its Temple as Viewed by Clement of Rome." *Analecta Bruxellensia* 5 (2000) 97–112.
Unnik, W. C. van. "Studies on the So-Called First Epistle of Clement. The Literary Genre." In *Encounters with Hellenism: Studies on the First Letter of Clement*, edited by C. Breytenbach and L. L. Welborn, 115–81. Translated by Laurence Welborn. Arbeiten zur Geschichte des antiken Judentums und des Urchristentums 53. Leiden: Brill, 2004.

———. *Studies over de zogenaamde Eerste Brief van Clemens. I. Het Litteraire Genre.* Mededelingen der Koninklijke Nederlandse Akademie van Wetenschappen, Afd. Letterkunde. Nieuwe reeks, 33/4. Amsterdam: Noord Hollandische Uitgevers Maatschappij, 1970.

Verheyden, Joseph. "Israel's Fate in the Apostolic Fathers: The Case of 1 Clement and the Epistle of Barnabas." In *The Separation between the Just and the Unjust in Early Judaism and in the Sayings Source*, edited by Mark Tiwald, 237–62. Göttingen: Vandenhoeck & Ruprecht, 2015.

Wattenbach, Wilhelm. *Deutschlands Geschichtsquellen im Mittelalter*. 2 vols. 4th ed. Berlin: Hertz, 1877–1878.

Wehofer, Thomas M. *Untersuchungen zur altchristlichen Epistolographie*. Vienna: Gerold, 1901.

Welborn, L. L. "On the Date of First Clement." *Biblical Research* 29 (1984) 35–54.

———. "'Take up the Epistle of the Blessed Paul the Apostle': The Contrasting Fates of Paul's Letters to Corinth in the Patristic Period." In *Reading Communities, Reading Scripture: Essays in Honor of Daniel Patte*, edited by G. A. Philips and N. W. Duran, 345–57. Harrisburg, PA: Trinity, 2002.

———. *The Young against the Old: Generational Conflict in First Clement*. Lanham, MD: Lexington/Fortress Academic, 2018.

Wendland, P., ed. *Hippolytus Werke*. Die Grieschischen Schriftseteller der ersten drei Jahrhunderte 3. Leipzig: Hinrichs, 1916.

Windisch, Hans. *Taufe und Sünde im ältesten Christentum bis auf Origenes: Ein Beitrag zur altchristlichen Dogmengeschichte*. Tübingen: Mohr (Paul Siebeck), 1908.

Wölfflin, Eduard von. "Die lateinische Übersetzung des Briefes des Clemens an die Korinther." In *Archiv für lateinische Lexikographie und Grammatik*, vol. 9, edited by Eduard von Wölfflin. Leipzig: Teubner, 1984.

Wrede, William. *Untersuchungen zum ersten Klemensbriefe*. Göttingen: Vandenhoeck & Ruprecht, 1891.

Young, Patrick. *Clementis ad Corinthios epistola prior*. Oxford: Oxonii, 1633.

———. *Clementis ad Corinthios epistola prior*. 2nd ed. Oxford: Oxonii, 1637.

Zahn, Theodor. *Geschichte des neutestamentlichen Kanons*. Vol. 1. Erlangen: Deichert, 1888.

———. "Review of 'Germain Morin: Sancti Clementis Romani ad Corinthios epistulaeversio latina antiquissima.'" *Theologische Literaturblatt* 17 (1894) 197–200.

Zahn-Harnack, Agnes von. *Adolf von Harnack*. Berlin: de Gruyter, 1951.

———. *Adolf von Harnack*. Translated by William Henry Allison and William Henry Walker. 1951. Unpublished typescript.

Ziegler, Adolf. *Neue Studien zum ersten Klemensbrief*. Munich: Manz, 1958.

Ziegler, Leo, ed. *Italafragmente der Paulinischen Briefe*. Marburg: Elwert, 1876.

Ziwsa, Carolus. S. *Optati Milevitani Libri VII*. Leipzig: Freytag, 1893.

Indexes to 1 Clement by Harnack

I. Scriptural Citations

Genesis	1 Clement
1:9	20.6
1:26f	33.5
1:28	33.6
2:23	6.3
4:3–8	4.1f
5:24	9.3
6:8f	9.4
12:1–3	10.3
13:14–16	10.4
15:5f	10.6; 32.2
18:27	17.2
19	11.1
21f	10.7
22:7f	31.3
22:17	32.2
26:4	32.2
27:41f	4.8
28f	31.4
37	4.9

Exodus	1 Clement
2:14	4.10
3:11	17.5
4:10	17.5
14:13f	51.5
32:7f	53.2
32:32	53.4
34:28	53.2

Numbers	1 Clement
12	4.11
12:7	17.5
16	4.12
16:31f	51.4
17	43.2
18:27	29.3

Deuteronomy	1 Clement
4:34	29.3
9:9, 12f.	53.2
14:2	29.3
32:8f	29.2
32:15	3.1

Joshua	1 Clement
2	12.1f

1 Samuel	1 Clement
2:10	13.1
13:14	18.1
18f; 21; 29	4.13

2 Chronicles	1 Clement
2:6–8	512, 566

Psalms	1 Clement
2:7	36.4
3:5	26.2
12:3f	15.5f
18:26f	46.3
19:1ff	27.7
22:6ff	16.15
23:4	26.2

24:1	54.3	19:26	26.3
28:7	26.2	38:11	20.7
31:19	15.5f		
32:1f	50.6	*Wisdom*	*1 Clement*
32:10	22.8	2:24	3.4
34:11–17	22.1f	10:7	11.2
37:36f	14.5	11:22	27.5
37:39	14.4	12:12	27.5
38	14.4		
44:14	39.1	*Sirach*	*1 Clement*
45:6	16.2	4:29	34.1
49:15	51.4		
50:14f	52.3	*Esther*	*1 Clement*
50:16–23	35.7f	4:16	55.6
51:3–19	18.2f	7f	55.6
51:19	52.4		
62:4	15.3	*Judith*	*1 Clement*
69:4	39.1	8ff	55.4
69:31f	52.2		
78:36f	15.4	*Jonah*	*1 Clement*
89:21	18.1	3	7.7
104:4	36.3		
104:29	21.9	*Job*	*1 Clement*
110:1	36.5	1–2	303, 305
118:18	56.3		
118:19f	48.2	*Malachi*	*1 Clement*
132:1	7.3	3:1	23.5
139:7f	28.3		
139:15	38.3	*Isaiah*	*1 Clement*
141:5	56.5	1:16–20	8.4
		3:5	3.3
Proverbs	*1 Clement*	6:3	34.6
1:23–33	57.3	13:22 (14:1)	23.5
2:21f	14.4	26:20	50.4
3:12	56.4	29:13	15.2
3:34	30.2	40:10	34.3
7:3	2.8	41:8	10.1; 17.2
		53:1–12	16.3f
Job	*1 Clement*	59:14	3.4
1:1	17.3	60:17	42.5
4:16ff	39.3f	62:11	34.3
4:19–5:5	39.5f	66:2	13.4
5:17–26	56.6f		
11:2f	30.4f	*Jeremiah*	*1 Clement*
14:4f	17.4	9:23f	13.1
15:15	39.5		

Ezekiel	1 Clement		6:16f	45.6
33:11	8.2		7:10	34.6
37:12 (?)	50.4			
48:12	29.3		*Apocrypha*	
			8.3; (13.1?); 17.6; 23.3; 26.2; (29.3?);	
Daniel	*1 Clement*		24.8; 46.2; 50.4	
3:19f	45.7			

II. Allusions to NT Scriptures

Whether a dependeny exists must be investigated on a case by case basis.

[The two quotations of the Lord's words (indpendent of our gospels) found in the letter (1 Clem 13 and 46) are similar to or coincide with Matt 5:7; 6:14; 7:1f, 12; Luke 6:31, 37f and with Matt 26:24; Mark 9:42; Luke 17:2]

Matthew	*1 Clement*		*1 Corinthians*	*1 Clement*
11:29f	13.1; 16.17		1:1f	salutation; 65.2
23:11	48.6		1:10f	47.3
			1:31	13.1
John	*1 Clement*		7:7	38.1
10:9	48.4		7:7	38.1
17:18 (20:21)	42.1f		10:24, 33	48.6
			12:8f	48.5
Acts	*1 Clement*		12:12f	37.5
14:19	5.6		12:29f	37.3
20:35	2.1		13:1ff	49
			15:20, 36f	24:1f
Romans	*1 Clement*		15:23	37.3
1:21	36.2; 51.5		16:11	65.1
1:29ff	35.5f			
2:24	47.7		*Galatians*	*1 Clement*
2:29	30.3, 6		2:9	5.2
3:8	51.3		3:1	2.1
3:28	32.4		3:6f	31.2
4:1f	31.2		6:1	56.1
4:7	50.6f			
6:1f	33.1		*Ephesians*	*1 Clement*
9:4f	32.2		1:4	64
12:5	46.7		1:17f	59.5
13:2	61.1		2:12	7.7
			4:4f	46.6

4:18	36.2	2:7	36:2f
5:21	38.1	2:17	36:1
		3:1	36:1
Philippians	*1 Clement*	3:2	17:5
1:l5	5.1	3:5	43.1
1:27	3.4	4:12	21.9
1:30	7.1	4:14f	36.1
2:5f	16.2	10:23	27.1
		11:5ff	9.3ff
Colossians	*1 Clement*	11:11	27.1
3:14	49.2	11:37	17.1
		12:1	13.1; 19.1
1 Thessalonians	*1 Clement*	12:9	64
5:14	59.4	13:2	10.7
		13:7, 17, 24	1.3
1 Timothy	*1 Clement*	13:21	21.1
1:17	61.2		
2:3	7.3	*1 Peter*	*1 Clement*
2:8	29.1	1f	salutation
2:11	21.7	1:l7	salutation
5:21	21.7	1:19	7.4
		2:1	30.1
2 Timothy	*1 Clement*	2:9	36.2; 59.2
1:11	5.6	2:12	50.3
2:21	34.4	2:13f	37.3; 61.1
		2:25	59.3; 63.1
Titus	*1 Clement*	4:8	49.5
1:5	42.4	4:10	38.1
2:5	1.3	5:5	30.2; 57.1
3:5	32.3f		
		James	*1 Clement*
Hebrews	*1 Clement*	2:21f	31.2
1:3f, 5, 7, 13	36:2–5	2:24	30.3
1:8	16.2	4:16	13.1; 21.5

III. Names

Aaron, 4.11; 43.5
Abel, 4.1f, 6
Abiram, 4.12
Abraham, 10.1, 6; 17.2; 31.2
Adam, 6.3; 29.2; 50.3
Ananias, 45.7
Apollo, 47.3

Apostle, 5.3; 42.1f; 44.1; 47.1, 4
Arabia, Arabic, 25.1, 3
Azarias, 45.7

Bito, Valerius, 65.1

Cain, 4.1ff

Cephas, 47.3
Christ, as address, 1.2; 2.1; 3.4; 7.4; 16.1; 20.11; 21.8; 22.1; 24.1; 32.4; 36.1; 38.1; 42.1ff; 43.1; 44.1, 3; 46.6f; 47.6; 48.4; 49.1, 6; 50.3, 7; 54.2f; 57.2; 58.2; 59.2f; 61.3; 64; 65.2 (= servant of God 59.2, 4)
Claudius, *see* Ephebus
Corinth(ians), 47.6

Danaids, 6.2
Dathan, 4.12
Dircae, 6.2

Elijah, 17.1
Elisha, 17.1
Enoch, 9.3
Ephebus, Claudius, 65.1
Esau, 4.8
Esther, 55.6
Eygpt (Egyptian), 4.10; 17.5; 25.3; 51.5; 53.2
Ezekiel, 17.1

Fortunatus, 65.1

Heliopolis, 25.3
Holofernes, 55.5

Isaac, 31.3
Israel, 4.13; 8.2; 29.3; 31.4; 43.5f; 55.6

Jacob, 4.8; 29.3; 31.4
Jericho, 12.2
Jerusalem, 41.2
Jesus, address, 13.1; 16.2; 20.11; 21.6; 24.1; 32.2, 4; 36.1; 38.1; 42.1, 3; 44.1; 46.7; 49.6; 50.7; 58.2; 59.2, 4; 61.3; 64; 65.2

Job, 17.3; 26.3
Jonah, 7.7
Joseph, 4.9
Joshua, 12.2
Judah, 32.2
Judith, 55.4

Laban, 31.4
Lebanon, 14.5
Levites, 32.2; 40.5
Lot, 10.4; 11.1

Miriam, 4.11
Mishael, 45.7
Moses, 4.10, 12; 17.5; 3.1, 6; 51.3, 5; 53.2, 4

Ninevites, 7.7
Noah, 7.6; 9.4
Nun, 12.2

Ocean, 20.8

Paul, Apostle, 5.5; 47.1
Peter, Apostle, 5.4
Pharaoh, 4.10; 51.5

Rahab, 12.1, 3
Rome, salutation

Saul, 4.13
Sodom, 11.1
Spirt, Holy, 2.2; 8.1; 13.1; 16.2; 18.11; 22.1; 42.3; 45.2; 46.6; 58.2; 63.2 (Trinity 42.3; 46.6; 58.2)

Valerius, *see* Bito

III. Subjects

This hundred word index exhausts the author's religious and moral concepts. No main concept is lacking; it only lacks any form of originality. Nevertheless, the impression is not one of meagerness, but of ecumenicity. It is also strongly emphasized that religion is not a matter of thought to the writer, but of life.

abstinence, 62.2
Almighty, salutation; 2.3; 3.5; 32.4; (56.6); 60.4; 62.2
altar , 32.3; 41.2
athlete, 5.1, 2

baptism, 42.4
beauty, beautiful (καλός), 6.1; 7.3; 35.3; 49.3
bishop, 42.4f; 59.3 (by God)
bishop's office, 44.1, 4; 50.3 (by Christ)
blessed, 35.1; 40.4; 43.1; 44.5; 47.1; 48.4; 50.5ff; 55.4; 56.6
blood (of Christ), 7.4; 12.7; 21.6; 49.6; (55.1)
body, 6.2; 37.5; 38.1; 46.7
border of the west, 5.7
brotherhood, 2.4
brotherly Love, 47.5; 48.1

calling, 42.6
canon, 1.3; 7.2; 41.1
charis, salutation; 8.1; 16.17; 23.1; 46.6; 55.3; 65.2
charisma, 38.1f
chastity (ἁγνεία), 1.3; 21.7. 8; 29.1; 38.2; 40.1, 5; 64
Christology, *see* "Blood"; "Suffering"; "Redemption"; 16; 36; 49.6; 55.3; 65.2
church, salutation 44.3; 47.6
clique, 21.7; 47.3f; 50.2; 63.1
conscience, 1.3; 2.4; 34.7; 41.1; 45.7
cosmology, 20; 33

deacon, 42.4f
Demiurge, 20.11; 26.1; 33.2; 38.3; 55.3; 59.2
depths (of divine *gnosis*), 40.1

despot, frequently used of God, never of Christ
diakonien, 40.5

election, 1.1; 2.4; 6.1; 29; 30.1f; 46.3f, 8; 49.5; 52.5; 58.2; 59.3f; 60.4
example, 5.7; 16.17f; 33.8

Father (God), Eight times of God: 7.4; 8.3; 19.2; 23.1; 29.1; 35.3; 56.16; 16.2. twice in a citation; three times as the Father of the world and the eons; three times as the compassionate Father; once as the Father of Christ
faith, believe, 1.2; 3.4; 5.6; 6.1; 10.6f; 12.7f; 16.3; 22.1; 31.2; 34.4; 35.5; 39.4; 42.4; 43.1; 58.2; 60.4; 62.2; 64
flesh, 6.3; 25.3; 26.3; 32.2; 49.6; 59.3; 64

gate (Christ), 48.2f
gentleness (ἐπιείχεια), 13.1; 30.8; 56,1; 58.2; 62.2
gifts (δῶρα), 44.4; (προσφοραί) 36.1; 40.2, 4
glory, place of, 5.4
glory of faith, 5.6
gnosis, 1.2; (27.7); 36.2; 40.1 ("depths of *gnosis*); 41.4; 49.5; (ἀγνωσία 59.2)
God, proclamation, and doctrine, 20; 27; 32.1ff; 33.2; *see also* "Election" and 59f
gospel, 42.1, 3; 47.2

harmony (ὁμόνοια), 9.4; 11.2; 20.3, 10f; 21.1; 30.3; 34.7; 49.5; 50.5; 60.4; 61.1; 63.2; 65.1

herd (= the congregation of God and Christ), 16.1; 44.3; 54.2; 57.2; (59.4)
High Priest (Christ), 36.1; 61.3; 64
holiness, sanctify, 30.1; 35.2; 46.2; 59.3
holy Books, 43.1
holy Scriptures, 23.3, 5; 34.6; 35.7; 42.5; 45.2; 53.1
honorable (σεμνός), 1.1, 3; 7.2; 41.1; 47.5; 48.1
hope, 11.1; 12.7; 16.16; 22.8; 27.1; 51.1; 57.2; 58.2; 59.3
hospitality, 1.2; 10.7; 11.1; 12.2, 3 (ἀφιλοξενία 35.5)
humility, 2.1; 13.1, 3; 16.1f, 17; 17.2; 19.1; 21.8; 30.3, 8; 31.4; 38.2; 44.3; 48.6; 56.1; 58.2; 62.2

immortality, 35.2; 36.2

justification, 8.4; 16.12; 18.4; 30.3; 32.4 (see righteousness)

king of the ages, 61.2
kingdom of God (Christ), 42.3; 50.3

laity, 40.5
law, 1.3; 3.4; 40.4; 43.1 (ἐπινομή 44.2)
leaders (ἡγούμενοι), 1.3; 5.7; 32.2; 37.2f; 48.2; (63.1?); (προηγούμενοι 21.6)
life, 35.2; 48.2
liturgy (λειτουργία, λειτουργεῖν), 8.1; 9.2, 4; 20.10; 32.2; 34.5f; 36.3; 40.2, 5; 41.1f; 43.4; 44.2f, 6
logia, 13.4; 19.1; 53.1; 62.3
Lord (κύριος), 64 times (but 34 times in citations), 17 times of Christ, 13 times of God or uncertain
Lord's Supper, (41.1); 44.4
love, (3.1); 15.4; 18.6; 21.7f.; 22.2; 29.1; 33.1; 49.1ff; 50–56; 59.2f; 62.2

multitude (πλῆθος = congregation), 53.5; 54.2

neighbor, 38.1

obedience and submission, 1.3; 2.1; 7.6; 9.1, 3; 10.1f, 7; 13.3; 14.1; 19.1; 20.1; 34.5; 37.2, 5; 38.1; 39.7; 57.1f, 4; 58.1; 60.4; 61.1; 63.1f
offering, 4.1f; 10.7; 18.16f; 31.3; 35.12; 41.2; 52.3

patience, 5.5f; 34.8; 35.3f; 5.8; 62.2; 64
patron (of Christ), 36.1; 61.3; 64
peace, salutation; 2.2; 3.4; 15.1; 19.2; 20.1, 9ff; 5.2; 60.3f; 61.1f; 62.2; 63.2, 4; 64; 65.1
perfection, 50.1; 53.5; (1.2; 23.5; 33.6; 44.2, 5; 49.5; 50.3; 55.6; 56.1)
people of God (λαός), 29; 55.5f; 59.4; 64; and in numerous citations
person, 33.4f; 38.3
phoenix, 25
piety (εὐσέβεια), 1.2; 2.3; 11.1; 15.1; 32.4; 50.3; 61.2; 62.1
pillars, the apostles, 5.2
priest (priesthood), 25.5; 32.2; 40.5; 43.2, 4
presbyter, 1.3; 3.3; 21.6; 44.5; 47.6; 54.2; 55.4; 57.1

rank, order, 40.1ff; (37.3)
rebirth, 9.4
redemption (σωτηρία, λύτρωσις), 2.4; 7.4, 6f; 11.1; 12.1, 7; 21.8; 36.1; 37.5; 38.1; 45.1; 55.2; 58.2; 59.3f; 60.4
repentance, 7.4f; 8.1ff; 57.1; 62.2
resurrection, 24f; 42.3
reward, 5.4; 6.2
righteousness, righteous, act justly, 3.4; 5.2, 7; 9.3; 21.4; 27.1; 30.7; 31.2; 32.3; 33.7, 8; 35.2; 5.3f; 46.4; 48.2ff; 60.1; 62.2 (see also "Justification" and "Statutes")
ruler (ἄρχοντες), 32.2; 60.2; 61.1

savior, 59.3
scepter of God (= Christ), 16.2; (32.2)
Second Coming, 23.5
sedition, 1.1; 2.6; 3.12; 4.12; 14.2; 43.2; 46.7, 9; 47.6; 49.5; 51.1f; 54.2f; 55.1; 57.1; 63.1

servant (παῖς = Christ), 59.2ff
sin, 2.3; 4.4; 7.7, 11f., 14; 8.3f; 16.4f;
    41.2; 47.4; 49.5; 50.5f; 53.4;
    56.13; 59.2; 60.2f
slavery, voluntary, 55.2
sophrosyne, 1.2f; 62.2; 63.3; 64
stranger (παροικεπιν), salutation
statutes (δικαίωμα), 2.8; 35.7; 58.2
sufferings of Christ, 2.1

testimony, witness (μαρτυρία,
    μαρτυρεῖν), 5.4, 7; 17.1f; 18.1;
    19.1; 30.7; 38.12; 43.2; 44.3;
    47.4; 63.3

tradition (canon of tradition), 7.2
truth, 18.6; 19.1; 23.5; 31.2; 35.2, 5; 47.3;
    60.2, 4; 38.2; 39.6; 57.3, 5

way, the, 36.1
wisdom, 13.1; 18.6; 32.4; 38.2; 39.6;
    57.3, 5
words of Jesus, 13.2; 46.8
work, (good) works, 2.2, 7; 28.1; 30.3;
    32.3, 4; 33.1f, 7f; 34.1, 3, 4; 38.2;
    39.4; 43.1; 48.5; 59.3
wrath, free of (ἀόργητος), 19.3

Index of Authors

Bakke, Odd, xxii
Barclay, John M. G., xxvi
Bardy, Gustave, xxii
Bousset, Wilhelm, 169, 171–73, 184, 196–97
Breytenbach, Cilliers, xxii–xxiii
Bruno, Violet, 170, 176
Bumpus, H. B., xxii

Caspar, Erich, 193

Dibelius, Martin, xxii, 182
Diekamp, Franz, 190
Drews, Paul, 96

Fischer, Joseph, xxi
Funk, F., 109, 188, 191

Gebhardt, Oskar von, xxiv, 5, 9, 109–10, 113, 131, 141, 186
Grant, Robert M., xiii–xv
Gressmann, Hugo, 172

Hagner, Donald, xxi
Harnack, Adolf von, xi–xv, xvii, xix–xxvii, 1, 4–7, 9, 13, 50–51, 53, 68–69, 72–73, 75–76, 78, 84, 92, 94, 99, 102, 106–9, 111, 113, 131, 133, 141, 150, 168–69, 172, 191, 193, 199
Hauck, Albert, 121, 141
Hauler, Edmundus, 188
Hilgenfeld, Adolf, xxiv, 109, 131
Holl, Karl, 193

Jaubert, Annie, xx–xxi

Knopf, Rudolf, xii, 5, 45, 90, 92, 107, 147–48, 159
Kunze, J., 131

Lagarde, P. de, 120, 194–95
Lietzmann, Hans, xxv, xxvi, 91, 177, 188, 196
Lightfoot, J. B., xxiv, 5, 7, 45–47, 67, 88, 109–11, 113, 133–34, 136, 147, 162, 164, 179
Lindemann, Andreas, xii–xiv, xxi
Lipsius, Richard Adelbert, 172, 186,
Löhr, Hermut, xiv
Lommatzsch, C. H. E., 138–39
Lona, Horacio, xiii–xiv, xxii

Markschies, Chrsitoph, xxvii, 4, 69
Marsh, Charles, xxvi
Mikat, Paul, xxiii–xxiv
Morin, Germain xii, 8, 110–14, 116–17, 119, 122, 126, 128, 131–32

Paget, James Carleton, xxi
Preuschen, Erwin, 88, 190

Rösch, F., 8
Rothschild, Clare K., xxiv

Sanders, Louis, xxii
Schermann, Theodor, 179, 188, 193
Schmidt, Carl, 8, 194
Schmidtke, Alfred, 173–74

Smith, Jonathan Z., xxvii
Sohm, Rudolph, 72

Tomson, Peter J., xxi,

Unnik, W. C. van, xix, xxii

Verheyden, Joseph, xxi

Wattenbach, Wilhelm, 119–21
Wehofer, Thomas M., 146–47, 150, 154, 162
Welborn, Laurence L., xi, xxiv, xxv–xxvii
Wendland, P., 183

Windisch, Hans, 154
Wölfflin, Eduard von, 131–33, 135, 139, 142
Wrede, William, xx–xxii, 45, 54, 72, 90, 101, 137, 148, 150, 158–60, 162

Young (Junius), Patrick, xxiv, 7, 121, 123

Zahn, Theodor, xxiv, 132–33, 135, 140–41, 143
Zahn-Harnack, Agnes von, xix
Ziegler, Adolf, xxii
Ziegler, Leo, 137
Ziwsa, Carolus, 198

Index of Subjects

Aaron, 77, 91, 102
Abel, 91
Abraham, 62, 63n22, 94, 98, 146n1, 159n44, 170, 9n5
abstinence, 44, 69n38, 146
admonition, 9n5, 44–45, 49, 75, 77–78, 92, 95, 97, 105, 108, 146n2, 149, 153n21
Akhmimic, 8
Alexander von Humboldt, 67
Alexandria, 106
Ambrose, 124, 127–28, 128n5, 129–30, 130nn7–8, 176
angels, 97, 105, 152, 156n31, 185, 198n86
antilegomena, 7, 134n25
Antiphanes, 67, 164
apocalyptic/apocalypticism, 52n15, 71, 87, 144, 155
Apocrypha/apocryphal, xxn10, 54n3, 82, 93, 158, 172n19
apocryphon of Ezekiel, 93
Apollos, 75, 103
Apologists, 58n10, 84, 97, 155n28, 178n37, 184–85
apostle, xxii, xxiv, 9n5, 45–47, 59–61, 63, 66–67, 73n5, 75, 77–79, 87, 91, 101–4, 112, 155, 155n29, 156n34, 157–58, 158n40, 160, 164, 172, 175n26, 186n54, 195
Apostles Creed, 92

apostolic
    age, 3, 41, 46–47, 47n8, 75, 147n3, 152n20
    Constitutions, 179n42, 191
    succession, 78–79, 85, 101, 139n40
    teaching, 46
    writings, 46
ascetic/asceticism, 48, 50n11, 84, 100, 147n3, 148–49, 153n21
Augustine, 124, 126, 132n17, 1782n18
Augustinian churches, 51

baptism/baptize, 52, 58, 102, 157, 171, 177
Baur, 45
Beda, 176, 200
Bensly, 7
bishop
    general, 40, 43, 57n9, 73, 73n3, 73n5, 74, 76–81, 101–3, 73n3, 73n5, 74, 76–78, 105–6, 136n29, 160, 167, 188
    monarchial, 40, 73, 78–80
    Rome, 9n5, 136n29–30, 146n1
body (church), 76, 99–100, 149
British Library, 7n1
British Museum, 7, 7n1
Bryennios, 7, 109

Calvin, John, xxvii, 48, 148
Cambridge, 7, 109
canon law, 72, 85
Castrius, Leo, 190

219

catacombs, 41
Catholic
    church, 3, 78–79, 143, 159, 160
    monoepiscopacy, 78n14
    offices, 160
    pre-Catholicism, 4n2, 144, 145, 161
    priesthood, 117
Catholic Epistles, 7
Catalogus Liberianus, 136n30
Celsus, 184, 190, 198n84
charisma, 48, 75, 79n15, 100, 149, 151n14
charismatics, 75
charity, 81, 99
Chiappelli, 6
Christ
    appearance of, 56, 59, 64, 64n25, 69, 90
    blood of, xxi, 52–53, 59, 62–64, 85, 90, 93, 96, 104, 154n23, 156, 156n33
    christological/Christology, xxi–xxii, 85, 106, 155, 157, 198n86
    divinity, 59n13, 173
    flock of, xxi, 59, 47, 59, 61, 74, 86–87, 95, 159n44, 168
    high priest, 60, 63n22, 99, 108, 159n44
    in/through, xxi, 52–53, 56, 58–65, 77, 96, 102
    kerygma of, 9n5, 47n8, 54, 69
    Logos, 59n13, 96, 184, 187, 193
    mediator, xxii, 62, 88, 189
    parousia, xx, 49, 97
    party, 103
    patron, 60, 63n22, 99, 108
    pre-existence of, 59, 95, 155
    prophecies about, 56n7
    provisions of, 90
    resurrection, 97
    sacrifice, 98
    sending of, 60, 78–80, 101–2
    sufferings, 90
    words of, 47, 155n4, 56
church
    history, 3–4, 6, 42, 78, 81, 84–85, 87, 110, 144–145, 173n22, 178n37
    law, 4n3

Cicero, 89
Clement
    author, 40–42
    education, 41
    Jew, 41
    person, 8n5, 9n5, 40–41, 136n29, 143
Clement of Alexandria, 8, 9n5, 82, 95–97, 99–100, 103–4, 110, 112, 112n12, 113n15, 114n15, 140, 149, 166–67, 189, 199
clique, xxv, 75
Codex Vercellensis, 140
Columbus, 67, 164
consul, 41
covenant, 55n5, 56, 56n8, 57, 86
Craftsman, 53, 64, 96
creation, 66, 85, 92, 94, 96, 98, 106, 179, 198n86, 200n94
Creator, 9n5, 49, 51–52, 93, 95–96, 107, 151, 154, 196, 199
cult, xxi, xxiv, 48, 52, 57n9, 74, 100, 106, 118, 148, 148n4, 154, 158, 159n44, 172, 173n22, 177

Danaids, 92
danger, xxiii, 4, 91, 94, 104, 147n3
Dante, 6
David, 55n4, 63n24, 91, 95, 169–70, 175–76, 178, 178n39, 187, 198n86, 200
deacon, 43, 57n9, 73, 73n5, 77–79, 101–3, 105, 160, 167–68
death penalty, 77, 101, 159
democracy, 40, 72–73, 73n6, 74
demons, 50, 152
depose/deposition (of church officials), xxvi, 43, 72–80, 103, 105
Diaspora, 93
Dircae, 92
dismissal (of presbyters)
    general, 43
    majority decision, 43
dispute, 43–44, 75–76, 76n12, 77–78, 80, 102, 112, 113n15, 119, 147n2, 148, 148n4
Dionysius of Alexandria, 190
Dionysius of Corinth, 8, 9n5, 167

INDEX OF SUBJECTS

Docetism, 180n43, 183–84
doctrine, 4n4, 46–47, 47n8, 62, 63n23, 64n25, 72, 80n16, 84, 108, 118, 155, 157, 190
Domitian, reign, 3, 9n5, 42
Domitilla, 41
doxology, 96, 108, 147n2, 177, 177n32, 180, 188–89, 196n79, 198, 200n94
Dutch critics, 47n8

Ebionism, 46
ecclesiastical
　antiquity, 5
　general, 79, 82, 86, 120, 135, 159, 198, 201
　governance, 73n6, 179
　history, 147
　institutions, 56n9, 78n14
　law, 78
　office, 40, 71, 71n39, 72–80, 105, 108, 148, 160, 166–67
　order, 111
　prayers, 189
　present, 56n9
　principles, 5n4
　termini technici, 166–67
　tradition, 62
elect/election, xx, 48, 55, 55n5, 56, 59, 64, 77, 90, 106, 148
emigrate, 104–5
emperor, 89, 100, 107, 119, 163n58, 185, 193
empire, 42, 46, 86, 89, 89n3
Enoch, 94
enthusiasm, 48, 61, 84, 86, 144, 148, 148n4, 160, 160n49, 162n52
Epictetus, 68
Epicurious, 68
Esau, 68
escapism, 48, 148
eschatology/eschatological, 84, 106, 150
exorcism, 50, 152, 176, 196n79

faith, 4n4, 9n5, 44, 47, 50–53, 50n11, 52n.15, 58, 58n12, 59, 62, 63n22, 64, 66, 72, 87, 89, 92–94, 97–98, 104, 107, 146, 152–53, 152n20, 161, 185, 189
Fascist Italy, 6
Father, 9n5, 49n9, 53, 59, 64, 99, 108, 178, 180n43, 187–88, 197, 200n94
Florennes, 7, 119–22, 126, 136, 141n51, 142, 143n56
forgery, xii–xiii, 101, 107, 114, 116, 117n23, 119, 122, 141, 143
forgive/forgiveness, 51, 63n22, 90, 153, 196n81
foundational document, 3, 4, 5, 47, 54n2, 78, 146, 147n2
fraternity, 41

Gennadius, 124
Gentile, xiii, 3, 49, 51, 58, 85, 93, 106, 144, 146–47, 152, 154
gladiator, 66, 91
gnosis, 52, 52n17, 53, 65, 85, 90, 154–155, 156n34
gnostic, 4, 48, 52, 86, 106, 155, 155n26
Gnostic, 52n18, 87, 148, 154n26, 157, 160, 168, 183
gnosticism, 52
Gnosticism, 85, 160
government
　authorities, xxiii–xxiv, xxvi, 70, 107, 114, 116–17, 141, 143, 150, 150n12, 167, 169, 171
　Clement's stance, 70–71
grace, 51, 55–56, 59, 95, 156n33
Grapte, 8n5
guilt/guilty, 51, 62n21, 77

harmony, 44, 66, 81, 84, 182
healing, 50, 152, 196n79
heaven, 9n5, 6, 70, 197, 156n31
Hebrew, 41
Hegesippus, 8, 9n5
Hellenism, 6, 65, 80, 99, 145, 177
Hellenistic, 57, 65, 66, 68–69, 99, 107, 150n11, 165, 171, 178–79
Hellenistic-Roman, 66, 163
heresy, 4n4, 85
Hermas, 8, 40, 47n8, 51, 94
hero/heroic, 66, 75, 91–92, 94, 96

Herodotus, 67, 97, 164
Hesiod, 67, 164
Hieronymus, 95, 110, 121, 124, 136
Hilary, 176
Hippolytus, 180, 181n44
Holy Spirit, 49, 55n4, 57n9, 59, 61, 61n20, 65, 72, 73n3, 78, 80, 80n16, 84, 90, 93, 96, 101, 105, 108, 137n31, 162, 162n52, 182–83, 200n94
hospitality, 52, 52n15, 62, 89, 94
household code (*Haustafel*), 48, 96, 149
humility, xix, 41, 48, 84, 95, 148–49, 153, 153n21
hymn, 49, 96, 98–99, 104, 149, 189

Ignatius, 8, 47n8, 81
immortality, 53, 64–65, 67, 99, 154, 164
inheritance, 51
inspiration, 46, 137n31
Irenaeus, 8, 40–41, 94
Isaac, 98
Isidor, 124
Israel, xx–xxi, 56–57, 157n44, 169–70, 170n11, 171n15, 175–76

Jacob, 59n13, 67–68, 91, 156n30, 164, 170
Jacobson, 67, 164
Jerusalem, xxi, 80n16, 178
Jewish
  character, 65, 163, 96, 98, 163
  Christianity, 45, 47, 171, 177, 178n36
  cult, 177
  tradition, 55n3, 58n12, 93
  law, 58n12, 64n25
  legend, 94, 98
  liturgical practice, 96
  people, 82, 89n3, 107
  prayer, 107, 178–79, 197n84
  proselytes, 58
  religion, 90
  sect, ix
  synagogual propaganda, 86, 160
Johannes, deacon, 134n22
John (teaching of), 46
Jonah, 64

Judaism, xx–xxi, 41, 45, 47, 54–58, 58n12, 61, 64, 64n25, 65, 69–70, 83, 86, 94, 162, 177
judge, 49, 51, 56n8, 57n9, 70, 98, 151, 153, 185
judgment, 43, 45, 49, 61–62, 69, 86, 100, 133–34, 136n30, 153, 154n22, 160, 166
Judith, 105
Julius I, bishop, 106
Junius, Patrick, 7, 121, 123
justification, 57n9, 58n12, 62, 62n21, 79, 152n20
Justin Martyr, 57, 94–95

Kennet, 7
kerygma, 9n5, 47n8, 54n2, 69
king of England, 7
kingdom, xxiii, 46, 59, 61, 97, 102, 157, 158n40, 177n32

laity, 77, 100
laudatio, 66, 88–90, 146n2
law
  ceremonial, 56, 56n9, 57–58, 58n12, 64n25, 77, 193
  civil, 71
  priestly, 56, 57n9, 78
  ritual, 56
legalism, 58n12, 82
Levite, 57n9, 77, 98, 100, 167
living God, 49, 86, 151–52, 160
Lobbes, xii, 121, 121n30, 123, 123n1, 125–27, 136
Lord, 9n5, 51, 59, 59n13, 60, 60n16, 61, 64, 67, 77, 94–95, 102–4, 126, 150, 153n21, 155n30, 156n33, 158, 164, 168, 177, 198n86
Lord's Supper, 52, 74, 99, 104, 156–57, 157n36, 177, 188, 196n81, 197, 197n84
love, xix, 44, 48–49, 51, 55, 59–60, 63n23, 64, 66, 78, 80, 98, 104–5, 145–46, 146n2, 148–49, 153, 156, 159
Lucian, 94
Lucifer, 176

Marcion, 6
Marcionism, 85, 172, 183
martyr/martyrdom, 49, 91–92, 103, 126, 150, 163n58, 173
Master, 49n9, 64, 73n5, 93, 96, 156, 170
Manilius, 67, 164
manuscripts of Clement
    Codex A(lexandrinus), 7, 7n1, 8, 109–10, 112, 113n15, 114n15, 133–34, 145, 149n6
    Codex Argentinensis 8n4
    Codex Berolinensis, 8n3
    Codex C^1, 8, 40, 109n1
    Codex C^2, 8, 8n4, 109n1
    Codex H(ierosolymitanus), 7–8, 109, 109n1, 110, 112, 114n15, 127n4, 133
    Codex L, 7–8, 109–43
    Codex S, 7–8, 109–10, 112, 113n15, 114n15, 127n4, 133
    Constantinopolitanus, 7, 7n2, 109, 109n1, 133, 200n94
Melito of Sardis, 94, 185
mercy, 49n9, 51, 55n6, 56, 64, 153, 155n29
miraculous/miracles, 50, 61n20, 77, 102, 152, 176, 196n79
Miriam, 91
moderation, 41, 44–45, 147n3
monotheism, xxvii, 48, 148, 171n15, 172n15
Montanist, 84
monuments, 51, 51n13, 113, 113n14
moral
    general, 5n4, 41, 44, 52, 90
    moral ideal, 48, 69, 148
    moral law, 48, 148
    moral movement, 48, 86, 148, 160
    moral-philosophical, 90, 149
    moralism, 58n11, 65, 68, 96, 165
    moralistic, 56, 65–69, 152, 160n49
    morality, 48, 63n24, 148–49
Morin, 8, 110, 112n13, 113n15, 114, 114n16, 116, 116n17, 117n24, 119, 122, 126, 128, 131
Moses, 9n5, 78, 95, 101–2, 104, 169–70

Muratorian Fragment, 47n7, 92
mystery movement, 48, 52, 52n17, 100, 106, 118, 147n3, 148, 157, 157n37, 158, 169, 170, 189

Namur, 7, 110, 114, 126
natural phenomenon/law, xxii, 50, 97, 152, 158n42
New Testament, xiv, xix, 3, 4n2, 5, 7, 49n9, 62, 85, 94n10, 114n15, 131, 131n10, 134, 134n23, 134n25, 145, 165n62
Ninevites, 64
Noah, 93–94, 170

obey/obedience, xxi, 41, 46, 48, 51, 58n12, 62, 63n23, 70, 73–74, 74n7, 76, 78, 80–81, 90, 93–94, 102, 105, 116–18, 141, 149, 152, 152n18, 153, 153n21
Old Testament, xii, xx–xxi, xxiv, 47, 50, 52, 54–58, 58n11–12, 60n16, 63, 64n25, 65, 68–69, 78, 82, 85n2, 87, 93, 97–99, 101, 108, 137, 152–54, 159, 159n44, 162, 165, 171n15, 182
older traditions (of 1 Clement), 43n1
order, 41
Origen, 49, 69, 70n38, 96, 101, 111, 124n2, 130n8, 134n24, 138, 166, 172n15, 173n23, 184, 190, 190n60, 198, 199n92

paleontological epoch, 3–4, 4n1
papal infallibility, 80n16
paraenesis, 97, 100, 104, 147n2, 55n3
Pastoral Epistles, 83, 102
Patriarch Cyrillus Lukaris, 7
Patriarchal Library, 7
patriotism, 41, 70, 159n47
Paul, 8n5, 41, 44–47, 47n7–8, 51n14, 52n18, 56n8, 57, 62, 66, 78, 87–89, 91–92, 95, 102–4, 108, 149n6, 154n26, 155–56, 157n35, 159, 159n47, 161, 171n15, 197n83, 198n84

Pauline
- age, 159
- churches, 51
- Epistles, 7, 45–46, 48, 53, 83, 113, 149, 158, 167, 186
- thought, 45, 50–51, 57–58, 58n12, 62–63, 63n22, 64n25, 83, 85n2, 90, 98–99, 152, 152n20, 156–57, 159n44, 166n63

peace, 9n5, 41, 44, 44n2, 45, 48, 66–67, 81, 95–96, 107–8, 120, 146n2, 163–64
peaceably, 103
peaceful, 48, 61n20, 149
perfection, 55, 84, 104
persecution
- Domitian, 44n2, 70, 85, 88, 163n58
- general, 85, 88–89
- Nero, 70, 85, 88, 91, 92, 159n47, 167
- Trajan, 88, 167

perseverance, 44
Peter, 41, 44–47, 62, 66, 91–92, 102, 108, 110, 116, 136n30, 159n47, 161
Philo, 56n9, 58, 94, 101, 178, 178n37
phoenix, 50, 67, 67n30, 97, 118n25, 127–29, 152, 158n42, 164, 164n60
phenomena, 4, 6
photographical facsimile, 7
phototype, 7
piety, 52, 52n15, 58, 62, 64n25, 89, 92, 94, 154, 156, 171n15
pious, 44, 56, 56n7, 56n9, 58n12, 91, 100, 104, 107, 153n21
place of glory, 91
Plato, xxii, 65n27, 67, 96, 164, 185
Plutarch, 67–68, 164
pneumatic, 47, 49, 61, 72–73, 88, 101, 103, 148, 148n4, 150
Polycarp, 8, 145–46, 148
pope, xii, 80n16, 116, 118–21, 126, 143
post-apostolic
- age, 3, 6, 46, 151
- fathers, 47n8
- literature, 47n8, 52, 93, 109, 145–46
- tradition, 93

prayer
- authorities, 150, 150n12
- congregational, 44, 44n2, 55n5, 58n12, 59, 61, 63n22, 70, 106–7, 114, 136n31, 141n50, 146n2, 151n16, 156n30, 159, 175, 177, 179
- consecration of a bishop, 188
- consecration of a presbyter, 188
- evening, 189n59
- formula, 196, 196n79
- general, 60, 90, 98–99, 171, 174, 176, 176n30, 178–81, 185–89, 194, 198–200
- Jewish, 178–79, 196, 197n84
- liturgical, 186, 191, 193–94, 196
- Lord's Supper, 126, 177, 177n33, 180, 180n43, 188, 194, 196–97, 197n82, 197n84
- offering of the fruits, 189
- Polycarp, 180

predestination, 90, 124
presbyter, 40, 40n1, 43, 73, 73n5, 74–76, 76n12, 78, 102–3, 105, 111, 112n11, 138, 138n38–39, 139, 139n40, 148n4, 150n12, 159n45, 168, 188
primitive, 4
prisoner, 44n2, 107, 150
prophecy, 55, 67, 94, 101–2, 164, 195
prophet, 9n5, 47, 55, 55n5, 56, 73, 93, 95, 102, 147n3, 154, 162, 169, 184
prophetic word, 101–2, 160
Protestant,
- church, 3
- historiography, 6

Psalms, 50–51
Puritan, xxvii, 48, 148

Rahab, 60, 62, 94
rebellion, 74, 78
redeemer, 49, 95, 151, 156, 190n60, 198n86
redemption, 58n12, 62n21, 64, 94
religion
- Christian/Clement's, xx, xxvii, 48–49, 52–54, 57–58, 63n23–24, 66, 86, 90, 108, 112, 137n31, 144,

INDEX OF SUBJECTS

146–47, 147n3, 148, 151, 154, 158, 160–61, 168, 173n22
history-of-, 144, 173n22
Jewish, 90
mystery, 82, 148, 157
Old Testament, xx, 54, 54n3, 57–58, 69, 158
repent/repentance, 44, 51, 59, 63, 78, 93, 104–5, 146, 153, 156n33
resurrection, xxii, 50, 50n10, 60, 60n15, 97, 99, 101, 118n25, 152, 156n34, 157, 157n35
revelation, 52, 55–56, 90, 101, 154, 157, 187
righteousness, 53, 63n22, 64, 97–98, 101, 103
Roman intervention, 44n3

salvation, 46, 48, 55–56, 59–60, 62, 64, 64n25, 90, 93, 99, 107, 148, 154n23, 156
savior, 59, 107
Satan/devil, 9n5, 50, 50n11, 52n18, 152, 152n17
scepter, 59
Scripture, xx–xxii, 54n2, 55, 55n4–5, 56–57, 60, 60n16, 61, 61n19, 71, 77, 84, 93, 95, 97, 100–2, 130n7
Second Clement, book of, 7, 47n8, 51, 110, 133–34, 134n24, 135, 136n29, 136n30, 153, 159
seminar, 1, 6, 82–83, 82n1
Seneca, 68, 89
Septuagint, 55n3, 65, 82, 162, 170
servant of God, xiv, 106, 169–202
sin, 51, 90, 97, 152–53, 154n22, 155n29, 196n81
soldier, xii, 67, 70, 96, 118, 150, 164
Solinus, 67, 164
sophrosyne, 66, 146
Soter, 136n29
Spain, 92
Staatsbibliothek Berlin, 8

Stoic/Stoicism, xxii–xxiii, 65, 68, 68n34, 70, 80, 83, 89–90, 96–98, 165
Strabo, 67, 164
stranger, 88
structure (of 1 Clement), 43n1
student, 4–6
subscriptio, 40
synagogue, 56n8, 58, 93, 106, 158
syzygy, 6

Tacitus, 67, 164
Tertullian, 50n11, 100, 131–33, 135, 137–38, 138n38, 139, 166, 176, 187
Titus Flavius Clemens, 41
Tragedians, 67n31
transmission, 3, 5, 7–9
Trinity, 59, 69, 102, 184

unity, 41, 48, 59, 63n23, 76, 80–81, 99, 148–49, 152, 159
universalism, 63n22, 64
Urkunde, 3, 4, 5, 47, 54n2, 78, 146, 147n2

Valentine, 180n43
Vatican, 6
virtue, 10–11, 44, 48, 52n15, 63n23, 68n34, 69n38, 89, 94, 149, 152, 153n21, 154n24
young vs. old, xxv–xxvi, 48, 73, 76n11, 91, 149

Wettstein, 68
Whit Monastery of Shenute, 8
will of God, xxiii, 56n9, 60–62, 64–65, 77, 79, 93, 98, 101–3, 105, 141, 162
wisdom, 48, 62, 106, 149, 154, 158
wisdom cult, 52, 158
worship,
    of God, 5n4, 44, 169–70
    service, 44, 74, 76–78, 98, 100–101, 106, 136n31, 159, 189

Index of Ancient Sources

Old Testament

Genesis

1:9	20n62
1:26f	25n96
1:28	25n97
2:23	12n19
4:3–8	12n9
5:24	14n30
6:8ff	14n31
12:1ff	14n33
13:14ff	14n34
15:5f	15n35
15:5	24n93
18:27	18n54
19	15n37
21f	15n36
22:7f	24n91
22:17	24n93
26:4	24n93
27:41ff	12n10
28f	24n92
37	12n11
41:37f	171

Exodus

2:14	12n12
3:11	18n57
4:10	18n57
6:1	38n165
14:33f	34n144
32:7f	34n148
32:32	34n149
34:28	34n148

Numbers

12	12n13
12:7	18n57, 29n122, 34n144
14:18	38n164
16	12n14
16:22	37n161
16:23f	33n143
18:27	23n86
27:16	37n161, 39n169

Deuteronomy

4:34	23n86
7:9	38n163
9:9	34n148
9:12f	34n148
13:18	38n164
14:2	23n86
14:4	39n169
32:8f	23n85
32:14f	11n6
32:39	37n161

Joshua

2	15n39

Judges

19:19	170n5

1 Samuel

2:7	37n161
2:10	16n40
13:14	18n59
16:15ff	171
18f	12n15
18:22	171
18:26	171
21	12n15
29	12n15

1 Kings

8:60	37n162
9:4	38n164

2 Kings

19:19	37n162

2 Chronicles

20:7	14n32
31:14	23n86

Ezra

2:16	171
5:33	171
5:35	171

Nehemiah

1:7	170n9

Job

	58
1:1	18n55
4:16ff	28n119
4:19–5:5	28n120
5:11	37n161
5:17ff	36n157
10:12	37n161
11:2f	24n88
14:4f	18n56
15:15	28n120
19:26	22n77
35:16	179n42
38:11	20n63

Esther

4:16	35n152
7ff	35n152

Psalms

2:1	34n150
2:7	27n109
3:5	22n76
12:3f	17n49
17[18]:0	170n8
18:25f	31n127
19:1–3	23n81
22	58n11
22:6ff	18n52
23:4	22n76
28:7	22n75
31:19	17n48
32:1f	33n141
32.1	63n22
32:10	21n70
32(33):13	37n161
33:3	181
33:10	37n161
34:11–17	21n69
37:36–38	16n44
37:39	16n43
39(40):3	38n164
44:14	28n118
45:6	17n50, 155n30
48(49):14	33n143
49(50):14f	34n146
50:16–23	26n105
51	58n11, 63n24, 96
51:3–19	19n60
51:19	34n147
62:4	16n46
66(67):1	38n165
68[69]:17	170n7
69:4	28n118
69:31f	34n145
78:36f	17n47
85[86]:16	170n7
89:21	18n59
96:10	182

INDEX OF ANCIENT SOURCES

99(100):2	37n162	41:8	14n32, 18n54, 170n6
104:4	27n108		
104:29	20n68	42ff	171
110:1	27n110	42	179
112[113]:1	170n7	42:1f	171, 184
115:7	37n161	42.1	175n28
118:18	35n154	42:9	170n5
118:19f	32n133	42:19	170, 170n6
118(119):114	37n162	42:43	171
118(119):133	38n164	43:10	170n10
132	13n21	44:1f	170n6
139:7ff	23n83	44:21	170n6
139:15	28n117	44:26	170n10
141:5	35n156	45:4	170n6
144(145):8	38n166	46:3	170
		46:6	170
Proverbs		49:3	190n60
		49:5	170n11, 173n23
	58	49:6	170n10, 190n60
1:23ff	36n159	50:10	170n10, 171
2:21f	16n43	51:16	38n165
3:12	35n155	52:10–54	184
3:34	23n87	52:56	184
7:3	11n5	52:13	170n10, 175n28
20:27	20n65	53	58n11, 61n19, 63n24, 95, 171, 175n28
Ecclesiastes			
		53:1–12	18n51
4:13	190n60	57:15	37n161
		57:16	37n161
Song		59:14	11n8
		60:17	29n121, 101
1:6	191	62:11	25n99
13:1	179n42	64:4	26n103
		66:2	16n42
Isaiah			
		Jeremiah	
	95, 195, 201		
1:16–20	14n29	9:23f	16n40
3:5	11n7	21:10	38n165
6:3	25n102		
13:11	37n161	*Ezekiel*	
13:22	21n72		
26:20	33n140	33:11	13n27
29:13	16n45	34:16	37n162
29:19	37n161	37:12	33n140
37:35	170n8	48:12	23n86
40:10	25n99		

Daniel

2:7	171
2:22	100
3:19f	31n125
6:16f	30n124
7:19	25n102

Amos

4:13	37n161

Jonah

3	13n26

Zechariah

12:1	37n161

Malachi

3:1	21n72

Deuterocanonical Works

Judith

8ff	35n151
9:11	37n161
13:15	35n151

Wisdom of Solomon

	58
2:13	170n7
10:7	15n38
11:22	22n80
12:10	13n24
12:12	22n80

Sirach

4:29	25n98
16:18f	37n161
28:14	66, 163

1 Maccabees

1:6	171
1:8	171

2 Maccabees

4:1	96

Old Testament Pseudepigrapha

Apocalypse of Elijah

	26n103

Apocryphon of Ezekiel

	13n28

3 Maccabees

5:27	179n42

Psalms of Solomon

12:6	170n6
17:21	170n6

Sibylline Oracles

	69n35, 166n64
1.128f	13n25, 93
1.324f	191, 199, 199n88, 199n90
1.330f	191, 199, 199n88, 199n90
1.364f	191, 199, 199n88, 199n90

New Testament

Matthew

	95
5:7	16n41
6:14	16n41
7:1f	16n41

7:22	196n79	14:15	104
8:17	171	15	191
11:28f	61n18	17:3	102
11:29f	95		
11:29	89	*Acts*	
12	16n41, 184		95, 167, 179, 195,
12:17f	171, 174–75, 195		198n84
12:27f	171	3:13	171, 175–76, 197,
14:2	171		200
15:8	16n45	3:26	171, 175–76, 200
18:6	31n130	4:25f	175, 187, 175, 200
23:11	32n135	4:25	176, 187
26:24	31n130	4:27	171, 176, 187, 190
		4:30	171, 175–76, 196,
Mark			196n79, 175, 200
	95	8:26ff	171
4:3	22n74	14:19	12n18
6:6	140n44	14:23	102
6:36	140n44	15:28	80n16
7:6	16n45	20:35	10n3, 90, 95
8:23	140n44		
8:26	140n44	*Romans*	
9:38	196n79		83
9:42	31n130	1:17	92
11:2	140n44	1:21	27n107, 34n144
15:28	171	1:29–32	26n104
		1:29ff	99
Luke		2:24	32n132
1	175n27	2:29	24n89
1:54	175	3:8	33n142
1:69	175	4:1f	24n90
5:17	140n44	4:7	63n22
6:31	16n41	4:9	104
6:37f	16n41	6:1f	24n95
9:6	140n44	6:17	131n10
9:49	196n79	9:4f	24n93
17:2	31n130	12:5	31n129
19:12	140	13	70
22:37	171	13:2	38n167
24:13	140n44		
		1 Corinthians	
John			60n 17, 62, 83, 88,
1:21	190n60		104
1:29	171	1:1f	10n1
12:38	171	1:2	39n171

INDEX OF ANCIENT SOURCES

1 Corinthians (continued)

1:10f	31n131
1:31	16n40, 95
2:9	26n103
2:10	100, 154n26
7:7	27n116
10:24	32n135
10:33	32n135
12:8f	32n134
12:12f	27n115, 100, 100n14
12:24	67, 164
12:29f	27n114
13	149
13:3	105
13:4	32n137
13:7	32n137
15:3	171
15:20	21n73
15:23	27n114
15:34	179n42
15:36f	21n73
15:53f	178n37
16:11	39n170

Galatians

	88
2:9	12n17, 91
3:1	10n3
3:6f	24n90
6:1	35n153

Ephesians

	159
1:4	39n169
1:6	175n26
1:17f	37n161
2:12	13n26
4:4f	31n128
4:18	27n107
5:21	27n116

Philippians

1:1	137, 137n35
1:15	12n16
1:27	11n8
1:30	13n20
2:5f	17n50
2:7	173n23, 198n86
4:22	108

Colossians

3:14	32n136

1 Thessalonians

5:14	37n162

2 Thessalonians

2:4	131n10

1 Timothy

1:17	38n168
2:3	13n21
2:8	23n84, 68, 165
5:21	20n67

2 Timothy

1:11	12n18
2:21	25n100

Titus

2:5	10n2
3:5	24n94

Hebrews

	46–47, 57, 58n10, 63n22, 69, 69n36, 83, 94, 99, 155, 158, 166
1:3ff	27n107
1:5	27n109
1:7	27n108
1:8	17n50, 155n30
1:13	27n110
2:17	26n106
3:1	26n106
3:2	18n57

3:5	29n122	*1 John*	
4:12	20n68	2:5	104
4:14f	26n106	5:3	104
6:18	22n79		
10:23	22n78	*Revelation*	
11:5ff	94		7, 42
11:5–10	14n30	2:24	52n18, 100, 154n26
11:5	14n30	12	187, 189, 199
11:10	96, 165n62		
11:31	15n39		
11:32—12:3	95	*Codex Corb.*	
11:37	18n53, 95		
12:1	19n61	*James*	
12:9	39n169		138

James		*Codex d*	
	46–47, 94	*Acts*	
2:21f	24n90	3:13	176
4:16	20n66	3:26	176
		4:30	176

1 Peter		*Codex e*	
	8n5, 46–47, 47n7, 83, 95, 167	*Acts*	
1:1f	10n1	3:13	176
1:2	88	4:27	176
1:17	10n1, 88	4:30	176
1:19	13n23		
2:9	27n107, 37n160, 99, 179	*Codex Vercellensis*	
2:12	33n139	*Mark*	
2:13f	27n114	6:6	140n44
2:13	38n167	6:36	140n44
2:15	38n167, 179n42	8:23	140n44
2:17	90	8:26	140n44
2:23f	171	11:2	140n44
2:25	37n161		
3:8	94n10	*Luke*	
4:8	32n137	5:17	140n44
4:10	27n116	9:6	140n44
5:5	27n116, 36n158	19:12	140
5:9	90	24:13	140n44

2 Peter	
2:5	93
3:4	21n71

Gigas librorum

Acts

	138
3:13	176
4:27	176

Laudianius Oxoniensis

Acts

	138

Codex p

Acts

4:30	176

Graeco-Roman Authors

Celsus

I.49	172n15

Cicero

Mil.

93	66–67, 164

Cyprian

De oratione

	135

Ep.

22	167
52.1	137n33
55	167
67	167
68	167

Euripides

Frag. Aeol.

| 2 | 67, 164 |
| 21 | 67 |

Heliodorus at Galen

De Antid.

II.7	68, 165

Horace

Saec.

I.16f	66, 163

Josephus

Ant.

1.11.4	94
1.13.4	98
1.74	93

Livius

XXXVII.13.5	116n18

Plato

Leg.

902 E	67, 164

Timaeus

p. 40 DE	185

Seneca

Ep.

81.17	165

Med.

II.375	67, 164

INDEX OF ANCIENT SOURCES

Sophocles

Aj.

158	67, 164

Suetonius

Dom.

11	163n58

Somitianus

11	89

Tacitus

Ann.

XV.44	92, 163n58

Theophilus

Autol.

3.19	93

Xenophon

Hellenica

6.1.3	66, 163

Christian Literature[1]

1 Clement

1f	103
1–2	146n2
1	43n1, 50, 52, 97, 99, 147n2, 152
1.0	155n29, 159n44, 167
1.1—2.8	66, 89
1.1	44n3, 75, 88, 163n58
1.1c	75
1.2ff	88
1.2	58, 66, 69n35, 89, 113n15, 155n29, 163, 166n64
1.3	73, 73n5, 76n11, 90, 96, 113n15, 139
2	43n1, 50, 50n11, 51, 51n12, 152, 153n21, 156
2.1–2	150n14
2.1	59–60, 68, 90, 153n21, 165, 167
2.2	48–49, 58n12, 61, 90
2.3–4	153n22
2.3	90, 167
2.4	55n5, 90, 159n44
2.5–8	90
2.7	165
2.8	68, 165, 166n64
2.10	52n18
3–13	146n2
3	108
3.1	90
3.2–4	91
3.3	73n5, 76n11
3.4	58, 68, 155n29, 165
3.8	90
4.1ff	12n9
4.1–13	91
4.1	64n25, 82
4.8	91
5f	88
5–6	91
5	62, 66, 91, 159n47
5.1	91
5.2	91
5.3	91
5.4	91

---

1. Harnack's discussion of the contents of the Lobbes library along with the placement of 1 Clement within the catalog appears on pages 123–27. Three are numerous ancient works mentioned on these pages that are not readily identifiable.

INDEX OF ANCIENT SOURCES

1 Clement (continued)

5.5f	92
5.6	68, 165
5.7	92, 139
6	91, 159n47
6.1	68, 92, 159n44, 163n58, 165
6.3f	92
6.4	66, 163
7	55n6, 113n15
7.1f	92
7.1	165
7.2ff	93
7.2	54n2, 68, 131n10, 158n43, 167
7.4–6	154n23
7.4	52, 59, 64, 154n23, 156n33
7.5	93, 96, 117n21
7.6	93–94
8	55n6
8.1ff	93
8.1–2	154n23
8.3	93, 158n39
8.5	69n35, 154n23, 166n64, 167
9.1	66n28, 68, 94, 163n57
9.2	66n28, 163n57
9.3ff	14n30
9.3	94
9.4	68, 93–94, 165
10–12	52n15, 90, 99, 154n24
10	94
10.1ff	94
10.1—17.6	95
10.1	94
10.7	62, 152n20
11–12	94
11.1f	15n37
11.1	62, 68, 94, 152n20, 165
11.2	68, 94, 165
12	56n7
12.1	94
12.7	59, 156n33
13.2	158, 158n41
13.3	69n35, 166n64
18.2ff	19n60
12.1ff	94
12.1f	15n39
12.1	62
12.7f	94
12.7	52, 59, 64, 156n32
12.8	94
13	51n12, 153n21
13.1f	103
13.1	55n4, 60, 16n18, 69n35, 94–95, 153n21
13.2	60
13.3	153n21
14–30	146n2
14	95
14.1	95
14.3	95
15.1	95
15.2	95
15.5	95, 108n20
15.6	113n15, 117n20
16–19	51n12
16	56n7, 63n24, 153n21
16.1	59, 95, 153n21, 159n44
16.2	55n4, 59, 95, 153n21, 155
16.3ff	95
16.7	153n21
16.15	55n4, 95
16.17	59–60, 61n18, 62, 95, 153n21
17	56n7, 63n24, 113n15
17.1f	95
17.1	95
17.5	113n15
17.6	68, 158n39, 165
18	63n24
18.8	153n21
18.12	96, 165
18.17	153n21
19	63n24, 158n43

INDEX OF ANCIENT SOURCES

19.1	56n7, 95–96, 153n21	23.4	68, 158n39
19.2ff	96	23.5	97
19.2	49n9, 54n2, 66n28, 163n57	24–27	60n15
		24	50, 131, 152, 157
19.3	68, 96, 165	24.1	60, 97, 156n34
20	66, 98	24.2f	97
20.1ff	96	24.4	140n46
20.1	96	25	50, 67, 97, 118n25, 129, 131, 152, 163n58
20.3	67–68, 164–65		
20.5	67n31, 69n35, 96, 165n61, 166n64	25.1	127
		25.3	112n12, 130
20.8	67, 96, 118n25, 164	26	56n7
		26.2f	97
20.9	69n35, 166n64	26.2	158n39
20.10	68, 165	26.3	55n4
20.11f	96	27	97
20.11	49n9, 59, 68, 69n35, 96, 155n29, 165, 166n64	27.3	97
		27.4	59n13
		27.5	113n15
		28	97
21	51n12, 56n7, 157n36	28.2	97
		28.3	114n15
21.1ff	96	29	97
21.1	68, 165	29.1	55n5, 68, 159n44, 165
21.3	49n9		
21.4	96, 159n44	29.3	159n44
21.5–6	113n15	30	51n12, 97
21.6f	90	30.1	97, 159n44
21.6	52, 60, 73, 73n5, 76n11, 96, 118, 155n29	30.2	153n21
		30.3	68, 97, 152n20, 153n21, 165
21.7	76n11, 96, 149n6	30.6	69n35, 166n64
21.8	58, 97, 113n15, 153n21	30.7	159n44
		30.8	153n21
21.9	96, 113n15	31–36	146n2
22	95, 113n15	31–35	46
22.1	55n4, 59, 97, 155n29	31	51n12, 98
		31.1	166n64
22.2—27.7	97	31.2	63n22, 98, 159n44
22.2	97	31.3	98
22.6	114n15	31.4	69n35, 153n21
22.7	97, 114n15	32	56n9, 57n9, 69n35, 98, 166n64
22.8	114n15		
22.8a	97	32.1ff	48
23	49, 56n7, 61, 150n13, 165	32.2	59n13, 139, 155n30
23.3f	97	32.3ff	98

237

INDEX OF ANCIENT SOURCES

1 Clement (continued)

32.3f	24n94, 62
32.3	68, 165
32.4	59, 96, 152n20, 155n29, 167
33ff	96
33	66, 98
33.1	58n12, 98
33.3ff	98
33.3	68, 98, 165
33.4	98
33.7	98
33.8	63, 98
34.1ff	58n12
34.1	114n15
34.3	98
34.5	98, 152n18
34.6f	98
34.7	44, 68, 98, 165
34.8	98, 114n15
35	64–65, 99
35.1ff	99
35.1–3	53, 64
35.1–2	151n15
35.2	99, 99, 165
35.3	69n35, 166n64
35.4	48, 99
35.5ff	99
35.5	69n35, 99, 166n64
36–37	43n1
36	52, 60, 63n22, 64–65, 99, 108, 114n15
36.1–2	156n31
36.1	59, 64n26, 99
36.2	69n35, 99, 154n25, 155, 166n64
36.2a	64, 99
36.4f	59
36.4	155n30, 179
37ff	44
37–47	146n2
37–41	77
37	70, 76, 99–100, 158n42
37.1	96, 159n44
37.2	67, 99, 118, 139, 150n11, 164
37.3	100
37.4	67, 164
37.5	100, 164
38	51n12, 63n23, 76, 100, 114n15
38.1–2	49, 149n7
38.1	59, 75, 151n14, 155n29
38.2	48, 67, 69n35, 100, 149n5, 153n21, 164, 166n64
38.3	100, 153n21
38.4	96
39	77
39.1	100
39.4	139
39.7	139
40f	56n9, 57n9, 74, 76
40–44	160n48
40	77, 100, 118, 140, 167
40.1	52, 100, 114n15, 154
40.3	69n35, 166n64
40.5	100, 111n10, 166
41	52, 77, 147n2, 159n46
41.1ff	101
41.1	101, 159n44, 167
41.2	118n26
41.3	101
41.4	101, 155n27, 159n46
42.1ff	101–102
42	157
42.1–4	77
42.1	60, 158n40
42.2	101
42.3	59–61, 101, 103, 106, 157, 157n35, 158n40
42.4	73, 74, 102, 111–12, 113n15, 139, 156n34
42.5	52, 57n9, 73, 77

INDEX OF ANCIENT SOURCES

43	56n9, 77, 134n22	48	51n12, 52, 114n15
43.1ff	102	48.1	48, 69n35, 104, 166n64
43.1	59, 155n29	48.2ff	104
43.2	102	48.3	155n29
43.6	96, 102, 113n15	48.4	59, 156
44	51n12, 52, 54n2, 77, 157n36	48.5ff	104
44.1ff	102	48.5–6	50n11
44.1f	60	48.5	75, 155n27
44.1	59, 73, 102, 155n29	48.6	68, 153n21, 165
44.2ff	74	49	49, 78, 104, 146n2, 149n8, 155n29
44.2	102	49.1ff	104
44.3	59, 69n35, 73, 95, 153n21, 159n44, 166n64, 167	49.1	59, 104, 157
		49.3	65, 165n62
44.4	73–74	49.5	68, 104, 165
44.5	73, 103, 138n39	49.6	60, 64, 104, 156n33, 159n44
44.6	68, 165		
45	77	50	49, 51, 56n7, 78, 146n2
45.1ff	103	50.1ff	104
45.2	55n4	50.1	104
45.7	66n28, 96, 163n57, 166n64	50.3	59, 63n22, 68, 104, 112n12–13, 114n15, 139, 157
45.8	96, 103		
46	77	50.4	104
46.2	158n39	50.5	68, 154n22, 165
46.4	159n44	50.6f	55n5
46.6	59, 61, 103, 106, 155n29, 157n35	50.6	104
		50.7	96, 155n29, 159n44
46.7f	103		
46.7	60, 155n29, 159n44	51–59.1	104
		51–58	146n2
46.8	60, 95, 103, 158, 158n41	51–55	78
		51	50n11, 51, 159n46
46.9	68, 165	51.1	75–76, 104, 114n15, 152n17, 154n22
47	47, 62, 75, 78, 147n2, 158n40		
47.1	103	51.2	54n2, 68, 165
47.2	103, 113n15, 140n46	51.3ff	104
		51.5	139
47.4	103	52.1	68, 104, 165
47.5f	103	52.2	55n4
47.5	112n13	53	51n12
47.6	59, 73, 75, 155n29	53.1ff	104
47.7	68, 103, 147n2, 165	53.2	153n21
48f	104	53.3	108n20

1 Clement (continued)

53.5	104
54	66, 163–64
54.1ff	104
54.1–2	66–67, 164
54.2	73, 105, 111, 138, 159n44, 166n64
54.3	59, 105
54.4	68, 105, 159n44, 165
55	51n12, 70, 158n42
55.1	66, 69n35, 105, 139, 150n10, 156n32, 163, 166n64
55.2	105
55.4f	105
55.4	105
55.6	68, 69n35, 105, 153n21, 166n64
56	51n12, 159n44
56.1ff	105
56.1	61, 105–6, 153n21, 162
56.2–59.1	105
57.1	75–76, 76n9, 78, 105, 154n23
57.2	59, 159n44
57.3ff	105
57.3	55n4, 106, 166n64
57.5	73
57.6–65.2	7
57.7	106
58	51n12
58.1	106
58.2	59, 96, 103, 106, 153n21, 155n29, 157n35, 159n44, 165, 179n40
59–65	43n1
59–61	44, 146n2
59	51n12, 55n5, 156n30, 178, 196
59.1	61, 105–6, 108, 108n20, 137n31, 159n44, 162, 178
59.2ff	106
59.2	106, 155n29, 178, 197, 200
59.3	68, 73, 106–7, 111, 137, 153n21, 155n29, 159n44, 179, 196–97, 200
59.4	44n2, 59, 107, 150n9, 153n21, 179, 197, 200
60–61	141
60.1ff	107
60.1	66n28, 117, 163n57
60.1a	107
60.2	107, 118
60.3	44n2, 107, 150n9
60.4–61.2	115
60.4	68, 107, 139, 139n41, 165, 166n64, 167
61	60, 70, 107, 119, 150n12
61.1f	70
61.1	66n28, 68, 107, 142–43, 163n57, 165
61.2b	107
61.3	96, 107, 155n29
62–65	78, 147n2
62	51n12, 163
62.1–2	44
62.1ff	137n31
62.1	118n26
62.2	108, 153n21, 154n23, 167
62.3	108
63	146n2
63.1	108, 118
63.2	44, 61, 68, 105, 108, 137n31, 146n2, 162, 165
63.3	40, 78, 108, 118
63.4	108
64	39n169, 55n5, 59–60, 96, 108, 155n29, 159n44

64.1	66n28, 68n33, 69n35, 157, 163n57, 166n64	45.8	103
		46.8	103
		47.2	103, 113n15
65.1	40, 108, 165	48	114n15
65.2	96, 108, 159n44	50.3	104, 114n15
		51.1	114n15
	Codex A	51.3ff	104
		55.6	105
1.1	89	57.7	106
1.2	113n15	58.1	106
1.3	113n15	65.2	108
2.1	59, 90		
5.7	92		Codex C
7	113n15		
12.1	94	1.1	89
14.3	95	2.1	90
15.1	95	14.3	95
15.6	113n15	15.1	95
17	113n15	16.2	95
17.5	113n15	20.5	96
21.1	96	21.1	96
21.5–6	113n15	21.7	96, 149n6
21.7	149n6	21.8	97
21.8	97, 113n15	22.8a	97
21.9	113n15	33.1	98
22	113n15	33.3	98
22.6	114n15	33.4	98
22.7	114n15	33.7	98
22.8	114n15	34.3	98
22.8a	97	37.2	118
27.5	113n15	44.2	102
28.3	114n15	45.8	103
33.1	98	46.8	103
33.3	98	47.2	103
33.4	98	50.3	104
33.7	98	51.1	104
34.1	114n15	51.3ff	104
34.3	98	55.6	105
34.8	114n15	57.7	106
35.5	99	58.1	106
36.2	99	58.2	106
37.2	118	59.3	106
38	114n15	59.4	107
40.1	114n15	60.1a	107
41.1	101	60.2	107
42.4	113n15	60.4	107
43.6	113n15	61	107
44.2	102	61.1	107

Codex C (continued)

61.3	107
61.4	107
62.2	108
62.3	108
63.1	108

Codex H

1.1	89
1.2	113n15
1.3	113n15
2.1	90
2.4	90
5.7	92
7	113n15
12.1	94
14.3	95
15.1	95
15.6	113n15
17	113n15
17.5	113n15
21.1	96
21.7	96
21.8	97, 113n15
21.9	113n15
22.2	97
22.6	114n15
22.7	114n15
22.8	114n15
22.8a	97
25.1	127
25.5–6	113n15
27.5	113n15
28.3	114n15
33.1	98
33.3	98
33.4	98
33.7	98
34.1	114n15
34.3	98
34.8	98, 114n15
35.5	99
36.2	99
37.2	118
38	114n15
40.1	114n15
42.4	113n15
43.6	113n15
44.2	102
45.8	103
46.8	103
47.2	103, 113n15
48	114n15
50.3	104, 114n15
51.1	104, 114n15
51.3ff	104
55.6	105
57.7	106
58.1	106
58.2	106
59.3	106
59.4	107
60.1a	107
60.2	107
60.4	107
61	107
61.1	107
61.4	107
62.2	108
62.3	108
63.1	108
65.2	108

Codex L

1.1	89
1.3	139
2.1	90
5.7	139
7.2	131n10
7.5	117n21
12.1	94
14.3	95
15.1	95
15.6	113n15, 117n20
17	113n15
17.5	113n15
20.8	118n25
21.1	96
21.5–6	113n15
21.6	118
21.7	96, 149n6
21.8	97, 113n15
21.9	113n15

INDEX OF ANCIENT SOURCES 243

22	113n15	55.6	105
22.6	114n15	57.7	106
22.7	114n15	58.1	106
22.8	114n15	58.2	106
22.8a	97	59.3	106, 111, 137
24.4	140n46	59.4	107
25	118n25, 129	60–61	141
25.1	127	60.1	117
25.3	112n12, 130	60.1a	107
27.5	113n15	60.2	107, 118
28.3	114n15	60.4–61.2	115
32.2	139	60.4	107, 139
33.1	98	61	107, 119, 150n12
33.3	98	61.1	107, 142–43
33.4	98	61.3	107
33.7	98	61.4	107
34.1	114n15	62.1	118n26
34.3	98	62.2	108
34.8	114n15	62.3	108
35.5	99	63.1	108, 118
36.2	99	63.3	118
37.2	118, 139	65.2	108
38	114n15		
39.4	139	Codex S	
39.7	139		
40	118, 140	1.1	89
40.1	114n15	2.1	90
40.5	111n10	7	113n15
41.2	118n26	12.1	94
42.4	102, 111–12, 113n15, 139	14.3	95
		15.1	95
43	134n22	15.6	113n15
43.6	113n15	16.2	95
44.2	102	17	113n15
44.5	138n39	17.5	113n15
45.8	103	20.8	96
46.8	103	21.1	96
47.2	103, 113n15, 140n46	21.5–6	113n15
		21.7	96, 149n6
47.5	112n13	21.8	97
48	114n15	22.7	114n15
50.3	104, 112n12–13, 114n15, 139	25.1	127
		27.5	113n15
51.1	104, 114n15	28.3	114n15
51.3ff	104	33.1	98
51.5	139	33.3	98
54.2	111, 138	33.4	98
55.1	139	33.7	98

Codex S (continued)

34.3	98
34.8	98
35.5	99
36.2	99
37.2	118
42.4	113n15
43.6	113n15
44.2	102
45.8	103
46.8	103
47.2	103, 113n15
48	114n15
50.3	104
51.1	114n15
51.3ff	104
55.6	105
57.7	106
58.1	106
58.2	106
59.3	106
59.4	107
60.1a	107
60.2	107
60.4	107
61	107
61.1	107
61.4	107
62.2	108
62.3	108
63.1	108
65.2	108

2 Clement

2.1	179
9.5	200n94
11.2f	97, 179

Acts of John

11	186, 196n79, 198n87, 199n88

Acts of Justin

2	185, 190, 199, 199n88, 199n90

Acts of Paul and Thecla

17	186
24	186, 198n87, 199n88, 199n90, 200

Acts of Perpetua and Felicitas

3	137
13	139

Acts of Xanthippe and Polyxena

66.30	173n20
68.20	173n20
74.8	173n20

Ambrose

De fide resurr.

59	128

Expos. in Psalm

CXVII, sermo 19 c. 13	128

Hex

V.23	127

Apostolic Canons

conclusion	195, 198n87, 200n94

Apostolic Constitutions

I	194
VII	194
VII.25	194
VII.26	194
VII.27	194
VIII	194
VIII.5	194, 198n87, 200n94
VIII.12	194, 198n87, 199n88
VIII.14	194–95, 198n87, 199n88

INDEX OF ANCIENT SOURCES

VIII.39	194–95, 198n87, 200n94	VI.6.52	175n26
VIII.40	194–95, 198n87, 199n88	VII.4.1	189, 191, 198n87, 199n88–90
VIII.41	194		
VIII.11	179n42, 191		

Athenagoras

Quis dives salvetur

42.10	189–90, 198n87, 199

Commodianus

Carm. apolog.

v. 99	139

1

12	184, 190, 199
37	185

Suppl.

10	184
23	185

Instruct.

II.26–29	138

Augustine

De haer.

23	172n18

Didache

	7, 94, 179, 195, 197, 197n82, 198n84
7	177
9.2	177, 196
9.3	177, 196
9.4	177
10.2	177, 196
10.3	177, 196
16	177

Barnabas

	7, 47n8, 57, 58n10, 94–95
2.6	95
6.1	181, 195
8.5	182
9.2	181, 195

Didascalia apostolorum

191, 194, 199n88

Beda

De locis sanctis	8
Retract. 118	176

Diognetus

7.2	185
7.4	185
8.9	185, 199n89, 199n90
8.11	185, 199n90
9.1	185, 199n90
9.2	185
9.4	185
10.2	180n43, 185

Clement of Alexandria

Paedagogus

V.58f	189, 199n90

Stromata

I.1	167
IV.8.112	112n12
IV.17.105	9n5
V.12.80	9n5

Epiphanius

Panarion

29.7	173n24, 195n77, 199n93
78.3	194, 198n87, 199n90
78.6	94

Eusebius

Ad coetum sanctorum

IX.4	193

De laudibus Constantini

XVII.13	193
XI.8	193

Hist. eccl.

III.16	9n5
III.38.4	134n24
IV.22.1f	9n5
IV.23	167
IV.23.9f	9n5
IV.26.2	94
IV.26.7	185
V.6	146n1
V.19	157n35
V.19.2	167n66
V.20.6	
VI.25.14	69, 166
VII.6	190–91, 198n87, 199, 199n88, 199n90
X.4.56	193, 199

Vita Constantini

I.32	193, 198n87

Fabius Planciades Fulgentius

Opera Fulgentii

	121, 121n30, 123, 123n1

Hegesippus

Hypomnemata

	9

Hexaem.

V.23	129n6

Hippolytus

Church Orders of Hippolytus

	187–89, 198n87, 200, 200n94

Contra haeresin. Noeti

5	187, 199n89

De antichristo

3	187, 199n90
6	187, 199, 199n90

Haer.

V.6	52n18
VIII.10	183, 198n87

Philos.

V.6	154n26

Refut.

V.7	172n19
VI.42	172n19
X.33	187, 199

Ignatius

Romans

3:1	8n5

To the Smyrnaeans

10	106

INDEX OF ANCIENT SOURCES

Irenaeus

Haer.

I.13.5	138n37
I.14.7	138n37
I.15.6	139n40
II.22.3	154n26
II.22.5	139n40
II.28.9	154n26
III.2.2	139n40
III.3.3	9n5, 129n7, 146n1
III.12.5	176, 187
III.12.6	176x
III.23.3	139n40
IV.26.5	101
IV.27	139n40
IV.28.1	139n40
IV.30.1	139n40
IV.30.4	139n40
IV.32.1	139n40
V.5.1	139n40
V.17.4	139n40
V.33.3	139n40
V.36.1	139n40

Italafragmente

	137

Jerome

Comm. Isa.

29.20f	174n24
31.6ff	174n24

Johannes Diaconus Romanus

Spicil.

	134n22

Justin

1 Apol.

53	94

2 Apol.

2	185

Dial.

13	184
123	184
135	184

Lactantius

De phoenice

v. 102ff	131
v.102	130
v.105	130
v. 117f	130–31
v. 121f	130–31

Libellus Bedan presbiteri

	120

Liber pontificalis

	136n30

Magical Papyri from Fayum

	193

Martyrdom of Matthew

5	186n54

Maximus Confessor Prolog. in Opp. S. Dinoysii

xxxvi	134n24

Novatian

De Trinitate

	198n86
XI.10.13f	198n86

Optatus

II.25	198n86

Origen

Adnot. Jes. Nav.

III.4	94

Comm. Jo.

I.21	173n23, 190n60

Comm. Rom.

	138

Contra Celsum

I.67	184
II.9	184
V.2	184
V.52	184
VI.41	184
VI.42	184
VI.74	184
VII.9	184
VII.14	184
VII.39	184
VII.53	184
VIII.39	184
XIII.2	184
XIII.4	184

Ep. Afr.

	190, 199n90, 199n92

Hom. Luc.

8	70n38

Select. Ps.

Ps 36 hom. 4 c.3	139n40
Ps 36 hom. 4 c.60	139n40

Passiv S. Longini

	120

Photius

Cod.

114	172

Lexicon

126	67n30, 69, 97, 99, 164n60, 166

Polycarp

Mart. Poly.

	195
12	180n43
14.1	180–81, 186, 191, 196–97, 200
14.3	180–81, 188, 196, 200n94
20.2	180–81, 192, 196–97
21	108

Phil.

	8n5, 47n7, 118n25, 146
5	137
7	167

Pseudo-Athanasius

De virginitate

13	194, 198n87, 199n89

Pseudo-Clementines

	8, 120–21, 125

Pseudo-Cyprian

De montibus Sina et Sion

4	191–92, 198n84, 199–200

Pseudo-Tertullian

Adv. omn. haer.

14	131n9, 200

Carmen adv. Marcionem

V.204	192–94

Shepherd of Hermas

Mandate

11.9	167

Similitude

V.2	182–83, 200
V.5f	183

Vision

II.4	8n5, 40
II.4.1	173n21
III.3.5	107
III.10ff	173n21

Palatina Version of Vision

II.2.6	139
III.9.7	139

Vulgate Version of Vision

II.2.6	139
III.9.7	139

Tertullian

Adv. Apell.

	172n18

Adv. Jud.

28	187, 200

Apol.

14	200n95
15	92
34	140n45
39	111n11

Bapt.

	187, 200
7	176
17	111n9, 112n11, 137n33

De exhortat. cast.

7	117n22

De resurr.

12	131
13	131

Fug.

11	137n33

Jejun.

12	153n21

Mon.

11	137n33

Praescr.

3	137n33
32	136n29
41	111n9, 137n33

Prax.

28	176

Val.

1	52n18, 154n26

Vita Cypriani

1	139n41

www.ingramcontent.com/pod-product-compliance
Lightning Source LLC
Chambersburg PA
CBHW070242230426
43664CB00014B/2386